Against the Imperial Judiciary

AGAINST THE IMPERIAL JUDICIARY

The Supreme Court vs. the Sovereignty of the People

MATTHEW J. FRANCK

 University Press of Kansas

FOR MY MOTHER AND FATHER
AND THE MEMORY OF MY GRANDFATHER
HARRY A. FRANCK

© 1996 by the University Press of Kansas
All rights reserved

Published by the University Press of Kansas (Lawrence, Kansas 66049),
which was organized by the Kansas Board of Regents and is operated and
funded by Emporia State University, Fort Hays State University, Kansas
State University, Pittsburg State University, the University of Kansas, and
Wichita State University

Chapter 2 is a revised version of "Statesmanship and the Judiciary,"
Review of Politics 51 (1989): 510–32; permission granted by the editors of
Review of Politics at the University of Notre Dame.

Library of Congress Cataloguing-in-Publication Data

Franck, Matthew J.
    Against the imperial judiciary : sovereignty of the
people / by Matthew J. Franck.
        p. cm.
    Includes bibliographical references and index.
    ISBN 0-7006-0761-7 (hardcover)
    1. United States. Supreme Court. 2. Political questions and
judicial power—United States. 3. United States—Constitutional
law—Interpretation and construction. I. Title.
KF8748.F647 1996
347.73'26—dc20
[347.30735]   95-43073

British Library Cataloguing in Publication Data is available.

Printed in the United States of America

10 9 8 7 6 5 4 3 2 1

The paper used in this publication meets the minimum requirements of
the American National Standard for Permanence of Paper for Printed
Library Materials Z39.48-1984.

CONTENTS

ACKNOWLEDGMENTS

In the course of writing this book, I frequently had occasion to reflect on my debts, intellectual and otherwise, to those individuals whose friendship and instruction made it possible. Those debts cannot be repaid, only acknowledged.

Six teachers during my undergraduate and graduate education generated and sustained my interest in political theory, the American founding, and the Constitution. Professor Edmund D. Carlson of Virginia Wesleyan College set my feet on the path and remains the model of the teacher I should like someday to become. Professor Richard G. Stevens continues to instruct me in how to think straight about the Constitution and the philosophy that informs it. Professor Paul C. Peterson's graduate course on the *Federalist* is still memorable after more than a dozen years, and Professor Alfred F. Young continually challenged my thinking in his graduate seminars in American history.

Professors Morton J. Frisch and Gary D. Glenn of Northern Illinois University took me in hand as a graduate student, and each in his own way taught me more than I have yet been able to absorb about the interpretation of texts. Professor Frisch, with consummate patience, generosity, and care, directed the doctoral dissertation from which this book eventually grew, and he and Professor Glenn gave unstintingly of their time and knowledge both then and in subsequent stages of my research. Joining them on my dissertation committee were Professors Larry Arnhart and James King, both of whom offered helpful criticism of that earlier version of this work.

At various stages the work that follows was read in whole or in part by the following friends: Christopher Wolfe of Marquette University, whose close and careful review of the dissertation prompted much of the revision that made its publication possible; Robert L. Clinton, a colleague for two years at Southern Illinois University who continues to influence profoundly my view of judicial power; Thomas K. Lindsay of the University of Northern Iowa, who for fifteen years has tried to keep my wit sharp; and Sidney A. Pearson, Jr., of Radford University, who, along with other colleagues in Radford's political science department, has made it a wonderful place to work.

James R. Stoner, Jr., of Louisiana State University and another, anonymous reviewer read the revised manuscript for the University Press of Kansas and offered tough, constructive comments that made final refinements of the argument easier. At the press itself, editor-in-chief Michael Briggs has my enduring gratitude for shepherding a naive first-time author gently through the publication process. All of the individuals I have named of course bear no responsibility for any of the places where I have surely gone astray.

To my father and mother, Peter and Suzanne Franck, I owe, in addition to all that one always owes loving parents, the incalculable gift of their examples as lovers of learning. My wife, Gwen Brown, often interrupted her own work as teacher and scholar to listen to my latest idea or my latest frustration and cheerfully put up with me at my worst. This book would never have existed without her loving support.

CHAPTER ONE

Introduction: Our Present Straits

This book is about the extent to which the Supreme Court of the United States, considered in light of the principles of its origins, may be said to have a legitimate share of the authority to govern. I do not intend to subject any of the more controversial recent decisions of the Court to sustained analysis, nor will I examine to any significant degree the bewildering variety of policy effects that Court rulings have had on the shape of our contemporary politics. I will point out, however, some of the more curious twists and turns the evolution of judicial power has produced in the course of the most prominent public discussions of that subject, namely, during confirmation hearings held by the Senate on presidential nominations to the Court.

Some readers will share my view that the text of the Constitution and its meaning as originally understood provide durable standards for a critique of present-day judicial behavior and wish therefore for an explicit analysis of such behavior in particular cases. My neglect of such a task may be frustrating for these readers, yet they can probably draw their own conclusions on such matters from what is said in the pages that follow—even though not all will find what is said to be agreeable.

Readers who regard the Constitution as more fluid than fixed, and judicial interpretation of it as more a creative than a discerning art, will probably not like this book. My attention to the fairly distant past in constitutional history, and my neglect of much of what passes today for constitutional "theory," may sometimes strike them as being the quaintest sort of antiquarianism. But I believe that close analysis of the thoughts and decisions of the past provides the best instruction for understanding our constitutional predicament today. For the most part, I leave it to someone else to persuade them of what it means to "take the Constitution seriously."[1] I have assumed, for better or worse, that my readers and I all speak the language of constitutionalism rather than that of Lewis Carroll's Humpty Dumpty.

Until fairly recently, an author making such an assumption might have had few readers indeed. Beginning in the 1950s, much of the scholarship in the field of constitutional law, concerned with the theory and practice of judicial review by the U.S. Supreme Court, tended to concentrate on developing and modifying variations on the theme that there are essentially two models for the exercise of judicial power in constitutional law: judicial restraint and judicial activism. But in the 1980s, the debate over which of these models is more appropriate to a constitutional democracy took a more fruitful turn, as both academic and public debate centered on whether the justices of the Supreme Court (and by implication, all other judges as well) should attempt to guide their decisions by an "original intent" or an "original under-standing" that informed the Constitution at the founding. Thus, the debate between "restraintists" and "activists" came to be supplanted by one between "interpretivists" and "noninterpretivists" or between "originalists" and "nonoriginalists."

The fatal defect in the earlier controversy between judicial activism and judicial restraint comes to light as soon as the reader recalls that, properly speaking, the name of the second model is judicial *self*-re-straint. Both the judicial practitioners and the academic defenders of judicial restraint treated the issue as one of reconciling a Court that is entrusted with the ultimate, binding, and authoritative power to expli-cate the meaning of the Constitution with a polity that the same Con-stitution constructs along largely majoritarian lines. This "counter-majoritarian difficulty," as the late Alexander Bickel called it,[2] was often treated as though judicial restraint were simply a matter of the justices husbanding scarce resources to check democratic processes—choosing their opportunities like any other political institution—so as to avoid doing things dangerously unpopular or politically risky to the Court's long-term prestige and power. Hence, it soon became clear that the idea of judicial restraint, no less than that of judicial activism, means the power of judicial review is regarded as indistinguishable from a grant of judicial supremacy over questions of the meaning of the Constitution (so long as minimal requirements of a properly presented case are met).

All the arts and doctrines of self-abnegation attached to judicial re-straint can be described more accurately as policies of prudence than as being compelled by constitutional principles. People who appeared before the Supreme Court pleading for novel and perverse readings of the Constitution might be told by self-restrained judges "not today but perhaps tomorrow," but they were never told "not today, not tomorrow, never." It would not go too far to say that the model of restraint never accomplished more than its opposite number as far as illuminating a *constitutional* distinction between law and politics was concerned. Judicial restraint was thus doomed to lose the battle with judicial activism—and did.

The terms of debate since the 1980s have been an improvement over those of earlier years because they at least hold out the possibility of bringing the Constitution back into the theory and practice of constitutional law. Able defenders of originalism as the appropriate method of constitutional adjudication have emerged, and I believe they have far better arguments than their opponents. Yet even originalists, in surprising numbers, have continued to treat the Supreme Court as the decisive venue for the establishment of justice in the United States and for the settlement of varied claims of right brought forth in a society riven by factions.

But this book is not another in the long line of works reviewing the claims and counterclaims of originalism and nonoriginalism. Nor do I attempt a grand theory or model of constitutional interpretation to which some such label may be affixed—although I am tempted to adopt the label of "textualism" put forth in a recent work.[3]

Essentially, I am concerned with the issue of theoretical and historical support in the text, theoretical foundations, and early adjudication of the Constitution for three related propositions: one, that the Supreme Court more than the other branches of government holds the paramount and final position in determining the meaning of the Constitution; two, that the justices of the Supreme Court may properly embark on any enterprise deserving of the name "statesmanship"—by, for instance, using constitutional rulings to fill the "vacuums" left by other institutions that have neglected or failed to solve political or social problems; and three, that constitutional decisions can be grounded legitimately in natural law (or "higher law" or "unenumerated rights") located above, beyond, or apart from the text of the Constitution.

To state my argument briefly, each of these propositions depends in some measure on the one before. That is, only if the constitutional rulings of the Supreme Court on all subjects have a final authority, which is irrebuttable by other national institutions (except by extraordinary means such as the amending power), is it possible for the justices, who occupy an institution not singularly adept at policy-making, to reach out as "statesmen" attempting to resolve any of the nation's pressing problems. At least it may be said that only such constitutional author-ity can provide consistent opportunities for such statesmanship and relatively consistent noninterference from others in the process. And only a Court with final authority and a statesmanlike potential will see fit to reach "beyond the Constitution"[4] when the written text is in-sufficient for its purposes and attempt to "do justice" by the light of em-anations that the Constitution does not cast. But a Court without the power to enforce authoritatively all that is in the Constitution is hardly in a position to enforce principles that are *not* in it; it will also be in a far weaker position to practice statesmanship while the other branches believe firmly that such a task belongs to them.

Although it would seem, therefore, that the entire tripod of proposi-tions collapses when the leg of judicial finality is kicked out from under it, I examine the validity of all three. The first two propositions are con-sidered in Part One, with Chapter 2 being devoted to the founding per-spective on statesmanship and the scope of judicial power. Chapters 3 through 5 examine the legacy of John Marshall, the man thought to have been both the country's greatest "judicial statesman" and the ju-rist responsible for establishing the idea that the Supreme Court has the "last word" on constitutional meaning. I hope to recapture, among other things, a more modest sense of the Court's capacities as origi-nally conceived and as guided by Marshall.

Because so much of the debate over the third proposition—the legiti-macy of adjudicating extraconstitutional principles—turns on mis-taken assumptions about the history of the practice, Part Two considers the historical evidence concerning the place occupied by natural law in the decisions of the early Court (Chapter 6) and the rewriting of that history by the Court in the late nineteenth century (Chapter 7). I argue that today's advocates and critics of the resort to natural law for decid-ing cases are both mistaken in their view of the historical evidence of its appearance in the Court's opinions.

But revising one's historical understanding of this matter is not enough. Even if it can be shown that, in nearly every instance usually cited from the antebellum Court, natural-law principles do not play the role they are thought to play, it may still be asked, On what grounds should men who manifestly believed in natural law eschew a resort to it in the decision of constitutional cases? This theoretical question is approached in Part Three by examining the related problems of sovereignty, judicial power, and natural justice in the works of three think-ers who helped shape the understanding of the American founders as they set about the business of constitution-making: Thomas Hobbes (Chapter 8), John Locke (Chapter 9), and William Blackstone (Chapter 10). Although the focus is mainly on the issue of natural-law adjudica-tion, I hope these chapters also shed light on the propositions examined earlier. In the final chapter I return once again to the founders of the regime for some concluding thoughts about the meaning of constitu-tionalism.

Unlikely as it may seem, each of the major questions exam-ined in this book has been raised in hearings before the Senate Judici-ary Committee on presidential nominations to the Supreme Court. At various times the hearings on the nominations of Robert Bork, An-thony Kennedy, David Souter, Clarence Thomas, and Ruth Bader Gins-burg have been colloquies on the Supreme Court's final authority over constitutional law, on the possibilities of judicial statesmanship, and on the place of natural law in constitutional adjudication. Neither the questions asked by senators nor the answers given by the nominees have always been instructive, edifying, or even consistent, but the man-ner and the context in which the questions were raised and answered may reveal something about today's constitutional politics.

Regarding the first proposition, in the hearings mentioned Senator Arlen Specter (R-Pa.) continued a pattern of questioning that he had begun in the confirmation hearings of Chief Justice William Rehn-quist and Justice Antonin Scalia.[5] Voicing his concern that there "are some prominent people in our country today who appear to be question-ing the finality of Supreme Court decisions," Senator Specter wanted to know in 1987 whether Judge Robert Bork would be a Supreme Court justice who would entertain such questions. On this point, if not on oth-ers, the answer could not have disappointed him: "The Supreme Court—the courts and ultimately the Supreme Court, are the final de-terminers of what the Constitution is," said Bork. The senator pressed for a still more definitive statement:

Senator Specter: But you would agree, then, that a Supreme Court decision has more of a binding quality than simply on the parties to the case and on the executive branch to enforce that spe-cific decision?

Judge Bork: That is true.

Senator Specter: And unless there is an appeal and a change in the Court's decision, that such a decision does establish a supreme law of the land that is binding on all persons and all parts of the Government.

Judge Bork: That is true.[6]

Senator Specter returned to the same subject with Judge David Souter three years later. He identified *Marbury* v. *Madison*[7] as "the 1803 case where it was decided by the Supreme Court that the Supreme Court had the last word on what the Constitution meant." But because "there are some today who dispute that," the senator worried that if Congress "pass[ed] a statute to divest the Supreme Court of jurisdiction," the result could be that "*Marbury* v. *Madison* does not have any real substance nor does the ultimate authority of the Supreme Court have any real substance." Responding to this concern, Judge Souter agreed that "the consequences of assuming that the power to except from the jurisdiction is a power which Congress in effect can exercise in any way it sees fit is [*sic*] basically to deny the possibility of national unity in constitutional interpretation."[8]

In the 1991 Clarence Thomas hearings, Senator Specter returned to the issue of judicial finality only briefly, apparently having received a satisfactory answer on the same subject when Judge Thomas was nominated to the Court of Appeals less than two years before. According to *Marbury,* said the senator, "the Supreme Court has the last word, no doubt in your mind about that." Thomas replied, "No doubt, Senator."[9]

Only in the December 1987 hearings to confirm Anthony Kennedy did the senator from Pennsylvania encounter any apparent reticence on the subject of the Supreme Court's position as "final arbiter" of the Constitution's meaning. Kennedy, in a 1982 speech of which the senator reminded him, had remarked that "the Constitution, in some of its most critical aspects, is what the political branches of the government have made it, whether the judiciary approves or not."[10] Seeming unsatisfied with the nominee's initial explanation of his meaning in that speech, Senator Specter pressed ahead by asking whether Judge Kennedy agreed with the sentiments expressed by then–Attorney General Edwin Meese, in a well-known 1986 speech at Tulane University, that a constitutional decision of the Supreme Court "does not establish a supreme law of the land that is binding on all persons and parts of government henceforth and evermore."[11] After reading the attorney general's words, the senator asked, "Do you agree with that?"

Judge Kennedy: Well, I am not sure—I am not sure I read that entire speech. But if we can just take it as a question, whether or not I agree that the decisions of the Supreme Court are or are not the law of the land. They are the law of the land, and they must be obeyed.

I am somewhat reluctant to say that in all circumstances each legislator is immediately bound by the full consequences of a Supreme Court decree.[12]

Under further questioning, Judge Kennedy raised the hypothetical instance of the Supreme Court reversing *New York Times* v. *Sullivan*[13] and narrowing the First Amendment protection of newspapers in libel suits. It would be appropriate then, he opined, for members of Congress, holding a different view of what freedom of the press requires, to reinstitute *Sullivan*-level protection by legislation. But his example rather deftly avoided the dicier question of whether, under the real regime of *Sullivan* as it presently exists, Congress could disregard, because of a different constitutional view than the Supreme Court has taken, the Court's pronouncements on the First Amendment and the law of libel and act to narrow the protections afforded to the press. It is one thing to grant by legislation a broader category of rights than the Court has seen fit to mandate in the name of the Constitution and quite another to attempt to reverse by legislation a judicially created regime of rights that Congress regards as too expansive. On the latter possibility—the far more interesting possibility—Judge Kennedy quite prudently (under the circumstances) had nothing to say.

After a few more exchanges made it plain that the line of questioning was fizzling out, Senator Specter, again asserting that "it has been accepted that the Supreme Court is the final arbiter," pleaded that "I just want to be sure that you agree with that proposition."

Judge Kennedy: Yes, but there just may be instances in which I think it is consistent with constitutional morality to challenge those views. And I am not saying to avoid those views or to refuse to obey a mandate.

Senator Specter: Well, I think it is fine to challenge them. You can challenge them by constitutional amendment, you can challenge by taking another case to the Supreme Court. But, as long as the Court has said what the Court concludes the Constitution means, then I think it is critical that there be an acceptance that that is the final word.

Judge Kennedy: I would agree with that as a general proposition. I am not sure there are not exceptions.

Senator Specter: But you can't think of any at the moment?

Judge Kennedy: Not at the moment.

Senator Specter: Okay. If you do think of any between now and the time we vote, would you let me know?

Judge Kennedy: I will let you know, Senator.[14]

Nothing in the public record indicates that Judge Kennedy had any more thoughts on this subject to communicate to Senator Specter in the days before the vote on his confirmation.

The purpose of recounting these colloquies is to suggest that there is something strange going on in them. In the classic textbook account of the separation of powers, it is taught that the three branches of government are coequal in authority, each with its own battery of defensive (and perhaps offensive) weapons in the form of checks and balances. In these terms, there is no reason to suppose that judicial review is more than one of these self-defensive checks, designed like the others principally to enable the judiciary to "resist encroachments"[15] of the other branches. In other words, there is no reason to suppose, taking an elementary view of our constitutional structure, that one branch among the three possesses an extraordinary check on the other two, enabling it to maintain a position superior to theirs. Moreover, if the meaning of the Constitution itself raises the most important class of political questions, it would seem especially improper that one branch possess the "last word" on such matters—subject only to its own members' sense of self-restraint or of limited capacity or resources—no matter what the arguable need for "national unity in constitutional interpretation." Only some very strong inferences from the text or structure of the Constitution, such as Senator Specter apparently supposed he found in the *Marbury* case, could serve to rebut the presumption that among coequal branches of power, none plays the role of final arbiter on the document's meaning.

If this "textbook" account of the separation of powers makes sense, even provisionally, then Senator Specter provided a very strange spectacle on the four occasions described above. A member of the legislative branch applied to nominees to the judicial branch a rigorous litmus test demanding that the nominees commit themselves to the proposition that their branch of government was more powerful than his own, indeed simply authoritative against all rivals, on the most important questions that confront the regime: those that ask, What does the Constitution mean?

The surprise was not that nearly all the nominees should eagerly acquiesce in such a proposition, since it amounts to saying "yes, I will be your superior" to a man who interviews you for a job ostensibly equal to his own. The surprise is that the interviewer asked such a question and demanded such an answer. From where we stand today in the culture of constitutional politics, Senator Specter's litmus test was not surprising, as it represents contemporary orthodoxy. Yet it *should* be surprising that this is the orthodoxy, compelled as it is by neither the text nor the theory of the Constitution, nor, as we shall see, by the precedent cited by the senator. And when a senator subscribes to a doctrine so damaging to the privileges of his own office, it is not only a sign of the contemporary orthodoxy's power, but also, from the standpoint of history, a sign that the universe of checks and balances has been turned inside out.

On the subject of the second proposition, that the Supreme Court may "play the statesman" or "fill vacuums" or "take the lead" in addressing national problems, members of the Judiciary Committee performed a bit better, but without seeming to have a clear idea about what should concern them. During the Souter hearings, Senator Charles Grassley (R-Iowa) and the nominee had the following colloquy:

> *Senator Grassley:* Judge Souter, those who advocate a greater activist role for the Court say that the broad and spacious terms of the Constitution lend themselves to Court-made solutions when the political branches fail to act.
>
> What is your sense of this perception that the courts, rather than the elected branches, should take the lead in creating a more just society?
>
> *Judge Souter:* I think the proper way to approach that is that courts must accept their own responsibility for making a just society. One of the things that is almost a factor or a law of nature, as well as a law of constitutional growth, is that if there is, in fact, a profound social problem if the Constitution speaks to that, and if the other branches of the Government do not deal with it, ultimately, *it does and must* land before the bench of the judiciary. . . .
>
> I guess the law of nature I am referring to is simply the law of nature and political responsibility, constitutional responsibility, abhor a vacuum. . . .
>
> *Senator Grassley:* Are you saying the Supreme Court should act

because there is a vacuum there, or because there is a cause within the Constitution for the courts to act; as opposed to because the political branches have not acted?

Judge Souter: The Supreme Court should only act and can only act when it has the judicial responsibility under the 14th amendment *or any other section of the Constitution.* But the Supreme Court is left to act alone when the political branches do not act beforehand.[16]

On the next day of the hearings, Senator Grassley, having had a weekend to think about this exchange, confessed, "I am a little troubled by this vacuum concept" and wondered if it were not "terminology likely to come from a judicial activist." Judge Souter was "going to be a very busy person," opined the senator, "if we are going to have a Supreme Court that thinks it can fill vacuums every time there is a perceived problem."[17] The nominee reassured him with a twofold reply: that courts only act where they have formal jurisdiction, which is not based on "perceptions at the moment about what ought to be done"; and that what "I had in mind . . . was the example . . . in *Brown*," referring of course to the 1954 desegregation ruling[18]—and here again he centered his reply on the issue of formal jurisdiction to act.[19]

With just a few more exchanges, Senator Grassley was satisfied. The reference to *Brown* provided just the right answer for this line of questioning, for it is certainly beyond the pale of respectable opinion today, at least in a hearing room of the U.S. Senate, to question whether the Court in that case acted properly in "filling the vacuum" left by the other branches. But it must be said that the senator allowed himself to be diverted from the most interesting aspect of Judge Souter's reply and quit the field too soon.

The judge had clearly indicated that two conditions must be met for the Court to "fill vacuums": first, that a case properly within the Court's jurisdiction arise, and second, that the political branches have failed to act on the constitutional problem raised by the case. But the first condition is a red herring; Judge Souter confounded, whether deliberately or not, the issues of jurisdiction and justiciability. Many cases may be properly within the Court's formal jurisdiction to hear them, yet raise constitutional issues over which the Court does not have final authority—and perhaps no proper authority at all. Today so much damage has been done to the notion that the Constitution does not award the Court final authority over all interpretive issues that jurisdiction and justiciability may have become indistinguishable for both interlocutors in the hearing. But that is only part of the bad news, for Judge Souter thus posed a false dichotomy when he said that "the jurisdiction of the Supreme Court . . . is derived from the [Constitution] that . . . create[s]" it, not "from perceptions at the moment about what ought to be done."[20] Of course this is true of jurisdiction; no one ever thought otherwise. But a Court with final authority to rule definitively on "constitutional solutions" to social problems wherever it has formal jurisdiction and wherever the other branches have failed (in the Court's view) to act has, on these terms at least, no reason *not* to be guided by "perceptions at the moment about what ought to be done."

In actuality Judge Souter had not retreated at all from the position he had taken on the previous day of the hearings: that insofar as the Constitution "abhors a vacuum," all problems amenable to solutions fashioned out of ostensibly constitutional materials "must land before the bench of the judiciary" and will be resolved with a final, authoritative character there. And Senator Grassley was mollified at just the moment when things could have gotten really interesting: Why, it might have been asked, should it be assumed that all aspects of constitutional law, if they may be brought to bear on some perceived need or other, require the judiciary's attention, even in the absence of action proceeding from elsewhere? Inaction on the part of Congress may be the result of purposeful neglect of a "problem" not seen to be a problem. More to the point, even inadvertent (or callous) neglect of a very real problem hardly constitutes a *constitutional* ground for action by the judiciary, even on the subject of a real issue in constitutional law. That is, it constitutes no such ground unless we presuppose what Senator Grassley and Judge Souter both apparently presupposed: that the Supreme Court has final authority over all constitutional issues out of which a piece of litigation may be fashioned. In seeking assurances that "judicial activism" will not result from "this vacuum concept," Senator Grassley had come up empty and seemed not to know it.

In the 1993 hearings to confirm Justice Ruth Bader Ginsburg, a similar colloquy occurred and with similar results. In Judge Ginsburg's case, the issue of "statesmanship" or of "the Court leading the way" to social change arose because of remarks she had made on the subject prior to her appointment. In a March 9, 1993, speech discussing the firestorm that followed *Roe* v. *Wade*,[21] the judge had given her now well-known "moderate" critique of that ruling that reversed every abortion statute in the land. The Court had only overstepped its bounds, argued Judge Ginsburg, by making too bold a move all at once rather than accomplishing its goal more stealthily, by smaller steps over time. The issue in the speech was not whether the Court had been right or wrong, only that it had been "divisive," and the judge counseled her listeners on a more appropriate way of proceeding: "But without taking giant strides and thereby risking a backlash too forceful to contain, the Court, through constitutional adjudication, can reinforce or signal a green light for a social change."[22] In similar terms, the judge once remarked that thus the Court "can moderately accelerate the *pace* of change."[23]

It was probably with remarks such as these in mind that in the hearings, according to one press account, "Sen. Dennis DeConcini (D.-Ariz.) asked whether the court should ever be a leader or only a follower of public sentiment." The reply was reported as follows:

> "When political avenues become dead-end streets," Ginsburg said, quoting a law professor, "judicial intervention in the politics of the people may be essential in order to have effective politics."
> . . .
> Ginsburg nonetheless suggested that "the imprimatur of the law" should be in sync with "the direction of change" in society.[24]

As an example of this appropriate "judicial intervention," the judge cited the 1962 reapportionment decision in *Baker* v. *Carr.*[25] Leaving aside the fact (if press accounts are correct) that she mistakenly characterized *Baker* as having to do with racial discrimination in voting rights, both Judge Ginsburg's reply and her example begged more than one important question that the senators failed to ask. In reaching its conclusions in constitutional cases, as opposed to explaining them, why should the Court take stock of public sentiment at all? Why should the risk of "backlash" be part of the calculation of how to decide who wins and who loses such cases, or of how much is won and lost? How does the Court recognize a "dead-end street" when it sees one? How does it know these dead ends are not good things? How does it know how to get out of them? How does the Court know, better than others know, what "effective politics" are? How does it know what the "direction of change" is at any given moment, whether it is a good direction, and how to calibrate its own contribution to that change in such a way as to accomplish neither too little nor too much "acceleration" of it? Finally, on what constitutional grounds can most of these questions legitimately be asked by the Court as it goes about its business? Such questions, and the answers to them, might have made for a far more interesting seminar between the legislative and judicial branches. Judge

Ginsburg's suggestive remarks on a Court that has such leadership responsibilities are difficult to square with her statement, also in the confirmation hearings, that "a judge is not a politician. . . . If [a decision] is legally right, it's a decision the judge should render."[26]

The final proposition to be considered—that natural law, "higher law," or "unenumerated rights" can form an independent basis for adjudication apart from the Constitution's text—came up most prominently in the confirmation hearings of two recent nominees, Robert Bork and Clarence Thomas. On both occasions, Chairman Joseph Biden (D-Del.) was the lead questioner.

In 1987, confronting a nominee with a substantial written record in defense of "original intent" jurisprudence and opposed to the judicial "creation" of rights, Senator Biden had this to say in his opening statement on the first day of hearings:

> I believe all Americans are born with certain inalienable rights. As a child of God, I believe my rights are not derived from the Constitution. My rights are not derived from any government. My rights are not derived from any majority. My rights are because I exist. They were given to me and each of my fellow citizens by our creator and they represent the essence of human dignity.[27]

During one of his colloquies with Judge Bork, Senator Biden elicited from the judge rejections of the reasoning, though not necessarily the results, in cases such as *Griswold* v. *Connecticut*[28] and *Skinner* v. *Oklahoma*[29] on "reproductive rights," which clearly bore some connection to the case the senator was most interested in defending, namely *Roe* v. *Wade*. But in a series of exchanges that must have been frustrating for both men—though for different reasons—a good deal of clarity did emerge about where the two stood on the question of such rights. At one point, for instance, the following exchange occurred, which typified their differences:

> *The Chairman:* So that you suggest that unless the Constitution, I believe in the past you used the phrase, textually identifies, a value that is worthy of being protected, then competing values in society, the competing value of a public utility, in the example you used, to go out and make money—that economic right has no more or less constitutional protection than the right of a married couple to use or not use birth control in their bedroom. Is that what you are saying?

Judge Bork: No, I am not entirely, but I will straighten it out. I was objecting to the way Justice Douglas, in that opinion, *Griswold* v. *Connecticut,* derived this right. It may be possible to derive an objection to an anti-contraceptive statute in some other way. I do not know.

But starting from the assumption, which is an assumption for purposes of my argument, not a proven fact, starting from the assumption that there is nothing in the Constitution, in any legitimate method of constitutional reasoning about either subject, all I am saying is that the judge has no way to prefer one to the other and the matter should be left to legislatures who will then decide which competing gratification, or freedom, should be placed higher.

The Chairman: Then I think I do understand it, that is, that the economic gratification of a utility company is as worthy of as much protection as the sexual gratification of a married couple, because neither is mentioned in the Constitution.

Judge Bork: All that means is that the judge may not choose.

The Chairman: Who does?

Judge Bork: The legislature.

Subsequent wrangling over particular cases produced no more enlightenment than this; the judge and the senator never saw eye to eye on whether judges may enforce rights not found in the Constitution's text.

In the majority report from his committee to the full Senate, Senator Biden made Judge Bork's refusal to endorse extraconstitutional rights a central reason for his rejection as a nominee. Borrowing freely from the critical testimony of Professor Laurence Tribe of Harvard Law School,[30] Senator Biden titled one section of the report "Judge Bork's Approach to Liberty and Unenumerated Rights Is Outside the Tradition of Supreme Court Jurisprudence."[31] The earliest cases cited to prove the existence of this tradition, first by Tribe and then by the senator, were *Fletcher* v. *Peck*[32] and *Terrett* v. *Taylor*[33] (in Chapter 6 I discuss whether these cases were what the professor and Senator Biden made them out to be and hence just how venerable such a "tradition" really is). But as a preliminary matter, it should be noted that these two cases, the only ones cited from before the Civil War, had to do with property rights and thus could hardly be much help in attacking Judge Bork's refusal to endorse the reasoning of recent cases vindicating rights of a different character altogether.

Perhaps more important, Senator Biden had from the first day of the

Bork hearings couched his arguments on "unenumerated rights" (language that understandably enough he frequently linked to the Ninth Amendment) in terms of the fact that as human beings we possess rights antecedent to the formation of any government, any Constitution. This fact is both true and traditional in American politics, echoing the language of the founders themselves. Whether Senator Biden's conclusion about judicial vindication of all such rights follows is a matter that will be discussed in Parts Two and Three. But Senator Biden was using, in 1987, the language of natural law and natural rights. Hence it became very peculiar when, in 1991, faced with a nominee who had a well-documented commitment to the notion that there is natural law and we all have natural rights, Senator Biden made precisely that commitment the grounds of his opposition to the nominee, Clarence Thomas.

Two days before the hearings began on the Thomas nomination, the chairman wrote in the *Washington Post,* "If Clarence Thomas believes that the Supreme Court should apply natural law above the Constitution, then in my view he should not serve on the Court."[34] But Senator Biden had not forgotten the position he had taken in 1987 and attempted both in the newspaper and in the hearings to distinguish between those judicial resorts to "higher law" that deserve approbation and those that do not.[35]

In his opening statement in the hearings, the chairman said that because Judge Thomas was on record as "an adherent to the view that natural-law philosophy should inform the Constitution," he proposed to spend a good deal of time inquiring into just what this would mean in the nominee's interpretive approach as a justice. He then offered the following set of distinctions:

> Judge, to explain why this is such an important question, at least to me, we need only look at the three types of natural law thinking which have, in fact, been adopted by the Supreme Court of the United States in the past and which are being discussed and debated by constitutional scholars today.
>
> The first of these views: Seize natural law as a moral code, a set of rules saying what is right and what is wrong, a set of rules and a moral code which the Supreme Court should impose upon the country. In this view, personal freedom to make moral choices about how we live our own lives should be replaced by a morality imposed on the conduct of our private and family lives by the Court.[36]

The second variety of "natural law thinking," said Senator Biden, appeared in the "so-called *Lochner* era":[37]

> When the Court used natural law to strike down a whole series of Government actions aimed at making the Nation a better place for Americans to live, those natural law rulings struck down such laws as the child labor laws, minimum wage laws, and laws that required safe working conditions. They held that the natural law of freedom of contract and the natural law right to property created rights for businesses and corporations that rose above the efforts of Government to prevent the ills they created. They put these so-called economic rights into a zone of protection so high that even reasonable laws aimed at curbing corporate excesses were struck down.[38]

"And there is a third type of natural law, Judge," said the chairman.

> It is this view of natural law that I believe—I personally, to be up front about it, think is appropriate. In this view of natural law, the Constitution should protect personal rights falling within the zone of privacy, speech, and religion most zealously. Those rights that fall within that zone should be most zealously protected. These personal freedoms should not be restricted by a moral code imposed on us by the Supreme Court or by unjust laws passed in legislative bodies.[39]

Although he had combined here certain rights that are enumerated (speech, religion) with one that is not (privacy), Senator Biden tightened his focus a moment later by alluding to cases such as *Griswold, Loving* v. *Virginia,*[40] *Meyer* v. *Nebraska,*[41] and *Pierce* v. *Society of Sisters*[42]—all of which he apparently grouped under the rubric of "privacy." And noting that the modern Court has given up on *"Lochner-* era" natural law, thus permitting more economic regulation, but has adopted this "third kind" of natural law of which he approves, the chairman observed that "adopting a natural law philosophy that upsets that balance ... would, in my view, be a serious mistake and a sharp departure from where we have been for the last 40 years."[43] This is what he claimed to worry that Judge Thomas might do.

In examining Senator Biden's lecture on "three types" of natural law, the "first kind" can be eliminated as largely irrelevant to later colloquies with Judge Thomas and because his account of it is simply incoherent on its own terms. The senator's notion of seizing natural law as a moral code and imposing it upon the country is an unrecognizable portrait of what the judicial function is capable of accomplishing. Again appearing to borrow from his mentor in these matters, Professor Laurence Tribe of Harvard,[44] Senator Biden offered the 1873 case of *Bradwell* v. *Illinois* as his one concrete example of this practice.[45] But contrary to the statements of both the professor and the senator, the Court in that case did not "deny a woman the right to practice law" (Tribe)[46] or say that "women could not become lawyers" (Biden).[47] The Court did, rightly or wrongly, affirm a judgment of the Illinois courts that state law forbade women to be admitted to the bar, and that this did not violate the federal principle of equal protection. The most that can be said is that a state's imposition of a particular moral view on its female citizens was not interfered with by the Court. This can be transformed into the Court's imposition of its own moral view on the nation only by an initial confusion of courts with legislators.[48] How the Court with or without Judge Thomas on it could, to take an example from Professor Tribe, "decree that abortion is murder"[49] and make that decree stick should be a mystery to anyone who knows how our institutions operate.

At least with his second and third categories of natural-law thinking on the Supreme Court, Senator Biden was speaking in recognizable historical terms. But where his argument nevertheless collapsed into incoherence once again was in his complete failure to tell his listeners what principle helped him to conclude that "*Lochner*-era" natural law was bad and "*Griswold*-era" natural law good. If neither the liberty of contract nor the right of reproductive freedom is to be found in the text of the Constitution, if both are variants of the oxymoronic "substantive due process," if both entail adjudication of natural-law principles, then nothing other than the Senator's *choice* between them, his choice to regard one as archaic and obstructive of the nation's progress and the other as progressive and enlightened, can produce a distinction between them. But this is—must we say it?—a political choice, not one compelled by anything in the Constitution. For once having departed from the Constitution's text, and from reasoning about the principles contained in it, no constitutional tether remained to rope this argument back into the universe of constitutional discourse. The chairman was apparently also unaware that the *Meyer* and *Pierce* rulings of the 1920s, to which he alluded approvingly, came from the *Lochner* era— deciding supposed "family rights" cases on exactly the same principles as the "economic rights" cases of that day—and form the link to the modern "privacy" cases (since *Griswold*) that he was so interested in defending.

In short, the chairman's position was in contradiction with itself before the Thomas hearings had fairly begun. He did not see, or refused to see, that he was asking the nominee to both embrace and reject judges deciding constitutional cases by resorting to extraconstitutional principles. If resorting to such principles is a kind of Pandora's box for the aggrandizement of courts at the expense of other institutions (including the Senate), he was asking Judge Thomas to open the box, permit the escape of only the evils approved by progressive opinion, and then slam the lid shut again.

Matters did not improve as the chairman questioned the nominee. During his tenure as chairman of the Equal Employment Opportunity Commission, Thomas had indeed given a number of speeches discussing the natural law and natural rights that lie at the foundation of the American regime. But he had not, as he frequently pointed out to the senators, spoken as a judge—which did make a difference even if certain senators could not see a difference—and he never in any of the remarks entered into the record of the hearings had endorsed the notion that judges should resort to natural-law principles divorced from the Constitution's text in deciding cases. Unlike Robert Bork, Clarence Thomas could not be plausibly charged with being a legal positivist, who holds that there are no principles of natural justice; but neither could he, any more than Bork, be plausibly charged with holding that judges may reach "beyond the Constitution."[50]

Senator Biden was or should have been aware of the emptiness of this charge. An early and persistent line of questioning by the chairman was to ask what the judge had meant in a 1987 speech when he said that "I find attractive the arguments of scholars such as Stephen Macedo who defend an activist Supreme Court that would strike down laws restricting property rights."[51] The chairman had reason to know—from his own staff's compilation of Thomas excerpts that he entered into the record—but did not say, that the next three sentences of the same speech were these: "But the libertarian argument overlooks the place of the Supreme Court in a scheme of separation of powers. One does not strengthen self-government and the rule of law by having the non-democratic branch of the government make policy. Hence, I strongly support the nomination of Bob Bork to the Supreme Court."[52] To repeat: nothing in the record of Thomas's speeches shows him contradicting the position taken here, which deliberately rejects as "making policy" the course suggested by those who would revive the "*Loch-*

ner-era" defense of property rights by the Court that so concerned Senator Biden.

It must be said that Judge Thomas might have acquitted himself better than he did in response to the chairman and other senators. At times he seemed to fall back on a rote response that the issues of slavery, equality, and racial discrimination were his main concern in his speeches on natural rights, even when the specific context of particular remarks suggested that he was ranging farther afield than that. But there was no "confirmation conversion" from an earlier position on natural-law judging to a "safer" position that would win him the votes of senators. Yet the judge was clearly in a precarious position, under hostile questioning, and faced with a well-laid trap—although it may have been a better one than its makers knew. If he rejected a commitment to natural law altogether, he would appear to be an opportunist forming himself to fit the wishes of his interviewers and he would declare himself opposed to the "unenumerated rights" currently fashionable. If he attempted to explain how natural rights can underlie the regime and yet not be a means of adjudication independent of the Constitution—an explanation he did attempt[53]—he would not only risk being misunderstood by those who would not or could not understand such an argument, which in fact happened, but he would yet again become liable to attack under the banner of Senator Biden's "third kind" of natural law, his endorsement of which was demanded.

To a considerable degree, in Parts Two and Three I make out a case that Clarence Thomas was exactly correct on the subject of natural law. It does lie at the basis of the American regime; nothing else can give the regime a legitimate basis. Yet this fact does not compel the conclusion that judges may ever abandon the positive law for the natural in constitutional adjudication. This book, however, is not a vindication of Justice Thomas. I was at work on this project before his nomination and had already reached the same conclusion that he expressed in his confirmation hearings. For what it is worth, I too came away from those hearings doubting whether Justice Thomas had adequately explained the role he saw for natural law in the business of judging. It was only after examining the record more carefully than casual television viewing or newspaper reading make possible that I saw that he had both a consistent and a correct position. Yet that position was not complete, for this will be added to it in Part Three: the principles of natural law themselves should compel judges to the conclusion that it is improper to decide cases on such grounds, without a proper textual basis in the Constitution.

Part One
Political Prudence vs. Juris Prudence

In the four chapters that follow, I attempt to make out a kind of prosecution's case against the use of the word "statesmanship" as a term—even or especially as a term of praise—appropriate to describe the work of justices of the Supreme Court of the United States. In making out that case, I know that I run certain risks: of appearing to endorse some version or other of "mechanical jurisprudence";[1] of appearing to ignore the very real rhetorical requirements of constitutional adjudication, particularly in the writing of opinions; of appearing not to take account of the role played by prudence on a Court with an often delicate relationship to the democracy. The argument of these chapters may also strike the reader initially as playing a merely semantic game—as an exercise purely academic (in the hollowest, that is to say, most popular and most frequently accurate sense of that term), geared toward scoring points against other constitutional commentators. But if the reader shares my conviction that words matter, that they matter to us (as citizens, at least) perhaps most of all in the shaping of our politics, I hope that impression will not last to the end of the discussion.

Perhaps the best place to start is with a provisional definition of "statesmanship" (Chapter 2 will approach a definition somewhat differently). Here I follow Morton J. Frisch and Richard G. Stevens, who have defined the statesman as one who "does as much good as he can get away with," further refined as "removing the greatest amount of evil while disturbing the least amount of prejudice."[2] If this definition sounds unduly "conservative," particularly in its apparent obeisance to prejudice, it may be enough to say that in a democracy the overcoming of one prejudice held to be evil must usually be approached with an appeal to another held to be good. As Frisch and Stevens also indicate, the task of statesmanship is inextricably bound up with a vision of the political good, but they argue persuasively "that the doing of political good at any given moment is, for the most part, a negative thing."[3] And pursuing a Platonic metaphor of politics as medicine, they characterize statesmanship as

> chiefly . . . a business of cure. The excellent statesman will, if he can, play the nurse, but he can and he will, if he must, play the surgeon. . . . [W]hether one engages in quiet nursing or in radical surgery and harsh purgatives, the central problem is the same—to alleviate wrongs while saving the patient. In politics, to save the patient means to preserve the country.[4]

Already it should appear that statesmanship, by this definition, seems a task far more radical (in the original sense of that word) than judges can reasonably be asked to perform. That they might at times play the nurse is plausible; but the surgeon? In ordinary times, none is needed; in extraordinary times surely the judge is institutionally unsuited to be a surgeon. He sits too far from the operating table; his instruments are the wrong ones; at best he may play the auxiliary role of anaesthetist. If the "excellent statesman . . . can and . . . will, if he must," take radical steps to save the regime-patient, it makes the most sense for someone other than even our highest jurists to do the cutting.

Another, less metaphorical way of approaching the problem here is to reflect on two aspects of the statesman: his peculiar quality or virtue, and his characteristic instrument. The first is prudence; the second is rhetoric. Though he is not always thought to be very relevant to discussions of American democracy, the best guide here is Aristotle.

Let us consider the subject of prudence first. In *Nicomachean Ethics,* Aristotle defines prudence as a "truth-attaining rational quality, concerned with action in relation to things that are good and bad for human beings."[5] In distinguishing prudence (practical wisdom) from wisdom simply (prudence "is [not] the loftiest kind of knowledge, inasmuch as man is not the most serious thing in the world"),[6] and by way of attaching it to politics, Aristotle tells us:

> Prudence . . . is concerned with the affairs of human beings, and with things that can be the object of deliberation. For we say that to deliberate well is the most characteristic function of the prudent man; but no one deliberates about things that cannot vary nor yet about variable things that are not a means to some end, and that

end a good attainable by action. . . . Nor is prudence a knowledge of general principles only: it must also take account of particular facts, since it is concerned with action, and action deals with particular things.[7]

Thus far prudence is said to be that species of knowledge connected with the political art; with deliberation; with "variable things" rather than with Being; with "particular facts" as much as or more than with "general principles"; and, repeatedly, with action. It might be said, in the American context, that those who deliberate with a view to means, which in turn serve good ends "attainable by action," are legislators and executive policymakers. Moreover, judges arguably are, or ought to be, concerned with the priority of "general principles" over "particular things," at least in their adjudication of constitutional issues. And if deliberation with a view to action as the means to ends is a necessary (though insufficient) ingredient in the definition of prudence, then it is difficult to see any aspect of the American judicial function partaking of prudence as Aristotle understands it. Even today's most energetic advocates of a powerful judiciary would probably agree generally with Alexander Hamilton that it "has no direction either of the strength or of the wealth of the society, and can take no active resolution whatever."[8] The use and abuse of the equity power have expanded;[9] the entry of judges into social policy proceeds apace;[10] and the capacity of the Supreme Court to affect profoundly our notions of justice has been much noted. But we have never yet heard of the judiciary taking the nation to war or concluding a peace; of a judicial attempt at resolving the dilemma of the budget deficit (although ideas like a balanced budget amendment may invite just such folly); or, until recently, anyway, of court-ordered taxation.[11] In short, the most ambitious practitioners and partisans of judicial power still appear to subscribe to some limits on that power, stemming less from limited ambition than from institutional realities, and those limits seem to be marked out largely by the difference between the realm of action and the realm of judgment.

Aristotle also remarks, although only in passing, that the political art is "subdivided into deliberative art and judicial art."[12] The judicial art is, then, political for Aristotle, but it would seem to be so only in the sense of "having to do with the regime," for even this subdivision of the political divorces the judicial from the deliberative, and in both previous and subsequent passages only the latter has any firm connection to his conception of prudence.[13]

Some little distance from his remark on the nondeliberative character of the judicial art, Aristotle abruptly takes up the faculty of "understanding," distinguishing it from prudence in the following way:

> [U]nderstanding does not deal with the things that exist forever
> and are immutable, nor yet with all of the things that come into
> existence, but with those about which one may be in doubt and
> may deliberate. Hence it is concerned with the same objects as pru-
> dence. Understanding is not however the same thing as prudence;
> for prudence issues commands, since its end is a statement of what
> we ought to do or not to do, whereas understanding merely makes
> judgments.[14]

Though no explicit link is made here to the judicial art, it is plausible
that understanding is the quality Aristotle expects of judges as opposed to rulers. Yet it is more likely to be a quality desired of citizens
generally, called upon as they are to give assent to those who actively
rule in their name. In any event, being "concerned with the same objects as prudence," understanding too may be said to "stud[y] that
which is just and noble and good for man,"[15] and thus to deliberate; but
in failing to command, it falls short of the action-oriented, ruling character of prudence. We might say that judges, like citizens generally,
should possess a "discerning" prudence, while the active statesman
possesses a "creative" prudence.[16] It remains to be seen, in subsequent
portions of this book, whether constitutional judging in America, as opposed to citizen understanding and deliberation, is ever properly concerned with "that which is just and noble and good" in the highest
sense.

Turning from the statesman's virtue to the instrument of his activity, Aristotle says in his work on rhetoric that it "may be defined as the
faculty of discovering the possible means of persuasion in reference to
any subject whatever."[17] Its function "is to deal with things about
which we deliberate,"[18] and it comes in three essential kinds—deliberative, forensic, and epideictic. The three kinds of speeches are distinguishable in terms of their different audiences, the different times that
they address, and their ends, i.e., the different kinds of judgments that
they are intended to elicit. Deliberative speech is directed to a political
assembly, looks to the future, and aims to persuade its hearers of what
is expedient or harmful for the community. Forensic speech is addressed to a jury or judge, with a view to the past, and accuses or de-
fends with regard to the just and the unjust. Epideictic speech, ad-

dressed to "the mere spectator" and with a view "most appropriately [to] the present," praises or blames with regard to what is noble or shameful.[19]

As indicated above, rhetoric generally invites the deliberative efforts of the hearer, and so all three kinds (remembering Aristotle's remarks in the *Ethics*) may be said to be political in nature. But as Larry Arnhart has written,

> Although all three types of rhetoric are in some manner political, deliberative rhetoric concerns the ultimate aims of political life as manifest in the character of the regime; for as with the character of an individual man, so too is the character of a political community defined by that conception of happiness or goodness that guides all activity. Therefore, insofar as deliberative rhetoric involves happiness or goodness, it is the architectonic form of rhetoric.[20]

It may seem odd that deliberative rhetoric, with its concern for the expedient, takes pride of place over forensic rhetoric, with its concern for the just. But in the context of the *Rhetoric*, the justice to which forensic speech appeals is almost wholly a function of the established laws of the regime[21]—the "is" of convention—whereas the expediency to which deliberative speech appeals is, at its best, the justice sought by the regime as such—the "ought" of happiness or what is good by nature for human beings living together.

Even though in practice any given example of rhetoric will often be a mixture of two or all three kinds of speech described here,[22] it should be clear by now that Aristotle's analysis assigns to the statesman the function of deliberative speech. The deliberative orator speaks of those things that concern prudent action by the rulers of the community, "to wit: ways and means, war and peace, the defence of the country, imports and exports, [and] legislation," discussing "happiness and the things which conduce or are detrimental to it," and inviting deliberation principally "not about the end, but about the means to the end, which are the things which are expedient in regard to our actions."[23]

Though he discusses in his *Politics* the possibility of the rule of law supplanting the rule of men,[24] Aristotle does not, of course, advance either of the two typically modern doctrines that will be discussed in the chapters that follow: constitutionalism and judicial review. Still, if he has comprehensively accounted for the different sorts of rhetorical activity used in political life, the question may be asked, Where in the picture thus painted do American jurists fit, in their exercise of judicial review under a constitution? What, in terms of Aristotelian categories, is the rhetorical function of the characteristic speech of such jurists, namely, the written constitutional opinion?

Following the schema used above, we would want to know about the audience for which such speech is intended, the time with which it is principally concerned, and the end it has in view or the kind of judgment it intends to elicit. The audience to which any judicial ruling is addressed is the parties and advocates to the instant case. In the case of constitutional rulings from the Supreme Court, the audience will include relevant lower courts to which a case may be remanded or which may be called upon to treat the ruling as precedent in future cases; it will also include those political authorities responsible for the laws and policies either affirmed or reversed. Professional legal and scholarly opinion may also be considered here. But in what is perhaps the paradigmatic case of judicial review, in which a court invalidates the popular act of a contemporary national majority, citizens generally are the audience. On this score we seem to see an aspect of deliberative rhetoric.

The element of time in Aristotle's rhetorical categories is less easily sorted out here. Strictly speaking, judicial review is oriented to the past: was such a law or action really a law or action permitted by the Constitution? Of course, it seems that increasing numbers of cases today come to the Court following preliminary injunctions entered against laws newly enacted, which might be said to "freeze" such laws in the "present" until final judgment on them is pronounced, but still the essential question is in the past tense: was a thing done properly? And although it is also more common today to hear the Court pronounce or argue that certain things shall be done in certain ways hereafter (e.g., that "*Miranda* warnings" shall be given), these explicitly future-oriented rulings are usually the most controversial and are openly called into question by many who would say they fall outside the proper ambit of judicial review. While it would be absurd to deny the effect of judicial review on future actions to be taken in the polity, that effect is classically negative rather than positive: *this* action *was* unconstitutional, and *by implication only* it is not to be attempted again. Hence, with their most characteristic orientation being toward the past, here the constitutional opinions of the Supreme Court seem to fall into the forensic category.

Finally, with what end in view, with an intention to elicit what sort of judgment from their audience, are constitutional opinions delivered by judges? At one level, this seems an odd question to ask because, as the power of decision is in their hands, the persuasion involved in a case would seem to be more of them than by them. But judges do not (in the momentous cases anyway) simply indicate tersely their having been persuaded by one party or the other. They give an account of how they have been persuaded, and if this exercise is to have any meaning, it must be as a rhetorical effort to persuade their audience as they have been persuaded.

But to persuade the citizens of what? Of which sort of conclusion: about the expedient, the just, or the noble? The relationship between judicial review and the just by nature will be considered fully later. Yet surely it is not controversial to say that the Constitution that judicial review seeks to vindicate represents some kind of established agreement (or contract) that is the standard at least of conventional justice. In vindicating constitutional justice, then, judicial rhetoric appears to be forensic in character. But this is not a perfect fit; although the advocates to cases before the Court are surely engaged in forensic argument, the opinions rendered by the justices are the resolutions of the arguments of which they have been the hearers and as such are in some ways less persuasive than explanatory. Yet the forensic category is the nearest fit: unlike deliberative speech, it does not seek knowledge of expedient action; unlike epideictic speech, it is not primarily concerned with praise and blame.

In sum, constitutional opinions are characterized by a type of speech that is difficult to classify. In its audience, it seems to rise to the deliberative category. In its concern for time, and again in the end it seeks, it seems forensic. But in its very hybrid quality—the difficulty of its classification—its political character, certainly its partaking of the architectonic function of political speech, is called into question.

One other possibility remains. Walter Berns has made this fruitful suggestion:

[I]n their role as faithful guardians, the judges must act to strengthen, or "fortify," the popular attachment to the Constitution, or, to cause it to be venerated by the people. They must come to revere it and, therefore, to be guided by it even when it might appear to be not in their interests to be so guided. . . . The President may be said to employ rhetoric to reconcile the people's wants with the genuine needs of the country; the judges employ rhetoric to reconcile the people's wants with the institutions of republican government.[25]

What is described here is chiefly an epideictic function, persuading the people to maintain allegiance to the framework of the regime because of its goodness or nobility. Recalling that the epideictic is also political for Aristotle, this description of the judicial function reveals perhaps its highest calling: honoring, and persuading others to honor, not men (unless they be the framers), but the law itself.

This may be the nearest the judiciary comes to statesmanship classically understood. But it is distinctly one notch below statesmanship and in the latter's service. Constitutional law may instruct the people what to think, even teach them in a limited way what justice is. But it does not meet particulars in a timely fashion or shape means to ends or look to the future with a view to action. In almost no way can it tell us what to do today for the sake of tomorrow. It does not either deliberate or command, as does prudent statesmanship. In short, although speaking to the understanding of the people, jurisprudence in a constitutional regime does not speak directly to their will. Jurisprudence is not political prudence.

CHAPTER TWO

Statesmanship and the Judiciary

> The federal judges therefore must not only be good citizens and men of education and integrity, qualities necessary for all magistrates, but must also be statesmen; they must know how to understand the spirit of the age, to confront those obstacles that can be overcome, and to steer out of the current when the tide threatens to carry them away, and with them the sovereignty of the Union and obedience to its laws.
>
> —*Alexis de Tocqueville*[1]

As the crowds of reporters and interested spectators roiled about the steps of the U.S. Supreme Court building in Washington on the morning of July 3, 1989, reporting, hailing, and denouncing the Court's ruling in *Webster* v. *Reproductive Health Services*[2] (on the constitutionality of a Missouri abortion statute), a strange spectacle presented itself in a constitutional democracy. What, after all, were all those people doing there? What, indeed, were many of the rest of us doing glued to our television sets? They and we were there to hear the justices of the Supreme Court (or five of them, anyway) "say what the law is."[3]

What made the spectacle strange was that it took on the aspect of waiting for the Pythia at Delphi—that, unfit to govern themselves, the American people were there to hear a mysterious oracle pronounce the new order under which they would henceforth be governed. That the Supreme Court in fact returned some small measure of self-government to the people makes as little difference as the fact that the oracular judgment did not meet with a universally pious reception. The larger point is that we have become accustomed to thinking of the Court as the appropriate and final arbiter for identifying those matters in which we will govern ourselves and those in which we will not. This habit has become so pervasive that even on those occasions when the Court apparently eschews government by judiciary, it is not perceived as such: just a week before *Webster,* when the Court announced its refusal to overturn capital punishment for sixteen- and seventeen-year-olds, ABC's "World News Tonight" opened its broadcast with the statement that "the Court today expanded the reach of the death penalty."[4] If that struck many viewers as an accurate depiction of events, it is a fair measure of the trouble we are in.

That major decisions of the Supreme Court seldom please everyone is no surprise; I do not propose that they should. Nor is such controversy, in itself, necessarily alarming. What is alarming is the degree to which ordinary citizens seem to expect that the Court will resolve the nation's deepest political difficulties in a statesmanlike fashion; citizens are pleased or displeased at the outcomes of hotly contested "constitutional" issues, but pleased or not they seem convinced that the Court is the right place to have them resolved. This is true, as the examples above attest, even when the issue itself is the extent of the Court's willingness to be involved in certain political controversies. We may wait to see if the Court will be "active" or "restrained" in this or that case; what is noteworthy is that, often after attempting to pressure the Court as though it were a legislature, we then revert to our Delphic view of it as wise, inscrutable, above politics—and wait.

On the other hand, for citizens generally, this response to judicial power may be quite sensible, the result of calculating that, no matter how the Court became so authoritative over so much of our lives, its present position invites us to treat it as just another institution to be lobbied and pressured. In the recent case of *Planned Parenthood of Southeastern Pennsylvania* v. *Casey* (ruling on a Pennsylvania abortion statute, much awaited after *Webster*), Justice Antonin Scalia put it well when he pointed to

> the twin facts that the American people love democracy and the American people are not fools. As long as this Court thought (and the people thought) that we Justices were doing essentially lawyers' work up here . . . the public pretty much left us alone. . . . But if in reality our process of constitutional adjudication consists primarily of making value judgments . . . then a free and intelligent people's attitude towards us can be expected to be (ought to be) quite different. The people know that their value judgments are quite as good as those taught in any law school—maybe better. If, indeed, the "liberties" protected by the Constitution are, as the Court says, undefined and

unbounded, then the people should demonstrate, to protest that we do not implement their values instead of ours.[5]

Justice Scalia, elsewhere decrying the "statesmanlike" pretensions of the Court's opinion in *Casey*,[6] seems here to find perverse cause for optimism in the public pressure that has been brought to bear on the Court from both sides in the abortion dispute: that pressure at least shows that the American people can still tell the difference between legal and political institutions. The bad news is that they have surmised quite correctly that the distinction has collapsed in many respects.

More disturbing perhaps than public attitudes, because less excusable, are the frequent calls for judicial statesmanship that come from those who study and write about the Constitution and the business of the Supreme Court. In the debates of recent years between friends and foes of "original intent" (often infelicitously called "interpretivists" and "noninterpretivists"), it is perhaps to be expected that those who reject a jurisprudence guided by the text and its original understanding have a high regard for the statesmanlike potential of the judiciary. Explicit references to "statesmanship" are rare, but the scent of it is in the air. Thus Michael Perry writes, "Noninterpretive review in human rights cases represents the institutionalization of prophecy . . . designed to enable the American polity to live out its commitment to an ever-deepening moral understanding."[7] Or Owen M. Fiss sees in the judiciary "a special competence to interpret the public morality of the Constitution."[8] Or Leonard W. Levy says, "The Court has the responsibility of helping regenerate and fulfill the noblest aspirations for which this nation stands. It must keep constitutional law constantly rooted in the great ideals of the past yet in a state of evolution in order to realize them."[9]

Again, none of these statements is surprising, coming from scholars who range themselves against the binding character of the text's original intent. But statements of remarkable similarity can be gleaned from those who take the original understanding of the document more seriously. John Agresto, for example, although warning of the dangers of judicial supremacy, tells us that the "primary defense . . . of judicial review . . . is the possibility of using that power as a guide to the democracy in its desire to live a principled life, a life in accord with certain formative national ideals."[10] More explicitly, Gary J. Jacobsohn has written an entire book advancing a theory of judicial statesmanship.[11] Like Jacobsohn, Harry M. Clor finds "judicial statesmanship" a moderate mean between a too-rigid interpretivism and a too-freewheeling noninterpretivism.[12] And it is difficult to read the recent writings of

Harry V. Jaffa on the place of natural law in constitutional interpretation without seeing in them an invitation to judges to assume the mantle of statesmanship.[13]

It is not my intention here to catalogue exhaustively, much less to meet on all fronts, the various exponents of statesmanship in the judiciary.[14] This chapter is devoted to the much more limited task of showing that, from the perspective of the framers, any notion that we should expect statesmanship from the judiciary (particularly on constitutional questions) constitutes a great forgetting on our part; the framers believed that the judicial branch should be expected least of all to exhibit statesmanship. On the contrary, the founding perspective on statesmanship locates it mostly in the executive and secondarily in the Senate of a powerfully flexible Congress. The framers envisioned the judiciary as quite limited in authority; moreover, even within the admitted sphere of judicial authority, the notion of judges as statesmen would have been alien and dangerous in their eyes. In short, I propose to show that the statement of Tocqueville with which this chapter opens is one the framers would have regarded as strange and revolutionary.[15]

THE RELIANCE ON TOCQUEVILLE

Nearly everyone is familiar with Tocqueville's famous statement that there "is hardly a political question in the United States which does not sooner or later turn into a judicial one."[16] It is seldom noticed, however, that this remark occurs not in his explicit discussion of judicial authority under the Constitution (as is the case with his statement that judges "must also be statesmen") but in a section of his chapter titled, "What Tempers the Tyranny of the Majority in the United States"—the section itself titled, "The Temper of the American Legal Profession and How It Serves to Counterbalance Democracy."[17] The theme of the section is the way in which the legal profession fills the void in America left by the absence of a traditional aristocracy: conservative by virtue of both the training and the habits of their profession, lawyers as a class form a salutary check on the excesses of majority rule.[18]

And, though Tocqueville does refer in this section to the power of courts—e.g., the courts "are the most obvious organs through which the legal body influences democracy" and an American judge, "armed with the right to declare laws unconstitutional, is constantly intervening in political affairs"[19]—he subsequently informs us that "no one should imagine that in the United States a legalistic spirit is confined strictly to the precincts of the courts; it extends far beyond them."[20] Following this statement is the famous one about political questions ultimately becoming judicial ones; between the two, Tocqueville remarks on the heavy presence of lawyers in all public offices, not least in the legislatures.

In short, the celebrated comment about political questions turning into judicial ones cannot be read unequivocally as a statement, much less as an endorsement, of the view that all the greatest political questions in America are ultimately confided to the judiciary for resolution. An equally if not more plausible reading, I think, is that the dominant presence of lawyers in American politics has the effect of casting most political questions in legal (and even constitutional) language. "The legislatures are full of [lawyers]," says Tocqueville, "and they head administrations; in this way they influence both the shaping of the law and its execution."[21] It is only natural, therefore, that political controversies come to be understood, in all institutions of government and on the public hustings, in terms reminiscent of the courts of law; hence, political questions commonly come to look much like judicial questions. Indeed, the immediate sequel to the famous sentence reads as follows: "Consequently the language of everyday party-political controversy has to be borrowed from legal phraseology and conceptions."[22] It is difficult to get from the theme of this section of *Democracy in America* to a Tocquevillean doctrine of judicial supremacy, on the basis of one sentence alone.

The statement appearing much earlier in the work, that Supreme Court Justices "must also be statesmen," is more problematic and bears partial repetition: they "must know how to understand the spirit of the age, to confront those obstacles that can be overcome, and to steer out of the current when the tide threatens to carry them away."[23] This seems a fair account of the task confronting statesmen, but is it appropriate to apply it to judges? The passage appears immediately following some other remarks worth noting: that "one might even say that [the Court's] prerogatives are entirely political, although its constitution is purely judicial" and that its "power is immense, but it is power springing from opinion."[24] Consider the gloss on Tocqueville's statement by Harry Clor:

This remarkable passage speaks of a court which must possess and exercise considerable political judgment, including judgment about the temper of public opinion and consequently about what is possible or impossible to accomplish (or dangerous to attempt) by judicial decisions. This hardly looks like a simple court of law which only registers the compulsory dictates of given legal norms. The statesmanship referred to here apparently involves the virtues of courage and prudential wisdom: the courage to affirm demanding principles and the wisdom to know when and when not to do so.[25]

It is possible to accept Clor's reading of Tocqueville's meaning without joining in his enthusiasm for it, especially after examining one more statement by Tocqueville, located in the midst of those cited above (and omitted by Clor): "Now, of all powers, that of opinion is the hardest to use, for it is impossible to say exactly where its limits come. Often it is as dangerous to lag behind as to outstrip it"[26] (this is the antecedent to the "therefore" in the passage that opens this chapter).

If the authority of the Court rests on opinion rather than on, say, "the compulsory dictates of given legal norms," can we indeed "say exactly where its limits come"? It seems that Tocqueville (and Clor as well) has placed the cart before the horse. It is one thing to say that favorable public opinion is important, even essential, to the continued vitality of the Court's work, and quite another to say that the Court's authority is *derived* from public opinion, consists in *using* it, and is maintained by a careful attention to neither "lagging behind" nor "outstripping" it. Clor rightly notes that judges "of the highest court are, of necessity, custodians of the ethical respectability of the law."[27] But it is difficult to see how judges can fulfill that responsibility by attempting to gauge the breezes of public opinion. For even—or precisely—if, as suggested above, favorable public opinion is vital to the Court's performance of its functions, that "ethical respectability," hinging on the perceived legitimacy of the Court as a *legal* institution, is likely to be damaged when its members pay explicit attention to the political forces around them. It is an institutional paradox of judicial power, but unless we suppose a populace quite corrupted, it is probably the case that fidelity to law alone, and relative oblivion to the vagaries of public opinion, is what brings the justices the good opinion of the many—as suggested by Justice Scalia in his *Casey* opinion. Only thus can they deserve it, at any rate.

It may be instructive to compare Tocqueville's views with those of one roughly his contemporary, Justice Joseph Story, whose *Commentaries on the Constitution* Tocqueville cites approvingly on several occasions. "It is manifest, that the constitution has proceeded upon a theory of its own, and given, and withheld, powers according to the judgment of the American people, by whom it was adopted. We can only construe its powers, and cannot inquire into the policy, or principles, which induced the grant of them."[28] Note that Story is not saying that judges are not to inquire into the principles of the Constitution, only that it is irrelevant to constitutional judgment what any man or set of men had as a motive for adopting it. As he states elsewhere,

> The reason is obvious: the text was adopted by the people in its obvious, and general sense. We have no means of knowing, that any particular gloss, short of this sense, was either contemplated, or approved by the people; and such a gloss might, though satisfactory in one state, have been the very ground of objection in another. It might have formed a motive to reject it in one, and to adopt it in another. The sense of a part of the people has not title to be deemed the sense of the whole. Motives of state policy, or state interest, may properly have influence in the question of ratifying it; but the constitution itself must be expounded, as it stands; and not as that policy, or that interest may seem now to dictate. We are to construe, and not to frame the instrument.[29]

A judiciary thus forbidden to inquire into the complexities of public opinion at the time of the Constitution's adoption cannot legitimately be expected to attend to the state of it when rendering judgment:

> Arguments drawn from impolicy or inconvenience ought here to be of no weight. . . . Temporary delusions, prejudices, excitements and objects have irresistible influence in mere questions of policy. And the policy of one age may ill suit the wishes, or the policy of another. The constitution is not to be subject to such fluctuations. It is to have a fixed, uniform, permanent construction. It should be, so far at least as human infirmity will allow, not dependent upon the passions or parties of particular times, but the same yesterday, to-day, and for ever.[30]

It is the mark of a statesman to attend with particular care to the prejudices and passions of the moment, to inquire whether policy must fluctuate to meet the demands of the age. This does not, of course, mean that he must be simply a barometer of what currently excites popular passions. Lincoln may have put it best in 1858:

> In this and like communities, public sentiment is everything. With public sentiment, nothing can fail; without it nothing can succeed.

Consequently he who moulds public sentiment, goes deeper than he who enacts statutes or pronounces decisions. He makes statutes and decisions possible or impossible to be executed.[31]

Story's point is that judges must eschew exactly this role. They must, in reaching a constitutional judgment (though not entirely in explaining it), turn a blind eye to public sentiment and, Tocqueville to the contrary notwithstanding, not consider the question whether they are "lagging behind" or "outstripping" public opinion. It is Story, and not Tocqueville, who stands with the framers of the Constitution on this question.

PUBLIUS ON THE MEANING AND LOCUS OF STATESMANSHIP

"The opinion of the *Federalist* has always been considered as of great authority. It is a complete commentary on our constitution; and is appealed to by all parties in the questions to which that instrument has given birth."[32] Thus wrote John Marshall in *Cohens* v. *Virginia,* and the chief justice was not given to hyperbole.

The word "statesmanship" appears nowhere in the *Federalist*. The words "statesman" and "statesmen" appear only rarely,[33] and on all but two occasions their use is strictly for rhetorical effect. One exception is in No. 58, where Madison makes the case against too-numerous legislative assemblies by noting that in ancient republics they often came under the sway of "an artful statesman,"[34] a use of the word that hardly has a positive connotation. The other exception is in No. 10:

It is in vain to say that enlightened statesmen will be able to adjust these clashing interests and render them all subservient to the public good. Enlightened statesmen will not always be at the helm. Nor, in many cases, can such an adjustment be made at all without taking into view indirect and remote considerations, which will rarely prevail over the immediate interest which one party may find in disregarding the rights of another or the good of the whole.[35]

The passage appears in the context of Madison's discussion of the problem of factions, forming the transition from his conclusion that the causes of faction are ineradicable in a free society to his new beginning, in which he turns his attention to controlling the effects of faction.

The balance of the tenth *Federalist* is taken up with an exploration of how a "well-constructed Union," governed by politicians of the ordinary sort, can nevertheless "break and control the violence of faction."[36] Note, however, that in the above passage Madison seems to be saying that a steady supply of "enlightened statesmen" would reduce the need to "extend the sphere" of republicanism to "take in a greater variety of parties and interests,"[37] and the intricate institutional arrangements discussed elsewhere in the *Federalist* would not be so vitally required. An inexhaustible, permanent supply of statesmen would be better able to "adjust these clashing interests and render them all subservient to the public good." The first two sentences in the paragraph quoted above, if taken alone, suggest that the problem is not the incapacity of statesmen to cope with factions, but the scarcity of statesmen. Provided statesmen were always present, the problem with factions would disappear. The final sentence, however, introduces a severe qualification of this suggestion: even "enlightened statesmen" may sometimes (perhaps even "in many cases") find the problem of faction to be intractable. This is so because the rhetorical powers of even the wisest public men may prove inadequate to the task of freeing shortsighted factions from their attachment to what they perceive as their immediate interest. But those who truly govern with a view to "the good of the whole" are obliged to make the attempt. Here and throughout the *Federalist,* of course, Publius argues that the Constitution will maximize the potential and opportunities for such statesmen to arise in the national government. But he is realistic enough to concede, indeed to make it central to his argument, that they will "not always be at the helm."

In any case, a critical aspect of the above passage deserves attention. Madison provides here one of the few statements supplying a definition of statesmanship in the *Federalist,* and, if not compendious, it is a good one: the adjustment of clashing interests in the name of the public good. Is this a function Publius expected the judiciary to perform? Assuming for the sake of argument that the framers did expect or hope for statesman-judges (even if they were few), would not their permanent tenure in office place them "at the helm" if not "always" at least for considerable lengths of time?[38] (And, in the nature of things, the Supreme Court is much more a "continuous" body than even the Senate.) Why did Madison not consider the Court as an institution that could provide a near-steady supply of statesmen? The answer, I think (modern doctrines of "interest-balancing" jurisprudence to the contrary notwithstanding), is that neither he nor his coauthors of the *Federalist* thought that the judicial function included anything akin to the adjustment of clashing interests.

It is much clearer that Publius regarded statesmanship as desirable, and to be anticipated hopefully, in the case of the executive. Hamilton, as is well known, regarded an energetic executive as "a leading character in the definition of good government," for "a government ill executed, whatever it may be in theory, must be, in practice, a bad government."[39] Just what does Hamilton consider as characteristic of good government? The answer can be found in *Federalist* No. 71, when Hamilton offers a view of democratic statesmanship even more pointed than the one offered by Madison in No. 10:

> When occasions present themselves in which the interests of the people are at variance with their inclinations, it is the duty of the persons whom they have appointed to be the guardians of those interests to withstand the temporary delusion in order to give them time and opportunity for more cool and sedate reflection.[40]

Readers familiar with the *Federalist* essays on the judiciary may see in this passage a similarity to Hamilton's remarks there on the constraints the judges may impose on the popular will. But the reference above to the "interests of the people" clearly sweeps more broadly than any reminder the judges might provide of the people's duty under the Constitution. The people's "interest" surely includes veneration of and obedience to the Constitution to which they have bound themselves, but it certainly also includes far more than that.

One of Hamilton's central concerns in his essays on the executive is to show how its design is conducive to "courage and magnanimity enough to serve [the people] at the peril of their displeasure," to the executive's capacity "to dare to act his own opinion with vigor and decision."[41] It is to be hoped, continues Hamilton, that with the strength that comes from unity, and with a sufficient duration in office, the executive will be able to "make the community sensible of the propriety of the measures he might incline to pursue."[42] This account of the executive shows it to be (in contrast to the judiciary, as will be discussed later) an emphatically *public* office, vitally concerned with the relationship of deliberative rhetoric to public opinion; with the moderation and balancing of factious interests; and with the leadership qualities conducive to obtaining the public good even in the face of strong civic inclinations to the contrary.[43]

Like Hamilton on the executive, Madison when writing of the Senate also stresses the requirements of "good government," which he says "implies two things: first, fidelity to the object of government, which is the happiness of the people; secondly, a knowledge of the means by which that object can be best attained."[44] Like the executive, the Senate is designed to "possess great firmness," enabling it to resist "the impulse of sudden and violent passions" or being "seduced by factious leaders into intemperate and pernicious resolutions."[45] As such an "anchor against popular fluctuations,"[46] it is described by Madison in terms substantially identical to those used later by Hamilton in describing the executive:

> As the cool and deliberate sense of the community ought, in all governments, and actually will, in all free governments, ultimately prevail over the views of its rulers; so there are particular moments in public affairs when the people, stimulated by some irregular passion, or some illicit advantage, or misled by the artful misrepresentations of interested men, may call for measures which they themselves will afterwards be the most ready to lament and condemn. In these critical moments, how salutary will be the interference of some temperate and respectable body of citizens, in order to check the misguided career and to suspend the blow meditated by the people against themselves, until reason, justice, and truth can regain their authority over the public mind?[47]

What these theories of statesmanship in the executive and Senate have in common, and what is utterly lacking in the *Federalist*'s treatment of the judiciary, is the emphasis on discerning and serving the public interest amidst the violent winds that are often set blowing by the coming together and breaking apart of democratic majorities in a society characterized by a "multiplicity of interests."[48] Statesmen have both particular and general constituencies, which they must learn to both serve and oppose as circumstances require. Judges, it cannot be repeated too often, properly have no constituency but the Constitution and the laws. Though judges must also possess independence, firmness, and integrity, there is no indication in the *Federalist* that the requirement of these qualities *in the judiciary* has anything to do with the complex interplay of opinions, interests, and public policies that characterize the business of the executive and legislative branches.

A STRICTLY LIMITED JUDICIARY

Hamilton's *Federalist* essays on the judiciary are devoid of any statement that can plausibly be called into support for a theory of judicial statesmanship. If, as I have argued, statesmanship should be regarded as a preeminently deliberative political function, this should not be surprising. As David F. Epstein has written, the *"Federalist's* account of the judiciary stands somewhat apart from the rest of the book, just as the judiciary stands somewhat apart from politics."[49]

Hamilton does indicate, in the course of arguing for their permanence in office, that "fit characters" for the bench are not common:

> [T]here can be but few men in the society who will have sufficient skill in the laws to qualify them for the stations of judges. And making the proper deductions for the ordinary depravity of human nature, the number must be still smaller of those who unite the requisite integrity with the requisite knowledge.[50]

The judiciary thus will require men a cut above the ordinary, but there is no indication that such men will be as scarce on the ground as statesmen. Hamilton is confident of a constant supply of "fit characters" so long as their duration in office is not mistakenly made temporary, and he is relatively confident that such men will "always be at the helm" of the federal courts.

More important is the question, What does Hamilton expect the judges to do? The case for judicial review made in *Federalist* No. 78 has been recounted many times. But Hamilton's argument for it is more limited than the usual interpretation supposes.[51] A familiar but crucial passage reads as follows:

> The complete independence of the courts of justice is peculiarly essential in a limited Constitution. By a limited Constitution, I understand one which contains *certain specified exceptions to the legislative authority;* such, for instance, as that it shall pass no bills of attainder, no *ex post facto* laws, and the like. Limitations *of this kind* can be preserved in practice no other way through the medium of courts of justice, whose duty it must be to declare all acts contrary to the manifest tenor of the Constitution void. Without this, all the reservation of *particular rights and privileges* would amount to nothing.[52]

No wide-ranging review power seems contemplated here; even the reference to "all acts contrary to the manifest tenor of the Constitution" must be understood by reference to the antecedent examples of "specified exceptions to the legislative authority." This passage does not indicate what other provisions of the Constitution are to be enforced by courts as "the like" of the examples given here. But a similarity to these examples is insisted upon: that the judicially enforceable provisions will be particular and textually specific—and perhaps that they will also be provisions, like those Hamilton mentions, that raise questions uniquely within the competence of courts of law.[53]

At the very end of the portion of the essay discussing judicial review, however, is perhaps the strongest statement pointing in the direction of judicial statesmanship. After considering the worst-case scenario in which not only the legislature but the great mass of the people in support of the former combine to violate the Constitution, Hamilton admits that "it is easy to see that it would require an uncommon portion of fortitude in the judges to do their duty as faithful guardians of the Constitution, where legislative invasions of it had been instigated by the major voice of the community."[54] Courageous guardians indeed will be needed in such circumstances to be the "bulwarks of a limited Constitution against legislative encroachments."[55] But taken in context, Hamilton's confidence that this can be ensured again comes through, as he appears certain that securing the independence of the judiciary will supply this "uncommon portion of fortitude." As he indicates two paragraphs later, the Constitution secures the independence of judges in order to accomplish that "inflexible and uniform adherence to the rights of the Constitution, and of individuals, which we perceive to be indispensable in the courts of justice."[56]

This emphasis on "inflexible and uniform" fidelity to law is thematic throughout *Federalist* 78. Hamilton's declaration that, in a system of separated powers, "the judiciary, from the nature of its functions, will always be the least dangerous to the political rights of the Constitution,"[57] is probably the best-known quotation from the essay. The judiciary will be "least dangerous" because it exercises "neither FORCE nor WILL but merely judgment."[58] Relatively few scholars have drawn attention to the fact that Hamilton regards this as true only "so long as the judiciary remains truly distinct from both the legislature and the executive."[59] No one, so far as I know, has noticed that Hamilton is really making a twofold argument in this part of the essay. The paragraph that follows the one with the "least dangerous" remark begins this way:

This simple view of the matter . . . proves incontestably that the judiciary is beyond comparison the weakest of the three departments of power; that it can never attack with success either of the other two; and that all possible care is requisite to enable it to defend itself

against their attacks. It *equally* proves that though individual oppression may now and then proceed from the courts of justice, the
general liberty of the people can never be endangered from that quarter; I mean so long as the judiciary remains truly distinct.[60]

Hamilton's use of the phrase "it equally proves" shows that the argument is twofold in the following sense: first, he wishes to demonstrate
that the judiciary will be incapable of aggrandizing itself at the expense of the other two branches; and second, he wants to assure the
reader that the people's liberties will not be endangered by an independent judiciary. This twofold character of the argument is apparent
again later in the essay, in a statement already quoted above: that it is
"indispensable in the courts of justice" to have an "inflexible and uniform adherence to the *rights* of the *Constitution, and* of individuals."[61]

In light of this reading, it can fairly be said that the famous "least
dangerous" language is easily misunderstood unless Hamilton is allowed to complete the thought. Least dangerous to what? To the "*political rights* of the *Constitution,*" that is, to the rightful prerogatives of
the other branches of the national government (and conceivably to
those of the states as well).[62] The "least dangerous" remark is thus connected to the first part of the twofold argument sketched above.
Throughout the essay, the (often unnoticed) emphasis by Hamilton is
on the expectation that the judiciary will be relegated by "the nature of
its functions" to a position from which it cannot invade the province of
other institutions. Hamilton advances the case for judicial review and
independent courts much more cautiously than is commonly thought.[63]

Before leaving *Federalist* No. 78, one more point must be made. To
support his thesis of judicial statesmanship, Clor tells us that

> Hamilton does not mean, literally, that the judges are expected to
> consult nothing but the Constitution and the laws. He suggests
> that the judicial magistracy will have an important duty to per-
> form in mitigating or limiting the operation of unjust and partial
> laws which might not be unconstitutional laws. It would seem,
> then, that the federal courts were expected to have in view certain
> standards of justice or right which are not necessarily to be found
> in the written Constitution. They were to be, among other things,
> courts of justice.[64]

Clor is referring to a passage in *Federalist* No. 78 immediately following the conclusion of the case for judicial review, in which Hamilton

speaks of another way in which judges can counteract the "occasional ill humors in the society." Clor is on the right track when he notes that these "unjust and partial laws . . . might not be unconstitutional"; Hamilton, having done with judicial review, is speaking now of laws that are clearly not unconstitutional.

The paragraph in question has always been somewhat enigmatic, considering the reassurances throughout the essay that the judicial power will be limited. It begins as follows:

> But it is not with a view to infractions of the Constitution only that the independence of the judges may be an essential safeguard against the effects of occasional ill humors in the society. These sometimes extend no farther than to the injury of the private rights of particular classes of citizens, by unjust and partial laws. Here also the firmness of the judicial magistracy is of vast importance in mitigating the severity and confining the operation of such laws. It not only serves to moderate the immediate mischiefs of those which may have been passed but it operates as a check upon the legislative body in passing them; who, perceiving that obstacles to the success of an iniquitous intention are to be expected from the scruples of the courts, are in a manner compelled, by the very motives of the injustice they meditate, to qualify their attempts.[65]

Again, as Hamilton's own words indicate, the power he has in mind here is not judicial review. Indeed, it may clarify matters to imagine him defending a Constitution and a judiciary from which judicial review is wholly absent—to imagine him writing here in the context of a regime of legislative supremacy. What then could be this power to "mitigat[e] the severity and confin[e] the operation" of "unjust and partial laws"?

A number of alternatives present themselves. For Clor this power is a clue to a buried theme in Hamilton's essay, that the courts will exercise a politically significant statesmanship. James Stoner sees in this passage a power to "limit statutes which, though not infringing the document itself, nonetheless threaten justice or constrict rights."[66] True enough as far as it goes, but this says both too little and too much. For if this is, in Stoner's account, only a "limiting" and not an "invalidating" power, it nevertheless may be asked, What justice, what rights, are threatened or constricted yet ungrounded in either the Constitution or statutes? If, in the absence of a constitutional review power, all courts have the power examined here, it is easy to see that it can rapidly expand to fill the void, with judges invalidating statutes behind the thin veil of a claim only to "limit" them. It is doubtful that Hamilton had any such thing in mind and probable that he would wish to avoid even the hint of it in these essays. Finally, David Epstein, seeing Hamilton suggest "that courts may be lenient against the lawmakers' intention," concludes that "the judiciary can discourage injustice by dragging its feet in applying the law to anyone."[67] But, not to put too fine a point on it, judges "dragging [their] feet" in the enforcement of legitimate statutes are in violation of their oath of office.

I think that the only way to make sense of this passage is to read it as an implicit reference to the power to be lodged in the federal courts to hear cases in equity as well as in law.[68] Contrary to Epstein's suggestion, Hamilton refers not to a judicial reluctance "in applying the law to *anyone*" but to redressing in some way the injuries received by "particular classes of persons." And there seems to be more than mere statutory construction involved here, i.e., "mitigating the severity" of the laws; there is also "confining [their] operation," i.e., ruling that persons whom the law by its own terms affects are not in fact to be affected by it. Only the equity power can produce that result. And as Gary McDowell has pointed out, Hamilton's assurances of a limited judiciary apply here as well: this "power was to be confined by adherence to the precedents that had evolved in equity jurisprudence" by 1788.[69]

Hence Stoner's view is correct but incomplete; protection of a certain kind of justice is contemplated here, against those "hard bargains"[70] in which the law sometimes traps individuals. The most that can be said of Hamilton's remarks on the subject in *Federalist* No. 78 is that he hoped that judges construing statutes equitably, in appropriate cases, would induce legislatures to exercise restraint and avoid the passage of vindictive statutes. But those remarks will not bear a reading that supports a broad "judicial statesmanship" thesis; the paragraph immediately succeeding it contains our (by now familiar) "inflexible and uniform adherence" language, and the paragraph following that one contains the warning that to "avoid an arbitrary discretion in the courts, it is indispensable that they should be bound down by strict rules and precedents which serve to define and point out their duty in every particular case that comes before them."[71]

The digression of the last few paragraphs should not divert us from the main thrust of the essay. Hamilton hardly breaks stride in *Federalist* No. 78, moving from the need for judicial independence to the case for judicial review, to a brief treatment of the equity power, to the imbecility of temporary appointments, all the while striking what is the primary theme of the essay: that an independent judiciary will pose no threat to the rightful powers of the political branches because the nature of its functions under the Constitution will not permit it (a point that Hamilton repeats in a later essay), not that the judiciary is empowered to interpret the Constitution in order to protect individual liberties (this theme is present but secondary).

This interpretation of Hamilton's intent is the more persuasive when we recall that all of his essays on the judiciary are written in response to the alarums of the Anti-Federalist "Brutus," whose essays warning of judicial supremacy had appeared in New York some six weeks earlier.[72] For Hamilton to make his compelling case for judicial review in the course of quieting the fears raised by Brutus is a calculated risk. He can do no less than expound the clear implications of the Constitution, but he appears very concerned about not giving the opposition any ammunition to say, when he is through, that such fears are justified.[73]

THE CHECK ON JUDICIAL ADVENTURISM

If there is one place where Hamilton falters slightly in No. 78, failing to comfort entirely the anxious readers of Brutus, it is here:

> It can be of no weight to say that the courts, on the pretense of a repugnancy, may substitute their own pleasure to the constitutional intentions of the legislature. This might as well happen in the case of two contradictory statutes; or it might as well happen in every adjudication upon any single statute. The courts must declare the sense of the law; and if they should be disposed to exercise WILL instead of JUDGMENT, the consequence would equally be the substitution of their pleasure to that of the legislative body. The observation, if it proved anything, would prove that there ought to be no judges distinct from that body.[74]

This is a good argument, but not quite good enough—and from the evidence of a subsequent essay in which he returns to the subject of the potential abuse of judicial power, I believe Hamilton knows it. But it is interesting that at this point in his discussion of judicial power Hamilton is willing to leave the argument at this. From the standpoint of contemporary orthodoxy, it seems that he is missing a crucial fact: today it

seems obvious that if the courts go too far afield in construing any statute, the remedy is available in the ordinary legislative process,
whereas their errors or abuses in constitutional construction are only
reversible by the extreme exertion of amending the Constitution. The
two situations, therefore, would not seem exactly analogous today, nor
equal as risks to be run with an independent judiciary. Yet Hamilton
appears to think they really are analogous. In the very essay advancing
and vindicating the power now called judicial review, he draws in this
passage no distinction between the prospect of judicial misconstruction
of statutes and the prospect of judicial misconstruction of the Constitution. A plausible (though not the only possible) reason is that Hamilton
foresaw an environment of "coordinate review" in which Congress had
as much power to construe the Constitution authoritatively in the exercise of legislative functions as the judges had to construe it authoritatively in the exercise of judicial functions. Thus the legislative "correction" of judicial errors regarding both statutes and the Constitution
could, conceivably in some instances, have come about through the regular exercise of lawmaking authority.

Yet even taking this into account, it is not so that the danger described here, "if it proved anything, would prove that there ought to be
no judges distinct from" the legislature. Another thing it might
"prove," at least where the Constitution's opponents are concerned, is
that that instrument goes too far in Article III by extending the judicial power to all cases "arising under this Constitution." This argument of Hamilton's is amply anticipated by Brutus,[75] who with his own
reasons for regarding the Constitution as granting the Court "final arbiter" status never once reaches the conclusion that there ought to be
no distinct judiciary.

Perhaps realizing the incompleteness of the argument quoted above,
Hamilton returns to the subject of the potential for judicial abuse of authority in *Federalist* No. 81, the only occasion in his essays on the judiciary (and, I suspect, in the whole of the *Federalist*) where Publius responds more or less directly to Brutus. Without, however, naming his
adversary, Hamilton places in quotes what amounts to a synopsis of
much of Brutus's argument about the uncontrollable power of the judiciary to construe the Constitution loosely to suit itself. Both the objection Hamilton puts in the mouth of his unnamed opponent and the answer he puts to it deserve partial quotation here:

> The arguments or rather suggestions, upon which the charge is
> founded are to this effect: "The authority of the proposed Supreme

Court of the United States, which is to be a separate and independent body, will be superior to that of the legislature. The power of
construing the laws according to the *spirit* of the Constitution will
enable that court to mould them into whatever shape it may think
proper, especially as its decisions will not be in any manner subject
to the revision or correction of the legislative body. This is as unprecedented as it is dangerous. . . . [The "adversary" then con-
trasts this with Britain and the states.] But the errors and usurpations of the Supreme Court will be uncontrollable and remediless."
This, upon examination [continues Hamilton], will be found to be
made up altogether of false reasoning upon misconceived fact.

In the first place, there is not a syllable in the plan under consideration which *directly* empowers the national courts to construe
the laws according to the spirit of the Constitution, or which gives
them any greater latitude in this respect than may be claimed by
the courts of every State. I admit, however, that the Constitution
ought to be the standard of construction for the laws, and that
wherever there is an evident opposition, the laws ought to give
place to the Constitution. But this doctrine is not deducible from
any circumstance peculiar to the plan of convention, but from the
general theory of a limited Constitution.[76]

This is a somewhat better performance by Hamilton than is his treatment of the same issue in *Federalist* No. 78. It is still not quite a complete reply to Brutus, who argues that Article III's grant of equitable
jurisdiction "under this Constitution" empowers the courts to construe
the document "according to the reasoning spirit of it, without being
confined to the words or letter."[77] Nevertheless it is significant that
Hamilton, here as in No. 78, again emphasizes the limited character of
the judicial function—in No. 78 he only claimed a judicial authority to
invalidate laws "contrary to the *manifest tenor* of [specified exceptions
to the legislative authority in] the Constitution," and here in No. 81 he
concedes such a power only "wherever there is an *evident* opposition [to
the terms of] a limited Constitution,"[78] the latter phrase having been
given a fairly precise formulation in No. 78.

Hamilton might still be accused of inadequately quieting the fears
raised by Brutus—and the question asked, Where is there a substantial
institutional check on runaway courts?—if we overlook the fact that
he begins his rebuttal to his unnamed adversary with the words, "in
the first place." His "in the second place" rebuts the counterexample
from the British constitution. His "in the last place" begins about as

strongly as his previous attempts here and in No. 78, asserting that the "danger of judiciary encroachments . . . is in reality a phantom," which "may be inferred with certainty from the general nature of the judicial power" and so forth.[79] So far there is nothing new here; the judiciary poses no danger simply by virtue of the kind of institution it is and the kind of business it conducts. But Hamilton is not quite through yet:

> And the inference is greatly fortified by the consideration of the important constitutional check which the power of instituting impeachments in one part of the legislative body, and of determining upon them in the other, would give to that body upon the members of the judicial department. This is alone a complete security. There never can be danger that the judges, by a series of deliberate usurpations on the authority of the legislature, would hazard the united resentment of the body intrusted with it, while this body was possessed of the means of punishing their presumption by degrading them from their stations. . . . [T]his ought to remove all apprehensions on the subject.[80]

The message could not be clearer. Insofar as there is "not a syllable" in the Constitution to directly support a judicial power to reason according to its "spirit," any court that goes too far in this respect is engaging in a usurpation of legislative authority, which Hamilton manifestly regards as an impeachable offense. This constitutes the complete reply to Brutus: there is a power of control, short of the amending process, which can be held over the heads of federal judges like the sword of Damocles. If the judges depart from their "strict rules and precedents"; if they "substitute their own pleasure to the constitutional intentions of the legislature"; if they invade the "political rights of the Constitution" accorded to other offices, they may be "degrad[ed] . . . from their stations."[81] This sword is unlikely to fall in the absence of a "series of deliberate usurpations," but it is hanging there just the same, and it is clearly up to the Congress to decide how much provocation is enough.

Brutus might be said to have anticipated this argument of Hamilton's by offering a "strict construction" of the congressional impeachment power. In his essay 15, after noting the language of Article II, section 4, that impeachment is to be used in cases of "Treason, Bribery, or other high Crimes and Misdemeanors," Brutus reasons that "civil officers, in which the judges are included, are removable only for crimes":

Errors in judgement, or want of capacity to discharge the duty of the office, can never be supposed to be included in these words, *high crimes and misdemeanors.* A man may mistake a case in giving judgment, or manifest that he is incompetent to discharge the duties of a judge, and yet give no evidence of corruption or want of integrity. To support the charge, it will be necessary to give in evidence some facts that will shew, that the judges commited [*sic*] the error from wicked and corrupt motives.[82]

Why Brutus should strictly construe the impeachment power of Congress while broadly construing the judicial function is readily apparent: it suits his purpose in claiming that the Constitution establishes judicial supremacy. We have already seen Hamilton's reply. It is interesting, however, that the view of Brutus rather than of Hamilton is espoused by most, if not all, modern scholars. According to Jesse H. Choper, the "use of [the impeachment] power simply because Congress disapproves of a Justice's votes or opinions cannot be seriously defended."[83] John Agresto thinks that "Hamilton shocks us in *Federalist* No. 81" when he "rather cavalierly" recommends impeachment as a solution to judicial abuse.[84] Agresto is correct to point out that, historically, impeachment has "verge[d] on the politically impossible"; he further asserts that it "seems extremely inappropriate morally," for "impeachment to remedy judicial decisions smacks too much of a punishment imposed for the expression of an opinion, for the exercise of a duty laid upon one by force of oath and office, for the statement of a thoughtful judgment."[85] These may be persuasive arguments of policy (or of defense in a judge's Senate trial), but in principle the Constitution leaves it entirely to the discretion of Congress to determine what actions constitute impeachable "high Crimes and Misdemeanors."[86]

Some, like Robert G. McCloskey, think that the Senate's acquittal of Justice Samuel Chase in 1805 "set a precedent against loose construction of the impeachment power."[87] Chief Justice Rehnquist has written that "the Chase acquittal has come to stand for the proposition that impeachment is not a proper weapon for Congress to employ" in confronting the justices; but then he moves too facilely from a historical "is" to a moral "ought": "No matter how angry or frustrated either of the other branches may be by the action of the Supreme Court, removal of individual members of the Court because of their judicial philosophy is not permissible."[88] The complex nature of the Chase trial defies such a simple conclusion.[89] Henry Adams, although more friendly to the Federalists than to the Republicans of 1805, offered a more measured judgment:

> The acquittal of Chase proved that impeachment was a scarecrow; but its effect on impeachment as a principle of law was less evident. No point was decided. The theory of Giles, Randolph, and Rodney [of broad construction] was still intact, for it was not avowedly applied to the case. The theory of Judge Chase's counsel—that an impeachable offense must also be indictable, or even a violation of some known statute of the United States—was overthrown neither by the argument nor by the judgment. . . . [A]lthough the acquittal of Chase decided no point of law . . . it proved impeachment to be "an impracticable thing" for partisan purposes.[90]

Impeachment may be awkward, impracticable, and generally undesirable—who could desire a remedy for judicial abuse that can be invoked too conveniently?[91]—but if Hamilton is to be taken at his word, it is clearly available to Congress in the event that the judiciary strays too far from its "strict rules and precedents." Despite what he must have regarded as the reassuring failure of the Chase impeachment, Joseph Story felt constrained to say twenty-eight years later:

> It is almost unnecessary to add, that, although the constitution has, with so sedulous a care, endeavoured to guard the judicial department from the overwhelming influence or power of the other co-ordinate departments of the government, it has not conferred upon them any inviolability, or irresponsibility for an abuse of their authority. On the contrary for any corrupt violation or omission of the high trusts confided to the judges, they are liable to be impeached, . . . and upon conviction to be removed from office. Thus, on the one hand, a pure and independent administration of public justice is amply provided for; and, on the other hand, an urgent responsibility secured for fidelity to the people.[92]

I believe that Story's words here can be read to sweep as broadly as Hamilton's in *Federalist* No. 81.[93] Hamilton and Story, two great advocates of judicial independence, seem to be in accord on this point.

To reiterate the logic of Hamilton's reply to Brutus: since there is "not a syllable" in the Constitution that "*directly* empowers" the judiciary to act on its "spirit," any judgment that stretches the meaning of the Constitution beyond reasonable boundaries (say, any doubtful ruling that invalidates a law for creating something less than an "evident opposition" to the Constitution's "manifest tenor") violates the separation of powers by substituting will for judgment, the pleasure of the judiciary for the "constitutional intentions of the legislature."[94] In the event of a "series of deliberate usurpations" of this nature, Congress is entitled to impeach the judges and "degrad[e] them from their stations."[95] Note that Hamilton does not deny that there is such a thing as the "spirit" of the Constitution or that the judges may reason from it (otherwise he would not say that nothing "directly" authorizes this). He only wishes to make the much more moderate point that judicial adventures into the "spirit" of the Constitution are, and should be, fraught with danger to the judges. Congress, if it does its duty, will see to it that judicial reasoning that strays too far from the letter of the Constitution, consistently invading the legislative sphere of authority, is a high-risk enterprise.

However one conceives of a theory of judicial "statesmanship," it seems unavoidable that such a theory must prescribe frequent recourse to the "spirit" of the Constitution, whether described moderately as "infusing constitutional provisions with regime considerations"[96] or immoderately as "seizing . . . opportunities for moral reevalution and possible moral growth."[97] The founding perspective we gain from the *Federalist* is at least suggestive of the thesis that judicial "statesmanship" conceived in any such terms is not only ungrounded in the framers' thought but is an impeachable offense. True, the use of the impeachment power for restraint of such misbehavior is unlikely, but the completeness of the founders' robust system of checks and balances should not be forgotten, even if we are unlikely today to put all of them to use.

CHAPTER THREE

John Marshall on Statesmanship

Although he led an important diplomatic mission and was not an otiose Secretary of State, the decisive claim to John Marshall's distinction as a great statesman is as a judge. And he is the only judge who has that distinction.

—*Felix Frankfurter*[1]

In the preceding chapter, I purposely excluded anything more than a passing mention of Chief Justice John Marshall; the problem of Marshall's "statesmanship" deserves a full and separate treatment and will receive it in this and the next two chapters. But I anticipate that the most common response to the argument so far will be, "What about Marshall?"

There is no shortage of literature in constitutional law presenting the Great Chief Justice as a judicial statesman. It is very interesting, however, that the appellation (or its functional equivalent) appears to be commonplace on both sides of a very great fence in current constitutional disputes. There are those, on the one side, who approve of a good deal of judicial activism, acknowledge a kind of debt to Marshall for making it all possible, but attack him for *his* alleged activism; and those on the other who defend (though not always wholeheartedly) Marshall's career on the bench and decry the judicial activism of more recent years. It is not possible to review here in any comprehensive way the mountains of Marshall commentary that have been produced in law, history, and political science; an example of each tendency must suffice.

Among those in the first camp, a curious split personality reveals it-self. When Leonard W. Levy, for instance, refers to Marshall as "the most activist judge in our constitutional history," he does not intend that as a compliment.[2] This is borne out by Levy's titling the very next chapter in his 1988 book "*Marbury* v. *Madison:* Judicial Activism Run Amok." Yet he just as clearly likes judicial supremacy over constitu-tional interpretation, as long as it leads to expansive readings of, for in-stance, the Ninth Amendment rather than the contract clause.[3] One might well ask how, if *Marbury* was somehow illegitimate, any present-day exercise of judicial review can be otherwise. Levy at least, among all the Marshall critics, has the fortitude to face up to that question: "To the extent that national judicial review rests on *Marbury* it rests on rubbish"—and therefore only long "acquiescence by the people and their representatives has legitimated judicial review."[4]

Bravery, however, does not a sensible argument make. To distill it somewhat, what Levy is saying would run roughly as follows: The un-democratic power of judicial supremacy (although it does, paradoxi-cally, serve democracy when its results are "progressive") is a wonder-ful device for keeping an eighteenth-century Constitution properly in touch with recently evolved social needs and claims of right, even though it has no real foundation in law, precedent, or original intent; and it's a good thing that judicial supremacy exists—so long as the "progressives" hold the balance on the bench—even though it was in-stituted by that "conservative" John Marshall. Levy never explores why the "long acquiescence by the people" in judicial review should continue the day after his revelation of its illegitimate origins, nor does he stop to consider what value a Constitution has when its (allegedly) most admirable institutional feature is revealed to be not really there at all "from reflection and choice" but rather as a result of "accident and force."[5] Why John Marshall is a villain rather than a hero for this Machiavellian masterstroke of inventing the judicial activism that Levy so admires is only to be inferred, again, from the apparent fact that he practiced the wrong sort of activism most of the time.

Levy is a convenient exemplar of the first school mentioned above be-cause his is the most openly extreme recent account of Marshall's leg-acy by a defender of judicial activism. Others evince a more usual ten-dency to grant the chief justice a respectful hearing, ranging from the grudging to the admiring, while stamping approval on modern Su-preme Court rulings that clearly violate Marshall's canons of interpre-tation—including some that flatly overturn his precedents.[6]

On the other side of the fence are those modern critics of judicial activism who, in general, defend Marshall's jurisprudence but have a problem fitting his rulings into their doctrines of restraint. Here the most prominent recent exemplar is Robert H. Bork, who honestly admits that an "explanation of sorts is required, for even those of us who deplore activism admire Marshall, and it is clear that Marshall was, in some respects, an activist judge."[7] The explanation offered is that "his activism consisted mainly [but not exclusively?] in distorting statutes in order to create occasions for constitutional rulings that preserved the structure of the United States. Although he may have deliberately misread the statutes, he did not misread the Constitution."[8] Others who share some of Bork's views on judicial power may be less charitable to Marshall's readings of the Constitution.[9] Nevertheless, it is difficult to understand why a verdict of "guilty" on any count of activism, constitutional or statutory, does not fatally damage the esteem for Marshall held by this school. One surmises that Marshall is the tragically flawed hero who performed the signal service of defending the Union from the "centrifugal forces"[10] of Jeffersonianism but could do so only by yielding to the temptations of judicial power. In admiring much, we forgive much.

And so we have the basic tenets of the "Levy school"—thank goodness John Marshall inaugurated judicial activism, though it's too bad he often used it for the wrong ends—and of the "Bork school"—thank goodness John Marshall kept the Constitution from expiring in its infancy, though it's too bad he could only do so by succumbing to judicial activism. Both schools, in some measure, owe a debt to an earlier generation of scholars and biographers who fixed in the modern mind the John Marshall everyone knows: Corwin's "political strategist" advancing a "nationalistic creed";[11] Thayer's judge who "acted on his convictions," assured that he knew what was "the permanent necessity of the country";[12] Beveridge's Marshall of "perfectly calculated audacity," who resolved to use *Marbury* to effect "a coup as bold in design and as daring in execution as that by which the Constitution had been framed."[13] All three of these writers give assurances in various places that Marshall was a "statesman." Justice Felix Frankfurter, whose words open this chapter, might be said to stand at the end of this earlier tradition, echoing Beveridge in stating that "Marshall's intrinsic achievements are too solid . . . to tolerate mythical treatment";[14] echoing his teacher Thayer that the reasoning in *Marbury* "is not impeccable and its conclusion, however wise, not inevitable";[15] echoing Corwin that there is "little doubt that Marshall saw and seized his opportunities to educate the country to a spacious view of the Constitution";[16]

and concluding withal that the Great Chief Justice was America's only judicial statesman.[17]

Another strain in Marshall scholarship should be discussed briefly: the partially successful attempt to find Marshall's place amidst the political thought of the founding generation. Robert Kenneth Faulkner's 1968 book *The Jurisprudence of John Marshall* presents itself as "less a treatise on American constitutional law than a study of one comprehensive political, economic, and legal persuasion by which the Constitution was to be interpreted."[18] As such, however, the work tends at times to obscure as much as it reveals of Marshall's judicial behavior, since Faulkner builds his case for "statesmanship" by intermingling the chief justice's legal rulings with statements from his pre-judicial career, his nonjudicial writings as chief justice (chiefly the *Life of Washington*), and his private letters. The "whole Marshall" emerges nicely from Faulkner's book, but, as I hope to show in this and the next two chapters, that "whole Marshall" can be misleading if we are interested in the chief justice's self-understanding of his role as a judge.

Anticipating Faulkner by ten years (and partly inspiring him, as Faulkner acknowledges),[19] is Morton J. Frisch's more compact treatment of "John Marshall's Philosophy of Constitutional Republicanism."[20] Like Faulkner after him, Frisch very capably sets Marshall's jurisprudence in the context of his overall political thought; however, it is revealing that the section of Frisch's article where Marshall himself speaks most clearly on the subject of democratic statesmanship contains not a single reference to a judicial opinion.[21]

In contrast to all the writers considered above, I believe that Marshall, as he spoke from the bench, was neither an activist nor a nationalist.[22] Nor did he craftily foist judicial supremacy on an unsuspecting nation. Nor, finally, did he view himself as engaged in an enterprise he would have called statesmanship. In attempting to recover Marshall's self-understanding, I will argue as follows: that he essentially shared with others of the founding generation the understanding of democratic statesmanship of which I have written in Chapter 2; that he likewise shared their view that constitutional adjudication is a function quite apart from that of the statesman; and that none of his constitutional opinions either aggrandizes the power of his Court or "enlarges by construction" the powers of the national government generally. In this chapter I look at Marshall on the subject of statesmanship, and in the next two I discuss his views on the judicial power and on the use of that power in relation to federal power generally.

A partial recapitulation of the argument of Chapter 2 may be in order. The *Federalist* states that an "enlightened statesman" is one who attempts to "adjust . . . clashing interests and render them all subservient to the public good."[23] In the course of their papers on the presidency and the Senate, Hamilton and Madison enlarge on this theme, arguing that the purposeful design of those institutions is to give those who occupy them the capacity to lead, shape, respond to, restrain, and withstand the forces of popular opinion in a complex society characterized by a great diversity of interests. This is by no means to suggest that democratic statesmanship consists of nothing more than the skillful politician's dance of pluralism. The "clashing interests" are "adjusted" not for the sake of the statesman's power or political survival, but for the sake of something higher—the "permanent and aggregate interests of the community," as *Federalist* No. 10 puts it.[24]

The public good as the end and the interplay of deliberative rhetoric, public opinion, and diverse factions as the means constitutes the framers' (or at least the *Federalist's*) understanding of statesmanship. Already it seems to have, at best, an uneasy fit with any familiar notion of the judicial function because this conception of statesmanship emphasizes governing. Throughout Hamilton's papers on the judiciary, this idea is conspicuously absent: the judges clearly do not govern, but only judge; they are to be "bound down by strict rules and precedents"[25] that seriously trammel their discretion, whereas discretion is virtually the sine qua non of statesmanship in the other branches; and they are never said to have any "constituents" in the ordinary sense. It has often been said that judges have a constituency in an extraordinary sense, namely the whole polity as it expresses itself through the Constitution. But that can be said of the other branches as well and a difference would still remain: where the other branches are given a mandate to lead, the judiciary is given an assignment to serve. The justices of the Supreme Court do indeed perform a preservative function and speak to public opinion through their judicial opinions. But, as I have previously suggested, that task at its highest is to encourage veneration of our institutions—no mean feat but still preservative only—not to speak to the public will and inspire action.[26]

John Marshall never produced a systematic extrajudicial exposition of the Constitution (such as the *Commentaries* of his friend and associate Joseph Story) or any free-ranging work in political thought or in the theory and practice of republican government (such as the *Defence of the Constitutions of Government of the United States of*

America by the man who placed Marshall on the bench, John Adams). Aside from his judicial opinions, to be discussed in subsequent chapters, the only other work written for public consumption to which Marshall signed his own name was the *Life of George Washington*. The massive first edition of this work was published in five volumes from 1804 to 1807; Marshall later condensed the last four volumes somewhat for a two-volume second edition that appeared in 1832, the original first volume having been published separately in 1824 as a history of the colonies.

The *Life of Washington* has not always enjoyed a good reputation, from the time of its publication to the present. It was originally conceived by Marshall and Justice Bushrod Washington (the late president's nephew and heir, who was in possession of his private papers) as a way for both to memorialize the late president and to make some money, although their financial expectations proved to be too high at least in the short run (the second edition sold better). Albert Beveridge ably recounts the pains Marshall suffered in preparing the work and the decidedly mixed critical reception it received in its day.[27] Jefferson, who feared while the work was in progress that it would all be published in time to influence the election of 1804, was in later years to call it a "five-volumed libel" (although he never pointed to any factual errors) for its portrait of the origins of the Federalist and Republican parties during the Washington administration.[28] Joseph Story called it "invaluable for the truth of its facts and the accuracy and completeness of its narrative,"[29] which of course says nothing with regard to the *Life*'s literary merits, which were widely criticized. On that score even Marshall's own biographers have not been kind: Allan Magruder adjudges him "not a literary man nor a scholar; he did not understand the art of composition,"[30] while Beveridge calls him a "literary composer temperamentally unfitted for the task, wholly unskilled in the art."[31] As Marcus Cunliffe has observed, even Marshall seems to have been conscious of a need to correct a certain stylistic heaviness when preparing the second edition.[32]

Robert Faulkner, taking up the work with a view to Marshall's political thought, regards the *Life of Washington* as representing the core of Marshall's "thoughts on political education," notably in its treatment of "noble republican statesmen" and especially in its placing always "before the reader's eyes . . . the character of Washington" as a model for those who might also seek political fame.[33] This describes the book's essence very well, yet I would offer one clarification: it is not literally the case that Washington is always "before the reader's eyes," although he is no doubt before the mind's eye. Any reader of the *Life* must note immediately that it is less a biography than a political history; Washington makes no appearance until the very end of the first volume (naturally, as this is the colonial history), is often absent from major portions of the middle volumes on the revolution, and even drops from view for pages on end in the crucial (and best-written) chapters on his presidency. References to any aspect of Washington's life outside his public career are few, far between, and terse—a neglect of the private Washington that irked some reviewers.[34]

The reader of the *Life* must, therefore, confront the question, What is it Marshall was trying to accomplish? To make some money, certainly; to honor his friend, his general, the father of his country, absolutely; to educate his countrymen, there is little doubt. I would suggest that there is another probable reason as well: that Marshall regarded the *Life* as an opportunity to explore, through the writing of political history, themes in republican government and statesmanship not open to him in the exercise of his judicial duties.

Admittedly, there is a dominant theme through much of the *Life of Washington* that will be familiar to readers of his great opinions as chief justice: the theme of union. In his chapters on the revolution, for example, Marshall ascribes many of the difficulties Washington faced as commander-in-chief to the disunited character of the wartime confederation. Even though all the states shared the same goal, the league exhibited the imbecility of an "empire" in which "the essentials of government resided in the members."[35] Perhaps worst of all were the persistent financial troubles, with which Washington coped with a "degree of energy seldom found" but which could be attributed to the lack of a central power of taxation.[36]

As for the Articles of Confederation, finally adopted in March 1781, Marshall damns with faint praise: "If the confederation really preserved the idea of union until the good sense of the nation adopted a more efficient system, this service alone entitles that instrument to the respectful recollection of the American people, and its framers to their gratitude."[37] Yet immediately preceding this judgment, Marshall enters a harsher one. Comparing the original draft of the Articles reported to Congress by John Dickinson's committee to the final product, Marshall finds the latter inferior to the former, particularly in its barrier to any "incidental powers" of Congress. The result of the Articles' defect soon manifested itself, yet it "required the repeated lessons of a severe and instructive experience to persuade the American people that their greatness, their prosperity, their happiness, and even their safety, imperiously demanded the substitution of a government for their favourite league."[38]

Experience taught most but not all Americans that the "great and radical change"[39] of adopting the Constitution was effected over the objections of those who "seemed firmly persuaded that the cradle of the constitution would be the grave of republican liberty."[40] Just how radical the change was, in terms of the relationship between the nation and the states, is clear in those judicial opinions where Marshall had occasion to contrast the old system with the new, e.g., *Gibbons* v. *Ogden*[41] and *Cohens* v. *Virginia*.[42] But in the narrative of the *Life,* a thematic corner is turned in the pages describing the Constitutional Convention, the ratification debates, and Washington's decision to accept the presidency.[43] From that point on, the theme of union begins to recede into the background—although in his discussion of the origins of the parties of the 1790s, Marshall significantly remarks that the opposition Republicans grew out of "the party opposed to the constitution,"[44] which may partly account for Jefferson's acrimony towards the biography—and discussions of the statesmanship involved in making the new system work come to the fore.

In roughly the last quarter of the work, Marshall treats the Union as essentially an accomplished fact, thanks to the Constitution (that "sacred instrument," as he was to call it years later),[45] and turns his attention to the great political debates over foreign and domestic policy in the executive and legislative branches in the 1790s. Now there was a government truly capable of governing, and Marshall wades into the details of the period with a palpable relish that leads one to suspect that he misses the cut and thrust of partisan politics from which John Adams had removed him in 1801. He is usually scrupulously fair in his presentation of both sides of the major issues; it is just as clear, however, that he is a Federalist in political economy, a severe skeptic with regard to the French revolution and French policies toward America, and a Hamiltonian in his belief in the virtues of an energetic executive.

Marshall's account of the rising tensions in 1794 over relations with France and Britain, then at war with each other, brings out his view of executive statesmanship most sharply. In his view, pro-French sentiment was lending credence in America to principles that had already ravaged France under a "tremendous and savage despotism." Moreover, "those statesmen who conducted the [Republican] opposition" seemed unmindful of the danger facing the nation if the feelings of their followers went unchecked and "the physical force of [the] nation usurp[ed] the place of its wisdom."[46] Under these daunting circumstances, Washington, determined to maintain the neutrality he had proclaimed the year before, sent John Jay to Britain to negotiate the treaty that would historically bear that envoy's name.[47]

Even before Jay's return, this bold move accomplished two purposes: showing the people that "their President did not yet believe war to be necessary" and putting opposition members of Congress in the defensive posture necessitated by not wishing to appear to undermine the executive's policy initiative. No act of Washington's presidency drew "a greater degree of censure," according to Marshall, and none exhibited so well the statesmanlike concern for policy over popularity.[48] Beset by "loud, angry, and unceasing declamation," a veritable "assemblage of passions and of prejudices," Washington stayed the course, and his "firmness of mind" paid off when the Jay Treaty became the subject of public debate. Washington's steadfastness, says Marshall (combined with public opinion of his "judgment and virtue"), produced "more moderate opinions" in those who had previously "yielded to the common prejudices."[49]

On the domestic front, Marshall reports, Washington displayed qualities equally firm and statesmanlike. He concludes his account of the suppression of the 1794 Whiskey Rebellion as follows:

Thus, without shedding a drop of blood, did the prudent vigour of the executive terminate an insurrection, which, at one time, threatened to shake the government of the United States to its foundation. That so perverse a spirit should have been excited in the bosom of prosperity, without the pressure of a single grievance, is among those political phenomena which occur not unfrequently in the course of human affairs, and which the statesman can never safely disregard.[50]

This is followed by an extended rumination on the "evils generated by faction," the temptation of factious parties to adopt "the detestable doctrine . . . that the end will justify the means," and their ability to agitate at least some portion of the public mind, "inflamed by suppositious dangers," against "an administration whose sole object was [the people's] happiness."[51] In the case of the Jay Treaty, and in foreign policy generally, Washington led by persuasion, force of personality, and shrewd maneuvering; in the case of the Whiskey Rebellion, a timely show of force coupled with prudent foresight proved appropriate.

In each notable episode of Washington's presidency, Marshall stresses again and again the problematic relationship of reason and passion. Jefferson was later to say "that though the will of the majority is in all cases to prevail, that will to be rightful must be reasonable."[52] Marshall, following the lead of the *Federalist,* would probably have stated this somewhat differently. It would not, for Marshall, be true that "in *all* cases" the majority is to have its way; instead, the popular will is to be restrained, so far as possible, when it is unreasonable, and is to prevail in such cases only after constitutional arrangements and the efforts of statesmen have done their best to render it "cool and deliberate."[53] Washington, as depicted by Marshall, excelled in this task of exercising deliberation, and using rhetoric, to combat the "ascendancy which, in the conflicts of party, the passions maintain over reason."[54] In the lengthy character sketch of his subject that concludes the work, Marshall returns to this theme:

> Respecting, as the first magistrate in a free government must ever do, the real and deliberate sentiments of the people, their gusts of passion passed over, without ruffling the smooth surface of his mind. Trusting to the reflecting good sense of the nation for approbation and support, he had the magnanimity to pursue its real interest, in opposition to its temporary prejudices; and, though far from being regardless of popular favour, he could never stoop to retain, by deserving to lose it. In more instances than one, we find him committing his whole popularity to hazard, and pursuing steadily, in opposition to a torrent which would have overwhelmed a man of ordinary firmness, the course which had been dictated by a sense of duty.[55]

Although Washington has no equals in the encomia bestowed by Marshall in this work, two other leading figures of the 1790s receive special attention: Hamilton and Jefferson. In addition to their appearances at all the expected moments in the narrative, Marshall pauses for a brief sketch at the point in the tale when each departs the Washington administration. The contrasting portraits certainly reveal Marshall's partisan view of the period, but they also show his notion of statesmanship at work, with its consistent themes of reason and passion, policy and popularity.

Hamilton is described as having taken on his responsibilities at the Treasury "under circumstances peculiarly unfavourable to the fair action of the judgment." Called to a "duty . . . to contend with . . . prejudices" regarding the national debt, he responded with a program designed to "retrieve the reputation of his country." "While the passions were inflamed" with controversy over the relations between federal and state authority, Hamilton showed a "firm determination" to "give the [national] experiment the fairest chance for success." And when "a raging fever" in favor of all things French "seized the public mind, . . . he remained uninfected by the disease. He judged the French revolution without prejudice; and had the courage to predict that it could not terminate in a free and popular government."[56]

The corresponding sketch of Jefferson, placed in the narrative at the moment of his departure as secretary of state, is not exactly damning, but neither is it effusive in praise as is the treatment of Hamilton. It is a far subtler performance, suggesting by indirection that Jefferson had fewer of the qualities of statesmanship than his nemesis in the cabinet, let alone the president they both served. Describing Jefferson as a gentleman who "withdrew from political station at a moment when he stood particularly high in the esteem of his countrymen," Marshall suggests that his actions at the Department of State had been—purposefully?—designed to court favor with "that immense party whose sentiments were supposed to comport with his" on a variety of subjects. His recently published correspondence with the French minister Edmond Charles Genet had shown that he could defend administration policy ably when called upon to do so. But even that fact is turned to the negative side of Marshall's ledger; he could not walk much longer on both sides of the street, serving Washington and leading an emergent opposition party.

> It would have been impracticable, in office, long to preserve these dispositions [of friendliness toward France]. And it would have been difficult to maintain that ascendancy which he held over the minds of those who had supported, and probably would continue to support, every pretension of the French republic, without departing from principles and measures [of the administration] which he had openly and ably defended.[57]

In these lines (or between them) Jefferson appears as something of an opportunist, and one who very nearly boxed himself in by a kind of imprudence. Opposing, from within, the administration he served, he did perhaps more than anyone to germinate a party more passionate than reasonable; called to account by the extremities of the Genet affair, he found himself unable to play a double game any longer. Then, rather than lose his "ascendancy" in that party by a continued embrace of (in Marshall's view) sound policy, he bailed out of the cabinet in timely fashion. This is a clever Jefferson (almost too clever by half), a near-demagogue, but no real statesman by Marshall's standards.

Whatever today's views of the Hamilton-Jefferson discord are, certain conclusions may be abstracted from those personalities and policies. For Marshall, the figures who would be called statesmen are the consistent pursuers of wise policy, even in the face of popular firestorms; realizing their responsibility to both the people's interest and the people's will, they endeavor to unite the two through a combination of persuasion and firmness. The mere politician, on the other hand—even or especially the clever politician—sows the wind of popular passions, and if he is not to reap the whirlwind, he must be protean in his ability to be all things to all those over whom he has ascendancy. For both types of men, rhetoric and timing matter enormously, but in both the ends sought and the means chosen they could not be more different.

It should be clear by now that Marshall undertook the *Life of Washington,* at least in part, so that he could bring certain lessons of statesmanship, of political prudence, and of republican virtue and vice before the eyes of his countrymen. They were lessons, moreover, that his judicial duties afforded him virtually no opportunity to teach in an official capacity. In all his many statements from the bench on the role of the judiciary in American political life there is nothing like his reflections on statesmanship in the *Life.* Whatever relationship he contemplated between judicial power and the will of the democracy, it was distinctly different from the relationship, about which the reader is instructed in the *Life,* between active public men and their constituents.

Two more points need to be made about the *Life of Washington.* First, the work never reads like a lawyer's or judge's history of the United States; in the lengthy chapters on the early constitutional period, Marshall says next to nothing on the subject of significant legal cases, judicial power, or even the inauguration of the third branch of government. The Judiciary Act of 1789 receives two sentences, the Bill of Rights less than two pages, the first appointments to the Supreme Court less than a page.[58] Granted, the Washington administration was not the most exciting period in judicial history, but neither *Hayburn's Case,*[59] *Hylton* v. *United States,*[60] *Ware* v. *Hylton* (which Marshall argued and lost),[61] or even *Chisholm* v. *Georgia*[62] and the Eleventh Amendment are ever mentioned by Marshall at all. This is emphatically *political* history—the chief justice's own department of government is all but invisible.

A second, related point is that there is no dearth of *constitutional* history in the *Life of Washington.* All the major debates of the 1790s over constitutional interpretation are treated at length: the executive removal power,[63] the reporting powers of the Treasury secretary,[64] the national bank,[65] the first reapportionment of the House,[66] the neutrality proclamation,[67] and the conflict between the House and the president over executive privilege in treaty negotiations.[68] But there is a dog that does not bark, as Sherlock Holmes might put it.[69] Marshall never so much as hints that the judiciary has or should have had any participation in resolving these questions, much less that its participation could have settled them with an authoritative finality.

On the contrary, choosing just two of the above, Marshall states that since the Department of Foreign Affairs bill passed, affirming executive removal power, "it has ever been considered as a full expression of the sense of the legislature on this important part of the American constitution";[70] and that when the House reapportionment bill passed both chambers, the president had "the solemn duty of deciding, whether an act of the legislature consisted with the constitution; for the bill, if constitutional, was unexceptionable."[71] There is no indication that the judiciary should, or perhaps even could, revise the constitutional judgments reached in these instances. It seems from the evidence in these pages that for Marshall these constitutional questions are also political questions to be settled with finality by debate in the departments vitally concerned with them. How odd Marshall's treatment of these events must seem, to those who are convinced that he and his Court moved aggressively in 1803[72] to assert their final authority over coordinate branches of government in all matters of constitutional interpretation.

CHAPTER FOUR

The Breadth of National Judicial Power in the Marshall Era

In *Marbury* v. *Madison* the Marshall Court . . . served notice that it intended to be the last word on the delineation of sovereign relationships under the Constitution.

—*G. Edward White¹*

The belief that the Supreme Court under John Marshall's leadership went about systematically aggrandizing its own power, setting itself up as the ultimate arbiter of all constitutional questions, is the core of the modern convention that Marshall was an "activist" or a "judicial statesman." The gravamen of this charge—and I hope to show that Marshall himself would have regarded it as a serious charge, and an unjust one—is *Marbury* v. *Madison*.²

The possibility of a distinction between judicial activism and judicial statesmanship should not be overlooked. Not all constitutional scholars equate the two; some who embrace the latter would question the "ultimate arbiter" characterization of the Supreme Court, while others (whether foes of activism or judicial statesmanship or both) would accept that characterization while narrowing the range of constitutional questions in which judicial finality should prevail. Yet even this more cautious assortment of scholars tends to read Marshall, particularly in the *Marbury* case, as claiming either judicial power over virtually all major constitutional questions, or judicial finality over a considerable range of them, or both.³ And, whether accepting his reasoning in that case or seeking to improve upon it, this camp is generally one of admirers of Marshall's rulings on judicial power. For how can the Supreme Court be called upon to exercise a statesmanlike guidance over American politics other than by asserting an expansive judicial authority, either in its extent or in the depth of its contribution to the spirit of constitutional self-government? However, if Marshall's doctrines of judicial authority are found to be far more limited than they are usually thought to be, I think the distinction between judicial activism and judicial statesmanship, to the extent that it rests on a reading of his jurisprudence, must in practice break down. Both the judicial activist and the judicial statesman must claim more authority over constitutional interpretation than Marshall ever did.

THE *MARBURY CASE*

On the subject of *Marbury,* the most complete analysis yet done is in the recent book by Robert Lowry Clinton, *Marbury v. Madison and Judicial Review.*[4] In this section, I shall unabashedly follow Clinton's lead, attempting to resolve some difficulties his argument raises; in subsequent sections, I hope to add force to his basic thesis with additional evidence.

For starters, Clinton lays to rest, one hopes for good, the following myths about the case: one, that it was unprecedented; two, that it was ungrounded in the intentions of the framers; three, that the opinion takes the questions in the case in an improper order; four, that Marshall unnecessarily "lectured" the executive branch on its legal duty in passages that are pure dicta; five, that he misread section 13 of the Judiciary Act of 1789; six, that he misread Article III of the Constitution; seven, that Judge Gibson's 1825 dissent in the Pennsylvania case of *Eakin* v. *Raub*[5] presents arguments refuting the *Marbury* opinion; and eight, that Marshall asserted in *Marbury* a general supervisory power of the Supreme Court over coordinate branches of government, the power to say with finality whether they had breached the limits of the Constitution.[6]

If none of the above is true, then what *did* Marshall do in *Marbury?* According to Clinton, Marshall's opinion conformed to a principle Blackstone expressed in his "Tenth Rule" of statutory construction, which instructs a court to disregard a legislative act "impossible to be performed."[7] Furthermore, it conformed to Madison's remark in the Constitutional Convention, to which the delegates generally assented, that the provision of Article III granting the judicial power in all cases "arising under the Constitution" was "constructively limited to cases of a Judiciary nature," meaning those in which the performance of the judicial function was implicated by the law and facts of the case.[8] Conjoining these two points, judicial review becomes "a special case of statutory construction." That is, when a statute is directly addressed to the judiciary, it presupposes (as part of the statute) the related constitutional provisions that also speak directly to it; and the Court is obliged to resolve any internal contradictions that arise in the commands it receives from the law. It is not likewise obliged to resolve similar contradictions arising in the acts of Congress that presuppose the constitutional provisions speaking only to that body.[9]

Marshall, Clinton argues, implicitly recognized this in *Marbury* by treating as separate issues the *fact* of an unconstitutional act being a nullity and the *right* of the Court to invalidate such an act.[10] The Court is not entitled to exercise the right to invalidate an act, with finality, in all situations in which a factual nullity presents itself; in keeping with the principle of departmental self-defense implicit in the separation of powers, Congress is just as entitled to the final word over the extent of purely legislative authority as is the Court over the extent of judicial authority. Should the Court declare an act unconstitutional in a case not of a "judiciary nature," Congress legitimately may provide for continued execution of the law.

Clinton is not the only scholar to have argued for some version of "departmentalism,"[11] though he is the first to make a comprehensive argument for this precise version of "functional" or "coordinate" review. Andrew C. McLaughlin, for instance, appears to have advanced a "departmental" thesis early in this century.[12] William W. Crosskey advanced a " 'tripartite' theory of constitutional interpretation" some forty years ago.[13] And Ralph Rossum has linked Madison's remark at Philadelphia on "cases of a judiciary nature" to the holding in *Marbury,* although he has not fully explored the implications of this connection.[14] Another careful treatment, but closer to the typical view, is that of R. Kent Newmyer, who writes that in *Marbury* "Marshall did not explicitly claim that the Court was the sole or final interpreter of the Constitution,"[15] but then goes on to argue that this was implicitly there. From there it is a short step to the orthodox view expressed by Edward Corwin in 1914 that "the finality of the judicial view of the Constitution . . . is the very essence of judicial review."[16]

It should be noted that Supreme Court authority over state enactments is not implicated by this debate over judicial finality but is implicit in the conjunction of Articles III and VI and was made explicit in section 25 of the 1789 Judiciary Act.[17] As regards judicial review over acts of Congress, however, *Marbury* is exactly the kind of case within the parameters of judicial review—as described by Clinton—since the Court was deciding a question of its own function where an act of Congress empowered it to do what the Constitution forbade. By contrast, *Dred Scott* v. *Sandford,* the truer model of most subsequent actions of the Court as final interpreter of the Constitution, did not fall within the scope of legitimate judicial finality, as Lincoln well knew.[18]

A potential problem with Clinton's thesis arises in connection with some of the particular language on judicial review and hypothetical examples of its exercise given by Marshall in his *Marbury* opinion. If final judicial authority vis-à-vis acts of Congress is confined to those constitutional *questions* that are of a "judiciary nature," as Clinton interprets that phrase, then the beginning point for understanding this power would seem to require the identification of a limited class of constitutional *provisions* that would most readily give rise to such questions. This is not to say that judicial review of this narrow sort is utterly clause-bound or textually confined; the crucial thing is the centrality of the judicial function as an issue in the case at hand and the preservation of that function's integrity as a means for the resolution of particular cases. But notwithstanding the necessity of remembering the Constitution's context or whole and not simply its text considered as parts, the question "what gives rise to cases where the Court's word is final?" is as an initial matter best answered by focusing on particular provisions.[19] A list of such provisions, not exhausting but typifying the grounds of appropriate cases, would include Article III, in nearly all its parts; the prohibition on federal ex post facto laws and bills of attainder in Article I, section 9; and those provisions of the Bill of Rights having to do directly with the judicial process (easily amendments five through seven, arguably four through eight). These are provisions that literally cannot be violated without the connivance of courts of law; conversely, as provisions "directly addressed to the courts,"[20] they may form the source of rulings whose final (and thus binding) character literally cannot be undone by the other branches.

Now back to Marshall's *Marbury* opinion. In a passage discussing the nature of limited constitutions based on popular consent, the chief justice notes that that consent

> assigns to different departments their respective powers. It may either stop here, or establish certain limits not to be transcended by those departments. The government of the United States is of the

latter description. The powers of the legislature are defined *and* limited; and *that those limits* may not be mistaken or forgotten, the constitution is written.[21]

It would seem from this that generally described powers of Congress may not give rise to fit occasions for judicial review; only express limitations may do so.

Later in the opinion, considering whether "an act of the legislature, repugnant to the constitution . . . notwithstanding its invalidity, bind[s] the courts,"[22] Marshall has recourse to several "peculiar expressions of the constitution" that raise examples of the exercise of an appropriate review power. As Alpheus T. Mason has written, the "examples cited . . . are, without exception, clear, unambiguous provisions of the Constitution."[23] The examples are four in all: one, the Article III, section 2, provision that the "judicial power of the United States is extended to all cases arising under the Constitution";[24] two, the prohibition on federal export taxes in Article I, section 9; three, the ex post facto law/bill of attainder clause of the same section; and four, the Article III, section 3, requirement of two witnesses in treason trials.[25] According to Marshall, "many other selections . . . might be made,"[26] but these are the only ones he offers.

Leaving aside the third and fourth examples as causing no trouble for Clinton's thesis, let us turn to the first. It is not, as most interpretations would have it, a general principle of judicial authority followed by and encompassing three discrete examples of its exercise. As Marshall couches it, it is the first of his "peculiar expressions" that may occasion a legitimate judicial invalidation of a law—a point that is indicated by his saying, in the next paragraph, that there are "many *other parts* of the constitution which serve to illustrate" the power in question, thus leading to examples two through four above. In other words, the "arising under the Constitution" clause of Article III appears in Marshall's catalogue of examples as one clause among several that the Court is obliged to enforce and *not* as a statement of a broad authority to enforce all constitutional provisions against the acts of coordinate branches simply because the issues they generate, in some wider sense, "arise under" the Constitution.

I would argue that Clinton's interpretation of the "arising under" clause as limited to "cases of a judiciary nature" is the only way to make sense of Marshall's use of the clause as an example in this manner. Two points are relevant. First, Marshall's purpose here is to give examples in which judicial power is to be used to prevent congressional power from acting as though constitutional "limits may be passed at pleasure."[27] But it must be admitted that Congress's plenary power over the jurisdiction of lower courts combined with its power to make exceptions to the appellate jurisdiction of the Supreme Court is complete enough to prevent the federal judicial power from resolving a vast array of constitutional issues that may be said to "arise under" the document in a general sense. Therefore, Marshall could not be suggesting that the judicial power, regardless of any congressional acts to the contrary, reaches *all* constitutional issues—much less that it reaches all such issues with a finality that cannot be undone by Congress and the executive. But if the "arising under" clause provides for judicial finality only in the case of provisions affecting the performance of the judicial function, that version of judicial review may be called forth to invalidate even those acts of Congress that purport merely to regulate or make exceptions to the judicial power, including the Supreme Court's appellate jurisdiction—if such acts adversely affect the integrity of the judicial process.[28] The peculiar limit on Congress's power that may not be passed at pleasure, contemplated in this first example, is this: Congress may not legislate in such a way that it prevents the judiciary from fulfilling its duties in the cases properly before it.

Second, only this interpretation makes sense of the last two sentences of the paragraph containing this first example, which might otherwise be said to contradict one another or else to be nonsensical in light of other statements in *Marbury:* "In some cases, then, the constitution must be looked into by the judges. And if they can open it at all, what part of it are they forbidden to read or to obey?"[29] The second sentence, taken alone, would indicate that all provisions of the Constitution are fit subjects of judicial enforcement. But this would contradict Marshall's own statement, earlier in the opinion, of the doctrine of political questions—i.e., *constitutional* questions that "can never be made in this court."[30] Thus the second sentence must be predicated on the first: only in the "some cases" in which "the constitution *must* be looked into by the judges" are they free to consider all those provisions in the document necessary to a decision of the case.

But what are those "some cases"? All cases brought in procedurally proper form and raising a constitutional question? That cannot be, again by virtue of the same political questions doctrine. In fact, the "some cases" language is not, as is usually thought, a reference back to some broadly stated "arising under the Constitution" (i.e., "any constitutional question") principle; it is instead a transitional statement, following discussion of the narrow example of the "arising under" provision. Thus some constitutional cases—not all—will require the judges to "look into" the text, and once there, provisions other than the one that triggered the inquiry may become relevant to a decision. The "arising under" clause is used here merely as one provision giving rise to the "some cases" Marshall has in mind.

It is the second example of the four that Marshall gives, however, that raises the most serious obstacle to Clinton's thesis and to my own argument here, namely Article I, section 9, prohibition on federal export taxes:

> It is declared, that "no tax or duty shall be laid on articles exported from any state." Suppose, a duty on the export of cotton, of tobacco or of flour; and a suit instituted to recover it. Ought judgment to be rendered in such a case? ought the judges to close their eyes on the constitution, and only see the law?[31]

Insofar as the levying and collection of an export tax would not require in the first instance any participation of the judicial branch or implicate the performance of any of its functions, this is far from being a clear example of a constitutional issue from which could be made out a "case of a judiciary nature." Of course, Marshall knows that tax collection from the recalcitrant may require judicial decision of an executive branch prosecution of a "suit instituted to recover" the tax. Would a decision in favor of the executive's collection of an unconstitutional export tax harm the integrity of the judicial process? Not unless the notion of "cases of a judiciary nature" is expanded to mean some broad category of cases potentially involving judicial complicity in any and all unconstitutional actions of the coordinate branches, whatever the constitutional principle or provision involved. Is Marshall proposing an example of a constitutional case not touching directly on the judicial power or its necessity of self-defense and suggesting that a Court ruling on an export tax could be the last word on the subject? Perhaps he is. But if so, we are, after all the argumentation above, only a few steps away from the judicial supremacy Marshall seems elsewhere in the opinion to eschew.

There are only a few plausible interpretations of this passage. First, Marshall could have made a mistake here, including in his examples one that simply does not fit the pattern of the others or the principles of the *Marbury* opinion as a whole. Second, he could mean that this clause, like those in his other examples, makes out an express limit on the federal legislative power (rather than describing a power of ambiguous extent); that the Court's duty is to enforce all such provisions, not merely those that are addressed to the judicial function; and that the Court has a final, irrebuttable authority in such enforcement. Third, Marshall might have consciously chosen an example where judicial review might be exercised in response to a properly brought suit challenging an invalid statute but without having the last word on the constitutional issue involved. I will consider each of these in turn.

In the first place, it is not inconceivable that the normally careful Marshall made an error in the inclusion of this example, which is after all an obiter dictum. Two things point to the possibility. For one thing, it is well known that Marshall made another, arguably greater error in *Marbury:* that Congress may not give the Court appellate jurisdiction where Article III makes it original.[32] On this point, he should have known better from the adjudication of exactly that issue in *U.S.* v. *Ravara* in 1793.[33] But he retracted his remark in *Cohens* v. *Virginia,* in terms that clearly signaled the importance of distinguishing between dictum and holding.[34]

In *Cohens* Marshall also made an admission regarding the limits on judicial power to enforce the Constitution that is of some importance here. In that case, while making the argument that the appellate jurisdiction of the Court did not reach all cases arising under the Constitution in the state courts, the "counsel for [Virginia] . . . mentioned instances in which the constitution might be violated without giving jurisdiction to this Court":

> One of these instances is, the grant by a State of a patent of nobility. The Court, he says, cannot annul this grant.
>
> This may be very true; but by no means justifies the inference drawn from it. [Article III] does not extend the judicial power to every violation of the constitution which may possibly take place, but to "a case in law or equity," in which a right, under such law, is asserted in a Court of justice. If the question cannot be brought into a Court, then there is no case in law or equity, and no jurisdiction is given by the words of the article. But if, in any controversy depending in a Court, the cause should depend on the validity of such a law, that would be a case arising under the constitution, to which the judicial power of the United States would extend.[35]

Marshall's remarks here, devoted to the question of jurisdiction over state actions, seem limited to the doctrine later to be known as "standing to sue." But like its counterpart under the "cases and controversies" language of Article III, the doctrine of political questions, it is rooted in the notion that the "province of the court is, solely, to decide on the rights of individuals," as Marshall said in *Marbury*.[36] Indeed, Marshall never distinguished between the two doctrines as we would today; for him, a litigant who has claimed no injury to a right requiring a judicial remedy has raised a nonjusticiable political question.

But let us delve deeper into the implications of the *Cohens* remark. If a state were to grant a title of nobility, it would raise an issue resolvable by the Supreme Court only if the aristocratic patent carried legal rights not enjoyed by other citizens—rights that came into play in a case between the "nobleman" and a "commoner." Then and only then could the Supreme Court invalidate the patent in the course of reviewing a case. Yet Marshall's own comments make it clear that if, after the patent of nobility were invalidated in such a case, the state were to grant it once again without any special legal privileges (i.e., a purely honorary title), this clause of the Constitution would not be vindicable by a federal court.

This conclusion applies with equal force to a similar violation by Congress of the ban on titles of nobility in Article I, section 9. The question is purely a political one, with no other citizen receiving an injury from the violation, unless peculiar legal rights, unequal and therefore injurious in litigation, vest with the title. Only when such rights are at issue is the Court's performance of its functions at stake; only then does the title of nobility clause become a clause directly addressed to the courts. Then the Court must resolve the conflict between two individuals by refusing to give effect to the rights attached to the aristocratic patent. And it is possible that even then Congress (though not a state) might ignore a judicial ruling and continue to assert its power to grant such titles—perhaps with the last word, through legislation on federal court jurisdiction.

Thus, in the two prohibitions on titles of nobility are express limitations on the legislative power, federal and state, which may not be enforced by federal courts unless the faithful performance of the judicial process under the Constitution is implicated by the violation. If Marshall could not see in the ban on state patents of nobility a limitation generally enforceable by his Court, surely he could not see it in the identical ban on congressional power. And if one of the express prohibitions in Article I, section 9, is not generally enforceable by his Court, what other such limitations on congressional power are judicially unenforceable besides this one? Is, for instance, the requirement that "No Money shall be drawn from the Treasury, but in Consequence of Appropriations made by Law" subject to routine judicial enforcement? Perhaps his example of the export tax in *Marbury* is not fully thought through.

Some of the ground of the second possibility has been covered already. That is, perhaps Marshall means to claim for the Court a final authority over every express limitation of legislative power. This would still be short of judicial supremacy generally speaking, since there simply are not many such limitations compared with the grants of legislative power whose boundaries are flexible. But it would be more power than merely to uphold the integrity of the judicial function.

Yet could the Court really have the last word on the subject of an export tax? When, as Marshall says, an executive suit is brought to collect unpaid export taxes, the judges cannot "close their eyes on the constitution, and only see the law."[37] Because of the express character of the prohibition, a right not to be so taxed is at stake and must, it seems, be defended. But could Congress not provide for the continued collection of the tax? And if sufficiently annoyed by the victories of the recalcitrant taxpayers in court, could Congress not remove the subject of the tax's constitutional validity from the cognizance of the federal courts? If either of these questions, let alone both, can be answered "yes," then Marshall's example here is one of judicial review without the last word on a constitutional question.[38]

After consideration of the first two possibilities, a final one remains. Unlike the other examples given in *Marbury*, where the constitutional violation cannot take place without judicial participation, and where judicial enforcement of the prohibition therefore has a final character, the example of the export tax is not one where the Supreme Court, in practice, can have the last word. If Marshall made no error in raising the example, then his point was limited to this: if such a tax should come before the Court, it will not respect it; it will refuse to order the recovery of monies to be paid by him who challenges it; but the Court will not pretend that on this subject its ruling would have any necessary force beyond the case at hand. Marshall's Court will "see the Constitution" and not only the law whenever the former makes out a clear right against the latter. But should the other branches see the Constitution differently, even on so explicit a limitation as this, Marshall gives no indication of believing that the judicial view will finally prevail (whereas it must, by logical necessity, in the case of the other examples).

In short, the logic of *Marbury* dictates either the first or the third possibility described above: Marshall's example here was in error, perhaps careless as he had been on one other point in *Marbury;* or he had in mind one of those express prohibitions (of which there are few in the Constitution) of which the Court would be obliged to take notice in a proper case but without any illusions that its enforcement could be final in the face of determined opposition from coordinate branches. Far from claiming, as G. Edward White says in the quotation that begins this chapter, the "last word on the delineation of sovereign relationships under the Constitution," Marshall's *Marbury* opinion, with the possible (but improbable) exception of one ill-considered example, claims the last word over only one aspect of those "relationships": that which has to do with preserving the sphere of judicial authority.

THE POWER AND JURISDICTION OF MARSHALL'S COURT

If the *Marbury* case is restored to its proper dimensions, it can be seen to fit quite naturally into a pattern of other Marshall opinions on the scope of judicial power—without, of course, losing its uniqueness as a refusal to act under a federal statute.

The narrow scope of final judicial authority can be seen six years after *Marbury* in *United States* v. *Peters.* Responding to an act of the Pennsylvania legislature attempting to interpose in and annul a ruling of a federal district judge, Marshall wrote,

> If the ultimate right to determine the jurisdiction of the courts of the Union is placed by the constitution in the several state legislatures, then this act concludes the subject; but if that power necessarily resides in the supreme judicial tribunal of the nation, then the jurisdiction of the district court of Pennsylvania, over the case in which that jurisdiction was exercised, ought to be most deliberately examined; and the act of Pennsylvania, with whatever respect it may be considered, cannot be permitted to prejudice the question.[39]

Note that inasmuch as the effort of the Pennsylvania legislature was to interfere with judicial processes established or sanctioned by the Judiciary Act of 1789 (upon a pretext drawn from the Eleventh Amendment),[40] the issues at stake in this case included congressional power as well as federal judicial power. Nevertheless, Marshall clearly stakes out against all rivals one area of constitutional interpretation where an "ultimate" authority "necessarily resides" in the Supreme Court:

the "right to determine the jurisdiction of the courts of the Union." And a review of all of Marshall's constitutional opinions will reveal that this is the *only* passage where Marshall ever claimed for the Court an "ultimate" authority over *any* constitutional issue. It is reasonable to suggest that the judicial supremacy claimed here is all the supremacy there ever was for Marshall.

Yet notice too the boldness, from one point of view, of Marshall's declaration of supremacy here. As he knows, the "jurisdiction of the courts of the Union" is subject to considerable control by Congress, which creates the lower courts and defines their jurisdiction, and exercises significant power over the appellate jurisdiction of the Supreme Court. Was he only asserting his Court's power as against the power of a state—given the circumstances of this case—and forgetting that congressional role? That is unlikely. Marshall was not apt to make such sweeping statements unthinkingly, especially when writing of the powers of the judiciary. He must mean just what he says: that the "ultimate right . . . resides in the supreme judicial tribunal of the nation" when questions of judicial authority are at stake. As indicated previously, Marshall's *Marbury* principle would encompass a power to gainsay congressional acts regarding the judiciary if it were concluded that such acts damaged the courts' capacity to carry out their duties properly.

Thus the "*Peters* principle," if I may so call it, is that the Court has final authority over questions of its own and other federal courts' functions as those functions are defined in the Constitution and relevant acts of Congress (assuming the latter are constitutional, as one proved not to be in *Marbury*). But this does not mean that Marshall took this power to be a brief for playing fast and loose with the terms of either Article III or the acts of Congress affecting the judiciary. In other words, the *Peters* principle (and *Marbury*) are perfectly consistent with a pattern of cases in which Marshall either declined jurisdiction for the Court on Article III grounds or deferred to Congress (in taking or not taking jurisdiction) in setting the boundaries of judicial power. The remainder of this section illustrates this pattern by examples.

In *Hodgson and Thompson* v. *Bowerbank,* Marshall declined jurisdiction for the Court on Article III grounds regarding the character of the parties, despite an argument by counsel that section 11 of the 1789 Judiciary Act gave it jurisdiction. Interestingly, although Marshall's remark that "the statute cannot extend the jurisdiction beyond the limits of the constitution" called the constitutionality of section 11 into question if counsel's interpretation of it were correct, he did not rule on that question, simply dismissing the case.[41] This is certainly not the Marshall renowned for his alleged predilection for reaching out to make constitutional rulings.

In *Owings* v. *Norwood's Lessee,* Marshall declined jurisdiction by strictly interpreting the "arising under a treaty" provision of Article III, such that a mere implication of a claim under a treaty proved insufficient if no direct claim were put forward.[42]

In *Cherokee Nation* v. *Georgia,* Marshall held that the Court could not accept the suit under its Article III diversity jurisdiction because by a literal construction the Cherokees could not be shown to be a "foreign state" within the meaning of the Constitution, particularly due to the distinction drawn between "foreign Nations" and "the Indian Tribes" in the commerce clause of Article I, section 8.[43]

In both *United States* v. *More*[44] and *Durousseau* v. *United States*[45] Marshall ruled that, absent any act of Congress on the subject, the Supreme Court's appellate jurisdiction is fully defined by Article III; nevertheless the affirmative description by Congress of cases in which the Court has such jurisdiction can be taken to imply a negative regarding the cases in which it has not. Thus, pursuant to its Article III power to make exceptions to the Court's appellate jurisdiction, Congress is not necessarily required to state the exceptions in terms if it chooses instead to grant a new class of appellate cases "arising under the laws."[46]

In *United States* v. *Bevans,* Marshall opined that a federal circuit court could not take jurisdiction of a murder case, on the grounds that the place in which the murder occurred did not clearly fall within the terms of the act of Congress under which jurisdiction was claimed.[47]

In *Bank of the United States* v. *Deveaux,* Marshall ruled (by literal interpretation) that the act of Congress creating the Bank did not accord it a general right to sue in federal courts, the right not being expressly granted. However, he held that the suit could go forward on other grounds, despite some misgivings that a corporation is "certainly not a citizen," because "in this case the corporate name represents persons who are members of the corporation."[48]

A digression on *Deveaux:* in the course of the opinion, Marshall also offers the following observation:

> The duties of this court, to exercise jurisdiction where it is conferred, and not to usurp it where it is not conferred, are of equal obligation. The constitution, therefore, and the law are to be expounded, without a leaning the one way or the other, according to

those general principles which usually govern in the construction of fundamental or other laws.

A constitution, from its nature, deals in generals, not in detail. Its framers cannot perceive minute distinctions which arise in the progress of the nation, and therefore confine it to the establishment of broad and general principles.[49]

It is tempting for scholars who think they know the Marshall of *McCulloch* and *Gibbons* to seize upon the second paragraph without recognizing that its principle is conditioned by, and premised on, the first. The first paragraph, after stating one of the elements of what I have called the *Peters* principle, proceeds to bear out the view that "constitutional interpretation [is] a special case of statutory construction."[50] The same "general principles" apply "in the construction of fundamental *or* other laws"; the salient difference between Constitution and statute is not in the interpretive canons, which are the same for each, but in the relatively greater difficulty in applying those canons to the Constitution, for the reasons of generality in draftsmanship alluded to in the second paragraph.[51]

Three more cases illustrate Marshall's consistent refusal, even when deciding questions of judicial power, either to read more into a statute than Congress put there or to gainsay a congressional act for an expansive use of power. In *Hepburn* v. *Ellzey* Marshall ruled by careful statutory construction that residents of the District of Columbia could not sue in the Virginia federal circuit court because they were not residents of "a State" as that term is consistently used in the Constitution and acts of Congress. He admitted that "it is extraordinary that the courts of the United States, which are open to aliens, and to the citizens of every State in the Union, should be closed upon them. But this is a subject for legislative, not for judicial consideration."[52] And in *Sere* v. *Pitot*[53] and *American Insurance Co.* v. *Canter*,[54] he upheld the power of Congress to create "legislative courts" in the federal territories, defining their jurisdiction without regard to Article III, on the grounds of its plenary power over territories granted in Article IV, section 3, clause 2.[55]

A final case illustrates how Marshall understood federalism to affect the judicial power. In *Elmendorf* v. *Taylor* he held that while the Supreme Court can offer interpretations of federal law binding on state courts, likewise the highest court of a state gives the authoritative construction of the enactments of its state legislature, which the Supreme Court is obliged to accept.[56]

This review of Marshall's opinions on the nature and scope of the judicial function should help to place *Marbury* in perspective as one
among many cases in which Marshall's court ruled quite narrowly on a
question of its own legitimate power as conditioned by the conjunction
of Article III and acts of Congress. The single thing that sets *Marbury*
apart is that it is the only case in which that conjunction created a re-
pugnancy that the Court was forced to resolve. It is implausible, after
setting that case beside the others just reviewed, to view *Marbury* as
representing either a precedent for judicial supremacy or even a habit-
ual tendency by Marshall to grasp after greater judicial power in creative, "statesmanlike" fashion.[57]

The only case that remains to be considered on the subject of judicial
power, although portions of it were relevant earlier, is *Cohens* v. *Virginia.*[58] Whatever might be said about *Cohens,* from Beveridge's rather
florid account of it[59] to David Currie's complaint that Marshall
"reach[ed] out for issues not necessarily presented,"[60] there can be little
doubt of two things: a contrary jurisdictional holding would have flatly
contradicted both Article III and legitimate federal legislation, thereby
upsetting the balance of federal-state relations; and therefore it is at
least as much the power of Congress as of the Court that is supported
by the denial of Virginia's motion to dismiss for want of jurisdiction.

Those inclined to see "statesmanship" in Marshall's best-known
opinions point to *Cohens,* among others, for its lengthy treatment of
"nationalistic" constitutional doctrine.[61] Why did the chief justice simply not cite section 25 of the 1789 Judiciary Act and summarily deny
Virginia's motion for dismissal of the Cohens' application for a writ of
error? The answer is that the counsel for the state offered arguments
on the nature of the Union and the extent of national power so manifestly absurd and so completely divorced from the express terms of the
Constitution that Marshall clearly felt obliged to give them a full reply—so as not to permit a perversely alleged "spirit of the constitution
[to] justify this attempt to control its words."[62] Moreover, the challenge
by Virginia was directly aimed at the one area of constitutional law
over which the Court has final authority. Marshall's tone of surprise
and exasperation at the temerity of the challenge is apparent: "The
propriety of entrusting the construction of the constitution, and laws
made in pursuance thereof, to the judiciary of the Union, has not, we
believe, as yet, been called into question."[63]

Yet, consistent with *Marbury* and *Peters,* Marshall refrained from
claiming Supreme Court finality over any issue not of a "judiciary nature," as was apparent in the passage on titles of nobility discussed ear-

lier. Marshall is so far from claiming for the Court final authority over all constitutional questions that throughout *Cohens* he maintains this careful distinction, claiming only that the federal judiciary "must be capable of deciding every *judicial* question which grows out of the constitution and laws"; that the framers gave it the power of "preserving [the constitution and laws of the Union] from all violation from every quarter, *so far as judicial decisions can preserve them*"; and again that the object of the judicial power is "the preservation of the constitution and laws of the United States, *so far as they can be preserved by judicial authority.*"[64] The furor with which *Cohens* was met by Jefferson and the Republicans says more about their faulty understanding of the Constitution and of Marshall's opinion than it does about the substance of the decision.

THE VIEWS OF MARSHALL'S CONTEMPORARIES: MADISON, HAMILTON, AND STORY

Robert Clinton has capably assembled much evidence on the views of various founders on the subject of judicial review, pointing in particular to the doctrinal differences between Jefferson and Madison. Jefferson seemed, after 1801 at least, to advance a doctrine that Clinton calls "arbitrary" coordinate review as opposed to the "functional" coordinate review claimed in *Marbury.*[65] Madison, on the other hand, not only made the remark on "cases of a Judiciary nature" in the Philadelphia Convention—expressing a functional limitation on judicial review "generally supposed" by the delegates in voting unanimously to extend judicial power to cases arising under the Constitution[66]—but he also may be seen, as Clinton notes, taking essentially the same position in 1789 in the debate on executive removal power.[67] As Chapter 3 illustrated, Marshall reported the outcome of that debate, in the *Life of Washington,* in terms that took on Madison's position without question.

Madison and the "Forms of the Constitution"

Still more evidence may be amassed on Madison's generally consistent position, opposed to judicial supremacy and wedded to a functional review power in the Court. Some of the evidence, however, is in the nature of significant silences. Yet in most of the great constitutional controversies in which he was involved, Madison rarely mentioned the federal judiciary as the locus of decision of those controversies—still less as the locus of final authority. And a silence so significant should be understood as saying something.

In *Federalist* No. 44, discussing the "necessary and proper" clause— probably one of the provisions most frightening to Anti-Federalists— Madison mentions the judiciary only in passing while attempting to counter the fears of implied powers run amok:

> In the first instance, the success of the usurpation will depend on the executive and judiciary departments, which are to expound and give effect to the legislative acts; and in the *last resort* a remedy must be obtained from the people, who can, by the election of more faithful representatives, annul the acts of the usurpers.[68]

Precious little sign is given here of just what instances Madison might have in mind when he refers to a judicial authority to check legislative "usurpation" in the course of "expound[ing] and giv[ing] effect" to statutes. It is certainly not enough to go on for a thesis that Madison embraced a broad judicial review power. And the conclusion that "in the last resort" the people are to check the usurpers is more revealing of Madison's consistent position on the efficacy of constitutional limitations.

In his five "Helvidius" essays attacking Hamilton's position on Washington's neutrality proclamation of 1793, Madison never once mentions judicial review as a check on executive power over foreign affairs. Given the nature of the controversy, this is hardly surprising. But in the course of excoriating his erstwhile partner's attachment to a theory of executive authority that, in his view, trod upon legislative ground, Madison made an interesting aside consistent with a "functional" view of judicial review:

> It may happen also that different independent departments, the legislative and executive, for example, may in the exercise of their functions, interpret the constitution differently, and thence lay claim each to the same power. This difference of opinion is an inconvenience not entirely to be avoided. It results from what may be called, if it be thought fit, a *concurrent* right to expound the constitution.[69]

The "inconvenience not entirely to be avoided" appears to be a natural consequence of a system of separated powers: namely, that branches of equivalent constitutional authority will clash over the exercise of powers to which both may make plausible claims. There is no sign here or elsewhere in the "Helvidius" essays that Madison sees a role for the Supreme Court in authoritatively refereeing such clashes. The reader is left to conclude that such clashes over constitutional authority, thanks to each branch's "concurrent right," are part of the normal stuff of interbranch and electoral politics. Indeed, that the Court itself might be a party to such clashes rather than the referee of them is indicated shortly after the passage above, when Madison writes that "the judiciary department may find equal occasions in the execution of *its* functions, for usurping the authorities of the executive"—and, it may be added, for usurping the authority of the legislature as well.[70]

Next, consider the two notable documents Madison authored in defense of states' rights following the passage of the Alien and Sedition Acts. In the Virginia Resolution of 1798, judicial review is completely absent as a check on congressional power to pass those acts. More than a year later, in the lengthier "Report to the Virginia General Assembly," Madison replied directly to those who claimed that "the judicial authority is to be regarded as the sole expositor of the Constitution."[71] It is well known that his reply was to refer "great and extraordinary cases" to "the ultimate right of the parties to the Constitution." An apparent change from his position at Philadelphia occurs, however, when he states,

> However true therefore it may be that the Judicial Department is, in all questions submitted to it by the forms of the constitution, to decide in the last resort, this resort must necessarily be deemed the last in relation to the authorities of the other departments of the government; not in relation to the rights of the parties to the constitutional compact, from which the judicial as well as the other departments hold their delegated trusts. On any other hypothesis, the delegation of judicial power, would annul the authority delegating it.[72]

But to read this passage as supporting judicial supremacy among the branches of the federal government begs the question, What are the "questions submitted to" the judiciary "by the forms of the Constitution"? In the previous paragraph, before giving his "proper answer" (regarding the "great and extraordinary cases") to those who hold the "sole expositor" view, Madison begins by saying that

> it might be observed, *first,* that there may be instances of usurped power, which the forms of the constitution would never draw

within the control of the judicial department: secondly, that if the decision of the judiciary be raised above the authority of the sovereign parties to the constitution, the decisions of the other departments, not carried by the forms of the constitution before the judiciary, must be equally authoritative and final with decisions of that department.[73]

Madison does not pause here to explain those "forms of the constitution" and their consequences for judicial power. Yet it seems clear that for him, there are some principles of the Constitution that are never enforceable by the courts.

Following the Marshall Court's decision of *McCulloch* v. *Maryland,* Madison complained in a letter the same year to Judge Spencer Roane of "a latitude in expounding the Constitution" that "substitutes for a definite connection between means and ends, a Legislative discretion as to the former to which no practical limit can be assigned."[74] Madison passed over in silence his own conclusion, in signing the charter of the second national bank, that the law at issue in *McCulloch* was constitutional. Yet in wondering "by what handle could the Court take hold" of congressional abuses of power after *McCulloch,* he may be read as taking the position that the judiciary has a potentially greater role in checking those abuses generally, rather than merely in cases affecting the judicial function. Or, perhaps equally plausibly, he may be ruefully admitting that while "few if any" at the time of the "birth of the Constitution" could have anticipated that "a rule of construction would be introduced as broad & pliant as what has occurred," there really is no "handle" of which to take hold. Hypothesizing an unconstitutional grant of monopoly, Madison writes to Roane that "it seems clear that the Court, adhering to its doctrine, could not interfere without stepping on Legislative ground, to do which they *justly* disclaim all pretension."[75]

In his last public statement on the states' rights controversies of his lifetime, Madison once again qualified, without further elaboration, his view of the scope of judicial authority. In an 1830 critique of the nullification doctrine he referred to the "power [of] the Supreme Court, in cases falling within the course of its function."[76] In his final private notes on the same subject, Madison only referred obliquely to the "provision made by [the] Constitution for its own exposition, thro' its own authorities & forms"[77]—without saying more on what those authorities and forms are.

This discussion may warrant another look at the younger Madison, who is famous for saying in 1788 that any construction of the Constitution that "makes the Judiciary Dept paramount in fact to the Legislature . . . was never intended, and can never be proper."[78] What view did he take of the judiciary in relation to his second great act of midwifery, the Bill of Rights? Writing to Jefferson in the fall of 1787, Madison remarked that George Mason had refused to sign the Constitution at the close of the convention because, among other reasons, Mason "consider[ed] the want of a Bill of Rights as a fatal objection," but there is no reason to suppose that Madison himself disagreed at this time with the reasons not to add a Bill of Rights given by Hamilton in *Federalist* No. 84.[79] Jefferson indicated some agreement with Mason when he replied that the lack of a "declaration of rights" was the Constitution's "principal defect,"[80] and Madison came around to a position of cautious acquiescence in the idea at least by the following fall. But in writing to Jefferson of how such amendments "might be of use . . . if properly executed," Madison initially said nothing of judicial enforcement, and he was, after all, writing this letter only days after penning the lines quoted above, to the effect that a judiciary "paramount" to the legislature "can never be proper." He saw the utility of a bill of rights in "counteract[ing] the impulses of interest and passion," thus forming a "good ground for an appeal to the sense of the community."[81] But in his wish to avoid "*absolute* restrictions" on power for fear of the effect of "repeated violations" when they are "opposed to the decided sense of the public,"[82] Madison implied that judicial enforcement—which could prevent those violations—would not be part of the equation.

Did his mind change by the following summer? In the meantime Jefferson had written to chide Madison that he had omitted as an argument in favor of a bill of rights "the legal check which it puts into the hands of the judiciary," although even Jefferson immediately followed this remark by insisting cryptically that the judges be "kept strictly to their own department."[83] Subsequently, in his speech in the House of Representatives introducing his draft version of the amendments now known as the Bill of Rights, Madison did say (as he is often quoted) that if

they are incorporated in the Constitution, independent tribunals of justice will consider themselves in a peculiar manner the guardians of those rights; they will be an impenetrable bulwark against every assumption of power in the legislative or executive; they will be naturally led to resist every encroachment upon rights expressly stipulated for in the constitution by the declaration of rights.[84]

But what is the antecedent to the word "they" and the phrase "those rights"? The paragraph in which this famous passage appears is one in which Madison is responding to those who have said that "it is unnecessary to load the constitution with this provision, because it was not found effectual in the constitution of the particular states."[85] But again the question must be asked, What is "this provision" that has been criticized as unnecessary? Is it the entire Bill of Rights or some part or parts of it?

This matter becomes murkier, not clearer, when we delve into the whole of Madison's great speech of 8 June 1789. He introduced a total of nine resolutions for amending the Constitution, each of them to be inserted into an appropriate place in the text rather than all appended to it. The provisions that are known today as the "Bill of Rights" (i.e., most of the first eight amendments) were largely contained in his fourth resolution, to be inserted between the third and fourth clauses of Article I, section 9.[86] But while he often used "bill of rights" as a general expression for various sorts of amendments in his correspondence with Jefferson, in his great speech Madison seemed more consistently to narrow the use of the phrase. "Bill of rights" was not his expression for the provisions in his fourth resolution, much less for his entire set of nine resolutions; in Madison's view, it was his first resolution that "relate[d] to what may be called a bill of rights."[87] That resolution, proposed to precede even the Constitution's preamble, declared

That all power is originally vested in, and consequently derived from the people.

That government is instituted, and ought to be exercised for the benefit of the people; which consists in the enjoyment of life and liberty, with the right of acquiring and using property, and generally of pursuing and obtaining happiness and safety.

That the people have an indubitable, unalienable, and indefeasible right to reform or change their government, whenever it be found adverse or inadequate to the purposes of its institution.[88]

Is this the part of his proposal (the "declaration of rights") that Madison has in mind when he responds later to the objection that it is "unnecessary to load the constitution with this provision"? If so, this would be extremely strange, as the provisions of this "pre-preamble" are broadly declaratory and political in character and hardly constitute a statement of the kind of "rights expressly stipulated for" that could be shielded behind an "impenetrable bulwark" of judicial protection.

Another possibility is raised by the fact that immediately prior to discussing "this provision" said by some to be "unnecessary," Madison referred to "the last clause of the 4th resolution."[89] If he meant by "this provision" only that last clause, it happens to be Madison's draft of what became the Ninth Amendment.[90] Under this reading, Madison's argument here would appear to be that the rights reserved in the *state* constitutions would be "incorporated into the [federal] constitution," bolstering the determination of the *states'* "independent tribunals of justice [to] consider themselves in a peculiar manner the guardians of those rights."[91] Thus interpreted, Madison would not be referring at all to routine judicial enforcement by the federal courts of the entire "Bill of Rights" as that enforcement is known today.

Finally, it is possible that "this provision" whose terms are to be "incorporated into the constitution" and judicially protected is not merely "the last clause of the 4th resolution" but the entire resolution containing nearly all the parts of the present "Bill of Rights." But even under this reading, a hasty conclusion should not be made about Madison's commitment to judicial review of *every* "assumption of power in the legislative or executive." First, he cautiously notes that "*some* of the most valuable articles . . . may have, to a certain degree, a salutary effect against the abuse of power"—hardly a ringing declaration of the utter impenetrability in every respect of judicial bulwarks.[92] Second, he immediately follows his famous remarks about judicial enforcement with an even firmer assurance that would not be necessary if judicial protection were truly complete as to every particular right:

> Beside this security, there is a great probability that such a declaration in the federal system would be inforced; because the state legislatures will jealously and closely watch the operation of this government, and be able to resist with more effect every assumption of power *than any other power on earth can do.*[93]

It should not be surprising that Madison, just after raising the subject of judicial review, should downplay its significance in comparison with other mechanisms for preserving the integrity of the Constitution. Moments before in the same speech, pausing to make a point about the implied powers arising under Article I, section 8, he unequivocally states that "it is for [Congress] to judge of the necessity and propriety to accomplish those special purposes which they may have in contemplation."[94] This is consistent with the Madison of the Report of 1800, as well as the one who stated some months before that the paramountcy of the judiciary "can never be proper." And in what is really his most acute statement in the June 8 speech on the efficacy of his proposed amendments, judicial review does not figure at all:

> It may be thought all paper barriers against the power of the community, are too weak to be worthy of attention. I am sensible they are not so strong as to satisfy gentlemen of every description who have seen and examined thoroughly the texture of such a defence; yet, as they have a tendency to impress some degree of respect for them, to establish the public opinion in their favor, and rouse the attention of the whole community, it may be one mean to controul the majority from those acts to which they might be otherwise inclined.[95]

Thus, it is the force of public opinion on which Madison most decisively relies for the maintenance of his "paper barriers."

Taking into consideration a single oblique statement in *Federalist* No. 44, one possible (but only possible) apparent deviation from his usual position in the letter to Roane in 1819, and the confusing and downplayed reliance on courts in the 1789 speech on amendments, it may be concluded that Madison's remarkably consistent position on judicial power was to ignore its role in enforcing the Constitution most of the time—and when he mentioned it at all, to hedge it round with qualifications about the limited range of questions properly submitted to the judiciary and to expatiate at much greater length on the nonjudicial mechanisms for preserving the Constitution that he clearly thought far more important.

Hamilton's "Specified Exceptions"

Next to be considered is Alexander Hamilton, the alleged apostle of judicial supremacy, whose argument in *Federalist* No. 78 has been discussed in Chapter 2. It should be noted once again that, like Marshall in *Marbury*, Hamilton described the judicially enforceable limits on government in terms of "specified exceptions to the legislative authority," and (unlike Marshall) his only examples were indisputably within the scope of the functional review for which I have argued: "such, for instance, as that it shall pass no bills of attainder, no *ex post facto* laws, and the like." He continues: "Limitations of this kind can be preserved in practice no other way than through the medium of courts of justice."[96]

And limitations of other kinds? As Ralph Rossum has noted (though his conclusion differs from mine), Hamilton "did not so much as allude to the Supreme Court" when discussing the limits on implied powers in *Federalist* No. 33 nor again when giving his doubts of the efficacy of a bill of rights in *Federalist* No. 84.[97] Likewise, in his 1791 opinion supporting the constitutionality of the Bank of the United States, he never said a word about the possibility of judicial review of the bank act's validity.[98] It would be a surprise if the Hamilton ready to recommend impeachment of justices for encroachment on the legislative domain, always the advocate of flexible legislative power in the central government, were to embrace a broad version of judicial review capable of hamstringing the authority of Congress to govern a growing nation.

Story and the "Final Judge"

Finally, let us turn once again to Joseph Story, Marshall's great colleague on the Court. In his *Commentaries on the Constitution,* Story titled one of the chapters, "Who Is Final Judge or Interpreter in Constitutional Controversies?"[99] The real aim of the chapter is to rebut those states' rights advocates who so often challenged the Marshall Court's authority over the states as "final judge" in the structure of the federal system. Thus Story generally supports the federal judicial power in the strongest terms. But even against this backdrop, he has some revealing remarks on the limited capacity of the Court to enforce the Constitution against coordinate branches of the same government.

There is more than the narrow modern version of the doctrine of political questions[100] at work in Story's pages. In its insistence on the differing characters of constitutional issues that may arise, Story's position is perfectly consistent with the thesis on functional review advanced by Clinton and which I defend here. As Story says:

[I]n many cases the decisions of the executive and legislative departments . . . become final and conclusive, being from their very nature and character *incapable* of revision. Thus, in measures exclusively of a political, legislative, or executive character, it is plain, that as the *supreme authority,* as to these questions, belongs to the legislative and executive departments, they cannot be reexamined elsewhere. Thus, congress having the power to declare war, to levy taxes, to appropriate money, to regulate intercourse and commerce with foreign nations, their mode of executing these powers can *never* become the subject of reexamination in any other tribunal. So the power to make treaties being confided to the president and senate, when a treaty is properly ratified, it becomes the law of the land, and no other tribunal can gainsay its stipulations. Yet cases may readily be imagined, in which a tax may be laid, or a treaty made, upon motives and grounds wholly beside the intention of the constitution. The remedy, however, in such cases is *solely* by an appeal to the people at the elections; or by the salutary power of amendment, provided by the constitution itself.[101]

At the conclusion of this passage, Story cites Madison's *Federalist* No. 44 for making the same point about the reliance on the people to enforce the Constitution. On the commerce clause, he could just as easily have cited *Gibbons* v. *Ogden,* where Marshall makes much the same point.[102]

Story then describes a different class of issues, in the very next section of his work:

But where the question is of a different nature, and capable of judicial inquiry and decision, there it admits of a very different consideration. The decision then made, whether in favor, or against the constitutionality of the act, by the state, or by the national authority, by the legislature, or by the executive, being capable, in its own nature of being brought to the test of the constitution, is subject to judicial revision. It is in such cases, as we conceive, that there is a final and common arbiter provided by the constitution itself, to whose decisions all others are subordinate; and that arbiter is the supreme judicial authority of the courts of the Union.[103]

Those who are determined to see in Story an advocate of judicial supremacy are apt to quote this passage only partially—e.g., beginning after the second comma in the final sentence, as does Robert Burt.[104] But even the "brought to the test of the constitution" language here must be qualified by the context supplied in the previous section. There is more than one way in which the acts of elected officials may be brought to that test, and the nature of the case will point out which way is appropriate. Some such acts will be tested before the constitutional judgment of the people; some before the constitutional judgment of judges.[105] Even though Story combines consideration of state and federal acts in the last passage quoted, he knew full well that once distinguished, they were subject to different standards for the appropriateness of judicial review.

Story's functional distinction regarding how the acts of the federal government are "brought to the test of the constitution" permeates the remainder of this chapter of the *Commentaries*. He refers to judicial settlement of a controversy "*if* it is capable of judicial examination and decision,"[106] a qualification that must be understood to condition his subsequent statement that the Supreme Court's "interpretation, then, becomes obligatory and conclusive upon all the departments of the federal government,"[107] unless the supposition is made that Story contradicted himself within the space of a few pages. As most of the remainder of the chapter is devoted to rebutting the proponents of nullification and of the position that lost in *Cohens* v. *Virginia*, Story's tone regarding judicial finality becomes stronger with each turn of a page; but as discussed earlier, his thesis of a "final arbiter" in the system of federalism coexists with a theory of multiple arbiters in the system of separated powers.

Even the structure of the *Commentaries* supports this reading. In the penultimate Chapter 44, "Amendments to the Constitution," Story first reviews in general the arguments for and against bills of rights under republican governments. At one point he cites Chancellor James Kent generally on the educative function of such declarations of rights but concludes with Kent's words that "they become of increased value, when placed under the protection of an independent judiciary instituted, as the appropriate guardian of the public and private rights of the citizens."[108] In both Kent and Story, this reference to judicial enforcement of bills of rights is almost an afterthought, a mere half sentence after extended ruminations on what might be called their effect on a community's political culture.

Moreover, since Kent's statement was in regard to bills of rights in the state constitutions and Story's use of Kent comes in his discussion of the utility of bills of rights in general, the answer to the following question is uncertain: does Story mean to say that all the provisions of the *federal* bill of rights are submitted to the judiciary for final, authoritative interpretation? As Story goes on in this chapter to consider each provision in turn, the subject of judicial enforcement slips from view.[109]

And then something curious happens; after discussing the first four amendments, Story says, the "next amendment is, 'Excessive bail shall not be required,'" and goes on to quote the whole of the Eighth Amendment. What happened to the fifth through seventh? Those provisions are discussed in Chapter 38, "Judiciary—Organization and Powers." The Seventh Amendment is folded into Story's treatment of common law trials before the federal courts,[110] and the fifth and sixth into his treatment of criminal trials.[111] This partition of the Bill of Rights for two separate discussions is at least suggestive of the thesis that I have argued, following Robert Clinton, in this chapter. On the one hand, despite his methodical, article-by-article and section-by-section discussion of the Constitution, Story may simply have found it most sensible to pull in those three amendments most closely tied to the judicial process when covering Article III. On the other hand, he is generally methodical, and so the out-of-order discussion of these amendments may be more than mere convenience. It might have made the most sense to include in the treatment of Article III those amendments that come under the special care of the judiciary, leaving for a later chapter the remaining amendments whose enforcement is not primarily or ultimately judicial in form.

Also in his chapter on the judiciary, Story considers "what constitutes a *case*"[112] under the clause of Article III, section 2, regarding "cases . . . arising under the Constitution." As he had done earlier in the work, Story conditions the reach of the judicial power in terms of whether a question "shall assume such a form, that the judicial power is capable of acting upon it."[113] The form Story has in mind must consist of more than mere formality in the making out of a constitutional controversy brought into court: first, because his next paragraph gives substantive examples, none of which deviates from the "judiciary nature" thesis I have argued here;[114] and second, because Story had earlier declared that certain exercises of authority by the other branches of the national government "can never become the subject of reexamination" in courts of law.[115]

Elsewhere I have written of Robert Clinton's book that " 'functional coordinate review' seems to have been so taken for granted by early judges and constitution-makers alike, that one wonders how it was lost sight of."[116] I would suggest that if we cannot find anyone of Marshall's generation stating unequivocally that the Supreme Court is "supreme in the exposition of the law of the Constitution"[117]—if we find instead that such prominent statesmen and judges as Madison, Hamilton, and Story consistently qualify their accounts of judicial power along functional lines—that mystery deepens still further.

CHAPTER FIVE

The "Nationalism" of *McCulloch v. Maryland*

> As ends may be made to beget means, so means may be made to be-
> get ends, until the co-habitation shall rear a progeny of unconstitu-
> tional bastards, which were not begotten by the people. . . . [The
> principles of *McCulloch*] squint at consolidation, and ingeniously
> undermine the state spherical sovereignty admitted by the court.
> —*John Taylor[1]*

In addition to *Cohens* v. *Virginia,* a number of other Marshall opinions are frequently adduced in evidence of the chief justice's
alleged "nationalism." These usually include such cases as *Gibbons* v.
Ogden,[2] Brown v. *Maryland,[3]* and *Craig* v. *Missouri.[4]* But the "nationalist" characterization, and thus much of the supposed activism of Marshall, stands or falls by the reader's understanding of *McCulloch* v.
Maryland.[5]

Albert J. Beveridge tells us that in *McCulloch* "John Marshall rose
to the loftiest heights of judicial statesmanship."[6] Edward S. Corwin,
after reviewing the contemporaneous politics of state sovereignty, observes that "chance presented Marshall with the opportunity to place
the opposing doctrine of nationalism on the high plane of judicial decision."[7] Robert Kenneth Faulkner argues that Marshall's opinion
makes certain "inadequate" arguments and "begs the question at issue" on the nature of the Union.[8] Each such judgment must at least imply that there was something preeminently political about the *McCulloch* opinion; more than that, each implies that Marshall was somehow
substituting his will for a constitutional judgment.[9] Even the milder
judgment of Richard E. Ellis implies as much: "Marshall elaborated on

the need for a loose and expansive interpretation of the powers of the federal government."[10] But as Marshall was anonymously to write some months after the decision, "not a syllable uttered by the court, applies to an enlargement of the powers of congress."[11]

Yet it is surely the case that the thesis on the scope of the judicial power for which I have argued so far seems peculiarly vulnerable to attack from virtually any familiar perspective on the *McCulloch* opinion. The case presented two questions to the Court: Is the creation of the Bank of the United States a legitimate exercise of congressional power? Can a state levy a tax on the operations of such a federal instrumentality? Only the second question was genuinely new in 1819; the constitutionality of the Bank, and the related question of the extent of implied powers, had been extensively debated in the other branches of government repeatedly since 1791. Yet that first question occupies roughly two-thirds of Marshall's opinion.[12] If the performance of the judicial function is not affected by the validity or invalidity of the Bank (that is, if the issue presents nothing of a "judiciary nature"),[13] why did Marshall simply not dismiss summarily the contentions of Maryland on the first question, on the grounds that the issue had been settled by constitutional practice in the other branches?

A necessary but insufficient answer to this question would be to note, as David Currie does, that since "McCulloch claimed federal incorporation as his defense, Congress's authority to establish the Bank was in issue."[14] In other words, the case invoked both "constitutional" grounds for a writ of error under section 25 of the 1789 Judiciary Act, since an act of Congress had been "drawn in question" by the ruling of a state court, and an act of a state legislature, alleged unconstitutional by one party, had been upheld by that same ruling.[15] And in the nature of the case it was necessary to the decision of the state-tax issue to say something on the subject of the Bank's validity.

Did Marshall, however, need to say so much? Considering the views the Court heard at the bar during nine days of oral argument, it would seem that Marshall felt the same sense of responsibility he was to feel two years later in *Cohens,* namely, a responsibility to reply at some length to the states' rights arguments put forward by the counsel for the state. In fact, Marshall did so in fairly compact fashion. The relevant portion of *McCulloch* on the nature of the Union and the powers of the national government is about half the length of the portion of *Cohens* devoted to denying Virginia's motion to abjure jurisdiction of that case. In the roughly twenty-five pages answering the case's first question, Marshall refers directly or alludes to the arguments of Maryland's counsel at least eleven times and does so at every crucial turn in the argument.[16] It is the counsel for Maryland that force consideration of the following arguments, some of them quite astonishing in their sweeping character: that the Constitution does not emanate from the people, but is "the act of sovereign and independent states";[17] "that the people had already surrendered all their powers to the state sovereignties, and had nothing more to give";[18] that the framers granted powers directed toward certain ends but withheld the "choice of means";[19] that "the power of creating a corporation, is one appertaining to sovereignty, and is not expressly conferred on congress";[20] that the "necessary and proper" clause is not, as it appears, "a grant of power" but is "really restrictive" of congressional power;[21] that the word "necessary" in that clause "always import[s] an absolute physical necessity";[22] and again, that "the intention of the convention" was to diminish the powers of Congress by the inclusion of the clause.[23]

The replies to these arguments comprise nearly all of the implied-powers reasoning in *McCulloch* that has traditionally been taken to be grandiloquent constitutional theorizing. Edward S. Corwin surely had these portions of the opinion in mind when he referred to Marshall's "audacious use of the *obiter dictum.*"[24] This has somehow become the conventional wisdom among twentieth-century admirers of Marshall's handiwork; ironically, it has its roots in the hostile reaction to *McCulloch* on the part of the Virginia Republicans of 1819. In the months following the decision, the *Richmond Enquirer* ran two series of scathing, pseudonymous articles accusing the chief justice, among other sins against states' rights, of "travelling out of the case" to expound unnecessarily on the nature of the Union.[25] Marshall's answer (in his own, unprecedented, pseudonymous essays in reply) is essentially the one I have given above: that the issue "was brought regularly before [the Court] by those who had a right to demand, and did demand, its decision."[26] Should the charge that Marshall engaged in a statesmanlike enlargement of congressional power in *McCulloch* really be hung on a peg originating in the discredited views of those who saw in that case a "judicial *coup de main*"?[27] Marshall was doing no more and no less than his judicial duty, and with remarkable patience, all things considered, in following the train of argument advanced by a party to a case—and a party with the dignity of a state itself.

Moreover, a preoccupation with Marshall's treatment of the issue as though it "were [a] question entirely new"[28] can obscure two other significant facts about the opinion's consideration of the Bank controversy: first, how clearly Marshall indicates that the question is anything but new; and second, how carefully he shies away from claiming for the Court any ultimate authority to gainsay what Congress has done, and the executive has approved, under the "necessary and proper" clause.

As to the first point, Marshall devotes roughly the first three pages of his opinion to remarks on how the validity of the Bank "can scarcely be considered as an open question, entirely unprejudiced by the former proceedings of the nation respecting it."[29] In 1791, in 1811, and again in 1816, the Bank's incorporation "did not steal upon an unsuspecting legislature, and pass unobserved"; it was hotly debated, and it "would require no ordinary share of intrepidity, to assert that a measure adopted under these circumstances, was a bold and plain usurpation, to which the constitution gave no countenance."[30] Indeed, well before this case reached the Court, the Bank law and the principle supporting it (the power of incorporation, "now contested") had "been acted upon by the judicial department, in cases of peculiar delicacy, as a law of undoubted obligation."[31] Marshall cites no precedents here, but he probably had in mind such a case as *Bank of the United States* v. *Deveaux*,[32] discussed in Chapter 4, in which the incorporation was treated as of "undoubted obligation."

> Such a "doubtful question" as the Bank incorporation, if not put at rest by the practice of the government, ought to receive a considerable impression from that practice. An exposition of the constitution, deliberately established by legislative acts, on the faith of which an immense property has been advanced, ought not to be lightly disregarded.[33]

All indications are that Marshall's own inclination is to take the first alternative stated in this passage—that the question *has* been "put at rest by the practice of the government"—and that he only writes at length on the issue because the "question was brought before" the justices by Maryland, and "they could not escape it."[34]

For one thing, Marshall had previously construed the "necessary and proper" clause in another context in substantially the same way he does in *McCulloch*, although more briefly. In *United States* v. *Fisher* fourteen years earlier, Marshall had dismissed similar (though less varied and creative) arguments against a congressional "choice of means" to enumerated ends by saying that they amounted to "an objection to the constitution itself."[35]

In addition, Marshall not only had his mind made up beforehand about the validity of the Bank (which will come as no surprise to many), but he had actually mapped out the essentials of his answer to *McCulloch's* first question *twelve years* before the case. In the *Life of Washington,* Marshall had discussed the congressional debates over the Bank bill in 1791 and had cursorily passed over, in a single paragraph in the text of the work, the cabinet opinions requested by Washington.[36] Then, however, he attached a lengthy note to the end of the work in which the opinions of Jefferson and Hamilton were condensed (Marshall ignored the opinion of Attorney General Randolph).[37] I say "condensed" because in the note Marshall simply reproduced, virtually verbatim, passages from the opinions of the two secretaries, choosing only those that went to the heart of the implied powers issue, compressing them slightly and inserting his own transitions within and between the two arguments. Needless to say, Hamilton's arguments win out over Jefferson's in substance in Marshall's account, just as they had in practice when Washington signed the Bank bill. Long before *McCulloch,* therefore, at a time when the Jeffersonian arguments were temporarily somewhat quiescent, Marshall had treated the subject of implied powers fairly thoroughly in a nonofficial capacity and had apparently regarded the constitutional issue as having been settled (nonjudicially, of course) in 1791.

The parallel between the endnote in the *Life of Washington* and major portions of the *McCulloch* opinion also supplies an answer to one of the critics of the latter. David Currie, although sympathetic to the general thrust of *McCulloch's* discussion of implied powers and supportive of the holding that the Bank was constitutional, argues that "Marshall devoted most of his effort to demolishing the straw man of indispensable necessity and slid over the real question of the propriety of the Bank itself"[38] because he did not emulate Hamilton in justifying in detail the utility of the Bank and its specific relation to ends enumerated in Article I, section 8. But what Currie regards as the "real question," Marshall clearly did not, at least where the constitutional issue was concerned. In *McCulloch,* once having affirmed the freedom of Congress to consider a bank as an appropriate means to enumerated ends, Marshall cautions that "to undertake *here* to inquire into the degree of its necessity, would be to pass the line which circumscribes the judicial department, and to tread on legislative ground. This court disclaims all pretensions to such a power."[39] Likewise, in the *Life of Washington* Marshall had selected those portions of Hamilton's 1791 opinion that went to the issue of implied powers in the most general way and then concluded his recitation (and the entire note) with the following paragraph of his own:

> The secretary of the treasury next proceeded, by a great variety of arguments and illustrations, to prove the position that the measure in question was a proper mean for the execution of the several powers which were enumerated, and also contended that the right to employ it resulted from the whole of them taken together. To detail those arguments would occupy too much space, and is the less necessary, because their correctness obviously depends on the correctness of the principles which have already been stated.[40]

Thus, in 1807 Marshall had already distinguished between the primary arguments (of constitutionality) and the secondary arguments (of utility or expediency), and he maintained that distinction in 1819, adding the further observation that the latter were none of the judiciary's business. Hamilton's arguments on the Bank's utility were necessary for him but not for Marshall, because unlike the chief justice he was urging a course of action in the legislative process, namely, Washington's approval of the Bank bill.

This leads to the second major problem of *McCulloch* mentioned above. Did Marshall consider the Court in a position of ultimate authority to gainsay the other branches on the constitutional issue of the extent of implied powers? I think not. It is true that Marshall did not regard the powers of Congress as made boundless by the "necessary and proper" clause—as when he stated that "if it does not enlarge, it cannot be construed to restrain the powers of congress" but was inserted to "remove all doubts" as to implied powers[41]—and that he defended himself vigorously in his newspaper essays against the charge that he had sanctioned unlimited national power.[42] But it is one thing to say that an act of Congress reaching beyond the limits of the power delegated to it by the people is unconstitutional; to say that the Supreme Court has a final, binding authority to invalidate such a law on constitutional grounds is quite another. Did Marshall hold the latter position in *McCulloch*?

In the *Fisher* case of 1805, Marshall noted that "the court can never be unmindful of its duty to obey laws which are authorised by that instrument [the Constitution],"[43] implying that it was free to disobey acts not so authorized. Yet on the same page he held that Congress "must be empowered to use any means which are in fact conducive to the exercise of a power granted by the constitution."[44]

This is reminiscent of Alexander Hamilton's "axioms as simple as they are universal; the *means* ought to be proportioned to the *end;* the persons from whose agency the attainment of any *end* is expected ought to possess the *means* by which it is to be attained."[45] As Hamilton explained in *Federalist* No. 23, wherever the national interests "can with propriety be confided, the co-incident powers may safely accompany them."[46] The safety of "unconfined authority" of this kind rests on the "internal structure" of the government—its dependence on direct and indirect elections and the checks and balances of the legislative process.[47] But Hamilton, in speaking this way of "unconfined authority" in the legislative choosing of means, could hardly have in mind an authoritative judicial review with ultimate power to confine that legislative authority after the choices are made.

So too with Marshall in *Fisher:* it is extremely difficult to square his mere implication of judicial review of implied powers with the breadth of legislative power mentioned just a few paragraphs later. In the latter passage, to be sure, Marshall writes of "any means which are *in fact* conducive" to fulfillment of enumerated powers. But such dealings in the facts and probabilities of policy-making, deciding (or guessing) whether certain ends are well served (or served at all) by certain means, are almost by definition the business of legislatures and executives. Would Marshall ever really contemplate involving his court in rendering authoritative judgments of whether a power claimed by implication was in fact a means well suited to its stated end? To state the question is virtually to answer it.

For David Currie, this aspect of *Fisher* "contradicts [its] simultaneous acknowledgment of the basic principle that the subjects of federal legislation are limited."[48] But no such contradiction occurs without the prior assumption that judicial supremacy exists to enforce those limits. Currie is on to something but closes his eyes to it as unacceptable when he says of *McCulloch* that it "threatened to eliminate judicial review of any measure adopted under the necessary and proper clause."[49] With appropriate qualifications, I suggest that that is exactly what *McCulloch* did: to eliminate *final* judicial authority over any such measure if it did nothing to threaten the sphere of the judicial function.

Two passages in *McCulloch* appear to controvert this view. At the outset, mindful of the seriousness of this dispute between nation and state, Marshall declares that the question "must be decided peacefully, or remain a source of hostile legislation, perhaps, of hostility of a still more serious nature; and if it is to be so decided, by this tribunal alone can the decision be made. On the supreme court of the United States has the constitution of our country devolved this important duty."[50] But exactly what question does "this tribunal alone" have an "important duty" to decide? In this opening paragraph of the opinion, Marshall's entire emphasis is on the federal supremacy question—taken up in the last third of the opinion—and the bare possibility that Congress has transgressed a constitutional limitation is considerably deemphasized. The case is described in the opening sentence as one in which Maryland "denies the obligation" of a federal law and McCulloch "contests the validity" of the state tax.[51] Does it make a difference that only the "obligation" and not the "validity" of the federal law is at issue, whereas the state law's "validity" is in question? Some will see a dubious distinction between these two words or suggest that the difference is merely a stylistic one of using synonyms rather than the same word for a concept in a single sentence.

But Marshall chose his words carefully. Later, in *Cohens* v. *Virginia*, he used similar language to suggest that the questions of obligation and validity are distinct. Speaking of Virginia's attempted defiance of a congressional act exercised under the power of "exclusive legislation" over the District of Columbia, Marshall admonished that

> Those who contend that acts of Congress, made in pursuance of this power, do not, like acts made in pursuance of other powers, bind the nation, ought to show some safe and clear rule which shall support this construction, and prove that an act of Congress, clothed in all the forms which attend other legislative acts, and passed in virtue of a power conferred on, and exercised by Congress, as the legislature of the Union, is not a law of the United States, and does not bind them.[52]

Since the validity of the Bank act is described in *McCulloch*'s second paragraph as "scarcely [to] be considered as an open question,"[53] the real challenge from Maryland, in Marshall's eyes, is its claim not to be bound by the strictures of a federal law "passed in pursuance" of valid legislative powers. *That* is the legal issue to be settled "by this tribunal alone."

Here the Court is unquestionably competent to act. Under the terms of Article VI (binding state courts to prefer federal to state law), Article III (granting appellate jurisdiction to the Supreme Court in cases arising under the Constitution and federal laws), and section 25 of the 1789 Judiciary Act (providing for Supreme Court review of state rulings on the conflict of federal and state laws and constitutions), the Court has a peculiar, perhaps unique, competence in the conflict-of-laws area of federalism. Certainly Congress has no specific tools for this job, an idea considered and rejected at the Constitutional Convention.[54] But nothing in or connected to the passage on "obligation" and "validity" quoted above evinces a general supervisory power of the Court over the extent of Congress's implied powers.

The only other passage in *McCulloch* that may be said to squint toward authoritative judicial review is this:

> Should congress, in the execution of its powers, adopt measures which are prohibited by the constitution; or should congress, under the pretext of executing its powers, pass laws for the accomplishment of objects not intrusted to the government; it would become the painful duty of this tribunal, *should a case requiring such a decision come before it,* to say, that such an act was not the law of the land.[55]

The phrase I have emphasized is a crucial qualification: what can Marshall mean by "a case *requiring* such a decision"? If this is simply a reference to any situation in which the congressional transgression has occurred or even any such situation where litigants have managed to obtain a hearing in court, then he has simply inserted a redundancy. After all, in this case it was alleged that just such a situation occurred, yet weeks later Marshall expressly stated the possibility that his *McCulloch* reasoning might be correct and the Bank nevertheless unconstitutional. Far more plausible is the conclusion that Marshall has a qualification in mind that this "painful duty" would apply only in cases of a "judiciary nature," in which the extension of congressional power beyond constitutional bounds has adversely affected the integrity of the judicial function, or of individual rights whose efficacy rests ultimately on the proper workings of the judicial process, which amounts to the same issue.

Even the first example given in the passage above falls under the qualification. Not even every case presenting an act of Congress "prohibited by the constitution" requires a decision from the Court that it is "not the law of the land," as demonstrated in the previous chapter by *Cohens* v. *Virginia.* There Marshall conceded that a state patent of nobility contrary to Article I, section 10, could probably not be invalidated by the Court;[56] it is more doubtful therefore that a federal patent of nobility contrary to Article I, section 9, could be so voided without some involvement in the case of uniquely judicial issues.

And assuming that the right sort of case came before the Court, why would the duty be such a "painful" one to fulfill? Perhaps Marshall is simply expressing a pro forma respect for acts of Congress. And to overturn a political program of the magnitude of the Bank would certainly entail some costs to the Court where the other branches are concerned. Yet he expressed no such sense of anguish or heavy burden when calmly overturning the mandamus provision of section 13 of the 1789 Judiciary Act in *Marbury* v. *Madison,* the only case in which Marshall's court did exercise judicial review over Congress. Perhaps the duty grudgingly conceded in *McCulloch* would be so painful to fulfill because Marshall knew full well that, generally speaking, Congress (checked by the people and the president) was entitled to judge the extent of its implied powers—with the sole exception of its crossing a constitutional boundary into that area where the Court must defend itself and its peculiar purview. And again, the invalidation of a policy so momentous as the Bank might be the source of considerable "pain" for the Court in the political arena, as the refusal to obey the mandamus provision in *Marbury* certainly was not. Assuming a properly judicial form to such a question, the Court would be obliged to exercise judicial review and would have the formal power to make it stick—but the aftermath might not be pleasant, "case of a judiciary nature" or not.

Note that the very next sentence following the passage I have been considering is one already discussed, in which Marshall disclaims any judicial pretension "to tread on legislative ground."[57] Although two pages earlier Marshall had indicated that whether "the end be legitimate"[58] was a crucial question regarding the validity of a congressional act, here he declines, as in *Fisher,* to inquire even into means; would not an inquiry into ends partake of far more political than legal considerations? As in *Marbury,* Marshall appears to treat separately the questions of whether an act is constitutional and whether the Court may invalidate it as such.

The lineal ancestors of those who today see in *McCulloch* an activist nationalism on Marshall's part are those, like John Taylor and Spencer Roane, who may have wished that his court had struck down the Bank act but were still more upset at the principles of the decision. Indeed, as Richard Ellis points out, the Virginia Republicans "were troubled not that the court had upheld the constitutionality of the Bank, but that it had justified loose and expansive interpretation of the Constitution."[59] Likewise, whether the Marshall scholar today approves or disapproves of the outcome of the case, he is usually inclined to agree with the Virginia Republicans of 1819 that the chief justice went far afield in unnecessarily embracing an expansive view of congressional power that neither the Constitution nor the circumstances of the case required him to embrace. Hence the assumptions common to his critics of yesterday and today are that Marshall's court had the power to take the option of overturning the Bank act, and that in taking the option of upholding the act, he said more than he needed to say in "authorizing" a broad expanse of national legislative power.

In his newspaper essays a few months after the ruling, Marshall himself had a reply to the second point that also sheds light on the first—i.e., on why a court without the last word on implied legislative powers should say so much in approval of them. First, detecting quite rightly that his critics were more incensed about his *McCulloch* opinion's principles than about its conclusion regarding the Bank, he had this to say:

> I hazard nothing when I assert that the reasoning is less doubtful than the conclusion. . . . [T]he principles laid down by the court for the construction of the constitution may all be sound, and yet the act for incorporating the Bank be unconstitutional. But if the act be constitutional, the principles laid down by the court must be sound. I defy Amphyction [pseudonym of one of his Richmond critics], I defy any man, to furnish an argument which shall, at the same time, prove the Bank to be constitutional, and the reasoning of the court to be erroneous.[60]

Now, it would be too much to say that Marshall is blasé about the outcome regarding the Bank—but would not a jurist, believing his court to be entrusted with ultimate interpretive power over coordinate branches as well as states, be interested in delivering a definitive "yes" or "no" on the validity of the Bank? Marshall's critics, now as then, want him to give a more minute reply in *McCulloch* as to exactly why the Bank was a "necessary and proper" law linked to legitimate congressional purposes. This he refused to do in the case, and in his defense above he indicates why: the constitutional judgment of the Bank's legitimacy is properly left to the legislative process, whose authoritative scope, sufficient to approve or disapprove the Bank, is amply supported by the reasoning in the case—and can be supported judicially by no other reasoning.

This interpretation is supported by an interesting silence years later on Marshall's part. In 1832 Andrew Jackson vetoed the recharter of the Second Bank, asserting that, as he read *McCulloch,* "it is the exclusive province of the Congress and the President to decide" the necessity and propriety of such an act.[61] Daniel Webster, who argued for the Bank in *McCulloch* and sat in the Senate at the time of Jackson's veto, asserted in partisan fashion (urging an override of the veto) that the "judiciary, alone, possesses this unquestionable and hitherto unquestioned right."[62] But this apparently was not Marshall's reaction. Beveridge reports that he was "infinitely disgusted" with Jackson's veto and wrote to Joseph Story of the baneful financial and political effects that would follow. But he apparently took no insult from the president's claim of legislative and executive supremacy over the issue of implied powers—nor (as Beveridge reports this letter) did he regard anything in Jackson's veto message as contradicting the principles of *McCulloch*.[63] As a political man, he could disapprove the veto; as a judge he had nothing to say, even privately.

Still, to return to his 1819 essay quoted above, if the reasoning of *McCulloch* amounts to announcing that the Court will step out of the way on issues of implied powers, Marshall's critics want to know now as then why his court, whether it did have authoritative power to review such issues or not, had to say so much in apparent authorization of broad legislative sway. If the Court had an ultimate review power, it is said that the opinion authorized too much; if it did not have such power, the opinion is so much obiter dicta. In the same essay, Marshall replies to this as well, beginning with the point made earlier—that answers had to be given to Maryland's antithetical arguments—and concludes as follows:

Suppose the court had said: "Congress has judged of the necessity and propriety of this measure, and having exercised their undoubted functions in so deciding, it is not consistent with judicial modesty to say there is no such necessity, and thus to arrogate to ourselves the right of putting our *veto* upon a law."

Or suppose the court . . . had said: "It is not our intention to bring that subject into discussion . . . because it has been repeatedly argued before Congress, and . . . was solemnly decided . . .

Would this reasoning have satisfied, or ought it to have satisfied the publick? . . .

But if . . . the court should be "unanimously and decidedly of opinion that the law is constitutional," would it comport with their honour, with their duty, or with truth, to insinuate an opinion that Congress had violated the constitution? If it would not, then . . . [i]t was incumbent on them to state their real opinion and their reasons for it.[64]

Here is a Marshall mindful of public opinion. But more to the point, he is mindful of the fact that appropriate expressions of judicial modesty do not consist of terse statements that questions left to the other branches have been decided by them, and that is that. Nothing at all, in Marshall's eyes, is *constitutionally* wrong about either of the supposed alternatives to *McCulloch's* extended reasoning given here. What is wrong with them is the possible rhetorical effect either alternative might have. "Congress is entitled to decide; Congress has decided; we have nothing to say" would have been, under the circumstances, a still more volatile fuel for the fires that raged in Republican circles—for it could indeed have been taken for an "insinuation" that the Bank law was invalid yet the Court powerless to overturn it. In supporting the validity of the Bank at some length—although without the minute consideration of its "necessity and propriety" more appropriate to the legislative chambers—Marshall hoped to avoid such an insinuation, without claiming a final review power that had simply been held in abeyance in this case. Lacking that final authority, Marshall and his court, strictly speaking, "authorized" nothing. But neither was the opinion larded with dicta, if the judges were to take seriously a responsibility to see to it that the challenge by a state to a valid law carried the day neither in their court nor in the court of public opinion.

In sum, the opinion in *McCulloch* is a very carefully crafted one, containing no excess of dicta and simultaneously expressing two principles entirely consistent with one another: that Congress possesses ample though limited implied powers under the Constitution; and that final authority over that amplitude and those limits does not rest with the Supreme Court.

In its rhetorical purposes, noted above by Marshall himself, *McCulloch* may come closer to true statesmanship than any other opinion he ever authored in his long tenure. But the statesmanship, if that is what it is, comes not in any crafting of a programmatic nationalism nor in the activist pursuit of any grand public policy aims. Consistent with Marshall's proper understanding of "judicial modesty," that "statesmanship" (if it was that) came in performing the epideictic function of reconciling to the Constitution itself those factions in society that would make the document say what it does not. If the epideictic rhetoric of *McCulloch* failed to some degree, as the Republican response indicated it had in some quarters, Marshall attempted to make up the defect with the forensic defense of the opinion in the later newspaper essays.

This rhetorical aspect of the judicial function raises once again the question of this and the last three chapters, of the hard-to-pin-down concept of statesmanship and its relationship to judicial review. The period of the late 1810s and the 1820s, fraught as it was with the partisan politics of states' rights and national supremacy, gave Marshall his handful of significant opportunities on the bench to expound on the nature of the Union (although, notably, always in response to the states' rights arguments of counsel). If in decisions such as *McCulloch, Gibbons,* and *Brown* v. *Maryland,* among others, Marshall endeavored to render peaceful legal resolutions of overheated political issues, can it not be said that he was acting in a statesmanlike fashion?

Marshall was the master of opinion writing, and a good judicial opinion is nothing if not educational. And he clearly believed that he was serving the public good, and helping in some fashion to quiet factious disputes, by his adherence to constitutional principle. But when comparing *McCulloch* (and his defense of it) and his always careful circumscription of judicial power with his reflections on statesmanship in the *Life of Washington,* it is apparent that Marshall understood what scholars of constitutional law sometimes forget: that adherence to the principles of the Constitution is a necessary but not sufficient condition of promoting the public good—and therefore also a necessary but not sufficient condition of the statesmanship needed for that promotion.

This is especially so in the case of the judiciary and for two reasons. First, its adherence to constitutional principles cannot guarantee the adherence of other institutions. Second, the best rhetorical efforts of constitutional jurists (and none is better than *McCulloch*), however educational they might be, still fall short of the deliberative aims, the preeminently political aims, of statesmanship—for education in the principles of constitutionalism is not the same as persuasion to action. To honor, respect, and live by the regime principles of constitutionalism and the rule of law is to place one's foot on the first stone of the political path to the good society. It is not even the beginning of knowing where to go from there. The author of the *Life of Washington* knew that better than most. He knew, too, that in 1801 he left the realm of true statesmanship for the remainder of his career.

Part Two
Natural Law in the Supreme Court

As I have indicated previously, the art of the statesman in a democracy is to seek, through the use of deliberative rhetoric and the commanding virtue of prudence, that state of "living well" that is more than the mere survival of the community. Thus, he is to seek to accomplish as much justice as is practically possible in the world of actual politics. In the modern conception of politics, of which America is the most durable experimental attempt, "living well" cannot be sought exactly along Aristotelian lines. Freedom replaces virtue as the architectonic political principle in modernity, and "living well" becomes chiefly the pursuit of the private rather than the public, of society rather than the state.

The natural law of classical political philosophy comes to be replaced by the natural rights of modern politics: the "Laws of Nature and of Nature's God" referred to in the Declaration of Independence are laws chiefly about the rights—and hardly at all about the duties—of man. A corresponding set of duties is imposed on those who actively govern: to preserve through the power of practical politics those conditions in which the private enjoyment of rights by each is given the widest possible latitude consistent with the public good of rights for all. "Justice is the end of government. It is the end of civil society," as Publius remarks.[1] But the statesman's pursuit of justice in a regime such as the United States is essentially conditioned by two things: first, by the need to be consistently aware of the primacy of freedom over virtue; and second, by the fact that the American people have already said, to a considerable if not complete extent, what they take justice to be in the ordination and establishment of the Constitution. They may change their minds and amend or abolish the Constitution. They may even do these things under the persuasive influence of a statesman (or a demagogue). But until they have done such a thing, the question of what justice is is largely a settled matter.

If this is true for the statesman, how much more is it so for judges? Richard G. Stevens has suggested the force of this argument where judges are concerned:

> [P]erhaps when we, "the people, in order . . . to establish justice," ordained and established the Constitution, we did not intend to *refer* the problem of justice to the Court which we made within the Constitution but rather believed that by the fact of ordaining and establishing the Constitution we had established that approximation of justice which is all men can hope for in an actual regime.[2]

In the seemingly endless debate among commentators on constitutional law over judicial activism and restraint or more recently over interpretivism and noninterpretivism, one of the hardiest perennials cultivated in the garden of scholarship has been a mythical history of the use by the Supreme Court of extraconstitutional standards of "higher law" or natural law in its exercise of judicial review. To the extent that the justices have engaged in this practice, they have usurped the position of the statesman in our politics, and perhaps even more: they have, by attempting to establish a justice that is not ordained by the Constitution, presumed to do over again that which the document has already done, or more precisely, what it considered and rejected doing.

The practice in question has few defenders;[3] but as Gary L. McDowell has suggested, most contemporary theories of noninterpretivism, even those that explicitly reject notions of natural law current at the founding, "seek to resuscitate and legitimate the notion of a higher-law background to the Constitution whereby to elevate the spirit above the letter of the document as *the* source for judicial decision making."[4]

Critics of natural-law judicial review are legion, from Roscoe Pound,[5] Benjamin Fletcher Wright, Jr.,[6] and Edward S. Corwin[7] decades ago to Walter Berns[8] and Gary J. Jacobsohn[9] more recently. Two widely read recent books by Leonard W. Levy[10] and Robert H. Bork[11] address the issue once again. In Chapter 2 these two authors' accounts of constitutional history were contrasted; yet despite their different views and agendas they join a consensus of long standing that extratextual natural-law considerations have formed a part of constitutional adjudication from the earliest days of the federal courts. Levy seems to want to prove that because this and other kinds of "rampant judicial activism"[12] have characterized the Supreme Court from the very beginning, it is inevitable; therefore, we should resign ourselves to it, or better still, applaud its modern manifestations, so long as the justices retain a "capacity to recognize at the propitious moment a need for constitutional evolution"[13]—so long, that is, as the evolution is of the kind Levy would regard as evolution. Bork, on the other hand, seeks to warn us of the dangers of result-oriented jurisprudence, especially of the sort that reaches outside the four corners of the Constitution to decide a case; he agrees with Levy, however, that "the impulse to judicial authoritarianism surfaced and was resisted at the beginning of our constitutional history."[14]

Between them, Bork and Levy introduce into evidence the testimony of the usual suspects: Justice William Paterson (on circuit) in *Van Horne's Lessee* v. *Dorrance*,[15] Justice Samuel Chase in *Calder* v. *Bull*,[16] Chief Justice John Marshall and Justice William Johnson in *Fletcher* v. *Peck*,[17] and Justice Joseph Story in *Terrett* v. *Taylor*.[18] In each case the common allegation is that the jurist in the dock has proclaimed a judicial authority to invalidate legislation as contrary to standards of natural law not inferable from the text of the Constitution. The list of cases in which a discussion of natural law appears can be expanded to include *Corfield* v. *Coryell* (Justice Bushrod Washington on circuit),[19] *Ogden* v. *Saunders* (Marshall),[20] and *Wilkinson* v. *Leland* (Story).[21]

These cases do not appear in the usual histories merely to make the point that the justices of the early Court believed in natural law or even to establish that a practice existed of reaching outside the constitutional text in the exercise of judicial review. The orthodox view, at least since Pound, Wright, and Corwin, is that the early Court's advancement of a "vested rights" doctrine under the rubric of natural law laid the logical groundwork and set the precedents for the post–Civil War development of substantive due process under a natural-law reading of the Fourteenth Amendment.[22] In the recently published *Encyclopedia of the American Constitution* (of which Leonard Levy is editor in chief),[23] this conventional wisdom reaches its apotheosis: in articles such as "Fundamental Law and the Supreme Court,"[24] "Higher Law,"[25] and "Substantive Due Process of Law,"[26] the cases cited above are directly associated with activist property rights decisions of the Chase, Waite, and Fuller Courts such as *Hepburn* v. *Griswold*,[27] *Loan Association* v. *Topeka*,[28] *Allgeyer* v. *Louisiana*,[29] and *Lochner* v. *New*

York.[30] Even a contributor to the more recent (and far superior) *Oxford Companion to the Supreme Court* manages to hint at the same association with the offhanded and misleading remark that during "the nation's first century . . . freedom of contract and other rights of property were considered fundamental."[31]

It is certainly true that the most strident defenders of private property on the Court of the late nineteenth century were wont on occasion to call the opinions of antebellum justices into service to support their views.[32] But as I argue in Chapter 7, in nearly every significant instance of this borrowing, what is borrowed is misread, taken out of context, or downright abused.[33]

In the two chapters that follow I contend that this misreading has infected scholarship for the last eighty years in two ways. First, the alleged natural-law opinions of the antebellum Court cannot be considered precedents for the property rights activism that arose decades later. Second, the allegation that these earlier justices felt free to reach beyond the confines of the Constitution in exercising judicial review is, in all but one or two instances, simply false (and in those exceptional instances, some reasonable doubt of the charge can be introduced). My second contention, which is the burden of Chapter 6, if successful will largely bear out the first. But any doubts may be dispelled by examining the Court's treatment of the early cases as precedents, which is the burden of Chapter 7.

Some limitations on the scope of the argument need to be made at the outset. It is not possible here to catalogue eighty years of scholarly error through all its permutations; it should be sufficient to point to the survival of an orthodoxy from 1909 through the work of contemporary observers as divergent on other issues as Leonard Levy and Robert Bork. In Chapter 7 I offer only a brief account of the causes of the rise of the natural-law–based due process doctrines of the late nineteenth century. A variety of scholars has already explored this topic, and I will offer an opinion as to which exploration seems most plausible.[34]

The principal task is to reexamine, in some depth, the usually suspect cases and judges named above.[35] I will argue that a search for justices who regarded natural-law standards not expressed in the letter of the Constitution as sufficient warrant to invalidate legislation will find them so rare before the Civil War as to be virtually nonexistent— and no justice appears to have held that view consistently. Instead we will find that nearly all of the suspect opinions existed fully within the judicial mainstream, once they are properly understood. (In Part Three I will explore why the justices of the early Court resisted the temptation to step beyond the bounds of the written Constitution to resolve concrete cases.) An examination of these cases' fates as precedents will confirm the distinctly modern character of today's misreading of them.

CHAPTER SIX

The Early Cases on "Natural Law"

[A]lthough the spirit of an instrument, especially of a constitution, is to be respected not less than its letter, yet the spirit is to be collected chiefly from its words.

John Marshall[1]

Any reexamination of the pre-Marshall and Marshall Court opinions allegedly advancing a power of "natural law" judicial review should be approached with certain caveats in mind. First, to discover a jurist discussing the precepts of natural law is not adequate grounds for concluding that he has abandoned the parameters of the written constitution. Even when the discussion seems to range quite far from the constitutional text at hand, it may have the purpose of illuminating, by means of purpose and context, the letter of that text. Second, it is important to notice what constitution enters into the merits of the decision. Some of the cases arise under the federal courts' Article III diversity jurisdiction, with the substantive issues located in state constitutions and not the federal Constitution. Finally, statements that natural law (or some equivalent concept) render a legislative enactment of doubtful validity should be approached with caution. As Robert Lowry Clinton has demonstrated, even Marshall's *Marbury* opinion, in a case where the letter and not merely the spirit of the Constitution was violated, distinguished clearly between the *fact* of a statute being void and the *right* of a court to invalidate it.[2]

VAN HORNE'S LESSEE V. DORRANCE (1795)

The record of this case consists of Justice William Paterson's instructions to a jury while presiding over the trial of a land dispute in the U.S. circuit court for Pennsylvania. The case seems to have arisen under the federal courts' Article III jurisdiction over "Controversies . . . between Citizens of the same State claiming Lands under Grants of different States." Paterson directed a verdict on behalf of the plaintiff on the grounds that an act of the Pennsylvania legislature, known variously as the "quieting" or "confirming" act and intending to confirm the defendant's title to the land in question (originally granted to the latter by Connecticut), was invalid from the moment of its enactment; if valid, had not been properly performed; had been subsequently suspended by the legislature; and still later was repealed altogether.[3]

The case has been the subject of some careless commentary. Leonard Levy apparently thinks Paterson invalidated a law (he does not say which one) under the contract clause of the U.S. Constitution.[4] In fact, Paterson held the confirming act itself invalid on the grounds that it violated the Pennsylvania constitution (see the first point above). He did indeed, at the conclusion of his instructions, consider whether the latest act repealing the confirming act (see the last point above) was a violation of the federal contract clause. He concluded, however, that it was not since, as he had already ruled, the original confirming act was invalid; hence the repeal impaired no legitimate contractual obligation the state might have towards Dorrance. This is the only portion of the opinion in which a substantive issue arises under the federal Constitution.[5]

It is in the portion of the opinion devoted to the Pennsylvania constitution that Paterson makes the remarks that have attained some notoriety.[6] As Levy comments, he "discoursed on the relationship between fundamental law and the rights of property. He found such rights inalienable, their preservation a primary object of 'the social compact.'"[7] Indeed, Levy conveys the impression that Paterson was reasoning in a vacuum: "'. . . It is a right not *ex gratia* from the legislature, but *ex debito* from the constitution. It is sacred. . . .'"[8] The ellipses both fore and aft are altogether too convenient. Here is a fuller sample of the passage in which these words appear:

> The constitution expressly declares, that the right of acquiring, possessing and protecting property is natural, inherent, and inalienable. It is a right not *ex gratia* from the legislature, but *ex de-*

bito from the constitution. It is sacred; for it is further declared, that the legislature shall have no power to add to, alter, abolish or infringe any part of the constitution. The constitution is the origin and measure of legislative authority.[9]

What is Paterson talking about? Simply this: the Pennsylvania constitution of 1776, under which the confirming act is held invalid, "expressly declares" exactly what Paterson says it does. All the language of "natural, inherent, and inalienable" rights is borrowed verbatim from that text.[10] It is not free judicial philosophizing, gratuitously importing natural law into constitutional interpretation. In fact, the entirety of Paterson's "discourse on fundamental law" is by way of explaining to the jury the operation of that *written* constitution on the law in question and immediately follows his reading to the jury of relevant portions of the constitution.[11] His repeated references to "a primary object of the social compact," "principles of the social alliance," the "sacred principles of the social compact," and so forth, are not abstractions of political theory; they are explications of the clear intent of a written text expressing the will of the sovereign people.[12]

The confirming act of 1787 had effectively settled all the disputed land titles on the claimants under the Connecticut grant, establishing a "board of property" to judge the competing claims of those divested of their land and to award "equivalent" parcels of land to those among the latter whose claims were held valid. According to Paterson, the act suffers from the following defects: there is no constitutional authority in the legislature to "excuse the seizing of landed property belonging to one citizen and giving it to another citizen"[13]—a taking that is, of course, not for a public use under eminent domain; assuming even that the legislature can, on grounds of necessity, exercise "this despotic power," the deliberations of the board of property established by the statute are no substitute for a jury trial in fixing compensation for divested proprietors (or for some other form of arrangement in which the consent of the claimant is preserved);[14] and the principle of just compensation requires money, not some board-determined "equivalent" in land.[15] (This final ground, like the second, is again premised on the hypothetical falsehood of the first.)

Considering the broadly stated strictures on the legislature in the state constitution, the first ground above was probably sufficient to establish the act's invalidity. Given the text Paterson had to work with, his charge to the jury on this score may even be called a strict construction of that document. It is exceedingly farfetched to call it, as Levy

does, "judicial activism running wild," relying on "extraconstitutional" standards "reading his prejudices" into the law.[16]

Justice Paterson's accusers must ignore entirely the portion of his remarks that immediately precedes his discussion of the Pennsylvania
constitution. To prepare the laymen of the jury for what may be an un-
familiar idea to some of them, namely, that the court can rule on the
validity of a statute, he gives a brief lecture on constitutionalism. Quoting Blackstone, he refers to an "absolute despotic power, which must in
all governments reside somewhere."[17] In England this power is lodged
in Parliament, a fact that refutes those with "the boldness to assert,
that an act of parliament, made against natural equity, is void."[18] In
America, there are written constitutions, and these are "delineated by
the mighty hand of the people"; they contain "first principles" that are
"certain and fixed." And Paterson leaves no doubt that he agrees with
Blackstone that "absolute despotic power" must be located somewhere:
"The constitution is the work or will of the people themselves, in their
original, sovereign and unlimited capacity."[19]

In short, Paterson is no believer that "natural equity" can be invoked to invalidate a statute any more than Blackstone is. Only the
sovereign will, which in England rests in Parliament and in America is
embodied in written constitutions, can serve as a measure of what is
and what is not law, at least in courts of law. Only "certain and fixed"
first principles, expressed in writing, can be invoked against the act of
a subordinate authority. If the sovereign people establish a constitution
that affords insufficient protection for natural rights, or even one that
runs contrary to "natural equity," they have acted unwisely and unjustly—but they have done so in their "unlimited capacity" to make the
social contract, and no judge may deny them. What he must do is say
"nay" to a legislature that contradicts their sovereign will. And that is
precisely what Paterson has done here.

CALDER V. BULL (1798)

This case is well known as the precedent of first impression
interpreting the ex post facto clause of Article I, section 10 (and by implication the same clause of section 9 as well), as applying only to retroactive criminal laws and not to civil laws. There has been some controversy as to whether the Court correctly interpreted the intent of that
provision,[20] but the four justices who wrote seriatim opinions were
unanimous on this point (Chief Justice Ellsworth did not participate,

and the sixth seat on the Court, shortly to be filled by Bushrod Washington, was vacant at this time owing to the death of James Wilson). What is still better known, or thought to be known, about this case is that Justices Samuel Chase and James Iredell engaged in a more or less open dispute over the question of natural-law review of legislative acts.[21]

Considerable opprobrium has been heaped on Justice Chase in connection with his opinion here. One of his milder critics, Christopher Wolfe, tells us that he "held out the possibility that courts enforce 'principles of natural justice' independently of particular constitutional provisions,"[22] although the phrase placed in quotation marks is never used in Chase's opinion. More harshly, Robert Bork says Chase "was prepared to strike down laws that violated no provision of any constitution, federal or state," and, amazingly, that no "modern Court has been quite so candid in claiming a power beyond any written law."[23] Worse still, Leonard Levy tells us that because the ex post facto route for voiding retroactive civil laws was foreclosed, and the "main opinion" by Chase flirted with "higher law" review, the case virtually propelled the Court into its subsequent "expansion" of the contract clause and perhaps even laid the groundwork for substantive due process.[24] This account rests on the assertions that the entire Court was wrong about the ex post facto clause, which is more than doubtful;[25] that the Court in later years "expanded" the contract clause, a notion seriously called into question by recent scholarship;[26] and that Justice Chase affirmed a judicial power of natural-law review, a notion to be disputed herein.

Calder involved the validity of a resolution passed by the Connecticut legislature in 1795, setting aside a probate court judgment and ordering a new hearing. The result was that Caleb Bull and his wife were adjudged the legitimate heirs in the new hearing; Calder and his wife, who had been adjudged the heirs before the legislature's action, claimed that that resolution was an ex post facto law forbidden by the federal Constitution. As indicated above, all the justices rejected that claim as groundless. But all three of the justices who wrote at any length (Cushing's opinion was a mere two sentences) ventured into other territory as well. For despite the fact that the supreme court of Connecticut had found no errors, the legislature's action seemed so unusual that each justice saw fit to consider also the matter of state constitutional law.

This raised what is probably the most interesting aspect of the case: Connecticut had no constitution in the now-usual sense; like Rhode Island, it had as yet adopted no constitution after independence but was still governed under its royal charter of 1662. The charter contained no true separation of powers, with near-absolute governing authority lodged in the "General Court," which consisted of what today would be called both the executive and legislative branches. That authority was *nearly* absolute only because the charter contained an all-purpose provision securing to the citizens of Connecticut all the rights of the statute and common law of England.[27]

Justice Chase's often quoted ruminations on the "fundamental law" jump off from the problem the Connecticut charter presents:

> Whether the legislature of any of the states can revise and correct by law, a decision of any of its courts of justice, although not prohibited by the constitution of the state, is a question of very great importance, and not necessary now to be determined; because the resolution or law in question does not go so far.[28]

The resolution "does not go so far" because it merely reopens the judicial process to a second round of hearings and appeals; it does not simply reverse the probate court's ruling by legislative fiat. Chase offers no judgment on whether the Connecticut charter would permit the latter sort of enactment, although he seems to intimate that where there is a proper modern separation of powers, such an act would be of doubtful validity. His colleagues Paterson and Iredell are clearer on this point: insofar as the accepted practice since the beginning of Connecticut's charter government had been for the legislature (or "General Court") to exercise judicial as well as legislative authority, no state-constitutional difficulty presents itself in the awarding of a new trial.[29]

The rest of the paragraph just quoted and the succeeding one, which contain all there is of the alleged natural-law reasoning singled out by Chase's critics, consist of remarks, moving from general principles to particular instances, to the effect that legislatures possess only those powers duly authorized by their constitutional texts. That the remarks are pure obiter dicta is unquestionable, for Chase has already declared that "the sole inquiry" in the case is whether Connecticut has violated the federal ex post facto clause,[30] and he will come to that issue in due course. Dicta or not, the remarks do not affirm a judicial power to invoke "natural justice" from beyond the bounds of a constitution to invalidate legislation.

The first passage usually cited by those who see a power of natural-law review advanced in Chase's opinion is this: "I cannot subscribe to

the omnipotence of a state legislature, or that it is absolute and without control; although its authority should not be expressly restrained
by the constitution, or fundamental law of the state."[31] The second passage usually cited, appearing at the end of the same long paragraph, is
this: "An act of the legislature (for I cannot call it a law), contrary to
the great first principles of the social compact, cannot be considered a
rightful exercise of legislative authority."[32] These two sentences, removed from their context, might suggest that Chase is willing to look
outside the constitution (state or federal) for judicially enforceable restraints on the state legislature. Replaced in the context of his full
opinion, they stand for nothing of the sort.

Two paragraphs earlier Chase had written: "It appears to me a self-
evident proposition, that the several state legislatures retain all the
powers of legislation, *delegated to them by the state constitutions;* which
are not expressly taken away by the constitution of the United
States."[33] Here Chase is making a distinction somehow overlooked by
his critics, between the limits on a legislature's authority that emerge
from the powers it has been given (what might be called the "Thou
shalts") and those expressly *limiting* the powers given (the "Thou shalt
nots"). This is the true import of his subsequent remarks in the first
controversial paragraph (a few lines after the sentence already quoted
on the "omnipotence of a state legislature"):

The purposes for which men enter into society will determine the
nature and terms of the social compact; and as they are the foundation of the legislative power, they will decide what are the proper
objects of it. The nature, and ends of legislative power will limit
the exercise of it. . . . There are acts which the federal, or state legislature cannot do, without exceeding their authority. There are
certain vital principles in our free republican governments, which
will determine and overrule an apparent and flagrant abuse of legislative power; as to authorize manifest injustice by positive law; or
to take away that security for personal liberty, or private property,
for the protection whereof the government was established. [Now
comes the second sentence already quoted above:] An act of the legislature (for I cannot call it a law) contrary to the great first principles of the social compact, cannot be considered a rightful exercise
of legislative authority. The obligation of a law, in governments established on express compact, and on republican principles, must
be determined by the nature of the power on which it is founded.[34]

Harry Jaffa has asserted (approvingly) that the "great first principles of the social compact" referred to here "meant the principles of the Declaration of Independence."[35] This, to put it mildly, is implausible in the extreme. As a document telling us that we are equal and have unalienable rights, that only "just powers" are derived from the consent of the governed, and that the government must not become "destructive of these ends," the Declaration is singularly unhelpful in determining whether a particular legislative act, duly enacted under a social contract to which the people have consented, is or is not destructive of its principles. The social compact to which Chase refers is not the Declaration, nor is it any extraconstitutional source of law. The place to look for his "great first principles" is in the "express compact" simultaneously creating and limiting political power—a compact made by the people, who in following their own purposes "will decide what are the proper objects of it." (Notice the similarity here to Paterson's statement in *Van Horne's Lessee* that the people's power to set the terms of the compact is in practice unlimited.) The "compact," in short, *is* the constitution (or in Connecticut's case, the ancient charter), not some antecedent set of precepts declaring the people's natural rights or their sovereign power over their governments. Within its terms can be found that compact's "great first principles." Nothing less than its terms will do for the overturning of a statute.

Some might see Chase coming close to parting from constitutional moorings when he states that "certain vital principles" will "overrule" a legislature when it "authorize[s] manifest injustice by positive law."[36] This is quite vague; but the next paragraph (the second and last containing the dicta under consideration) begins, "A few instances will suffice to explain what I mean."[37] The examples then recited are of ex post facto laws, impairment of "lawful private contracts," laws that violate the principle that no man should be a judge in his own case, and direct expropriations of property from one man to give it to another— this last a violation of simple due process, as a later Supreme Court was to note.[38] Each of these examples describes a legislative enactment prohibited either by the federal Constitution or by the "laws of England" language of the Connecticut charter.[39]

It is, says Chase, "against all reason and justice, for a people to intrust a legislature with such powers; and therefore, it cannot be presumed that they have done it."[40] His "cannot be presumed" expresses a sound rule of construction: what if it were clear beyond a doubt that the people had entrusted such powers? The argument would not apply, and however unreasonable or unjust, the powers' validity would be unquestionable.

But even where the presumption governs, that is, even where powers "against all reason and justice" have not been granted to the legislature, what conclusion follows as to a judicial power to overrule the exercise of such powers? Since the "general principles of law and reason forbid" such powers, Chase concludes the second of these controversial paragraphs, "To maintain that our federal, or state legislature possesses such powers, if they had not been expressly restrained; would, in my opinion, be a political heresy, altogether inadmissible in our free republican governments."[41] I think it no accident that he refers to this notion as a "*political* heresy." It would certainly be a gross error for citizens and public officials thus to forget the true principles of "our free republican governments." But it does not inexorably follow that the judges of the United States, on grounds of vindicating the natural law and defeating this heresy, may overturn state acts contrary to "general principles of law and reason." Only by an undue focus on the two paragraphs that have been considered here, and by a blindness to the remainder of Chase's opinion, can his readers reach that conclusion.

In his very next paragraph Chase makes it clear that in order to restrain legislatures from doing that which by all reason and justice they should not do anyway, some restraining constitutional language is necessary. After reviewing the sorry history of British parliamentary abuses of due process, the rules of evidence, and the ex post facto principle, he remarks that to "prevent such and similar acts of violence and injustice, I believe, the federal and state legislatures were prohibited from passing any bill of attainder, or any ex post facto law."[42] This, in fact, forms the transition to his discussion of the merits of the case and of the meaning of that clause of Article I, section 10.

Although near the very end of his opinion Chase says that no property rights had vested in the Calders that the Connecticut legislature's action could be said to have taken away,[43] he remarks two paragraphs previously that the ex post facto clause was not intended "to prohibit the depriving a citizen even of a vested right to property; or the provision, 'that property should not be taken for public use, without just compensation,' was unnecessary."[44] It seems here that Chase mistakenly may have thought the takings clause of the Fifth Amendment to be applicable to the states (an error refuted thirty-five years later by John Marshall).[45] But far more interesting for our present purposes is how clearly he indicates that some textual provision is necessary for the judicial defense of vested rights of property against the depredations of legislative authority—so much for any attribution to Chase of a natural-law "vested rights" doctrine.

Finally, notwithstanding his dicta remonstrating against the "omnipotence of a state legislature" as a "political heresy" even in the absence of express restraints on its power, a few pages after those famous paragraphs Chase emphatically rejects a federal judicial power to overturn acts of the state legislatures that reach beyond their clearly—i.e., textually—authorized powers or even those that transgress express limits in the state constitution:

> It was argued by the counsel for the plaintiffs in error, that the legislature of Connecticut had no constitutional power to make the resolution (or law) in question, granting a new hearing, &c. Without giving an opinion, at this time, whether this court has jurisdiction to decide that any law made by congress, contrary to the constitution of the United States, is void: I am fully satisfied, that this court has no jurisdiction to determine that any law of any state legislature, contrary to the constitution of such state, is void. . . . I should think, that the courts of Connecticut are the proper tribunals to decide, whether laws contrary to the constitution thereof, are void.[46]

Following on the heels of his earlier discussion of the limited character of state legislative authority—a limited character made concrete by the "purposes for which men enter into society" and to be revealed by examining what those men set down as "the great first principles of the social compact"—this passage is hardly helpful for those interpreters who wish to make of Chase a freewheeling natural-law jurist. In the courts of the United States, the only inquiry for Chase is whether Connecticut has violated the express terms of the federal Constitution. (It might be otherwise in a case of diversity jurisdiction, but *Calder* is not one of those.) Whether the state legislature has violated principles of justice explicit in the state constitution, found either in its grants of power or in its explicit limitations thereon, is a matter for state courts. Whether it has violated principles of natural justice only implicit in the character of its own charter's purposes and powers is perhaps arguably a matter also for state courts, but being removed from the clear federal grounds that Chase's court would require for action ("I will not decide any law to be void, but in a very clear case," he says),[47] such principles have no capacity to make out a case for federal judicial decision.

The most that can be imputed to Chase on the basis of *Calder* is a strict constructionism of the strictest sort, as he does not subscribe to something like the doctrine of state "police powers" that was to develop on the Court of the nineteenth century.[48] He enunciates a rule of construction that will not impute to the people an intention to grant to the legislature those powers it would be unreasonable or unjust to grant without an express authorization. Notice again that three of his four examples of laws "contrary to the great first principles of the social compact" were forbidden by either the statute law or common law of England,[49] precisely the sources from which Connecticut's charter derives its limits on legislative power.[50] There is no natural-law constraint on the sovereign people here; again, Chase's remark that "it cannot be *presumed* that they have" consented to powers against "law and reason" without express constitutional grant implies that the people *may expressly* do so if they wish, and all matters of presumption will be at an end. This reasoning places Chase squarely in the tradition of Blackstone, who states just such a point regarding parliamentary sovereignty when he discusses the principle that no man should be judge in his own case—which is probably where Chase derived the example.[51]

More important, when the controversial paragraphs in Chase's *Calder* opinion are situated once again in the larger context of the opinion as a whole, they turn out to be little more than an aside in political theory with, practically speaking, no juridical significance. Even his strict rule for construing the powers of state legislatures is better understood as a political orthodoxy than as a judicially enforceable principle of law. Taken as a whole, his remarks may signify no more than a commentary on the antiquated Connecticut charter, which fails to a dangerous degree to separate powers or to restrain the legislative authority. But these paragraphs contemplate no judicial invocation of natural law to rein in any sovereign lawgiver or even any subordinate one. Only plausible inference from a written constitutional text will do, preferably one with explicit limitations on power written into it, but in any event the only limitations with which Chase is concerned as a judge are those in the U.S. Constitution. The rest penultimately is up to the judges of Connecticut but ultimately is up to the people, who alone can effectively resist the "political heresy" of unconstrained legislative power.

It should be noted that nearly the entire discussion is keyed to issues of state constitutional law and thus might be taken as, at most, an admonition to state judiciaries to be watchful of their legislatures. On the only federal issue in the case—the "sole inquiry" for his Court—Chase's reasoning sticks to the black-letter technicalities, although it is not necessary to call a judge so interested in the natural-rights basis of government "fiercely positivistic," as John Hart Ely has done.[52] Relying on Blackstone, the *Federalist,* and the context of Article I, section 10, Chase concludes that Connecticut's act is "not within the letter of the prohibition; and for the reasons assigned, I am clearly of opinion, that it is not within the intention of the prohibition; and if within the intention, but out of the letter, I should not, therefore, consider myself justified to construe it within the prohibition."[53] If this is any brief for a broad reading of judicial power, it certainly is not on behalf of the U.S. Supreme Court or on the basis of higher-law principles animating the federal Constitution. It is extremely difficult to square the usual account of Chase the natural-law jurist with his actual opinion. How likely is it that a judge who follows a strict technical construction of the only federal issue in the case, eschews any obligation to consider whether the state constitution has been violated, and emphasizes the need for textual support of vested rights should in the same opinion announce a federal judicial power to overturn state acts violating no textual provision whatsoever?

Those who read Chase's opinion in *Calder* in the usual way must take account of his views in *Ware* v. *Hylton* (1796). There, in only the second full-fledged opinion he wrote after joining the Court, he made it clear that for him "fundamental law" was, juridically speaking if not politically, a notion interchangeable with the explicit terms of a written constitution:

> I hold it as unquestionable, that the Legislature of Virginia, established as I have stated by the authority of the people, was forever thereafter invested with the supreme and sovereign power of the state, and with authority to make any Laws in their discretion, to affect the lives, liberties, and property of all the citizens of that Commonwealth, with this exception only, that such laws should not be repugnant to the Constitution, or fundamental law, which could be subject only to the controul of the body of the nation, in cases not to be defined, and which will always provide for themselves. The legislative power of every nation can only be restrained by its own constitution: and it is the duty of the courts of justice not to question the validity of any law made in pursuance of the constitution.[54]

The customary reading of Chase's *Calder* opinion cannot be squared with this passage in *Ware*. The orthodox interpreters must put forth the unlikely thesis that in the space of two years Chase either forgot these lines or moved knowingly to a completely contrary view of constitutionalism. None in the cadre of *Calder* critics appears to have even made the attempt.

Besides the common misreading of Chase's opinion, the other component of the orthodox *Calder* myth is that Justice James Iredell rebutted Chase's pretensions to a natural-law review power in the federal judiciary. But if, as already seen, Chase entertained no such pretensions, only two possibilities present themselves: either Iredell has been misunderstood as commonly as Chase, or he himself (like so many modern readers) misunderstood Chase. We know from Iredell himself, for instance, that he arrived in the Court's chamber without having "had an opportunity to reduce [his] opinion to writing."[55] Therefore, it is possible that he had no idea what he was to hear his colleague read from the bench. Did he respond extemporaneously to Chase? Did he fully understand Chase? These facts are unknown. And it is just as possible that his remarks on natural law were directed to the arguments of counsel in the case as to his fellow judge.

Iredell, not surprisingly for a jurist of his day, was not a legal positivist who rejected the existence of natural law. Indeed, although seemingly taking issue with Chase's stricter view that the positive grants of legislative power mark limits thereon just as the restraining provisions of a constitution do, he seems not far at all from Chase's view that the positive law's legitimacy rests on its consistency with the natural law:

> If, then, a government, composed of legislative, executive and judicial departments, were established, by a constitution which imposed no limits on the legislative power, the consequence would inevitably be, that whatever the legislative power chose to enact, would be lawfully enacted, and the judicial power could never interpose to pronounce it void. It is true, that some speculative jurists have held, that a legislative act against natural justice must, in itself, be void; but I cannot think that under such a government any court of justice would possess a power to declare it so.[56]

There is some degree of real disagreement with Justice Chase here. Iredell comes close to subscribing to what Chase has called a "political heresy": that whatever the legislature calls a law is a law, subject only to the explicit limitations of some constitution or other. Iredell comes close but does not go all the way. In denying that courts can invalidate statutes on grounds of natural justice, he does not deny either the existence or the moral force of natural law as a standard for the positive. And it would take something of a speculative leap on the reader's part to assume that his phrase "speculative jurists" is a caustic reference to Chase or for that matter even a pejorative reference to anyone at all. Those jurists he has in mind as "speculative" are probably the great theorists and commentators at whose feet Iredell and the lawyers of his day learned the basics (Blackstone, Pufendorf, Vattel), all of whom affirmed the relationship of the positive law to the natural that he describes here. Viewed in that light, Iredell is almost certainly in full agreement with the position he ascribes to his "speculative jurists."

The passage in which Iredell is usually read as taking Chase to task is this:

> If . . . the legislature of any member of the Union, shall pass a law, within the general scope of their constitutional power, the court cannot pronounce it to be void, merely because it is, in their judgment, contrary to the principles of natural justice. The ideas of natural justice are regulated by no fixed standard: the ablest and the purest men have differed upon the subject.[57]

Here quotations of Iredell usually end, leaving the impression that, if not a positivist, he holds that the variability of opinions means that judges ought never to traffic in the "ideas of natural justice" at all. But the sentence continues, "and all that the court could properly say, in such an event, would be that the legislature (possessed of an equal right of opinion) had passed an act which, in the opinion of the judges, was inconsistent with the abstract principles of natural justice."[58]

Thus, in Iredell's view, the judges could opine but not hold with the force of a legal ruling that a legislature had contravened the natural law. But at the very most—i.e., even by the orthodox reading of Justice Chase's opinion—this is all that Chase had actually done in *Calder*, since whatever may be thought of his pronouncements on natural law, he did, after all, hold with his colleagues that the Connecticut resolution was valid. Indeed, he did less than what Iredell endorses here, for he never said that the Connecticut law violated the natural law any more than he held that it did. And by the account I have given of Chase's opinion, his position and Iredell's are nearly indistinguishable; all that Chase had said in *Calder* was that the principles of natural law instruct the people to reject as "political heresy" the positivistic view that all laws that a legislature is not by written limits restrained from passing are valid. Never having moved from that political principle to a juridical one that would permit judges to enforce the political ortho- doxy he describes, Chase's holding and his rhetoric—both his action and his speech—are fully consistent with the position staked out by Ire- dell. If Iredell thought that he was rebutting a contrary view of Chase's, he was mistaken. It is more likely that the supposed disagree- ment was not seen as such by either of the justices, only by their mod- ern readers.

THE CONTRACT CASES: MARSHALL AND JOHNSON

Fletcher v. Peck (1810)

Fletcher declares that the contract clause governs public as well as private contracts, in this instance a land grant subsequently re- pealed by the state of Georgia. For many years this was regarded as an expansion of the clause beyond its original intent, but recent scholar- ship has supported the view of Marshall himself that the words of the contract clause "are general, and are applicable to contracts of every description."[59]

The two opinions in this case, by Chief Justice John Marshall for the Court and by Justice William Johnson for himself alone, have also been cited frequently for their allusions to "higher law" judicial review.[60] To most observers, Marshall's opinion appears moderate and restrained only by comparison to Johnson's, for the former is viewed as grounded at least partly in the constitutional text and the latter as departing from the text altogether.

The initial statement cited by Marshall's critics occurs where he is considering the state's deviation from the usual course of settling dis- puted property claims, particularly those in which it is itself one of the claimants:

> If the legislature of Georgia was not bound to submit its preten- sions to those tribunals which are established for the security of property, and to decide on human rights, if it might claim to itself the power of judging in its own case, yet there are certain great principles of justice, whose authority is universally acknowledged, that ought not to be entirely disregarded.[61]

One may be tempted to read this passage as launching a discourse on extraconstitutional limits on legislative power. But it is the fifth of some eighteen paragraphs in which Marshall recounts the unusual circumstance of the Georgia legislature, by its rescinding act of 1796, attempting to redress a "fraud" on the people of the state in the original bribery-tainted land conveyance, and addresses the effects of that attempt on subsequent purchasers—namely, that the legislature, "if the [1796] act be valid, has annihilated their rights also."[62] Marshall intends here only to show that in a case of allegedly fraudulent conveyance such as this, the usual course of judicial process is for a court of chancery, governed by "the clearest principles of equity, to leave unmolested" the lawful titles of innocent second- and third-generation purchasers (such as Peck and Fletcher, respectively)—even when the fraud of the first transaction is proven.[63] Those principles of equitable proceeding are the "great principles of justice" to which Marshall alludes here, as is indicated by the paragraph following the one quoted above:

> If the legislature be its own judge in its own case, *it would seem equitable* that its decision *should* be regulated by those rules which would have regulated the decision of a judicial tribunal. The question was, in its nature, a question of title, and the tribunal which decided it [i.e., the legislature] was either acting in the character of a court of justice, and performing a duty usually assigned to a court, or it was exerting a mere act of power in which it was controlled only by its own will.[64]

By intervening this way in a question of land title, the Georgia legislature had indeed performed what is usually a judicial duty, but since it did not follow "those rules which would have regulated" a judicial proceeding, namely the "clearest principles of equity," Marshall concludes that "its act is to be supported by its power alone."[65] These paragraphs clearly imply that the rules governing chancery courts need not, in strict legal terms, govern the legislature. It would be fairer if they did, but the legislature is free to disregard them and to proceed otherwise if its mere power, unrestrained by state or federal constitution, authorizes the divestiture of land titles originating in its own grant.

But does the legislature have that power? The last six paragraphs of this eighteen-paragraph section of the opinion treat this as an open question. Still keeping his focus on the subsequent purchasers who could not have been involved in the bribery of legislators—for the retaking of land might have been justified "so far as respected those to whom crime was imputable"[66]—Marshall considers the conflict between the ordinary power of a legislature to repeal its own previous acts and the rights these purchasers have in "vested legal estates."[67] Contrary to what might be thought by those modern readers who are predisposed to think of Marshall's opinion here as that of a natural-law jurist, he does not indicate that in the nature of things the vested rights automatically trump the legislative power of repeal. Vested rights are facts, but facts just possibly might be denied by power: "*If* those estates may be seized by the sovereign authority, still, that they originally vested is a fact, and cannot cease to be a fact."[68] Likewise, although it is a fact that "the law cannot devest those rights," Marshall states that "the act of annulling them, *if* legitimate," is so by virtue of a legal-political power copious enough to deny a legal fact. However much the legal fact of vested rights is rooted in nature, legislative power, if not positively restrained, may be quite competent to do what natural justice forbids. Marshall's "ifs" in the lines just quoted are not rhetorical flourishes regarding a question he has already answered for himself and whose answer he is about to spring on the reader. They show a real irresolution on his part about a question he is fortunate enough not to have to answer since he will shortly turn to the concrete terms of the contract clause for an answer that obviates the whole difficulty.

The section under consideration concludes with three brief paragraphs that deserve full quotation here, in which Marshall reflects on the nature and limits of legislative power:

> It may well be doubted whether the nature of society and of government does not prescribe some limits to the legislative power; and, if any be prescribed, where are they to be found, if the property of an individual, fairly and honestly acquired, may be seized without compensation?
>
> To the legislature all legislative power is granted; but the question, whether the act of transferring the property of an individual to the public, be in the nature of the legislative power, is well worthy of serious reflection.
>
> It is the peculiar province of the legislature to prescribe general rules for the government of society; the application of those rules to individuals in society would seem to be the duty of other departments. How far the power of giving the law may involve every other power, in cases where the constitution is silent, never has been and perhaps never can be, definitely stated.[69]

Portions of the first two paragraphs have been cited by those who think this is an invocation of natural-law limits on legislative power.[70] However, the third paragraph reveals that Marshall is ruminating on the separation of powers, a subject about which he confesses as much uncertainty as Publius, who states in *Federalist* No. 37 that "no skill in the science of government has yet been able to discriminate and define, with sufficient certainty, its three great provinces—the legislative, executive, and judiciary."[71] The three paragraphs just quoted are simply unintelligible except in the context of Marshall's concern that the Georgia repeal act has usurped the powers of a court of equity. But given his explicit puzzlement here over what can be "definitely stated" about the separation of powers, it would be strange indeed if he were about to conclude that his Court can (in Publius's words) "discriminate . . . with sufficient certainty" an improper legislative act from a proper one. And stranger still if he were about to say that his Court can take action judicially on such a conclusion about the separation of powers, as though it were a matter of judicially enforceable natural law.

Such uncertainties left murky by the science of government could not very well be expected to yield firm, enforceable answers in a court of law. They are by their nature political questions, not judicial ones. In the next paragraph of his opinion, Marshall leaves this murky realm for the more solid ground of the Constitution's text: "The validity of this rescinding act, then might well be doubted, were Georgia a single sovereign power. But Georgia cannot be viewed as a single, unconnected, sovereign power, on whose legislature no other restrictions are imposed than may be found in its own constitution."[72]

From this point on, he discusses Georgia's violation of the contract clause of the federal Constitution. On the ground merely of the separation of powers (whether that political principle expresses a standard of natural justice or not), all that Marshall will say is that the Georgia legislature's ad hoc intrusion into the business of an equity court "might well be doubted." Doubted only; he will not so much as opine, much less hold, that the repeal act is invalid on such grounds. Marshall, as he indicated elsewhere in this same case, was not prone to act merely on his doubts; he required more certainty than he expresses here before he would announce a holding.[73] Only the federal contract clause, to which he now turns, will provide an answer that can be given by his Court to the question of the legislature's power.

Much ado has been made of Marshall's holding at the conclusion of his interpretation of the contract clause. As Wolfe has remarked, this part of the opinion "end[s] rather ambiguously":[74]

It is, then, the unanimous opinion of the court, that in this case, the estate having passed into the hands of a purchaser for a valuable consideration, with notice, the state of Georgia was restrained, either by general principles, which are common to our free institutions, or by the particular provisions of the constitution of the United States, from passing a law whereby the estate of the plaintiff in the premises so purchased could be constitutionally and legally impaired and rendered null and void.[75]

Why the "either-or" in this holding? One possibility is that the "general principles" remark refers to the equity principle in fraud cases, which Marshall had been discussing earlier. The case had originated in the federal circuit court under its diversity jurisdiction (Fletcher was from New Hampshire, Peck from Massachusetts); had the circumstances of the case been such as to have it brought as a bill in chancery rather than as a suit at law for breach of covenant, the Supreme Court could well have checked the operation of the Georgia rescinding statute as inequitable when applied to subsequent purchasers such as these two parties, neither of whom had anything to do with the "fraud" of the original land grant. But as already discussed, that problem of the legislature violating principles of equity had for Marshall resolved itself into a dead-end political problem of the separation of powers, a quandary about the "limits of the legislative power" the solution to which "perhaps never can be, definitely stated."

Thus the more plausible reason for the "either-or" ambiguity in Marshall's holding, as David Currie has suggested,[76] is that it is the Court's "unanimous opinion." Justice William Johnson "entertain[ed], on two points, an opinion different from" Marshall's.[77] The first of these differences is that Johnson denies that the Georgia rescinding act could be held invalid on contract clause grounds and does appear to regard the natural law as justiciable against this act of the state. The second reason Johnson writes separately is that, unlike Marshall and the rest of the Court, he regards the Indian titles to the land originally conveyed by the Georgia legislature as still valid, which leads him to the conclusion that whether repealed or not the original land grant is void. There can be no meeting of the minds between Marshall and Johnson on this second point; thus in his holding on the question of the Indian titles, Marshall is only able to announce an opinion of the "majority of the court."[78]

Concerning the first point of difference between them, the fact that Marshall decided the case on contract clause grounds and Johnson

would prefer natural-law grounds can be made into an either-or holding on a common result, thus enabling Marshall to announce, on these
double grounds, "the unanimous opinion of the court."[79] Given the in-
conclusive ending to his own remarks on how "certain great principles
of justice"[80] could restrain the Georgia legislature, Marshall could
hardly be expected to be speaking for himself and the other three justices in the majority when he writes in the unanimous holding of the
"general principles, which are common to our free institutions."[81] As
we have seen, for any measure of certainty in deciding this case Marshall had to turn to the contract clause. The "general principles," as
opposed to "particular provisions of the constitution," are Johnson's,
not Marshall's.

Unlike so many of Marshall's modern readers, Justice Johnson did
see a real difference between his own view and Marshall's on this
point.[82] Since he is prepared to overrule the original land grant, his departure from the Court's views in the first part of his opinion is the purest obiter dicta. But in disputing Marshall's interpretation of the contract clause and instead offering the alternative ground of natural law,
Johnson reveals the extent to which he thinks Marshall's opinion is
solidly—and mistakenly, in his view—grounded in the text of the Constitution.

Johnson's most notorious remark on the principle restraining the
state's revocation of its land grant is this: "I do not hesitate to declare
that a state does not possess the power of revoking its own grants. But I
do it on a general principle, on the reason and nature of things: a principle which will impose laws even on the Deity."[83] Hoots of derision usually follow any quotation of this passage, owing to its invocation of a
standard to control the Deity. But before looking for Johnson's statement of just what this "general principle" is, it should be noted that he
was not alone in the thought expressed here. Even Blackstone (not a
"higher-law" jurist, as will become evident in Chapter 10) said much
the same, that natural law consists of "the eternal immutable laws of
good and evil, to which the creator himself in all his dispensations con-
forms."[84]

Johnson's general principle turns out to be a distinction between the
state's "right of jurisdiction" and its "right of soil." The former can
never be granted away to anyone, as it is an attribute of sovereignty; to
"part with it is to commit a species of political suicide."[85] But it can
part with the latter with no damage to itself, as it is merely the right
attaching to a material possession. And when the state does this, according to Johnson, it loses all subsequent claim to property other than

what it may assert under eminent domain for public use.[86] As a matter of political principle, this makes some sense of the often ridiculed passage above, and it might, at some stretch, be enforceable under a prohibition of such takings. But Johnson makes no issue of whether the Georgia constitution forbids such expropriation, and the Fifth Amendment takings clause does not apply to states. It must be concluded, therefore, that Johnson is the first of these jurists to venture into the wild blue yonder without regard to any relevant constitutional text.[87]

It may be, however, that if Johnson had been obliged to deliver the controlling opinion in *Fletcher,* he would have thought through the consequences of his principles more carefully. For there is an internal contradiction of sorts—an unwitting one—in his position on how his "general principle" can be brought to bear on a state legislature retaking property it has granted. This contradiction arises when Johnson remarks on the notion, which he rejects, that "the grants of a legislature may be void because the legislature are corrupt."[88] The reason he gives for rejecting such a view is this:

> The acts of the supreme power of a country must be considered pure for the same reason that all sovereign acts must be considered just; because there is no power that can declare them otherwise. The absurdity in this case would have been strikingly perceived, could the party who passed the act of cession have got again into power, and declared themselves pure, and the intermediate legislature corrupt.[89]

But if the "supreme power" in Georgia, responsible for the state's "sovereign acts," is the legislature, as Johnson appears to say; and if all such sovereign acts "must be considered just"; and if "no power . . . can declare them otherwise"; then two bewildering questions arise. First, what can possibly be unjust about the "absurdity" Johnson contemplates of one "sovereign" legislature undoing the grants of a previous one (or of this happening successively, one legislature after another alternately revoking and reaffirming such grants)? Second, should this occur—as it did in *Fletcher*—does his statement that "no power can declare" such "sovereign" acts impure or unjust not contradict his earlier assertion that a "right of soil" principle may be invoked to invalidate the legislative revocation of a grant?

In short, in the passage quoted above, does he not give back to the state a power he had denied it on the previous page of his opinion? First he "declare[s] that a state does not possess the power of revoking its own grants", then he announces that "no power can declare [sovereign acts of the legislature] otherwise" than just. Johnson offers no support for any principled exception that would state that the only sovereign acts of a legislature that may be declared unjust by another power are those in which it revokes a grant previously made. Stated flatly on subsequent pages as categorical assertions, Johnson's two principles cannot logically coexist.

Johnson's very next words place him on much firmer ground for resolving the dilemma of legislative injustice, though he still has in view only the problem of controlling the alleged corruption of the first legislature that had made the original land grant: "The security of a people against the misconduct of their rulers, must lie in the frequent recurrence to first principles, and the imposition of adequate constitutional restrictions."[90] In the people's power mentioned here—not in the acts of the legislature—Johnson would find his true "sovereign" if only he were to look a bit more closely. And in the sovereign people's "imposition of adequate constitutional principles"—not in the judicial invocation of "reason and nature of things" or the "right of soil"—is to be found some security "against the misconduct of their rulers," either in improvidently granting away state property in the first place or in attempting to regain it by expropriation. Like his mentor Jefferson, Johnson is most likely speaking here of the *people's* "frequent recurrence to first principles," not to such a practice on the part of judges. (It was Jefferson who advocated, in a draft of a constitution for Virginia in the 1780s, the alteration of that constitution whenever necessary for "correcting breaches of it"—a "frequent reference of constitutional questions to the decision of the whole society" severely criticized by Madison in the *Federalist*.)[91] Whatever the advisability of that expedient, it seems better to leave the ultimate control over legislatures to the electoral and constitution-making powers of the people than to assert a natural-law review power over them both on the part of judges.

In the end, as will be apparent in the next case to be considered, Justice Johnson appears to have preferred the power of the people to the power of the judiciary where no clear constraints of a written constitution could be brought to bear by the latter. Sandra F. VanBurkleo reports that after 1819 Johnson moved "away from abstract decisions rooted in political theory and natural law."[92] But this point could be taken still further: *Fletcher* appears to be Johnson's only flirtation with extraconstitutional natural law as a ground of decision; and as already discussed, his views in that case display the mind of a jurist who had by no means worked out the implications of or ironed out the inconsistencies in taking such a position.

Ogden v. Saunders (1827)

In this case, Marshall penned his one and only dissent in a constitutional case during his entire tenure on the Court.[93] Taking Justices Story and Duvall with him in a 4 to 3 decision, Marshall disputed the Court's ruling that a state law could, consistent with the contract clause, discharge private debts incurred after the passage of the law. The Court had already decided in *Sturges* v. *Crowninshield* (1819)[94] that "insolvency" laws with a retroactive effect violated the Constitution; in Marshall's view, similar laws with only a prospective effect were likewise forbidden. Typically, commentators have applauded the majority's view and condemned Marshall's,[95] but a few are more sympathetic to Marshall.[96]

My purpose is not to rehearse that debate; I include *Ogden* because some observers view it as another instance of Marshall's alleged predilection to import extraconstitutional standards of natural law into his jurisprudence.[97] True enough, there are pages of Marshall's opinion containing numerous references to rights "anterior to, and independent of society," "natural rights," the "state of nature," "the original right of individuals," and "the authority of those writers" who gave us "treatises on the laws of nature and nations" read by the framers of the Constitution.[98] But what point is Marshall attempting to make?

He is trying to find his way to the exact meaning of the word "obligation" in the prohibition against any state law "impairing the Obligation of Contracts." All the justices who write in *Ogden* have something to say on the subject of natural law and on its relation to positive law. But the majority of the Court, led by Justice Bushrod Washington in the first of four seriatim opinions, holds that the obligation of a contract has its foundation in positive law.[99] In the context of the prospective insolvency law at issue here, this means that for the majority (to simplify somewhat) the law impairs no obligation because it forms part of the obligation in the first place. Marshall, in addition to showing how this interpretation could obviate the principle of the contract clause altogether,[100] replies that it "assumes that contract is the mere creature of society."[101] Not so, he writes; in a state of nature men are perfectly capable of making contracts, although they must rely solely on their own efforts to enforce the obligations of them. Once entering society, they give up this latter "right of coercion" to government "but bring that right [of contract] with them into society."[102] Government is then responsible for fashioning the remedies to enforce the obligations of valid contracts. However, Marshall continues,

> We think, that obligation and remedy are distinguishable from each other. That the first is created by the act of the parties, the last is afforded by government. The words of the restriction we have been considering, countenance, we think, this idea. No State shall "pass any law impairing the obligation of contracts." These words seem to us to import, that the obligation is intrinsic, that it is created by the contract itself, not that it is dependent on the laws made to enforce it. [And if we turn for support to the treatises read by the framers,] we find them to concur in the declaration, that contracts possess an original intrinsic obligation, derived from the acts of free agents, and not given by government.[103]

Yet for all his reliance on the theory of natural rights and the social contract, Marshall should not be taken as endorsing some illimitable "freedom of contract" standing outside the positive law. In addition to its responsibility to provide remedies for the enforcement of valid contracts, government has the power, Marshall repeatedly stresses, to regulate the making of contracts and even to prohibit any species of contract it chooses. The relation between man's natural right and these positive laws is a simple one:

> So far as this power has restrained the original right of individuals to bind themselves by contract, it is restrained; but beyond these actual restraints the original power remains unimpaired. . . . [T]he right to contract is not surrendered with the right to coerce performance. It is still incident to that degree of free agency which the laws leave to every individual, and the obligation of the contract is a necessary consequence of the right to make it. Laws regulate this right, but, where not regulated, it is retained in its original extent. . . . [T]he right of government to regulate the manner in which [contracts] shall be formed, or to prohibit such as may be against the policy of the State, is entirely consistent with their inviolability after they have been formed.[104]

Small comfort here for the liberty of contract jurists of the *Allgeyer* and *Lochner* cases. Where the law does not act, the rule is freedom—this can hardly be called a revolutionary departure into natural-law reasoning. There are two reasons for Marshall's condemnation of the prospective insolvency law. First, there is no support in text or intent for limiting the application of the contract clause to retrospective laws; second, such laws seem to say to contracting parties that they are free to incur obligations to one another, but those obligations will cease to exist when the debtor goes broke. That, for Marshall, is more than a legitimate modification of the remedy available.

The phrase "legal positivist," with its distinctly modern connotations, conjures up the image of Oliver Wendell Holmes, Jr., who derided "jurists who believe in natural law" as being "in that naive state of mind that accepts what has been familiar . . . as something that must be accepted by all men everywhere."[105] Marshall would no doubt make short work of such Holmesian nonsense, yet in *Ogden* he reveals a view of judicially enforceable law that may well deserve to be called positivistic:

Law has been defined by a writer, whose definitions especially have been the theme of almost universal panegyric, "to be a rule of civil conduct prescribed by the supreme power in a State." In our system, the legislature of a State is the supreme power, in all cases where its action is not restrained by the constitution of the United States.[106]

The much praised but unidentified writer is Blackstone. Whether from memory or with the *Commentaries* at his elbow, Marshall has quoted him exactly; either way, he can hardly be unaware that this is not Blackstone's definition of law simply, but his definition of municipal (i.e., positive) law.[107] He must also know that in the *Commentaries* it follows hard on the heels of a discussion of the law of nature, which is declared to be "superior in obligation to any other. . . . [N]o human laws are of any validity, if contrary to this," nor "should be suffered to contradict" it.[108] Of course, when it comes to the judicial function, Blackstone will suffer no judge to overrule the sovereign will on such grounds.[109] Marshall's attachment to the natural law can be assumed to be as strong as or stronger than Blackstone's. Yet, if anything, his slightly altered quotation of the latter shows him to be stronger still in the conviction that judges have nothing to do with any laws but the positive ones made by men. The letter of the contract clause is his touchstone in *Ogden,* and the foray into social contract theory has only helped him to illuminate the meaning of that letter, as understood by those who wrote it under the influence of that theory. But no limits on power from any extratextual source are invoked.

And what of Justice Johnson? The critics of his *Fletcher* opinion do not prepare the reader for his opinion in *Ogden*. In the years since the former, he appears to have given up both his opposition to the contract clause's coverage of executed grants and his alternative grounding of vested rights in natural law—as witness *Dartmouth College v. Woodward,* in which he concurred without additional comment in Marshall's opinion.[110] Now with the majority in *Ogden,* Johnson speaks of the power of government over the subject of contracts in even stronger terms than the chief justice does, as when he asks, "Who can doubt the power of the State to prohibit her citizens from running in debt altogether?"[111] Like his brethren in the majority, Johnson regards even the obligation of a contract as a matter of positive law, though he does not of course deny the existence of natural law:

> The obligation of every contract . . . will be found to be measured neither by moral law alone, nor universal law alone, nor by the laws of society alone, but by a combination of the three,—an operation in which the moral law is explained by the law of nature, and both modified and adapted to the exigencies of society by positive law. The constitution was framed for society, . . . in which . . . *all* the contracts of men receive a relative, and not a positive [i.e., absolute] interpretation: for the rights of all must be held and enjoyed in subserviency to the good of the whole.[112]

If this leaves the reader in any doubt as to the operation of natural law in the adjudication of cases, Johnson admonishes us: "All the notions of society, particularly in their jurisprudence, are more or less artificial; our constitution no where speaks the language of men in a state of nature."[113] Gone is the justice who would invoke "reason and the nature of things" to rein in a state legislature; here is a peroration worthy of an adherent of judicial restraint in any age:

> It is true, that in the exercise of this power [to impose limits to avarice and tyranny of individuals], governments themselves may sometimes be the authors of oppression and injustice; but wherever the constitution could impose limits to such power, it has done so; and if it has not been able to impose effectual and universal restraints, it arises only from the extreme difficulty of regulating the movements of sovereign power.[114]

Somehow these remarks of Johnson's in *Ogden* are usually lost amid all the attention paid to his opinion in *Fletcher.* He is, for the most part, justly subject to the charges of his critics for what he said in 1810; yet the facts should be considered—that he offered one rather ill-considered invocation of natural law in just under two pages of dicta in a dissent; that he never again ventured into such extraconstitutional territory; and that seventeen years later, he devoted more than ten pages, in a case where he cast the critical fourth vote, to criticizing the notion that anything but the positive law can decide a case. True, he did not publicly recant his *Fletcher* opinion, but this may be more than should be asked, and the context in *Ogden* hardly provided an apt occasion to do so. I believe that Marshall was right in *Ogden* and Johnson wrong; yet neither of them invoked the law of nature as justiciable above the positive law.

As an aside (and because it was to be cited decades later), another of the seriatim majority opinions in *Ogden* deserves brief mention. Justice Smith Thompson gives the contract clause a reading as "positivistic" as Johnson's. But in the course of arguing that the contract clause, like those forbidding ex post facto laws and bills of attainder, should be understood to prohibit only retrospective laws, he then interjects, quite unnecessarily to the argument at hand, the following:

> No state court would, I presume, sanction and enforce an *ex post facto* law, if no such prohibition was contained in the constitution of the United States; so, neither would retrospective laws, taking away vested rights, be enforced. Such laws are repugnant to those fundamental principles upon which every just system of laws is founded.[115]

Shortly thereafter, writing ambiguously enough to refer either to the ex post facto clause or to the contract clause, Thompson says that where such a fundamental principle is concerned, "the provision [in the Constitution] was unnecessary," meaning that the principle could be vindicated by courts of law even without its appearance in the text.[116] In light of this passing remark, Thompson could be counted with the William Johnson of the *Fletcher* case as the only other justice during this era to state without equivocation that extraconstitutional natural law may form the basis of a judicial decision. But as with Johnson's *Fletcher* dicta,Thompson's remark here is not developed with any rigor and is contradicted by other statements in the same opinion—as when he writes that a "contract is a law which the parties impose upon themselves, subject, however, to the paramount law—the law of the country where the contract is made."[117]

JOSEPH STORY AND NATURAL JUSTICE

Terrett v. Taylor (1815)

This case involved the title to land of the parish of the Episcopal church of Alexandria and the effect on that title of a Virginia statute of January 1802. Before that enactment, Alexandria had been ceded by Virginia to Congress to form part of the District of Columbia. Terrett and others, the overseers of the poor for Virginia's Fairfax county, claimed the land under the Virginia act, which asserted the state's "right to all the property of the Episcopal churches" in the state and gave these county overseers the power to sell vacant parish lands and use the money for the benefit of the poor. Taylor and other vestrymen of the church desired that the overseers be "perpetually enjoined from claiming the land" and that the two wardens of the church "be decreed to sell and convey the land," with the proceeds devoted to the use of the church.[118] The case was tried in the federal circuit court for the District of Columbia, where Taylor and the vestrymen were victorious, and was appealed to the Supreme Court. Justice Story wrote a brief opinion for a unanimous Court, affirming the circuit court's ruling but with the proviso that while Terrett et al. could claim no title, neither could the wardens proceed with a sale without the minister's consent, he "also having the freehold, either in law or in equity, during his incumbency."[119]

Story found it appropriate to review the church's history under Virginia law. The land had been acquired by private conveyance in 1770 under the terms of acts of the colonial legislature; subsequent to independence, an act of 1776 "completely confirmed and established the rights of the church to all its lands and other property."[120] An act of 1784 made a corporation of each Episcopal parish in the state; this was repealed in 1786 but with no adverse effect on property rights. These last two acts and another of 1788 also modified slightly the status of the vestries or trustees of each parish. Then in 1798 all the previous acts since the revolution were repealed "as inconsistent with the principles of the constitution and of religious freedom," and in 1802 the act giving rise to this case was passed.[121]

Story questioned the supposition of the act of 1798 that all the previous acts violated the Virginia bill of rights, but be that as it may, it "will require other arguments to establish the position that, at the Revolution, all the public property acquired by the Episcopal churches, under the sanction of the laws, became the property of the State."[122] The land had not been a grant from the state or the Crown but had been privately acquired, and title to it "indefeasibly vested." Upon America's independence there was no loss of title, as it is "a principle of the common law, that the division of an empire creates no forfeiture." Even if that were not so, the Virginia act of 1776 "vested an indefeasible and irrevocable title."[123] True, that and the subsequent acts were repealed in 1798:

> But that the legislature can repeal statutes creating private corporations, or confirming to them property already acquired under the faith of previous laws, and by such repeal can vest the property of such corporations exclusively in the State, or dispose of the same to such purposes as they may please, without the consent or default of the corporators, we are not prepared to admit; and we think ourselves standing upon the principles of natural justice, upon the fundamental laws of every free government, upon the spirit and the letter of the Constitution of the United States, and upon the decisions of the most respectable judicial tribunals, in resisting such a doctrine.[124]

The final portion of this sentence, after the semicolon, is what has disturbed some commentators and prompted them to charge Story with succumbing to the same temptation alleged of Marshall, Johnson, Chase, and Paterson.[125] It is disquieting on the face of it: Story alludes to judicial decisions but names none; he refers to the federal Constitution but specifies no provision of it. Does he rest the case, in the final analysis, on "natural justice"? Yes and no. No, if what is understood by "natural justice" is an extraconstitutional ground for the exercise of judicial review. Yes, if note is now taken of what is almost universally overlooked about this case by its modern readers. None of Story's critics, to my knowledge, ever seems to have remarked that *Terrett* is an appeal of an equity ruling of the circuit court, in which the prayer of Taylor's "bill in chancery" had been granted, Terrett had been enjoined from making any further claim on the land, and the sale desired by Taylor and the vestry had been decreed.[126] (Only this last part of the circuit court's ruling, as has already been discussed, was modified by the Supreme Court.)

It is (or was) in the nature of an equity case that no principle of statutory or common law directly applies or can supply the relief prayed for. As Gary McDowell has remarked, "the jurisdiction of courts of equity extends only to the relief a court of law would grant if it could."[127] The jurisdiction of the federal courts extends to cases in both law and equity under Article III, and this is the one kind of case where it should not be surprising to see an opinion refer to "natural justice," an appellation commonly applied to the principles of equity jurisprudence. But, as we shall see, an equity case such as this does not, properly speaking, give rise to an exercise of judicial review, insofar as it does not invoke the judicial power of invalidating a statute as void ab initio. Rather, as McDowell writes, for Story (following Aristotle) equity entails the " 'correction of the law' whenever the strict law is defective by reason of its universality."[128] And although it is true that equity provides the vindication of rights grounded in natural justice (which rights, however, are not vindicated by the common law), it is not true that equity jurisprudence—for Story at least—is a realm of untrammeled judicial discretion to "do justice," as "nothing could be more absurd or more dangerous than the assumption that every case in equity 'is to be decided upon circumstances according to the arbitration or discretion of the Judge, acting according to his own notions *ex aequo et bono.*' "[129]

But if the equitable character of *Terrett* places it outside the ambit of judicial review, properly understood, why then does Story make any reference at all, even (or especially) such a vague one, to "the spirit and the letter of the Constitution of the United States"? The maxim of this branch of jurisprudence is that "equity follows the law," and certain principles of the federal Constitution (and of the state constitution) do protect certain species of vested property rights. The federal contract clause does so; so do sections 1 and 11 of the Virginia bill of rights of 1776.[130] But none of these provisions can be directly brought to bear on the case. The contract clause, in particular, is not directly applicable because the corporate charter bestowed on the church in the act of 1784 was repealed in 1786, before the federal Constitution existed. The 1786 act, however, explicitly refrained from any divestiture of preexisting property rights, which carried over until after the adoption of the Constitution. Vested rights resting at least in part on prior legislative acts then existed at the time of the 1798 repeal of all postrevolutionary acts. The connection to the contract clause thus seems too tenuous for a square holding on constitutional grounds—and any such holding would be more than could properly be asked for by the equity pleading of a bill in chancery—but its "spirit" may be strongly invoked in an equity ruling (it should be noted here that Justice Washington, and Story himself, were later to cite *Terrett* as upholding a *principle* associated with the contract clause).[131] It does seem clear that in legislating what amounts to an uncompensated expropriation of the property of one class of owners, namely Episcopal parishes, Virginia has committed what Hamilton described in the *Federalist* (while discussing equity) as an "injury of the private rights of particular classes of citizens, by unjust and partial laws. Here also the firmness of the judicial magistracy is of vast importance in mitigating the severity and confining the operation of such laws."[132]

Hamilton here may have the prospect of "unjust and partial" federal laws most clearly in view; yet in a diversity case such as *Terrett* the equity power may clearly be brought to bear on state laws as well. More important, this "mitigating the severity" is "not with a view to infractions of the Constitution," said Hamilton;[133] hence the reader should note what Story does and does not do in *Terrett*. In the very sentence following the passage under consideration, he does not declare any Virginia statutes unconstitutional but only (in Hamilton's terms) "confin[es] the operation" of them: "The statutes of 1798, c. 9, and of 1801 [1802], c. 5, are not, therefore, in our judgment, operative so far as to divest the Episcopal church of the property acquired, previous to the Revolution, by purchase or by donation."[134] To the modern reader this may seem a clear case of declaring a statute "unconstitutional as applied." But that sort of ruling, commonplace today, seems not to have been thought of in 1815 and indeed seems most likely to have emerged in the years since then precisely as a result of the blurring or merging of equity and law.[135] Story's narrow holding bears the hallmark of equity: to prevent, by standards of common sense, legislative intent, and the spirit of the law, the injustices the letter of the law would permit in a particular case—and to do so by fashioning remedies tailored to that case alone. What might be the fate of the law in any case not covered by this holding will have to await another day. It bears repeating that strictly speaking, *Terrett* should not even be regarded as an exercise of judicial review.

One loose end still dangles. Why did Story not simply rule, as a matter of law, that Virginia no longer had any jurisdiction over the Alexandria parish, as it had become part of the District of Columbia before the act of 1802? First, it is important to remember that *Terrett* was brought as a case in equity, not a case in law. But Story does fortify his ruling with reference to this fact: As to the "corporations and property within [the District of Columbia], the right of Virginia to legislate no longer existed."[136] However, it may be that the act of 1798, having been passed before the cession of Alexandria—even though it does not explicitly assert the state's ownership as the 1802 act does—bolsters Virginia's pretension that the church no longer owns the land and that its title has somehow been defaulted to the state. But as Story points out, the 1798 statute's only effect was to repeal all state laws since the revolution regarding the established church, "and, of course, it left in full force all the statutes previously enacted [i.e., in colonial times], so far as they were not inconsistent with the present [state] constitution."[137] As they arise, other cases involving perhaps the rights of parishes still within the jurisdiction of the state will necessarily be adjudicated by state courts, which will have to determine what force, if any, the property rights protected by those colonial statutes still have under the state constitution. But those cases are not Story's problem or his concern; in this case, equity has provided a proper adjustment of the competing claims of the vestrymen and the county overseers (even the winners have not obtained all that they asked), and there is no need for a blanket ruling on the constitutional validity of the 1802 Virginia statute. (Notice that Story's narrow holding does not even preempt the state's right to claim lands acquired by this parish since the revolution, although other things he says indicate that such a claim would be severely prejudiced.) And "natural justice," far from being a ground of any extraconstitutional judicial invalidation, has been invoked merely as a traditional description of that equity jurisprudence at work.

Contrary to what is suggested by David Currie, Story's "reliance on natural justice" is not an "alternative holding . . . along the way to his clear conclusion" that the federal Constitution has been violated by Virginia.[138] Story's opinion in *Terrett,* if seen in its proper light, holds neither that the federal Constitution has been violated nor that the Court is authorized to wield a general power to void statutes on extraconstitutional grounds. No law is held void in *Terrett* on any grounds, constitutional or otherwise. Certain public officials of a state are simply enjoined, on grounds of equity, from pressing the claims of the state to lands of a certain description.[139]

Wilkinson v. Leland (1829)

Wilkinson reversed a federal circuit court ruling in a diversity suit and upheld the validity of an act of the Rhode Island general assembly passed in 1792. The act was essentially a private bill, confirming the validity of a sale of lands in Rhode Island by the executrix of an estate to settle debts in that state owed by the testator, a late citi-

zen of New Hampshire. At the time of the sale, the will had been pro-
bated in New Hampshire but not in Rhode Island, and so the executrix
as yet had no legal right under Rhode Island law to sell the property.
The private bill retrospectively confirmed what was, before the legislative action, a void sale. Years later, second-generation heirs of the estate contested the sale and challenged the Rhode Island legislature's
authority to pass the act confirming it.

As noted already, the Court overturned no law in this case, but Justice Story, again for a unanimous Court, appears to discuss principles
of natural law at one point:[140]

> That government can scarcely be deemed to be free, where the
> rights of property are left solely dependent upon the will of a legis-
> lative body, without restraint. The fundamental maxims of a free
> government seem to require that the rights of personal liberty and
> private property should be held sacred. At least, no court of justice
> in this country would be warranted in assuming that the power to
> violate and disregard them—a power so repugnant to the common
> principles of justice and civil liberty—lurked under any general
> grant of legislative authority, or ought to be implied from any gen-
> eral expressions of the will of the people. The people ought not to
> be presumed to part with rights so vital to their security and well-
> being, without very strong and direct expressions of such an inten-
> tion.[141]

This passage echoes the dicta of Justice Chase in *Calder* v. *Bull,* a case
Wilkinson resembles in one decisive respect. Rhode Island, at this date,
was the only state governed under its old royal charter (it did not adopt
a constitution until 1842). As with the old Connecticut charter in 1798,
the Rhode Island charter provided, as Story puts it above, a "general
grant of legislative authority" to the general assembly, with no specific
enumeration of powers and providing only that the laws passed were
not to be "contrary and repugnant" to the laws of England. Also like
the old Connecticut charter, this one did not contain any meaningful
separation of powers.[142]

Could it be considered some form of natural-law review for Story to
urge upon his readers a limitation on legislative power that is not so
much in the Rhode Island charter as an emanation from the "fundamental maxims of a free government"? The question is revealed as the
wrong one to ask when Story's dicta on those "fundamental maxims"
are placed in their proper context. Like Samuel Chase in *Calder,* Story

has digressed briefly on the political principle of limited legislative power in general before returning to the precise question at issue in the case: exactly how is it that this legislature's power is limited by the organic law that brought it into being? Rhode Island in 1829, like Connecticut in 1798, is governed under no state bill of rights or comparable set of textual limitations on political power. Hence the only way for Story to ascertain the limits on power is to work from the other end of the problem, as it were: what are the limits implicit in the very authority granted to the general assembly?

Story thus faces a dilemma quite similar to that faced by Chase and Iredell thirty-one years before. The limits on the legislature are derived from standards of English common and statute law, and its nebulous authority must be considered from the perspective of what can reasonably be presumed to have been granted to it by the charter and by the tacit consent of the people. This context can be restored by noticing two passages in the same paragraph quoted at length above. The first appears just a few lines beforehand:

> What is the true extent of the power thus granted, must be open to explanation, as well by usage as by construction of the terms in which it is given. In a government professing to regard the great rights of personal liberty and of property, and which is required to legislate in subordination to the general laws of England, it would not lightly be presumed that the great principles of Magna Charta were to be disregarded, or that the estates of its subjects were liable to be taken away without trial, without notice, and without offence.[143]

And the second passage concludes his thinking on the subject: "We are not prepared, therefore, to admit that the people of Rhode Island have ever delegated to their legislature the power to devest the vested rights of property, and transfer them without the assent of the parties."[144]

As was mentioned already, these two passages bracket the longer one quoted above. They reveal that Story imports no extraconstitutional natural law as a limitation on legislative power but instead inquires into the source and extent of that power in a written text. As he indicates twice in these lines, the legislature would be perfectly competent to exercise the despotic power to which he refers if the people had delegated it by an express grant—and nothing in practice (certainly nothing justiciable) is interposed in the way of the people making such "strong and direct expressions of such an intention."

For those who are predisposed to view Story as a consistent expositor of some natural-law–based vested rights doctrine, it may come as some surprise to see him say in *Wilkinson* that it "is not sufficient, to entitle [Leland and others] now to recover, to establish the fact that the estate so vested has been devested; but that it has been devested in a manner inconsistent with the principles of law."[145] And should it be supposed that by "principles of law" he means the natural law, Story's very next statement, beginning a new paragraph, is this: "By the *laws of Rhode Island*, . . . the real estate of testators and intestates stands chargeable with the payment of their debts, upon a deficiency of assets of personal estate."[146]

In the end, Story holds the private bill of 1792 valid as no violation of any charter principle because one, the laws of the state, charging the real property of testators to the payment of "existing liens of paramount obligation,"[147] leave the complaining heirs no indefeasible but only a qualifiedly vested right; and two, under the state's charter vesting undifferentiated sovereign powers in the legislature, nothing precludes it from acting after the sale in a manner that a probate court might have done beforehand.[148]

It should be noted that, contrary to at least one commentator's assertion, no issue under the federal Constitution arose on the merits of *Wilkinson;*[149] that a fairly broad reading was given to the charter powers of the legislature in the Court's holding; and that the references to "fundamental maxims of free government"—if they are not taken as pure obiter dicta in a digression on political theory—allude principally to the rights protected by Magna Charta, which looms largest among those "lawes of this our realme of England" to which Charles II's charter specified the general assembly's statutes must be, "as neare as may bee, agreeable."[150] Nowhere, however, does Story suggest that the natural law (especially as it animates the federal Constitution) can substitute as a justiciable standard for the explicit statements of a written constitution.[151] An early commentator saw this much more clearly than do some of Story's more recent readers; Thomas Cooley, in 1868, used *Wilkinson* as his chief example for advancing the following proposition:

Nor can a court declare a statute unconstitutional and void, solely on the ground of unjust and oppressive provisions, or because it is supposed to violate the natural, social, or political rights of the citizen, unless it can be shown that such injustice is prohibited or such rights guaranteed or protected by the constitution.[152]

Moreover, Cooley correctly identified the issue in *Wilkinson* as the question, "What is the scope of a grant of legislative power to be exercised in conformity with the laws of England?"[153]

CORFIELD V. CORYELL (1823)

I include this case, a circuit court ruling by Justice Bushrod Washington, primarily because it was cited decades later by some of the justices who laid the groundwork for a natural-law reading of the Fourteenth Amendment.[154] Justice Joseph Bradley, relying on Washington's gloss on the privileges and immunities clause of Article IV, even went so far as to use this case as authority for his view that the similar clause of the Fourteenth Amendment rendered justiciable the "pursuit of happiness" declared inalienable in the Declaration of Independence.[155]

The case is actually a good deal more prosaic than that. Washington upheld the right of New Jersey, in the face of an Article IV privileges and immunities claim to the contrary, to reserve the use of the oyster beds on its shoreline to its own citizens, excluding those of other states. When inquiring into the nature of the privileges secured by Article IV, he wrote:

> We feel no hesitation in confining these expressions to those privileges and immunities which are, in their nature, fundamental: which belong, of right, to the citizens of all free governments; and which have, at all times, been enjoyed by the citizens of the several states which compose this Union, from the time of their becoming free, independent, and sovereign. What these fundamental principles are, it would perhaps be more tedious than difficult to enumerate. They may, however, be all comprehended under the following heads: Protection by the government; the enjoyment of life and liberty, with the right to acquire and possess property of every kind, and to pursue and obtain happiness and safety; *subject nevertheless to such restraints as the government may justly prescribe for the general good of the whole.*[156]

This statement was followed by a more detailed enumeration of rights possessed by the citizens of one state as they sojourn in another, most of them having to do with property rights and rights to judicial process. All the examples, however, are adduced to illustrate that the principle of Article IV is legal equality: the rights that a state accords to its own citizens must also, in general, be accorded to the citizens of other states. What seemed to escape Justice Bradley (as well as Justice Stephen Field) is the import of the portion I have emphasized above, namely, that the clause protects only civil rights and not natural rights.[157] Washington's prior reference to these rights being "in their nature, fundamental" recognizes that the purpose of securing civil rights by the positive law is to provide some practical effect for men's natural rights, but the emphasized portion indicates that the clause protects only those rights which have been codified by positive law, either constitutional or statutory.

Even Washington's apparent limitation of state power to "such restraints as the government may *justly* prescribe for the general good" introduces no justiciable issue, for he nowhere indicates that a court may judge the justice of such restraints or whether they are really calculated to serve the general good. Nor does he say the contrary; but that question of justice seems to be left to the political process—the day of such legislation being scrutinized under the rubric of "due process" was still a long way off. Even the constitutional principle that is enunciated, legal equality, is qualified: the oyster beds of New Jersey, since they are the common property of the state, which is entitled to consider itself holding them in trust for the use of its own citizens alone, may be legitimately closed to out-of-staters.

Before considering how the cases discussed here came to be treated (and mistreated) as precedents by later justices, a tally should be taken of these alleged uses of natural-law review by the earliest justices. Of the eight opinions often held to be examples of an "alternative tradition" of the enforcement of extraconstitutional principles, only one has proven, under close scrutiny, to be anything of the kind. Only the dissenting opinion of Justice William Johnson in *Fletcher* v. *Peck,* which propounded this view in self-contradictory fashion in a passage quite unnecessary to the result Johnson reached and which was effectively contradicted by the same justice years later in *Ogden* v. *Saunders,* fits the description in any way. Aside from that, there is the equally isolated—and equally self-contradictory—seriatim opinion of Smith Thompson in the *Ogden* case. If that is the final tally on this subject, then as Gertrude Stein is said to have remarked of the city of Oakland, California, so it may also be said of the thesis of much commentary on the subject of this "alternative tradition": there's no there there.

CHAPTER SEVEN

The Metamorphosis of the Early Precedents

Courts cannot nullify an act of the State legislature on the vague ground that they think it opposed to a general latent spirit supposed to pervade or underlie the constitution, where neither the terms nor the implications of the instrument disclose any such restriction. Such a power is denied to the courts, because to concede it would be to make the courts sovereign over both the constitution and the people, and convert the government into a judicial despotism.

—*Nathan Clifford[1]*

When penning these words in a lone dissent in 1875 from a ruling that a state may not authorize municipal bond issues to be applied to the support of private manufacturing, Justice Clifford was engaged, knowingly or not, in a rearguard action on the post–Civil War Supreme Court. Although the heyday of substantive due process was not to arrive for at least another fifteen years,[2] the immediate postbellum period witnessed much struggle over and experimentation with exactly the sort of jurisprudence Clifford condemns in the passage above (indeed, as will become evident, Clifford himself was not a consistent combatant on the side of the struggle he takes above). What has been noticed in some accounts of this period, but not sufficiently explored in any of them, is how the opinions discussed in Chapter 6 came to be used as precedents by the justices on the side of expanded judicial authority. The purpose of this chapter is to show how that use required a distortion and transformation of their meaning that would render those precedents unrecognizable to their authors but supply the mythical meaning commonly attached to them to this day. The telling of this overlooked history is important because if the now customary reading (as resting on extratextual natural law) of the opinions discussed in the previous chapter is either absent in their use as precedents or delayed for several decades, it may be concluded that something suspect was going on at whatever time the cases took on their modern coloration in scholarly and judicial eyes.

For purposes of giving the best possible focus to this historical tale, the order in which the cases from Chapter 6 will be discussed is altered. Also, it is not necessary to treat their precedential history exhaustively up to the present day. The watershed comes in the years immediately following the Civil War, as the rulings of the Marshall Court and its predecessors were put to highly "creative" new uses.

CORFIELD V. CORYELL

Corfield may be dealt with first and most easily. Before the adoption of similar language on "privileges or immunities" in the Fourteenth Amendment, Washington's ruling on the Article IV clause seems to have been little noticed. As late as 1868, the commentator Thomas Cooley said that "the precise meaning of [Article IV] 'privileges and immunities' is not very definitely settled as yet" and cited *Corfield* as one of only three federal cases on the subject.[3] As Raoul Berger has shown, *Corfield* was the subject of much discussion in Congress in 1866 when the "privileges or immunities" clause of the proposed Fourteenth Amendment was under consideration.[4] But the very carelessness and variety of the floor speeches documented by Berger evince a distinct lack of congressional consensus on the meaning of either *Corfield* or Article IV.[5]

Ironically, such a scattering of congressional views may have invited the abuse of the new "privileges or immunities" clause by both sides in the *Slaughter-House Cases*:[6] the familiar truncation of the clause by Justice Samuel Miller for the majority (on the way, however, to a correct result) and the constitutionalization of the "pursuit of happiness" in the dissents of Justices Stephen Field, Joseph Bradley, and Noah Swayne. Miller, wherever else he may have erred in this case, correctly characterized Justice Washington in *Corfield* as having "spoken of . . . rights belonging to the individual as a citizen of a State"[7]—not, it may be noted, of natural rights. Field, on the other hand, cited *Corfield* in support of the proposition that the new amendment protected "the natural and inalienable rights which belong to all citizens."[8] Bradley, reasoning similarly, concluded by contradicting Washington when he said that "the language of the [Article IV] clause . . . seems fairly susceptible of a broader interpretation than that which makes it a guarantee of mere equality of privileges with other citizens."[9]

Not surprisingly perhaps, with Miller's view on the new clause winning out, Fourteenth Amendment privileges and immunities law has all but disappeared and so has citation of *Corfield*, except for its rare use in an Article IV argument.[10] Not until 1961 would another justice use *Corfield* as standing for any natural-law principle,[11] and the dissenters in *Slaughter-House* largely gave it up as the due process clause proved more promising for their purposes.

VAN HORNE'S LESSEE V. DORRANCE

Van Horne's Lessee is something of a mystery, at least when inquiring into how it came to be understood by certain scholars today as a ruling based on natural law. Only four citations of the case have appeared in opinions of the justices, all of which support the reading of it that I have offered above. In the first, *Satterlee* v. *Matthewson* (1829), Justice Washington, for a unanimous Court, referred to *Van Horne's Lessee* as "founded expressly on the constitution" of Pennsylvania.[12]

The case's next two appearances are in opinions of Justice Levi Woodbury. Concurring in *West River Bridge Co.* v. *Dix* (1848), Woodbury cites *Van Horne's Lessee* as standing for the principle, grounded "on necessity," that "all the property in a State is derived from, or protected by, its government, and hence is held subject to its wants in taxation, and to certain important public uses, both in war and peace."[13] Paterson would probably have agreed with all of this except the notion that property is "derived from" government; Woodbury, if anything, makes him sound like a legal positivist. Then, dissenting in *Luther* v. *Borden* (1849), Woodbury quotes Paterson on the importance of written constitutions, again noticing nothing of the natural-law reasoning alleged of the latter today.[14]

Finally, Justice Mahlon Pitney, dissenting in *Southern Pacific Co.* v. *Jensen* (1916), cites *Van Horne's Lessee* to support the proposition that

the object of the framers of [the Constitution] was to lay the foundations of a government, to set up its framework, and to establish merely the general principles by which it was to be animated;

avoiding, as far as possible, any but the most fundamental regulations for controlling its operations, and these usually in the form of
restrictions. Vanhorne v. Dorrance, 2 Dall. 304, 308.[15]

This citation can hardly be a reference to the Justice Paterson so eager
to impose extraconstitutional limitations on the acts of legislatures.

CALDER V. BULL

Justice Samuel Chase's opinion in *Calder* v. *Bull* may be the
one opinion discussed in Chapter 6 that is most susceptible to misun-
derstanding—it certainly appears to be treated by many scholars as the
locus classicus of natural-law jurisprudence on the Supreme Court. Yet
the first eleven times *Calder* was cited by any member of the Court, its
import was confined to the holding on the ex post facto clause applying
only to criminal law.

The first time Chase's opinion was recalled for any other purpose was in
McVeigh v. *United States* (1871), in which Justice Swayne, for a unanimous Court, ruled that a wartime act for the confiscation of rebel property must not be construed to bar the owners of such property from appearing in court to answer the claims of the government. "A different
result," wrote Swayne, "would be a blot upon our jurisprudence and civi-
lization. We cannot hesitate or doubt on the subject. It would be contrary
to the first principles of the social compact and of the right administration
of justice."[16] At this point an asterisk appeared, and the corresponding
footnote was to *Calder.* No law was invalidated, the case being confined to
statutory construction. But this was the first time *Calder* was taken to
stand for anything but the textual meaning of the ex post facto clause.

The next time *Calder* appeared in an opinion from the high bench
was in the famous *Legal Tender Cases* in the same term of the Court.[17]
So many tattered threads of old law were woven into a new fabric by the
dissenters in this case that it will receive separate treatment below.[18]

In *Osborn* v. *Nicholson* (1872) the Court upheld the outstanding obligations of debtors under contracts for the sale of slaves freed before final payment was made, despite an attempt to annul such obligations in
the Arkansas constitution of 1868 and in the face of arguments
founded on the Thirteenth Amendment and the final clause of section 4
of the Fourteenth Amendment. Swayne, for an 8 to 1 Court, wrote:

Rights acquired by a . . . contract executed according to statutes subsequently repealed subsist afterwards, as they were before, in all re-

spects as if the statutes were still in full force. A different rule . . .
would be contrary to "the general principles of law and reason," and to
one of the most vital ends of government. . . . [It] would, in effect, take
away one man's property and give it to another. And the deprivation
would be "without due process of law." This is forbidden by the fundamental principles of the social compact, and is beyond the sphere of the
legislative authority both of the States and the Nation.[19]

In support of this conclusion, Swayne cites *Calder, Wilkinson* v. *Leland,*
and two New York rulings now associated with substantive due process,
Taylor v. *Porter* and *Wynehamer* v. *People.*[20] *Osborn* is something of a
close call and may be a fair application of the contract clause, but the
dicta and precedents shown above surely show the direction in which
the Court was already moving.

Noah Swayne had the full Court with him again in *Gunn* v. *Barry*
(1873), once more upholding the full force of prior contractual obligations despite an alteration of legal remedies legislated pursuant to a
new Reconstruction constitution in Georgia. To alter a vested right as
it had existed under preexisting law "is in effect taking one person's
property and giving it to another without compensation. This is contrary to reason and justice, and to the fundamental principles of the social compact. [Here Swayne cited *Calder.*] But we must confine ourselves to the constitutional aspect of the case."[21] The final sentence
quoted evinces an awareness on Swayne's part that he had just traveled
outside proper constitutional confines in the preceding sentence. Yet,
although *Gunn* purports to be a case under the contract clause, Swayne
cites none of the many cases decided thereunder. Only *Calder* is cited
in his brief opinion, perhaps because none of the contract clause precedents he might have used would have supported the result. Then again,
neither would the genuine *Calder* v. *Bull,* but that was coming to matter less and less as Samuel Chase's dicta took on a life of their own.

In 1878 and 1884, Justice Field used *Calder* in dissents arguing for
natural-law limitations on congressional power.[22] (More of Field's singular style of reasoning will be apparent in the *Legal Tender Cases.*) In
the generation after the Civil War, only one justice seems to have used
the *Calder* precedent properly. Nathan Clifford, dissenting in *Loan Association* v. *Topeka* (1875), cited Justice Iredell's *Calder* opinion in support of the following view:

Except where the Constitution has imposed limits upon the legislative power the rule of law appears to be that the power of legisla-

tion must be considered as practically absolute, whether the law operates according to natural justice or not in any particular case, for the reason that courts are not the guardians of the rights of the people of the State, save where those rights are secured by some constitutional provision which comes within judicial cognizance.[23]

As already seen in Chapter 6, there is no reason that Clifford could not have cited Samuel Chase along with James Iredell to exactly the same effect. But by this time the lines were already being drawn: Chase's *Calder* opinion had begun to be reshaped into an all-purpose precedent for judicial activism, and so Iredell's opinion was beginning to look appealing to the defenders of restraint.

FLETCHER V. PECK

Fletcher v. *Peck* is cited in scores of subsequent cases under the contract clause. Marshall's own colleagues, however, appear not to have understood his opinion as standing for any absolute natural-law protection of vested rights. In *Satterlee* v. *Matthewson* (1829), Justice Washington observed that retrospective state laws are valid if they are neither ex post facto criminal statutes nor impair the obligation of a contract. Then, after quoting a portion of *Fletcher* that has already been discussed—that it "may well be doubted whether the nature of society and of government does not prescribe some limits to the legislative power"[24]—Washington explained the chief justice's view as follows: "It is nowhere intimated in that opinion that a State statute which devests a vested right, is repugnant to the constitution of the United States."[25]

Justice Story was in agreement. In *Watson* v. *Mercer* (1834), he cited *Calder, Fletcher, Ogden* v. *Saunders,* and *Satterlee* to make a similar point about retrospective laws and ruled that "this court has no right to pronounce an act of the state legislature void . . . from the mere fact that it devests antecedent vested rights of property."[26]

The first really novel use of *Fletcher* was in *Rice* v. *Railroad Co.* (1862). By a 4 to 2 vote, the Court upheld the repeal of a congressional act that had empowered the Minnesota territorial government to grant lands for the construction of a railroad. Counsel for the company had urged that the repeal act be held invalid, citing numerous cases, among them *Fletcher* on the irrescindable nature of land grants, *Van Horne's Lessee* on the principle of just compensation for takings, and *Wilkinson*

v. *Leland* on procedural due process as well as natural justice.[27] The repeal act had followed the original law by less than two months in the
summer of 1854, and the Court held for a number of factual and statutory reasons that no title to the lands had vested in the railroad company. But Justice Clifford opined for the majority that if title had
vested, it would have been "clear that it was not competent for Congress to pass the repealing act, and divest the title." For this dictum he
cited *Terrett* v. *Taylor* and *Fletcher* in support of the proposition that the
principle of the contract clause restrained Congress as well as the
states![28] Justice Samuel Nelson's dissent (joined by James Wayne) differed only in his view that the vested right of the company was real and
not hypothetical. *Fletcher* would not be so abused until Chief Justice
Salmon Chase's dissent in the *Legal Tender Cases.*

TERRETT V. TAYLOR, OGDEN V. SAUNDERS, AND WILKINSON V. LELAND

Terrett and *Ogden* have rather quiet histories, the former appearing in the last case discussed and the latter still to come in the
great greenback controversy. *Wilkinson* v. *Leland* seems to have been
well understood for quite some time. Three years after its decision, Justice Henry Baldwin correctly perceived that Story's holding had been
that Rhode Island's government, lacking a basis in a modern written
constitution, was restrained not by natural law but by the usage and
custom of the common law made binding by its ancient royal charter.
Such usage or custom was, Baldwin wrote, "always deemed to have had
its origin in an act of a state legislature of competent power to make it
valid and binding, or an act of parliament."[29] *Wilkinson* was also cited
as late as 1870, along with *Satterlee* and *Watson,* on the freedom of
states to pass certain kinds of retrospective civil laws.[30] The transformation of Story's intent occurred the following year in the *Legal Tender Cases.*

TURNING POINT: THE GREENBACK CONTROVERSY

The *Legal Tender Cases* (1871; also known as *Knox* v. *Lee*)
formally overturned the previous year's decision of *Hepburn* v.
Griswold.[31] The earlier case, in which Chief Justice Salmon Chase
wrote for a 4 to 3 majority, invalidated an act of Congress making fed-

eral paper money legal tender in payment of debts—at least it voided the law for payment of debts contracted before the act and possibly those contracted afterward as well.[32] In voiding the act whose passage he had supported as secretary of the Treasury,[33] Chase rested his ruling in *Hepburn* on three grounds: that the legal tender law "is not a means appropriate, plainly adapted, really calculated to carry into effect any express power vested in Congress; that such an act is inconsistent with the spirit of the Constitution; and that it is prohibited by the Constitution."[34]

Chase devoted twelve pages of his *Hepburn* opinion to the first ground, torturing Marshall's *McCulloch* ruling to show that the act was not authorized by the necessary and proper clause.[35] The second ground, the "spirit" of the Constitution, was asserted in less than two pages that reasoned that, one, the preamble speaks of the "establishment of justice"; two, one "efficient safeguard against injustice" is the contract clause; and three, despite the fact that "this prohibition is not applied in terms" to the federal government, "we think it clear" that the framers "intended that the spirit of this prohibition should pervade the entire body of legislation," federal as well as state.[36] Given that steps one and three in the argument both rest on an elusive "spirit" of the Constitution, Chase's reasoning here was at two removes from the letter of the document from which that spirit ought to be derived. But it is also noteworthy that his brief invocation of the contract clause (or its "spirit") against national legislation was accompanied by no citations whatsoever, not even to the convenient but dubious *Rice* v. *Railroad Co.*

After a further rumination on the just compensation clause of the Fifth Amendment, also admittedly not restraining such legislation "in terms," Chase's third ground (occupying less than a page) turns out to be the due process clause of the same amendment, which "cannot have its full and intended effect unless construed as a *direct prohibition*" of the legal tender act.[37] As David Currie observes, this was only the second time substantive due process was used by the Supreme Court to invalidate a law, the first being *Dred Scott*.[38] Again no citations of supporting precedent were offered, and Justice Samuel Miller, in dissent, remarked that the argument was "too vague for my perception."[39] Indeed, Chase cited none of the cases discussed in the previous chapter. Yet the way in which John Marshall's elegant edifice of *McCulloch* v. *Maryland* was torn down and reconstructed in the service of judicial expansionism should be taken as a sign that anything was possible by this time.

When the issue of the greenbacks was revisited the following year,

Chase (along with his fellow dissenters) was still more explicit about the sources of his view that the legal tender law was unconstitutional. So was the Court's reporter, who had recorded none of the arguments of counsel in his report of the *Hepburn* case. In the report of the *Legal Tender Cases,* a full and revealing account of those arguments was supplied.

Arguing against the constitutionality of the act in both cases was Democratic Congressman Clarkson Nott Potter of New York, who was to become one of the first presidents of the American Bar Association in the last year before his death in 1882.[40] His argument in the second case was a tour de force of tortuous reasoning, including an obeisance to the Court (not Congress) as the "ultimate judge" of the propriety, even the utility, of federal laws purporting to rest on the necessary and proper clause.[41] The final numbered portion of Potter's argument, however, was that the legal tender law impaired contracts.[42] Here he admitted that the federal government might not be compelled to keep its own contracts,[43] but that the preamble's object "to establish justice and secure the blessings of liberty" forbade any federal interference with private contracts.[44] He continued:

> Indeed, that Congress has power to impair the obligations of private contract is absolutely without authority. I find no court that has so decided. On the contrary, the very reverse has been declared by this very court, and other high constitutional authorities.*
> [Footnote:] * Wilkinson v. Leland, 2 Peters, 646, 657; Calder v. Bull, 3 Dallas, 386; Sturges v. Crowninshield, 4 Wheaton, 206; Ogden v. Saunders, 12 Id. 269, 270, 312, 303, 304, 327, 331, 336, 354; Federalist, No. 44.[45]

Only one of the cited authorities could plausibly be said to stand for any such proposition. Justice Smith Thompson's opinion (for himself alone) in *Ogden* v. *Saunders* had suggested that even in the absence of express constitutional restraints, no state court would enforce "retrospective laws, taking away vested rights," and further that it was unthinkable that the framers regarded the bankruptcy power of Congress as capable of violating the "great principles of justice" embodied in the contract clause.[46] Hence Potter might read Thompson as saying that the grant of the bankruptcy power really authorized no impairment of contractual obligations by Congress. But Thompson's view on both points was utterly idiosyncratic; his first point was repudiated by the full Court in *Satterlee* v. *Matthewson* and *Watson* v. *Mercer,* and his second was contradicted by every other justice who reasoned by analogy to the federal bankruptcy power in the state insolvency law cases of *Ogden* and *Sturges* v. *Crowninshield*. It was contradicted even by Chief Justice Chase's dissent in the case Potter was arguing.[47]

In any event, Potter may have been unsure of the strength of his "high constitutional authorities," as they all had to do with limits on the states rather than Congress. He fortified his argument, therefore, by reference to the takings and due process clauses of the Fifth Amendment:

> What do the amendments to the Constitution provide? Not particularly that Congress shall not impair the obligations of contracts; not particularly that it shall not intervene to declare what shall be a legal tender in discharge of pre-existing debts between citizens of any State; but they provide that private property shall not be taken for public use without just compensation, nor any person be deprived of property without due process of law.[48]

No cases were cited at this stage to support the planted axiom that the takings and due process clauses restrain the same sorts of laws at the federal level that the clauses of Article I, section 10, restrain at the state level.

No doubt Potter had made essentially the same points when successfully arguing the *Hepburn* case the year before. In that case, however, as already seen, the chief justice had not cited any of Potter's "authorities" on Congress's lack of power over private contracts. Therefore, the argument here appears to be, one, the second instance on the record of the Supreme Court (the first being the *Rice* case) that any of the cases discussed in Chapter 6 were cited as expressing principles restrictive of congressional power; two, the first time they were explicitly taken to signify natural-law principles, judicially enforceable, in the absence of express constitutional limitations; and three, the first time they were cited in association with the developing doctrine of substantive due process. And every one of Potter's "authorities" was pressed into service by the dissenters in the *Legal Tender Cases*, who pulled out all the stops in their frustration that the previous year's narrow victory had been upended.

Chief Justice Chase again argued that the legal tender act could not be justified as an implied power and again referred to it as a "manifest violation" of the due process clause.[49] Answering Justice William Strong's majority view that the clause applied only to "a direct appropriation, and not to consequential injuries resulting from the exercise of lawful power" nor to "laws that indirectly work harm and loss to individuals,"[50] Chase argued that the law "acts directly upon the relations of debtor and creditor. It violates that fundamental principle of all just legislation that the legislature shall not take the property of A. and give it to B."[51]

Then Chase went one step farther than Potter, enlisting Marshall's *Fletcher* opinion (specifically the passage Justice Washington had explained in *Satterlee*)[52] as "assert[ing] fundamental principles of society and government in which [the contract clause] had its origin."[53] And he moved immediately to Samuel Chase's opinion in *Calder,* which "had previously declared that 'an act of the legislature contrary to the great first principles of the social compact cannot be considered a rightful legislative authority.' "[54] The chief justice failed to see that the first Justice Chase, as I have argued in Chapter 6, meant by these "great first principles" the terms of a written constitution (or charter)—principles to be understood either from its express limitations on power or in light of the idea that the "obligation of a law . . . must be determined by the nature of the power on which it is founded."[55] Salmon Chase's quotation out of context loses Samuel Chase's nuances and gives the impression that a power arguably inferable from a constitution (the power to make paper money legal tender, inferred from the necessary and proper clause) may be trumped by a principle imported from outside the document ("great first principles" inferred from no textual source).

Justice Clifford also recorded a lengthy dissent in the *Legal Tender Cases.* Of the precedents at the center of this discussion, he cited one: in *Ogden* v. *Saunders,* he noted, both Justices Washington and Johnson had remarked on the firm policy of the framers to prevent the issue of paper money because of the vital need for a "fixed and uniform standard of value" of currency. Clifford conspicuously failed to mention that the framers saw fit to provide against this "evil to be repelled without modification" only in the case of the states and not in the case of Congress.[56]

Justice Stephen Field's dissent cited every one of Congressman Potter's "high constitutional authorities." He began by distorting the legacy of *McCulloch* v. *Maryland* much as Chief Justice Chase had, both in this case and in the previous year's *Hepburn* ruling—and Field went one step farther than Chase by enlisting the shade of Alexander Hamilton for the purpose of placing a novel restriction on Congress's implied powers![57] Likewise following Chase's lead on the question of the greenbacks' effect in impairing the obligations of contracts, Field used *Calder* to much the same effect as had the chief justice,[58] quoted Justice Thompson's lone dicta in *Ogden* v. *Saunders,*[59] and asserted without argument or quotation that Justice Washington in the same case had "repudiated the existence of any general power in Congress to destroy or impair vested private rights."[60] And he enlisted Story's opinion in *Wilkinson* v. *Leland* to argue that the legal tender act was "repugnant to the common principles of justice and civil liberty"[61] and could not therefore be upheld in the absence of an express grant of power—ignoring the fact that Story had been writing in the context of common law restrictions on the charter government of Rhode Island, and that he had upheld a law not expressly authorized by that charter that could plausibly be seen as divesting antecedent vested rights.

Given the record of their views on a whole panoply of issues from federal power to private rights, it is extremely difficult to imagine any of the justices considered in Chapter 6 siding with Chase, Clifford, and Field in the *Legal Tender Cases.* On the basis of his *Ogden* dicta, Smith Thompson might have come along, but even that is not a sure thing (as very little is about Smith Thompson).

THE ORIGINS AND COURSE OF POSTBELLUM NATURAL-LAW JURISPRUDENCE

Loren P. Beth has quite aptly characterized Stephen Field's judicial philosophy as "dictated by an attachment to an ideal of inalienable rights that, however, did not have specifically to appear in the Constitution. He was, in other words, strongly result-oriented; if he felt that a claimed right was inalienable he could find a place in the Constitution for it."[62] Field's result orientation on property rights in particular did not mean that he always sided with large corporate interests any more than so-called "Social Darwinists" of this period such as William Graham Sumner did.[63] In the *Slaughter-House Cases,* for instance, Field opposed them in defense of the small businessman squeezed by the combined efforts of those interests and a state legislature. But sometimes joined by and sometimes opposing his brethren Miller, Bradley, Clifford, Strong and Swayne, Justice Field left a remarkable record of consistency in three intertwined arguments: that the "pursuit of happiness" or some other principle of natural law in the Declaration of Independence was judicially enforceable; that the "spirit" of the contract clause, the due process clauses of the Fifth and

Fourteenth Amendments (and sometimes the privileges or immunities clause of the latter), secured this liberty of pursuit from both state and federal legislative interference; and that he could, at need, call on Samuel Chase, John Marshall, Bushrod Washington, and Joseph Story in support of the first two arguments.[64]

The *Legal Tender* dissents, however, reveal to what extent Field and his sometime allies also required a second strand of distorted precedent in order to expand judicial power at the expense of Congress rather than merely at the expense of the states. Only a virtual inversion of the meaning of *McCulloch* v. *Maryland*—and thereby also a tacit inflation of the judicial review power expounded in *Marbury* v. *Madison* (see Chapters 4 and 5)—could supply the principle of judicial finality needed to enable the justices' views of natural law to prevail over Congress's views of sound policy. In moving thus toward judicial supremacy over all matters arising under the Constitution, the dissenters in *Legal Tender* owed something to *Dred Scott* and presaged the astonishing audacity of the income tax ruling of 1895.[65]

As for the now transformed pre-Marshall and Marshall era cases that have been the focus of this and the previous chapter, their newly fashioned "natural law" significance came soon enough to be attached by Justice Field to the due process clause of the Fourteenth Amendment in such cases as *Munn* v. *Illinois*.[66] For a generation Field, most often with Bradley's help, attempted this melding of *Dred Scott*'s substantive due process with the newfangled reading of *Wilkinson, Calder, Fletcher,* and so forth, often in dissent, occasionally in concurrence. Field's vindication came in his final term of the Court, when his efforts of a quarter of a century bore fruit in *Allgeyer* v. *Louisiana*—a case in which Justice Peckham, for a unanimous Court, cited with approval the concurrence of Bradley in one of the cases where he and Field had pressed for judicial protection of extratextual natural rights.[67]

What lay behind this postbellum revolution in Supreme Court decision-making? Much of the story has to do with the creative opportunities glimpsed by the justices in the due process clause of the newly added Fourteenth Amendment. This often told tale has seldom been told exactly the same way twice and to a certain extent remains "one of the great mysteries of our constitutional law."[68] What is certain is that in " 'economic substantive due process,' the essential distinction between judging and legislating was broken down and judging became a different form of legislative power."[69]

As can be seen from the treatment here of the greenback controversy, however, this breakdown came about in the years following the Civil

War in other areas of constitutional jurisprudence aside from due process, for the justices intent on invalidating legal tender were perfectly willing as a matter of fact (if not of speech or even altogether wittingly) to repudiate the legacy of *McCulloch* v. *Maryland. Hepburn* v. *Griswold,* although overturned in just a year, was truly the beginning of such a trend when it came to judicial review of acts of Congress; a quarter century later, in the sugar trust and income tax cases, neither the *McCulloch* ruling nor *Marbury* v. *Madison* (nor *Hylton* v. *United States*[70] nor *Gibbons* v. *Ogden*)[71] was to be paid any heed.[72] In the words of warning penned by Justice Miller in the *Slaughter-House Cases,* the Court was on its way to becoming "a perpetual censor on all legislation"—of the national government as well as of the state governments to which Miller directed his solicitude in that opinion.[73] The "constitutional revolution" of 1937 to the contrary notwithstanding, it has remained so ever since.

On the subject of national judicial review, Robert Clinton avers that "it is possible to detect a nascent movement" after the Civil War "toward legitimization of a broader notion of judicial power than that conceived by the Founders and by the Marshall Court" and traces the beginning of that movement to the publication of Thomas Cooley's *Constitutional Limitations* in 1868.[74] Central to this movement, as Clinton reports it, was the transformation of *Marbury* v. *Madison* into a general warrant to annul acts of Congress, a transformation that in turn fed into the Progressive critique of *Marbury,* of Marshall, and of the framers themselves.[75]

It cannot be doubted that the postbellum aggrandizement of judicial power over national legislative power and that over state legislative power are parallel developments. Each necessarily entailed the abandonment of the jurisprudence of John Marshall or, what amounts to the same thing, the distortion of his legacy to suit novel purposes. But since, with a few exceptions, the usual vehicle for natural-law jurisprudence was the due process clause of the Fourteenth Amendment rather than that of the Fifth Amendment or other provisions addressing federal power, the focus in what follows will be on the development of substantive due process as a restraint on state power during what has come to be called the *"Lochner* era" (although much of this "era" considerably predates *Lochner* v. *New York).*[76]

Two competing interpretations of the *"Lochner* era" of recent vintage are those of Paul Kens[77] and Howard Gillman.[78] Kens, tracing the development of laissez-faire economic theory and "social Darwinism" in the decades prior to the *Lochner* ruling, argues that in nonjudicial circles there first appeared the doctrine of the "negative state," in which "government should do no more than make the rights of person and property as secure as possible."[79] Notably for our purposes, central to this politico-economic ideology was a "belief in immutable laws of nature and the benevolence of the system thereby created."[80] This new-fangled version of "laws of nature," having more in common with Newtonian laws of physics or the Darwinian law of the survival of the fittest than with the moral "Laws of Nature and of Nature's God" of the Declaration of Independence, nevertheless made a comfortable fit for many of its adherents with the "individualism [that] holds a revered place in American heritage or American myth."[81] When this ideology found jurisprudential expression in Cooley's *Constitutional Limitations,* the "seed for a theory . . . to become known as substantive due process" was planted.[82]

According to Kens, at the time of this writing "Cooley could point to only a few scattered state court opinions to support his extension of due process to the substance of legislation."[83] Yet the notion was very rapidly adopted on the federal Supreme Court by Justice Stephen Field; although he did not use an argument from the due process clause of the Fifth Amendment in his *Legal Tender* dissent (unlike Chief Justice Chase in that case as well as in the previous year's *Hepburn* ruling), he did not lag far behind, wielding the new substantive reading of the similar clause in the Fourteenth Amendment just five years after Cooley's publication and the ratification of the amendment.[84] Then too Field began to develop the "embryo of [the] liberty of contract" doctrine, which, grafted onto substantive due process, was to win the day in *Lochner.*[85] For that notable victory of the laissez-faire ideology, all it took was a majority of justices willing to view the police power so narrowly as to invert the traditional "principle that an act of a state legislature was presumed to be valid."[86]

For all its richness of detail—both in terms of personalities and events and of legal theory and case analysis—and its powerful explanations of politico-economic ideology in the late nineteenth century, Kens's work would offer a more complete pedigree of natural-law–substantive due process jurisprudence if he had followed up on something that he only briefly mentions. Remarking that "Field's argument [for liberty of contract] had roots that were imbedded in American soil far deeper than laissez faire–social Darwinism," Kens notes that others have linked liberty of contract to the abolitionist "free labor ideology" and to "an opposition to 'class legislation' and 'special legislation' [that] had been part of Anglo-American political philosophy since long before the Declaration of Independence."[87] A work that traces that strain of thought and connects it explicitly to the jurisprudence of the "*Lochner* era" is provided by Howard Gillman.

Exploring the reasons why "turn-of-the-century judges upheld a good deal of social legislation" while some was invalidated, Gillman flatly (and repeatedly) asserts that the true touchstone for American judges throughout the nineteenth and early twentieth centuries was not the economic ideology of laissez-faire but a "serious, principled effort to maintain . . . the distinction between valid economic regulation, on the one hand, and invalid 'class' legislation, on the other."[88] Finding this pattern of decision-making on state courts both before and after the Civil War[89] and on the Supreme Court following the adoption of the Fourteenth Amendment (and the publication of the ubiquitous Cooley),[90] Gillman argues that it can be traced to the "Jacksonian purification of America's founding ideology" and that it makes its way through mid-century in the vehicle of "the Republican party and its motto Free Soil, Free Labor, Free Men."[91] But he does not stop there; for Gillman, the "master constitutional principle of formal equality or government impartiality was first elaborated by the framers in the 1780s."[92] Hence, judges throughout the first 150 years of the nation's history were acting in accord with the framers' intentions when they struck down statutes advantaging some groups at the expense of others where no "public purpose"[93] justified the discrimination. (Interestingly, what Gillman regards as the de facto "amend[ment of] the Constitution" in *West Coast Hotel Co.* v. *Parrish*[94] is no cause for concern, for "new social facts," it seems, require a new Constitution.)[95]

The great strength of Gillman's work is in supplying two things that Kens, comparatively speaking, neglects: first, a way of accounting for the apparent vacillations of American courts in now upholding, now striking down social legislation; and second, an account of the ideological roots of "*Lochner*-era" jurisprudence that plausibly takes us as far back as the Jacksonian period.

But Gillman's version of legal history suffers from several significant weaknesses, which may be enumerated as follows. One, he posits an aspiration on the part of the framers to "faction-free" politics, dismissing with a cursory reliance on Garry Wills the most compelling evidence to the contrary in *Federalist* No. 10.[96] Two, he offers no textual basis in the Constitution for his "master constitutional principle," much less for its judicial enforcement, and the best he can do to support a thesis of the framers' intent with regard to the latter proposition is to misread *Federalist* No. 78.[97] Three, he undermines his own thesis with regard to the framers' design for judicial power when he admits that their (putative) "aversion to factional and class-based politics was transformed into constitutional ideology" only "well into the nineteenth century, during the period of Jacksonian democracy."[98] Four, his repeated assertion that judicial invalidations of statutes in the name of class neutrality had nothing whatever to do with a laissez-faire ideology even after the Civil War is blind to the fact that the former concept can quite readily be squared with a none-too-doctrinaire version of the latter, as legislation in the "general welfare" still leaves the market's playing field level.[99] Five, Gillman seems oblivious to the fact that no matter when this constitutional ideology emerged, it was the rankest form of judicial activism, as there is no warrant in the federal nor any of the state constitutions for judicial monitoring of what is "arbitrary" and what is "reasonable" legislation.[100]

Taking what is most useful from both Gillman and Kens, it seems most plausible to say that the conservative activism of the Chase, Waite, and Fuller Courts had political roots in the antebellum politics of both Jacksonian Democrats and (probably more importantly) Free Soil Republicans.[101] In terms of constitutional adjudication, however, those roots were only shallowly planted in scattered activist rulings of state courts (which Thomas Cooley later gathered together and gave his falsely orthodox imprimatur) and had no purchase whatever in the soil of the antebellum jurisprudence of the Supreme Court (aside from the *Dred Scott* case, to which understandably no one wished to point for support). As the ideology of laissez-faire economics gained a firmer hold in certain American intellectual circles after the Civil War, a fillip of pseudoscientific rationalism about "immutable laws" of economic "nature" gave additional impetus to the notion that the governing principle of a constitutional order ought to be a strict doctrine of the negative state. As William Graham Sumner wrote in 1880, "The truth is that the social order is fixed by laws of nature precisely analogous to those of the physical order."[102]

Ironically, in some minds this ideology was accompanied by a conscious abandonment and critique of the very principles of the Declaration of Independence that Lincoln had worked so hard to revive and place at the center of Republican politics. Sumner, remarking that "the country has, to a certain extent, outgrown some of its institutions in their present form," opined that it had "given its faith to some false and pernicious doctrines about equality and the rights of man."[103] And lest the reader think that these pernicious doctrines were only recent deformations of the original, genuine articles, this tireless advocate of

freedom later said bluntly that the "notion of natural rights is desti-
tute of sense,"[104] thus severing his theory of liberty from the only foundation that could give it life and substance.

But Sumner was, we might say, ahead of his time in so scorning the
most important legacy of the founding. Those justices of the Supreme
Court who, like him, wished to keep the state "neutral but benevolent"
rather than the "servant of envy"[105] were inclined, as is the wont of
American lawyers, to look to the past: to those founding principles that
Sumner derided and more particularly to the precedents in their own
reports that seemed to them expressive of those principles. If, as seems
likely, they, too, believed in a social order "fixed" by economic "laws of
nature," how convenient for them to find in the opinions of Samuel
Chase, John Marshall, and other early justices language about "natural law" that appeared to them to be prescriptive, justiciable principles
fitting nicely with the new descriptive language of Sumnerian political
economy. No particularly crass or narrow political agenda needs to be
ascribed to the postbellum justices; they need only have read their predecessors' opinions none too carefully, forgetting as they did so the jurisprudential categories of thought that lived in those old decisions and
supplied their true context. The Stephen Fields had doctrines in need
of precedents; they reached back and took them, distorting their meaning in the process. By now this is an old and familiar story.

A further irony is that as Sumner seemed to think he could abandon
the commitment to natural rights of the founders and of Lincoln and
still hold fast to liberty as a defensible principle of action, so could the
justices in the decades after the Civil War abandon Lincoln's critique of
judicial supremacy and still apparently think they exercised a defensible version of judicial power. In this respect, Lincoln's own appointees
(consistently in the case of Field and far too often in the case of Chase,
Swayne, and Miller) were only half the heirs to the core principles of
the Republican party that they thought themselves to be. And the part
they were forgetting was far from trivial.

There is little question that from 1857 the Republican party was as
committed to opposing the *Dred Scott* ruling as to any other practical
political agenda. Before, during, and after his great debates with
Stephen Douglas, Lincoln gave voice to this opposition not merely on
the grounds that the Taney Court had taken a wrecking ball to the
principles of the Declaration of Independence, but also on the grounds
that (in Douglas's phrases) "the supremacy of the laws" was not an expression interchangeable with "the final decision[s] of the highest judicial tribunal."[106] As he famously stated in his first inaugural address,

to acquiesce in such a proposition would mean that "the people will have ceased, to be their own rulers, having, to that extent, practically resigned their government, into the hands of that eminent tribunal."[107]

This was not mere opportunism or political maneuvering. Lincoln's settled position, like every other aspect of his political thought, had roots that went deeper than the issues of the day, deeper even than the Constitution; it was, like his opposition to slavery itself, grounded firmly in the natural law of the Declaration. Its self-evident truths, foremost among them the truth of human equality, supplied not only the basis of civil liberty under law but also the basis of legitimate self-government—of the sovereignty of a society of free men over their own affairs. It would be, for Lincoln, merely changing one species of oppression for another for his party to win the struggle against chattel slavery and then to give up the right of self-government to the life peerage of the judiciary, however well-meaning, however committed to principles of "class neutrality" or "free labor" the judges might be. Doubtless Lincoln would have been dismayed to see his appointee Stephen Field spend his career on the bench ostensibly pursuing one purpose of their common party at the expense of the other—and that other clearly the more fundamental of the two.

In Part Three of this book, I attempt to show that the natural-law principles that informed the thought of the founding—and Lincoln—eventuate in a prescription of constitutionalism under the sovereignty of the people and in fact forbid judicial decision-making by extraconstitutional principles. Before turning to such questions, however, it may be an instructive aside to take a glimpse at the modern fruits of Stephen Field's quarter-century effort to truncate to the point of repudiation the correct principles of the president who appointed him.

As noted previously, Field's long struggle for the constitutionalization of natural-law principles, accompanied by regular citation of the early cases examined in Chapter 6, came during his final term on the Court in the unanimous 1897 *Allgeyer* v. *Louisiana* decision. Considering that *Allgeyer* served as the chief precedent for the now notorious *Lochner* v. *New York*;[108] that both of these cases were vital to the decision in the early "privacy" case of *Meyer* v. *Nebraska*;[109] that *Pierce* v. *Society of Sisters*[110] was based in turn on *Meyer*; that *Allgeyer, Meyer,* and *Pierce* were cited by two of the dissenting justices in *Poe* v. *Ullman*;[111] that the latter two cases were important precedents for three of the majority justices in *Griswold* v. *Connecticut*,[112] which in turn was indispensable to the decision in *Roe* v. *Wade*,[113] it may be said that a wavering line of precedent, often meandering but easily traceable, connects the abortion furor of the last twenty years to the mistaken notion that the cases discussed in these two chapters endorsed a practice in the Court's early history of reaching beyond the Constitution's text to notions of natural law in the decision of cases. As absurd as it may sound, the liberal activism of today's abortion rulings is due in part to the success in 1871 of a congressman who hated paper money in persuading several Reconstruction-era justices that natural rights of property had triumphed over majority rule in the decisions of their pre-Jacksonian predecessors. Indeed, the argument of Clarkson Potter and the spadework of Stephen Field has been so durable that two justices in the contraception cases of the 1960s cited *Calder* v. *Bull* and *Corfield* v. *Coryell* for support.[114] Charity requires us to doubt that they had even read the cases.

Part Three
America's Philosophic Teachers and the Judicial Function

It is doubtless true that some constitutional commentators will be unpersuaded by the analysis in the preceding chapters to abandon a convenient account of history—an account that holds that members of the antebellum Supreme Court (sometimes) reached beyond the Constitution to enforce natural-law principles neither explicit in the written text nor clearly inferable from it as justiciable principles. Even the critics of such a practice seem to find that "history" useful, as it serves to illustrate the perennial character of the "political seduction of the law," to borrow the subtitle of Robert Bork's *The Tempting of America.*

For the proponents of natural-law jurisprudence, fewer in number though they may be, the early cases discussed in Chapter 6 have their obvious use. Men such as William Paterson, Samuel Chase, John Marshall, William Johnson, Joseph Story, and Bushrod Washington were all either members of the founding generation themselves or close enough in time to the framing of the Constitution to be presumptively strong witnesses as to the intent of the document and the meaning of its political and legal principles. If they occasionally saw fit to base the exercise of judicial review on something other than provisions of the written Constitution, they must have known what they were doing. Or so the argument appears to run, when stripped of its frills.[1]

But this argument that what was done early must have been done well (often made by the same people who maintain, for instance, that Marshall played fast and loose in *Marbury* v. *Madison*) could never be more than circumstantial, even if it had its history right. For even then, the natural-law opinions of the justices named earlier might be

criticized as aberrant, as outside the mainstream of the American judicial tradition,[2] or at best they might be treated as an "alternative" tradition, yet one lacking a theoretical grounding consistent with democratic institutions.[3]

On the other hand, for similar reasons even the historical correction
described in Part Two cannot deprive the argument for natural-law jurisprudence of all its force. Assume that historical correction to be successful. Assume further that even the friends of natural-law judging
would be loath to defend the property rights activism of Salmon
Chase's Court and its successors. (For the record, I know of no propo-
nent of a justiciable natural law who will adopt both these positions.)
Yet the argument might still run thus: the fact that the antebellum
Court did not rule on natural-law grounds is no proof that courts never
should, for one cannot infer from a thing not done that it must not be
done. And the fact that the natural-law rulings of the postbellum
courts were improper will not invalidate the practice either, for one
cannot infer from a thing done badly that it cannot be done well.

What is needed on both sides of the argument is a theoretical account of the logic of constitutionalism. On the side condemning or critical of natural-law jurisprudence, the best accounts have been given by
Walter Berns,[4] Leslie Friedman Goldstein,[5] and Christopher Wolfe,[6] all
of whose excellent arguments are nevertheless incomplete and may be
improved upon. On the side advocating or approving of such a practice,
by far the most formidable argument has been made by Hadley Arkes
in his recent book *Beyond the Constitution.*[7]

Arkes rarely uses the term "natural law" (and only a bit more often,
"natural rights"), but he clearly aims at regenerating our law and politics by recourse to such principles. He sets himself the task of showing
that "we cannot apply the Constitution" without encountering a "need
to appeal to those moral understandings lying behind the text; the understandings that were never written down in the Constitution, but
which must be grasped again if we are to preserve—and perfect—the
character of a constitutional government."[8] Arkes then crafts an argument that will frustrate legal positivists (than whom there is no one he
would rather frustrate), adherents of federalism as a principled limitation on national power (to whose sensibilities he is a bit gentler), and
anyone who clings to the historicist notion that political morality has
undergone progress since the American founding.

The book's interwoven elements may be reduced to three. One, the
Constitution can be "understood and *justified,* only in moral terms,
only by an appeal to those standards of natural right that existed *ante-*

cedent to the Constitution."[9] Two, the powers of Congress, or of the national government generally, are the powers of a real government, fully competent to pursue the moral ends marked out by those standards of natural right—and free to choose the most direct means to those ends, notwithstanding any apparent inconveniences arising from federalism or the Tenth Amendment. Three, the courts of such a regime, possessed of the power of judicial review, must be guided in the exercise of that power above all by those same standards—whether the guidance takes the form of illuminating the *"structure of moral argument* that lies behind" a particular constitutional provision[10] or of lighting the way to judgments unconnected to any particular clause or feature of the written Constitution.

Unfortunately, Arkes treats these elements as all of a piece with one another, as though the first cannot be affirmed without, as by an inexorable logic, affirming the second and third. For our purposes, it is not necessary to examine the connection of the first principle to the second, although it goes far beyond any "nationalism" even of Alexander Hamilton or John Marshall.[11] Here it should be pointed out that even if the first two elements of his argument are both borne out, the third simply does not follow. Eliminating the second proposition as unnecessary to establish the third (because both are conclusions directly from the first, which appears to be a major premise in need of no minor premise), the logic is that because the Constitution is incomprehensible except by reference to antecedent moral principles, therefore the courts (to put the hardest case of all) must invalidate any federal or state legislation that runs contrary to those principles, even in the absence of a textual basis for doing so.

As Arkes advances this argument, it turns out that the Constitution's principles are for him almost entirely a matter of jurisprudence—not of politics or of institutional structures. But no less is it true that his principles of jurisprudence, indeed his logic of constitutionalism, are finally heedless of the Constitution. It would not be going too far to say that his account of constitutional law as courts ought to practice it comes to this: if it is good, the Constitution commands it; if it is bad, the Constitution forbids it. This is no parody; Arkes's core argument is that "we have a natural right to be treated justly: We have a right not to have our lives taken, our freedom restricted, our property extracted, *without justification.*"[12] And it is essential to his thesis that judicial review is primarily concerned with the presence or absence of such justification.[13]

For instance, in a chapter quite ably rehabilitating the Federalist argument against the Bill of Rights, Arkes nevertheless goes off the rails by arguing in essence that courts would be authorized—perhaps obliged is more accurate—to invalidate statutes contrary to the moral principles marked out by the amendments even if they had never been added to the Constitution. Why? Because "the most critical premises of personal freedom [are] already reflected in the very structure of a constitutional government."[14] Indeed, Arkes seems to endorse a judicial power so expansive it could address such issues *even if there were no written Constitution.*[15] Somehow "the logic of constitutional government itself"[16] will do quite nicely, whether we bother to embody that logic in a written document or not.[17]

In his defense, it should be said that Arkes regards the good commanded and the evil forbidden by the Constitution as anything but subjective questions (and hence, it seems, trustworthily confided to judges): "The Founders did not think that they were entering the domain of arbitrary or 'subjective' judgment when they were compelled to move outside the text of the Constitution."[18] In a similar vein, he criticizes those who insist "that when a judge departs from the text of the Constitution, he has nothing to look to but himself."[19] In this Arkes is surely right, as he is equally right in the first element of his overall thesis: that the Constitution itself requires explanation and justification in terms of permanent principles of natural right. That is to say, when judges depart from the text, the thing they "look to" may indeed be (as the Declaration of Independence puts it) "the laws of Nature and of Nature's God"—the self-evident truths or first principles that undergird constitutional government. It is good to be reminded that legal positivism is mistaken when it supposes that the only alternative to constitutional or statutory text is the judge's own viscera.

But Arkes's reduction of judicial review to an exercise in Kantian rationalism[20] tells only half the tale of constitutional government. Were all judges to take *Beyond the Constitution* as their primer for the exercise of judicial review, a wise and just regime of law might well be the result. But the question left utterly unaddressed by Arkes, and dangerously so, given his prescription for the liberation of judges from textual constraints, is, Will they do so? Can the Arkesian judges be relied on to govern by the Arkesian first principles (for govern is what they will surely do, in any event)? James Iredell warned in 1798 that "the ablest and the purest men have differed upon the subject" of what natural justice may dictate in any given case.[21] Iredell's argument meant neither that there was no such thing as natural justice nor that correct answers are impossible to derive—only that recurrence to such standards of de-

cision was not a mechanical enterprise and made for a highly dangerous assignment to constitutional jurists. To go further, will Arkesian
judges be just as likely, nay, more likely, to govern by arbitrary decree?
As a practical matter, this is a question not for first principles of morals
but for human probabilities, probabilities that may be addressed by
quite another principle, that of the lodging of power in some safe place
and its grudging delegation to subordinate agents.

When he informs the reader that "the appeal to reason should be sufficient—and sovereign,"[22] Arkes commits the noble error of supposing
that constitutionalism is no more than the attempt to install reason in
the seat of sovereignty. It may largely be that, but it is assuredly more
besides. The intellectual struggle of the American founders and their
philosophic teachers was to arrive at a doctrine of politics and of law
that yielded the highest probability of solving the problem of what may
be called the two sovereignties: the sovereignty of law (or right, or reason, or justice) and the sovereignty of men. To flesh out the latter, that
other half of the tale of constitutional government, and to reconnect it
to the former, as Arkes has not done, is the purpose of the chapters that
follow.

Three works are the key to unlocking the problem of the two sovereignties: Thomas Hobbes's *Leviathan,* John Locke's *Second Treatise,*
and William Blackstone's *Commentaries on the Laws of England.* Each
of these thinkers struggled with the dilemma of how to constitute a regime that is durable, flexible, just, and founded on the broad basis of
consent by human beings who are by nature one another's equals. They
left the job unfinished, however, and it remained to America's founders
to complete it by the crucial innovation of a written constitution em-
bodying a new "science of politics."[23] Taken all together, the legacy of
Hobbes, Locke, Blackstone, and the founders culminates in a constitutionalism in which the sovereign people are ultimately, and their legislators penultimately, the ones responsible for the regime's accord with
the laws of nature. By contrast, judges entrusted with the preservation
of constitutions are not empowered to enforce standards that the sovereign people or their legislators have not set clearly in writing, however
much those standards might improve the regime's "fit" with the laws
of nature.

In this review of the philosophic works that paved the way for constitutionalism and in the conclusion that follows, I attempt to accomplish
two aims. First, it should become clear why the jurists discussed in
Chapter 6 could at once recognize the basis of the American regime in
principles of natural law and understand those principles as binding

them to the positive-law constraints of constitutional texts. (To grasp again this proper understanding of the connection of natural law to constitutionalism will also recapture what has been lost in American jurisprudence since the postbellum period discussed in Chapter 7.) Second, the argument will come full circle to the question of judicial statesmanship that was the subject of Part One. If there is a "spirit" of the Constitution (and there surely is), it is a spirit that is grounded in the modern doctrine of natural law. But that doctrine binds judges to the text, forbidding them to roam at large doing good or seeking justice. The latter are the concerns of republican statesmanship, with which the judicial function has nothing to do (other than in the fulfillment of epideictic obligations).

A caution at the outset: I do not mean to advance the dubious argument that the founders or the early jurists were simple followers of any one or more of the thinkers to be discussed in these chapters. Nor do I suggest that the deepest understanding of any one of these philosophers can necessarily be imputed to the founding generation.[24] On the other hand, it is demonstrably the case that the founding generation was steeped in the language of these thinkers, speaking and writing comfortably of human equality, natural and civil liberty, social contracts, and the right of revolution. Direct influence of a kind determinative of minute interpretive questions under the Constitution is not what should be sought. And including the "justly decried" Hobbes in a study of constitutionalism may only be asking for trouble in some quarters.[25] But the point is not that each successive contributor sailed by the same chart, which was then simply illuminated in the margins by America's founders. Each explorer (including the principal founders) navigated as much by sketching into his own chart the shoals on which he thought his predecessors had run aground as by following the course to the New World of constitutional government bequeathed to him.

CHAPTER EIGHT

Sovereignty and Judging in Hobbes's *Leviathan*

It is not wisdom, but authority that makes a law.

—*Thomas Hobbes¹*

Walter Berns has written that it "may seem paradoxical, but Hobbes, whose reputation is simply that of a teacher of absolutism, is the founder of self-government in the modern sense."² Richard G. Stevens has persuasively argued that, although "Locke leaves us with the impression that he differs greatly from Hobbes . . . the likenesses are far more consequential than the differences."³ My discussion in this chapter and the next will lead to a similar conclusion in general, although particular points along the way will focus much on the differences, especially as they bear on the development of the doctrine of constitutionalism.

One of the most persistent puzzles about Hobbes is whether he has any teaching about natural law that may properly be said to constrain the actions of those who govern.⁴ The overwhelming evidence seems to be negative, and Hobbes is for the most part rightly considered a "teacher of absolutism." But he gives frequent indications to the contrary in the *Leviathan*. Hobbes cannot simply be considered a legal positivist (though those who do deserve that label owe much to him). As Norberto Bobbio has framed the issue, why "should Hobbes eliminate every source of norms other than the state, if he then lets natural law survive, which is the most dangerous adversary of every positive law?"⁵ For, as Laurence Berns notes, "he who sets forth principles justifying authority by that very act provides standards for justifying the alteration or abolishment of that authority when it departs from those principles."[6] Grappling with this conundrum will lead us to see that even in Hobbes there is an effort to reconcile the sovereignty of law and the sovereignty of men.

In *Leviathan*'s crucial Chapter 13 on the state of nature, Hobbes states that in the war that prevails there of every person against every other, "nothing can be unjust. The notions of right and wrong, justice and injustice have there no place. Where there is no common power, there is no law: where no law, no injustice. . . . They are qualities, that relate to men in society, not in solitude."[7] In earlier chapters on speech and on the passions, Hobbes had presaged this point by treating the virtues and vices, and good and evil, as mere matters of opinion with "inconstant names," which are "ever used with relation to the person that useth them."[8] Elsewhere, however, he indicates that this inconstancy has a limit; men in the state of nature "who could not agree concerning a present, do agree concerning a future good," and that future good, declared to all men by reason itself, is peace.[9] With the establishment of peace comes the advent of justice; the latter term now has stable meaning given to it by the same means responsible for the former. The "fountain and original of JUSTICE," Hobbes tells us, consists in the faithful performance of covenants between and among men; but since "the bonds of words are too weak" to assure this, "before the names of just, and unjust can have place, there must be some coercive power, to compel men" to keep their covenants.[10] It follows then that justice is entirely conventional, a creature of contract and of the positive laws made to preserve that contract. But the origin of justice rests in the rational response to our natural need for peace as the condition of self-preservation. In that respect, justice has its origin in nature.

What the conventional character of justice appears to mean where the sovereign is concerned is clear enough. In addition to being a natural person like other men, he is, in his political character, an "artificial" person, the coercive force of whose every law and decree has been provided by the fact that all other men "*have made themselves every one the author*" of everything he commands.[11] "This is more than consent, or concord; it is a real unity of them all, in one and the same person, made by covenant of every man with every man."[12] But not quite literally of every man with every other: the one man not part of the social contract (hence, in an odd way, not partaking of this "real unity" with the rest) is the sovereign himself. The "right of bearing the person of them all, is given to him they make sovereign, by covenant only of one with another, and not of him to any of them."[13] This distinctiveness, this setting apart of the sovereign from other men, is clarified still further when Hobbes later reminds his reader

> that before the institution of commonwealth, every man had a right to every thing, and to do whatsoever he thought necessary to his own preservation. . . . And this is the foundation of that right of punishing, which is exercised in every commonwealth. For the subjects did not give the sovereign that right; but only in laying down theirs, strengthened him to use his own, as he should think fit, for the preservation of them all: so that it was not given, but left to him, and to him only; and (excepting the limits set him by natural law) as entire, as in the condition of mere nature, and of war of every one against his neighbour.[14]

I will discuss shortly the mysterious business indicated by the parenthesis in this passage, but the thrust of Hobbes's teaching at this point is that the sovereign is not altogether in the commonwealth over which he presides in the same way that other men are. Unlike the others, he is no party to the social contract; unlike them also, he alone retains the unlimited natural liberty that all men have in the state of nature. His unlimited liberty, coupled with the fact that all the rest are "authors" of whatever he does, is the source of his unlimited civil authority. It would not be accurate to say that his not being a party to the covenant instituting a commonwealth leaves him altogether in the state of nature either, for he, like his subjects, gains by that institution what had been absent in the state of nature, that highest of all ends in Hobbes's political science: peace. Thus it would perhaps be most accurate to say of Hobbes's sovereign that he has one foot in civil society and one in the state of nature. Be that as it may, his distinctive character leads Hobbes to the conclusion that "there can happen no breach of covenant on the part of the sovereign; and consequently none of his subjects, by any pretence of forfeiture, can be freed from his subjection."[15]

The theoretical consequence, then, is the principle of absolutism, which manifests itself in various ways. No man may justly accuse the sovereign of any injustice;[16] all rights to property flow from the sovereign;[17] and he is "not subject to the civil laws."[18] "So that it appeareth plainly . . . that the sovereign power . . . is as great, as possibly men can be imagined to make it."[19]

Yet scattered throughout *Leviathan* are assertions that the sovereign is answerable for his conduct before the tribunal of natural law. It is true that Hobbes ascribes to justice a precise meaning—even a narrowly technical meaning—as the creature of covenant and the command of the sovereign and therefore holds that the sovereign is incapable of injustice. Yet even in the very passage quoted earlier, where he speaks of the need for all men to "submit their wills" to him who "beareth their person," Hobbes implies a limit on political power when he insists that the sovereign's subjects acknowledge themselves as the authors of all his actions "in those things which concern the common peace and safety."[20] Thus the reader is told sotto voce that in indifferent matters, those not touching on the common peace and security, our will is not subordinated to the sovereign's. Still, the hard case is put by the question, What relationship obtains between subject and sovereign in those circumstances—inevitable in practice—under which the sovereign will collides with the requirements of peace and security?

The beginning of an answer comes when Hobbes states the following baffling distinction: "It is true that they that have sovereign power may commit iniquity; but not injustice, or injury in the proper signification."[21] "Iniquity" is one of the very words he uses when listing offenses, which "can never be made lawful," against the "immutable and eternal" laws of nature.[22] Elsewhere he tells the reader that "the commands of sovereigns" may be accused of being "contrary to equity, and the law of nature."[23]

Two possibilities present themselves when we inquire how it is that the sovereign can be charged with iniquity but not with injustice. First, iniquity's opposite, equity, is defined by Hobbes (as his eleventh of nineteen laws of nature) in terms of equality: If "*a man be trusted to judge between man and man, it is a precept of the law of nature, that he deal equally between them.*"[24] And inasmuch as the sovereign is supreme judge and he is described as "*trusted* with the sovereign power,"[25] Hobbes later refines this to mean "that justice be equally administered to all degrees of people; . . . for in this consisteth equity; to which, as being precept of the law of nature, a sovereign is as much subject, as any of the meanest of his people."[26] Throughout his works, Hobbes defines equity as the principle of proportional equality in distributive justice.[27]

The second possibility presents itself in Hobbes's *A Dialogue Between a Philosopher and a Student of the Common Laws of England.* When the philosopher states the same distinction between iniquity and injustice, the following colloquy takes place:

Lawyer: This is somewhat subtile [*sic*]. I pray deal plainly. What is the difference between injustice and iniquity?

Philosopher: I pray you tell me first, what is the difference between a court of justice, and a court of equity?

L.: A court of justice is that which hath cognizance of such
causes as are to be ended by the positive laws of the land; and a
court of equity is that, to which belong such causes as are to be determined by equity; that is to say, by the law of reason.

P.: You see then the difference between injustice and iniquity is
this; that injustice is the transgression of a statute-law, and iniquity the transgression of the law of reason.[28]

If these remarks are combined with those in *Leviathan,* it appears that
in so singling out "iniquity" in both works, Hobbes holds out the opportunity of charging the sovereign with being unreasonable in his
promulgation of laws and decrees, and that this lapse into unreason on
the sovereign's part might typically consist of a failure to treat his subjects equally before the law. But Hobbes holds fast to his refusal to call
this injustice; should a statute make invidious distinctions among "degrees of people," all subjects are nonetheless obliged to live under such
a law. And nothing in the *Dialogue* suggests that judges in a court of
equity may hold a law of the sovereign iniquitous and thus invalid under the law of reason. But that is to get ahead of the discussion up to
this point.

Hobbes's comments on equity and iniquity do not exhaust the subject
of whether the sovereign's actions may be held to account on the
grounds of natural law. In the important Chapter 26, "Of Civil Laws,"
the boundless legislative power again seems to have some bounds to it
when the reader is told that "whatsoever is not against the law of nature, may be made law in the name of them that have the sovereign
power."[29] In still later chapters similar strictures on the sovereign are
insisted upon: ex post facto laws appear to be forbidden,[30] as do governing by arbitrary decree rather than by standing laws,[31] punishing a
man "before he be judicially heard, and declared guilty,"[32] and all
"punishments of innocent subjects."[33]

The strongest statements Hobbes makes along these lines link the
strictures on the sovereign's power to his duty before God. In Chapter
21, "Of the Liberty of Subjects," Hobbes states that the sovereign
"never wanteth right to any thing, otherwise, than as he himself is the
subject of God, and bound thereby to observe the laws of nature."[34] And
in Chapter 30, "Of the Office of the Sovereign Representative," Hobbes
states that "the end, for which he was trusted with the sovereign power
[is] the procuration of *the safety of the people;* to which he is obliged by

the law of nature, and to render an account thereof to God, the author of that law, and to none but him."[35]

"To none but him" is a revealing addendum that keeps Hobbes from contradicting his principle that the sovereign cannot be charged by men with any breach of covenant or lawfully be deprived of his power. But even as indicating a responsibility enforced not by people but by divine power, such declamations will not do, for it is, to say the least, far from certain that Hobbes considered the sovereign—or anyone else—to be the "subject of God."[36] The major thrust of his project of enlightenment, after all, is to dispel the illusions that lead men to regard spiritual punishments as more terrifying than earthly ones. To replace men's fear of invisible powers (and the difference between "superstition" and "religion" is really no difference at all)[37] with the fear of death, first at the hands of their fellows, then at the hands of the sovereign, is central to Hobbes's political teaching. Hence a closer look at his doctrine of natural law is required.

The fearful character of the state of nature, itself an inference from the human passions, leads Hobbes to the first of his laws of nature, as a further inference from the same source: *"to seek peace, and follow it."*[38] Since this and the other laws that flow from it can never take precedence over the *right* of nature (namely, *"by all means we can, to defend ourselves"*),[39] and since "law, properly, is the word of him, that by right hath command over others,"[40] it appears that Hobbes's natural law is not properly law at all, at least not in the classical sense. Bobbio has stated the difference well: in the classical and Thomistic natural-law tradition, "natural law is superior to positive law in the sense that a positive norm contrary to natural law is not valid," but in Hobbes, while the law of nature "founds the legitimacy of [positive law] and makes it obligatory," what it makes obligatory is "the positive legal order as a whole, not the individual norms which comprise it."[41]

As Leo Strauss remarks, for Hobbes death "takes the place of the *telos.*"[42] That is, "Modern natural law as originated by Hobbes did not start as traditional natural law did from the hierarchic order of man's natural ends but from the lowest of those ends (self-preservation) which could be thought to be more effective than the higher ends."[43] Hobbes himself indicates the radically novel character of his natural-law teaching when, at the conclusion of his chapter on the state of nature, he shows the way out of that condition: reason "suggesteth convenient articles of peace . . . which otherwise are called the Laws of Nature."[44] That calling them such is questionable is made more explicit at the conclusion of Hobbes's catalogue of them:

> These dictates of reason, men used to call by the names of laws,
> but improperly: for they are but conclusions, or theorems concern-
> ing what conduceth to the conservation and defence of themselves;
> whereas law, properly, is the word of him, that by right hath com-
> mand over others. But yet if we consider the same theorems, as de-
> livered in the word of God, that by right commandeth all things;
> then are they properly called laws.[45]

The best that can be said about the final sentence here (with its crucial
"if") is that nothing in Hobbes's derivation of his laws of nature requires the reader to take seriously the possibility that they are, for
Hobbes, "delivered in the word of God." And so the sovereign, who "by
right hath command over others" but is subject to the command of no
other, is not "properly" fettered by any constraints deserving to be
called law.

But given the frequency with which apparent natural-law strictures
on the sovereign become visible in the *Leviathan,* the question necessarily arises, Why is a writer noted for "his almost boyish straightfor-
wardness . . . and his marvelous clarity and force"[46] equivocal about the
extent of sovereign power even to this degree? It is difficult to conclude
merely that Hobbes is writing esoterically for his own protection—
though that is probably a partial explanation[47]—for virtually his last
word on the subject is to criticize an "error of Aristotle's politics, that in
a well-ordered commonwealth, not men should govern, but the laws."[48]

A fuller explanation would be that Hobbes's purpose is to counsel[49]
sovereigns on the measures they should take, and refrain from taking,
in order to preserve the commonwealth (and thereby themselves). It is
"manifest, that law in general, is not counsel, but command,"[50] and if
Hobbes's laws of nature are not "properly" laws, then in the case of
the sovereign, to say nothing of other men, the natural law has more
the character of counsel than command. No less than other men in the
state of nature—and he is the only one who remains in some sense in
that condition vis-à-vis his fellow men—the sovereign is enjoined to
seek peace and to let nothing stand in the way of his self-preservation.
Even if Hobbes's sovereign takes all due care to rid the schools of "Aris-
totelity,"[51] to outlaw the teaching of various false doctrines that permit
distinctions between government and tyranny, he will not thus become
fully secure against a multitude of subjects each of whom believes himself (and rightly, says Hobbes) "more prudent in affairs of his own
house, than a privy-councillor in the affairs of another man."[52] In other
words, though private judgment of the justice of the regime is forbidden

by Hobbes, in practice it is impossible for an imprudent prince to avoid forever the massing of a great *collective* private judgment against the continuation of his rule. Hence the counsel on laws of nature against ex post facto laws and the like—"for there can arrive no good to the commonwealth"[53] from such practices. It is probably no accident that the most specific instances of Hobbes's counsel bear an uncanny resemblance to principles of the English common and statute law, some of which had been secured by the expedient of threatening a prince at swordpoint in 1215. No violation of these counsels will, in Hobbes's view, deprive a sovereign of his legitimate title to rule, but repeated flouting of them surely courts greater dangers than mere loss of title.

One of Hobbes's most explicit warnings to the sovereign comes in a surprising place. This is in the very chapter where the doctrine of absolute sovereignty is first presented in its fullest form—indeed in the very paragraph, already quoted, where Hobbes states that "there can happen no breach of covenant on the part of the sovereign":

> Besides, if any one [subject], or more of them, pretend a breach of the covenant made by the sovereign at his institution; and others, or one other of his subjects, *or himself alone,* pretend there was no such breach, there is in this case, no judge to decide the controversy; it returns therefore to the sword again; and every man recovereth the right of protecting himself by his own strength, contrary to the design they had in the institution.[54]

A second warning, still plainer, is in Chapter 21, "Of the Liberty of Subjects," in which Hobbes comes closest to sounding like the revolutionary Americans of 1776:

> The obligation of subjects to the sovereign, is understood to last as long, and no longer, than the power lasteth, by which he is able to protect them. For the right men have by nature to protect themselves, when none else can protect them, can by no covenant be relinquished. . . . The end of obedience is protection; which, wheresoever a man seeth it, either in his own, or in another's sword, nature applieth his obedience to it, and his endeavour to maintain it.[55]

In these passages, particularly in the second, Hobbes has all but let a Lockean cat out of the bag.[56] With slight modifications, the second passage could well have been drawn from Locke's discussion of the right of revolution in the *Second Treatise.* True, Hobbes's purpose in the first

passage is to underscore the importance of not supposing that the social contract is one that subsists between people and sovereign but one
between every man and every other man, excepting the sovereign
(hence every act of the sovereign is previously agreed to by every man
as his own act, done by his consent). But as the end sought by every
man upon entering the covenant was peace, as the arbitrary rule of a
sovereign by decree rather than by standing laws is to be regarded as
"an act of hostility,"[57] as the need for severity to his people is presumptively the fault of a sovereign ruling badly,[58] it is easy enough to suppose that subjects interested in their own preservation will quite naturally "pretend" just what Hobbes says they must not pretend—a
broken covenant between themselves and their ruler, if that ruler per-
sistently disregards the precepts of "natural law" counseled by Hobbes.
The sovereign cannot forfeit legitimacy, but practically speaking, in
the case of such foolishness all bets are off.

Now the question arises: short of that dire situation of which Hobbes
can barely bring himself to speak, what practical pressures can be
brought to bear on the sovereign to see that he keeps Hobbes's "natural
law" counsel? If the question requires a psychological answer, it is fear,
the sovereign's fear of his loss of power over other men. But if the question requires an institutional answer, the answer is that there are no
such practical means at all. This can be seen most clearly when Hobbes
discusses the duties of the judges who are to implement the sovereign's
standing laws.

Hobbes devotes more than half of *Leviathan*'s Chapter 26, "Of Civil
Laws," to the principles of legal interpretation that should guide "subordinate judges," appropriately beginning this long central portion of
the chapter with a section titled, "Some foolish opinions of lawyers concerning the making of laws."[59] Since he has only just told the reader
that the "law of nature, and the civil law, contain each other, and are of
equal extent,"[60] he is particularly alert to the dangers that may lurk in
the doctrines of the common lawyers who hold that legislative acts may
be held to a judicial test of reasonableness. Sir Edward Coke is singled
out for particular criticism[61] in a passage that deserves extensive quotation:

> That law can never be against reason, our lawyers are agreed. . . .
> And it is true: but the doubt is of whose reason it is, that shall be
> received for law. It is not meant of any private reason; for then
> there would be as much contradiction in the laws, as there is in the
> Schools; nor yet, as Sir Edward Coke makes it, an *artificial perfec-*

tion of reason, gotten by long study, observation, and experience, as
his was. For it is possible long study may increase, and confirm er-
roneous sentences: and where men build on false ground, the more
they build, the greater is the ruin: and of those that study, and observe with equal time and diligence, the reasons and resolutions
are, and must remain discordant: and therefore it is not that *juris
prudentia,* or wisdom of subordinate judges; but the reason of this
our artificial man the commonwealth, and his command, that
maketh law. . . . [T]he subordinate judge ought to have regard to
the reason, which moved his sovereign to make such law, that his
sentence may be according thereunto; which then is his sovereign's
sentence; otherwise it his own, and an unjust one.[62]

Hobbes is under no illusion that adjudication under the sovereign's
laws is a simple mechanical process. He admits that "it is not the letter, but the intendment, or meaning, that is to say, the authentic interpretation of the law (which is the sense of the legislator), in which the
nature of the law consisteth."[63] But it is for precisely this reason that
Hobbes insists on the sovereign's firm control over who the judges are
and how well they are doing their job, "For else, by the craft of an interpreter, the law may be made to bear a sense, contrary to that of the sovereign: by which means the interpreter becomes the legislator."[64]

The subordination of the Hobbesian judiciary is reinforced by two
other principles of jurisprudence. The first is a rule of statutory construction: The "intention of the legislator is always supposed to be equity: for it were a great contumely for a judge to think otherwise of the
sovereign."[65] The second is a healthy skepticism about the value of
precedents: "No man's error becomes his own law; nor obliges him to
persist in it. Neither, for the same reason, becomes it a law to other
judges, though sworn to follow it."[66]

The first of these principles requires a judge, insofar as it is possible,
to interpret the sovereign's law so as to avoid results that violate
Hobbes's "natural law" counsels against ex post facto laws, punishments without judicial hearing, and the like. A certain amount of discretion is called for here; Hobbes gives a bit of ground to the established practices of the common law, for where the positive law is silent
(there being "no commonwealth in the world, wherein there be rules
enough set down, for the regulating of all the actions, and words of
men; as being a thing impossible")[67] the judges will have to "fill in the
gaps" by reference to the natural law. But the second principle asserts
the primacy of the sovereign will over any established line of prece-

dents, whether of statutory interpretation or of common law, no matter its roots in immemorial usage. Each principle in its own way preserves that primacy, for should the sovereign expressly promulgate an ex post facto law, for instance, even the first principle here cannot prevent its execution.

It goes without saying that there is no room for judicial review in Hobbes's political teaching. Nor can there be where the supreme legislator and the "ordinary" legislator are one and the same. Nor is there even the essential precondition of judicial review, namely constitutionalism. Yet there are incipient ingredients indispensable to both these doctrines. First and foremost there is the doctrine of consent by fundamentally equal human beings as the foundation of government. Moreover, there is a sovereign constituted with the authority to make the highest laws of the society, a sovereign to whose dispensations all subordinate authorities must conform their actions. There is a clear teaching on a judicial power that must, one, uphold the fundamental positive law promulgated by the supreme legislator; two, assume (not merely *presume*) as a matter of principle the justice (or "constitutionality") of whatever that legislator pronounces; three, construe the letter of the law by reference to the original intention or "sense of the legislator"; four, by reasonable interpretation in the interstices or silences of the law, fill in the avowedly just intentions of that legislator; and five, prefer those laws and intentions to any common law precedents arrived at through the independent efforts of the judges. If this is not yet judicial review under a constitution, still it collects some of judicial review's necessary appendages or secondary principles and evinces an important role for the judiciary to play in assisting the sovereign to preserve the regime.

As a final consideration on Hobbes, it might be asked why he cannot bring himself to take further steps in the direction of constitutionalism as we understand it. After all, he provides a glimpse of what it would look like when he discusses the chartering of subordinate "bodies politic" in Chapter 22, "Of Systems Subject, Political, and Private." There, although the discussion is mostly in the context of corporations organized for trade or for the government of schools or churches, Hobbes does include the corporate government of provinces and colonies, which may be committed to an "assembly of men" whose "power [is] limited by commission."[68] The general principle for all such entities is stated near the outset of the chapter: "In bodies politic, the power of the representative is always limited; and that which prescribeth the limits thereof, is the power of the sovereign. For power unlimited, is absolute sovereignty."[69] If we let ourselves forget that Hobbes's category of "bodies politic" in this context cannot include the commonwealth itself, we have here a fair description of constitutionalism. As Hobbes states elsewhere, these representatives of limited power "personate" their respective bodies before the law, "as a church, an hospital, a bridge, may be personated by a rector, master, or overseer"[70]—and just as the sovereign represents or "personates" all the subjects in the commonwealth.[71]

So corporate associations of persons may themselves be "personated" by some representative. Add to this that for Hobbes sovereignty may be lodged in a plurality of persons; that the sovereign, whether singular or plural, assumes the character of an "artificial person"; and that consent is the basis of all of the above. All the essential ingredients are present here for a final combination: why may not the collective body of a society itself be the sovereign, assume its artificial personality, and delegate limited power through a constitution or "letters patent" issued to a governor or governors representing that body politic?

Hobbes will not allow this. His sovereign is always a particular natural person (or assembly of persons), who is no party to the social contract and to whom all the contracting parties are absolutely subject. But Hobbes's discussion of subordinate bodies politic reveals that all these stipulations are *choices;* they are not inexorably driven by principle. On the basis of his psychology, Hobbes argues that sovereignty cannot be lodged in the people at large, for there is no security for all individuals "from a great multitude" possessing this ultimate power, "unless directed by one judgment." For if the individuals in this multitude act "according to their particular judgments, and particular appetites," it will follow that they will be "distracted in opinions concerning the best use and application of their strength" and also that

> when there is no common enemy, they make war upon each other, for their particular interests. For if we could suppose a great multitude of men to consent in the observation of justice, and other laws of nature, without a common power to keep them all in awe; we might as well suppose all mankind to do the same; and then there neither would be, nor need to be any civil government, or commonwealth at all; because there would be peace without subjection.[72]

But Hobbes protests too much. We need not entertain any fancies about the capacity of "all mankind" to make peace in this fashion, to recognize that a powerful government, sufficient to keep men "in awe" of punishment, is perfectly possible on the basis of a consent that delegates limited authority over "those things which concern the common peace and safety"[73] but which leaves sovereignty collectively in the hands of citizens who are not subjects. Hobbes's rejection of that option in the passage above posits an alternative that all but confesses that, in his commonwealth, the instrument of the peace is a sovereign who from the people's perspective is the "common enemy." Only such an enemy can inspire the fear that keeps men from "mak[ing] war upon each other, for their particular interests." In short, although there is no "peace without subjection," that subjection itself amounts to something akin to perpetual war: not the natural state of war or the civil war that tears the fabric of society, but a kind of civilized war or cold war carried on between sovereign and subject, with the sovereign winning every skirmish so long as the enmity of the people is not collected into a force greater than his own.[74]

Clearly the key to Hobbes's preference for the sovereignty of men over the sovereignty of law, for the absolute rule of natural persons over the option of constitutionalism, is the chief end he assigns to every commonwealth, namely peace. And in Hobbes's opinion the passionate nature of man makes "peace without subjection" an impossibility. But what if men could be at peace with one another on some basis other than fear of and subjection to an absolute authority? What if peace were attainable more securely as the by-product of accomplishing something that people hold even more dearly? As we have seen, were Hobbes to opt for constitutionalism or any arrangement that leaves the sovereign less than absolute, indivisible, and inseparable from the ordinary legislative power, it would follow as a necessary consequence that the withdrawal of consent by the covenantors is possible. And that would amount to inviting the return to the state of war. But change the end of civil society from peace at any price to something prized even more highly, and the sovereignty of law, constitutionalism, and judicial review take a crucial step nearer the possible—and so too perhaps does a more certain peace. What that alternative something might be is at the heart of Locke's modification of Hobbes's political science.[75]

CHAPTER NINE

The Movement Toward Constitutionalism in Locke's *Second Treatise*

The great Question which in all Ages has disturbed Mankind, and brought on them the greatest part of those Mischiefs which have ruin'd Cities, depopulated Countries, and disordered the Peace of the World, has been, Not whether there be Power in the World, nor whence it came, but who should have it. . . . [I]f this remain disputable, all the rest will be to very little purpose; and the skill used in dressing up Power with all the Splendor and Temptation Absoluteness can add to it, without shewing who has a Right to have it, will serve only to give a greater edge to Man's Natural Ambition, which of it self is but too keen.

—*John Locke[1]*

Locke immediately changes the end of Hobbes's civil society when he says that the "great and *chief end* . . . of Mens uniting into Commonwealths, and putting themselves under Government, *is the Preservation of their Property*" (a term that Locke copiously defines to encompass men's "Lives, Liberties, and Estates").[2] Nowhere is the difference between Locke and Hobbes more stark than in the conclusions they draw from these purposes. Although the state of nature is in practice no more distinguishable from the state of war for Locke than for Hobbes,[3] Locke nevertheless finds Hobbes's absolutism, however much it seems to secure peace, to be no real escape from the state of nature at all—since an absolute sovereign (Locke is tacitly accepting Hobbes's terms here) is no party to the social contract and thus remains "Judge in his own Case."[4] And therein lies no security for property.

Likewise, in Chapter 26 of the *Second Treatise*, "Of Conquest,"

Locke takes pains (sometimes verging on the incredible) to constrain the "perfectly Despotical" power of even a just conqueror (not to mention an unjust one) in the name of the preservation of property.[5] Hobbes, on the other hand, distinguishes rule by consent and rule by conquest only on a practical level: Men "who choose their sovereign, do it for fear of one another," while conquered men "subject themselves, to him they are afraid of. In both cases they do it for fear."[6] For Hobbes, the efficient cause of government is fear, and the final cause is peace (which in turn is enforced by fear of the sovereign coming to replace fear of one another), whereas for Locke the efficient cause is fear, but the final cause is the preservation of property, which is enforced not so much by fear as by the rule of law.

This recasting of the end of civil society is the kernel of Locke's familiar doctrines of limited government and the right of revolution.[7] The priority of property over peace can be seen by contrasting what Hobbes and Locke say when each first introduces the subject of political power. For Hobbes, "all the *rights,* and *faculties* of him, or them, on whom the sovereign power is conferred" are directed "to the end" that men "live peaceably amongst themselves, and be protected against other men."[8] For Locke, on the other hand, "Political Power" is "a Right of making Laws . . . for the Regulating and Preserving of Property," with various ancillary rights, "and all this only for the Publick Good."[9] It is property as a higher end than peace that requires that political power be limited and *"never be suppos'd to extend farther than the common good,"*[10] thus permitting the withdrawal of consent when the limits are breached. Indeed, though Locke remarks that revolutions are not appropriate "upon every little mismanagement in publick affairs,"[11] he will permit the withdrawal of consent and the reconstituting of government under circumstances that appear to fall far short of the full-throated "appeal to Heaven." Such circumstances, in which "the *Legislative is changed,"* will be discussed later.[12]

Clearly, Locke's teaching on limited government moves closer to constitutionalism. The legitimacy of revolution against tyrannical government is the necessary but not sufficient condition of constitutionalism, as John Marshall recognized in *Marbury* v. *Madison.*[13] Only under a doctrine recognizing such a right can we refashion the consensual foundation of government on a non-Hobbesian basis. For Locke, all members of society are parties to the social contract, those who govern not excepted. Both Hobbes and Locke regard political power as a trust vested in those who govern. But the manner of the vesting is crucially different. Where Hobbes's men escape the state of nature by their submission to a sovereign who "personates" the entire power of the community and who is not altogether a member of the commonwealth he governs, Locke's men escape the state of nature by sharing among themselves the ultimate power, each equally with the rest, and delegating the immediate exercise of political power to subordinate agents who likewise each have their share (as private persons, however) of the collective self-governing right of the community.

Thus Locke, while not insisting too strenuously on a form of government where the legislative power is vested in an assembly "whose Members upon [its dissolution] are Subjects under the common Laws of their Country, equally with the rest,"[14] squarely renounces Hobbes's view that the legislator is not himself bound by the civil laws: *"No Man in Civil Society can be exempted from the Laws of it."*[15] However minimal we regard the limits on political power in Locke,[16] the limits are real enough so long as the people hold in reserve the right to alter or abolish the established government.

Yet from our perspective as heirs of the American founders, Locke seems oddly unable to grasp firmly the nettle of constitutionalism. This is nowhere more visible than in his treatment of sovereignty, the locus whereof is sometimes difficult to pin down. For one thing, although the terms "sovereign" and "sovereignty" are ubiquitous in the *First Treatise,* where Locke is busily refuting Sir Robert Filmer, these two words are used a total of only eight times in the entire *Second Treatise,* only once in terms that may be taken to show his approval of the word's use.[17] It could well be that Locke purposely avoids the use of "sovereign" and "sovereignty" as much as possible in order to make a clean break with the political science of Hobbes, at least on this score. Even when discussing doctrines with which he disagrees, Locke much oftener uses the term "dominion."

The term Locke uses most frequently to describe legitimate rule is "supream Power." Sometimes it is used virtually interchangeably with "the Legislative"; at other times the supreme power is set above the legislative authority, the former being the source of the latter. Thus, the supreme power is sometimes assigned by Locke to those who govern, sometimes to those who covenanted to make government, i.e., the society at large.[18]

A close reading reveals that Locke does in a sense mean to have it both ways. In fact, Locke provides three alternative readings of the relationship between the "supream Power" and "the Legislative," two of which hold them to be identical. In the first sense, following the *"original Compact"* unanimously forming a society of men, the "determination of the *majority*"[19] to constitute a particular form of government is at once an act of supreme power and a legislative exercise. This is clear despite the fact that Locke often refers to this exercise of majority rule in different terms or mixes his levels of meaning in one statement, as when speaking of men's agreement to "such Rules as the Community, or those authorized by them to that purpose, shall agree on" being the "original *right and rise* of both the *the Legislative and Executive Power,* as well as of the Governments and Societies themselves."[20]

In the second sense, Locke sometimes clarifies the priority indicated in the passage just quoted and distinguishes more sharply between supreme power and legislative power, stating that "the Constitution of the Legislative being the original and supream act of the Society, antecedent to all positive Laws in it, and depending wholly on the People, no inferiour Power can alter it."[21]

The most numerous passages are those in the third sense in which Locke again supposes no distinction between supreme and legislative power, but the context is one in which he has left behind the constituting of government and is speaking of its ordinary legislative operations. The greatest concentration of remarks identifying the supreme power and the legislative is in Chapter 11, "Of the Extent of the Legislative Power." Even here, a great portion of the chapter is given over to discussing the limits on this power, indicating its subordination to something higher, yet all the while it is characterized as supreme. At the outset, for instance, Locke informs us that

the *first and fundamental positive Law* of all Commonwealths, *is the establishing of the Legislative Power;* as the *first and fundamental natural Law,* which is to govern even the Legislative it self, is *the preservation of the Society,* and (as far as will consist with the publick good) of every person in it. This *Legislative* is not only *the supream power* of the Commonwealth, but sacred and unalterable in the hands where the Community have once placed it; nor can any Edict of any Body else, in what Form soever conceived, or by what Power soever backed, have the force and obligation of a *Law,* which has not its *Sanction from* that *Legislative,* which the publick has chosen and appointed.[22]

How close Locke comes here to a complete teaching of constitutionalism may be seen if the word "Constitution" is substituted everywhere "Legislative" or "Legislative Power" appears in this passage. Be that as it may, Locke immediately reverts to speaking of the ordinary legislative power as though it were the highest authority, telling the reader that "all the Obedience . . . any one can be obliged to pay, ultimately terminates in this *Supream Power*"—"it being ridiculous to imagine one can be tied ultimately to *obey* any *Power* in the Society, which is not *the Supream.*"[23]

The only way to make sense of this juggling, and it is not difficult (although Locke could have made it less so if he had not shied away from Hobbes's term "sovereignty"), is to consider who is obliged to obey whom in the context of each level of meaning. In the first, in our sovereign capacity as makers of the social contract, each individual is a legislator, for himself and his fellows alike. Each is likewise subject to move obediently with the body politic "whither the greater force carries it, which is the *consent of the majority.*"[24] In the second, the commanding party remains the sovereign individuals collected into society at large, and the obedient party is the legislative authority we have constituted by them, it "being only a Fiduciary Power" while "there remains still *in the People a Supream Power* to remove or *alter the Legislative.*"[25] In the third, most commonly used level of meaning, the people are no longer joined in their sovereign public capacity but are atomized as private individuals owing obedience to the high authority of the government they have constituted. That is the usual state of affairs in a commonwealth once constituted and continues so long as the regime is both stable and just—which will be most of the time, for Locke, if his principles are realized.[26]

It is at the second of these three levels of meaning, in which the people issue an original sovereign command, the ordinary legislative "being only a Fiduciary Power," that Locke approaches constitutionalism as such. Here also it is relevant that the rules legislators "make for other Mens Actions, must . . . be conformable to the Law of Nature."[27] But what practical mechanisms does Locke provide to ensure that conformity?

It is not quite the case that he only "hints at the separation of powers,"[28] for Locke does indicate that "in well order'd Commonwealths" the powers of legislation and execution "come often to be separated."[29] But nowhere does he subscribe to James Madison's "political truth" that the "accumulation of all powers, legislative, executive, and judiciary, in the same hands . . . may justly be pronounced the very definition of tyranny."[30] Even where such a prudential arrangement is adopted—even where some latitude remains for executive prerogative—ultimate political authority (subject only to the people's reserved right of revolution) resides in the legislative power, "to which all the rest [of the offices of government] are and must be subordinate."[31]

What is true of Locke's executive is doubly so of his judiciary. In fact, what strikes the reader who turns from Hobbes's *Leviathan* to the *Second Treatise* is how little Locke says, by comparison to his predecessor, on the two subjects under consideration here: the judicial power and natural law. On the role natural law plays in civil society, Locke appears to equivocate. At first it seems to have clarity and force, for at the very moment he declines to "enter here into the particulars of the Law of Nature," he assures us

> yet, it is certain there is such a Law, and that too, as intelligible and plain to a rational Creature, and a Studier of that Law, as the positive Laws of Common-wealths, nay possibly plainer; As much as Reason is easier to be understood, than the Phansies and intricate Contrivances of Men, following contrary and hidden interests put into Words; For so truly are a great part of the *Municipal Laws* of Countries, which are only so far right as they are founded on the Law of Nature, by which they are to be regulated and interpreted.[32]

Later these qualities of clarity and force are very much attenuated when Locke writes that the first signal advantage of civil society over the state of nature is the positive law, which is "*establish'd,* settled, known" and "allowed by common consent" for the decision of controversies: "For though the Law of Nature be plain and intelligible to all rational Creatures; yet Men being biassed by their Interest, as well as ignorant for want of study of it, are not apt to allow of it as a Law binding to them in the application of it to their particular Cases."[33] Still later, when speaking again of the positive law's advantages, Locke appears to synthesize these two remarks into one still more ambiguous, this time adding the "*known Authoris'd Judges*" who will interpret it: "For the Law of Nature being unwritten, and so no where to be found but in the minds of Men, they who through Passion or Interest shall mis-cite, or misapply it, cannot so easily be convinced of their mistake where there is no establish'd Judge."[34]

Little more than these few passages is said about natural law in the context of an established commonwealth—nothing like the detailed precepts Hobbes provides—and so the reader might conclude that Locke is highly confident that governments formed according to his teaching, unlike Hobbes's absolute sovereign, will need little counsel in how to govern justly or how to avoid the dangerous temptations of tyranny that lead to revolution. But the first and last of the three passages just quoted might nevertheless be taken to point toward a judicial role in keeping the government in line with natural law. Judges presumably will be "Studier[s] of that Law," perhaps less inclined by interest to "mis-cite" it, and thus safely called upon to "regulate and interpret" the positive law by the natural.

But for several reasons such an interpretation is implausible. First, the judicial power is nearly invisible in the *Second Treatise* (compared to Hobbes's treatment of it or to Locke's own treatment of the executive), and in every instance in which it is mentioned, it is strictly lashed to the mast of the positive law.[35] Second, Locke indicates, in what may be the only remark clearly setting a natural-law standard for the conduct of government, that "the Law of Nature and Reason" dictates majority rule as "pass[ing] for the act of the whole" in the promulgation of positive laws by legislative assemblies.[36]

Finally, what is it that judges, if empowered with a natural-law jurisdiction, would protect? What could be a more comprehensive object of such protection than life, liberty, and estate, all of which Locke gathers under the term "property"? Yet in several places he makes it clear that in society "property" is what the positive law says it is.[37] Until modern abortion and euthanasia law arrived on the scene it might have been said that in the nature of things it is impossible for the positive law to redefine life itself. But as to the other two rights comprehended by "property," it must be said that for Locke, even such questions as "Will Catholics be accorded religious liberty?" and "Are slaves legitimate property?" are to be answered in each society by the positive laws made by the supreme legislative authority.[38]

This is not to say that there are no right answers to such questions. It is to say that Locke provides no ground for subordinate judges to substitute the right answers for the wrong ones given by the positive law. The only recourse Locke provides in the case of a government gone consistently astray from the law of nature is the threat of the dissolution of government, upon which "the People are at liberty to provide for themselves, by erecting a new Legislative, differing from the other by the change of Persons, or Form, or both as they shall find it most for their safety and good."[39]

As Hobbes's *Leviathan* is full of counsel for the absolute sovereign who wishes to preserve the peace and his own rule, so the *Second Treatise* offers much counsel to the sovereign people regarding the circumstances under which revolution is justified and thus under which they may resume their original right as a society to legislate in the most authoritative manner. But no less than Hobbes, Locke leaves his highest authority in practice absolutely unfettered in the choices it is free to make. For Hobbes, a feckless sovereign will bring his own doom upon himself; for Locke, a feckless people, constituting government badly, only hasten the day when they will have to undo their handiwork and write a new social contract—as Americans had to replace the Articles of Confederation with the Constitution. In both cases, the ultimate legislator—and no one else—is responsible for the regime's conformity to natural justice.[40] And until such time as Locke's sovereign people resume their original legislative right, no authority subordinate to the ordinary legislative—least of all judges—can assume responsibility for that conformity.

This is not legal positivism, the view that "there is nothing higher to which one can appeal from the man-made laws or conventions,"[41] for no doctrine legitimizing a right of revolution can be so described. But it does entail a judicial commitment to forswear any recourse to the natural law in derogation of the positive law. And this commitment is inextricably linked to the principles of constitutional self-government. Hadley Arkes's assertion, noted previously, that in the adjudication of cases "the appeal to reason should be sufficient—and sovereign,"[42] contradicts the liberalism of Locke, who, though he goes far in rehabilitating Hobbes's consent theory in the direction of the sovereignty of law, nevertheless settles the ultimate practical choice of what is law, what is reasonable, on the sovereignty of the men who constitute government. The penultimate choice is lodged in the ordinary legislative authority. No choice at all is lodged in judges.[43]

Indeed, there are indications in Locke that, were judges to intervene to correct the positive law in the name of the natural, the result would be a change in the form of government justifying the resumption of sovereign power by the people. In the final chapter of the *Second Treatise*, "Of the Dissolution of Government," Locke discusses three sets of circumstances in which this dissolution may occur. The first is the dissolution of government from without, by foreign conquest; the other two concern its dissolution from within. Of these two, the one that has received the most attention is where the *"Legislative acts against the Trust* reposed in them," governing arbitrarily, invading the property of citizens, and bringing on "the state of War, wherein the Appeal lies only to Heaven."[44]

Comparatively neglected is the apparently less dire situation (perhaps resulting in a less violent response from the people) in which "the *Legislative is changed.*"[45] To illustrate, Locke supposes the tripartite legislative power of England and gives examples mostly of abuses by the monarch. But before those illustrations, Locke provides a principle broad enough to cover the phenomenon of judicial activism in a constitutional order:

> When any one, or more, shall take upon them to make Laws, whom the People have not appointed so to do, they make Laws without Authority, which the People are not therefore bound to obey; by which means they come again to be out of subjection, and may constitute to themselves a *new Legislative,* as they think best, being in full liberty to resist the force of those, who without Authority would impose any thing upon them. Every one is at the disposure of his own Will, when those who had by the delegation of the Society, the declaring of the publick Will, are excluded from it, and others usurp the place who have no such Authority or Delegation.[46]

Locke's use of "usurp" in this passage hints that his division in this chapter of "dissolution from within" into two categories reflects the different problems posed in the preceding two chapters, "Of Usurpation" and "Of Tyranny." The former he defines as the situation "where one *is* got into *the Possession of what another has Right to,*"[47] the latter as *"the exercise of Power beyond Right,"* which occurs when "the Gouvernour, however intituled, makes not the Law, but his Will, the Rule."[48]

In one paragraph Locke nearly collapses the distinction between the two forms of dissolution entirely but not quite. "In both the forementioned Cases, when either the Legislative is changed, or the Legislators act contrary to the end for which they were constituted; those who are guilty are *guilty of Rebellion.*"[49] The usurper as well as the tyrant "actually *introduce[s] a state of War,* which is that of Force without Authority." But then the usurpers of legislative power (whether they be executive, as Locke stresses, or judicial) are said merely to *"expose the People a new to the state of War,"* whereas a tyrannical legislative brings on such a war in actual fact.[50] It seems that usurpation does not necessitate the full-scale violence of revolution if the people can resettle the constitutional locus of legislative authority without resort to such extremity—as the English did, in relative peace, in the Glorious Revolution of 1688.[51]

Locke does not provide any guidance on how in practice the problem of usurpation can be kept from bringing on the complete fall of the regime to the same extent as it is brought on by the problem of legislative tyranny. But this inability to supply practical guidance is owing to

Locke not having taken the further step taken by our founders: the reliance on written constitutions as the foundation of political authority. Such constitutions, if amendable, may even provide a peaceful recourse when legislative tyranny arises. And I have already suggested in Chapter 2 that within the ordinary processes of the Constitution the framers provided a mechanism for redressing the problem of usurpation, whether the usurpers are executives or judges: impeachment. By that expedient the people, through their representatives, may punish those who are "guilty of rebellion" without taking the drastic measure of resuming directly their original sovereign right to rule themselves. Whether this is a practicable expedient will be up to them and their representatives.

Locke's advancement of liberal political science in the direction of constitutionalism was indispensable for the American founding, as no reader of both the *Second Treatise* and the Declaration of Independence can overlook. It is little wonder that Jefferson, the Declaration's principal author, placed Locke in his personal pantheon of the three greatest men who had ever lived.[52] But for a fuller account of law and judicial power in a liberal regime, an account that forms the last link in the chain from the power politics of Hobbes and the limited government of Locke to the formal constitutionalism of the American experiment, we must examine the *Commentaries* of William Blackstone.

CHAPTER TEN

The Political Science of Blackstone's *Commentaries*

But every man, when he enters into society, gives up a part of his natural liberty, as the price of so valuable a purchase; and in consideration of receiving the advantages of mutual commerce, obliges himself to conform to those laws, which the community has thought proper to establish.

—*William Blackstone*[1]

In certain respects, this endeavor to understand the relation of natural law to positive law, and the role in that relationship properly played by American jurists, becomes easier when turning from Hobbes and Locke to Blackstone. For one thing, he is a less original thinker than either of the others, and his political teaching may be explained largely by reflecting on points already explored in the thought of his predecessors. For another, there is little question about the depth of Blackstone's influence on the American legal mind.[2] Finally, far more than Locke or even Hobbes, he speaks directly on the issue of the duties of the judicial power. The *Commentaries on the Laws of England* are, after all, chiefly concerned with law as a judicial enterprise.

Blackstone's famous doctrine of parliamentary supremacy has led some American readers to identify him as a strict Hobbesian. James Wilson, in his "Lectures on Law" delivered at the College of Philadelphia (later the University of Pennsylvania) in 1790–1791, appears to be the earliest to lay this charge at Blackstone's doorstep. Tracing Blackstone's definition of law itself back through Pufendorf to an origin he attributes to Hobbes, Wilson condemns him on essentially Lockean grounds as not having embraced the principle that all legitimate political power flows from a consenting people.[3] This is not the place for a point by point comparison of Wilson and Blackstone, but such a comparison would reveal that on every essential point, the quarrel between them comes to nothing. Both legal theorists proceed from Lockean principles; Wilson misunderstood (willfully or carelessly remains obscure) either Blackstone or Locke or both.[4]

Only once does Blackstone sound a bit more like Hobbes than Locke, when he opines that "anarchy [is] a worse state than tyranny itself, as any government is better than none at all."[5] Yet even here and immediately beforehand in the same sentence, Blackstone evinces a distinctly un-Hobbesian recognition that there is such a thing as tyranny, by which "we have seen [the rights of Englishmen] depressed."[6] Locke himself might have expressed the point about anarchy and tyranny only slightly differently; recall that for him absolute arbitrary rule is only an apparent and not a real escape from the anarchic condition of the state of nature because absolute tyrants and their subjects remain in a state of war with one another. And revolutions are not undertaken in order to return to the "ill condition"[7] of the state of nature, i.e., to dissolve society itself, but to dissolve government only and reconstitute it as rapidly as possible. Blackstone, too, makes it clear that civil government characterized by the rule of law is preferable to either alternative, as the statement quoted above follows hard on the heels of a remark that "(as Mr Locke has well observed) where there is no law, there is no freedom."[8]

As befits a legal treatise, Blackstone begins with a definition of law: "that rule of action, which is prescribed by some superior, and which the inferior is bound to obey."[9] This definition, with its supposition of superior and inferior beings, is attacked by James Wilson;[10] but everything hinges on the question, Who are the prescribing superior and the obedient inferior? In the first instance, says Blackstone, the legislator is God, the author of the law of nature, of which men "discover the purport" through the "faculty of reason."[11] From the divine source of that law, it follows that it "is of course superior in obligation to any other" and that "no human laws are of any validity, if contrary to this."[12]

This hardly makes Blackstone an adherent of scholastic natural law. As with Hobbes and Locke, reason is in the service of the passions, and Blackstone explicitly reduces the natural law to a command that each man "pursue his own happiness": the Creator "has been pleased so to contrive the constitution and frame of humanity, that we should want no other prompter to enquire after and pursue the rule of right, but only our own self-love, that universal principle of action."[13] No other law obliges men in a state of nature, where "we are all equal," because "a law always supposes some superior who is to make it."

Blackstone does seem at one point to take an almost Aristotelian view of human nature when in the midst of his discussion of the state of nature, he remarks that "man was formed for society," immediately adding, "and, as is demonstrated by the writers on this subject, is neither capable of living alone, nor indeed has the courage to do it."[14] The writer cited by Blackstone is Pufendorf. The citation seems to be to his *On the Law of Nature and Nations*. But in his shorter subsequent work, *On the Duty of Man and Citizen According to Natural Law,* regarded by a recent editor as a "genuine compendium" of the longer treatise, Pufendorf essentially subscribes to the Hobbesian-Lockean view that man's natural state, although "seem[ing] extraordinarily attractive in promising liberty and freedom from all subjection," instead is "attended with a multitude of disadvantages" so frightening as to drive men from it into the state where there is "peace, security, wealth, splendour, society, taste, knowledge, benevolence."[15] Hence, although the reader may be lulled at first into thinking that "formed for society" signals a return by Blackstone to the teleology of the ancients, this is a red herring; his reliance on Pufendorf takes him right back to the modern liberalism of Hobbes and Locke. In Blackstone's view, man is "formed for society" only in the sense (with which his predecessors agreed) that the state of nature confronts him with the summum malum of violent death at every turn.

In any event, once man enters the state, municipal (i.e., positive) law takes hold—defined by Blackstone (quoting Coke's *Institutes*) as "a rule of civil conduct prescribed by the supreme power in a state, commanding what is right and prohibiting what is wrong."[16] Whence comes that "supreme power in a state"? Not by way of divine right, as Blackstone makes clear many pages later when criticizing the pretensions of James I.[17] Instead, though he finds the idea of a primeval state of nature "when there was no such thing as society" to be a "notion . . . too wild to be seriously admitted"[18] (and here again he seems to follow Pufendorf)[19] he agrees with both Hobbes and Locke in holding that the "only true and natural foundations of society are the wants and the fears of individuals." Hence "the original contract of society . . . must always be understood and implied" in any account of the basis of government.[20] But Blackstone's version of this contract is clearly Lockean, not Hobbesian; there is no individual who is not party to it, nor anyone free of the obligation that results from it to obey the laws.[21]

It also follows from the definition of municipal law that "sovereignty and legislature"—i.e., the power to legislate—"are indeed convertible terms," for "legislature . . . is the greatest act of superiority that can be exercised by one being over another."[22] If the reader looked no further, it would appear that Blackstone cannot see past the third and commonest meaning of "legislative power" used by Locke—that which conceives of men as private individuals daily subject to the laws of the land.[23] In his discussion of the powers of Parliament, Blackstone expresses this principle in its most stark and controversial form. Its power is

> transcendent and absolute . . . sovereign and uncontrolable [*sic*] authority . . . that absolute despotic power, which must in all governments reside somewhere. . . . It can, in short, do every thing that is not naturally impossible; and therefore some have not scrupled to call it's [*sic*] power, by a figure rather too bold, the omnipotence of parliament. True it is, that what they do, no authority upon earth can undo.[24]

Why is omnipotence a "figure rather too bold"? Because, as Blackstone makes clear in the very next paragraph, citing Locke, there is a power on earth that can undo what Parliament does, namely, the revolutionary action of an oppressed people. Blackstone is too conservative, too concerned with law-abidingness and stability, to mention this without immediately deemphasizing it:

> But however just this conclusion may be in theory, we cannot adopt it, nor argue from it, under any dispensation of government at present actually existing. . . . No human laws will . . . suppose a case, which at once must destroy all law, and compel men to build afresh upon a new foundation; . . . So long therefore as the English constitution lasts, we may venture to affirm, that the power of parliament is absolute and without control.[25]

The adjective "human" modifying "laws" in the second sentence here is the crucial qualifier, for the laws of nature, whether their source is divine or not, are decidedly not "human laws." And James Wilson to the contrary notwithstanding,[26] if Blackstone were a follower of Hobbes he would not have mentioned the right of revolution at all, much less have characterized it as "just in theory." His insistence that no political order can recognize that right as legal is perfectly consistent with Locke, who said that in "all Cases, whilst the Government subsists, the

Legislative is the Supream Power."[27] Indeed, it is perfectly consistent
with the state of things under our Constitution, which despite or indeed because its purpose is to fulfill ends marked out in the Declaration cannot recognize within its four corners any legal right the people
have to its own destruction (notwithstanding occasional addled theories of the Second Amendment).[28]

As gingerly as he approaches the subject, Blackstone is willing to
speak of the extralegal but truly sovereign steps that the English
people took in 1688 through a "convention"[29] of the Lords and Commons (it could not be "Parliament" without the Crown's participation)
to enthrone William and Mary in place of James II following what the
convention declared was his abdication. Such an extraordinary expedient was necessary under the circumstances, for, "whenever a question
arises between the society at large and any magistrate vested with
powers originally delegated by that society, it must be decided by the
voice of the society itself: there is not upon earth any other tribunal to
resort to."[30] Blackstone notes that the convention wisely avoided declaring that James had entirely subverted the constitution; this would
have resulted in a "total dissolution of the government, according to
the principles of Mr. Locke," and a consequent destruction of all preexisting positive laws.[31] Elsewhere too he cautiously softens Locke's
teaching on usurpation while admitting its validity. Writing that any
occurrence that upsets the "equilibrium of power" in England's tripartite legislative power would spell "an end of our constitution" because
the legislature would be changed, Blackstone asserts that "such a
change, however effected, is according to Mr. Locke (who perhaps carries his theory too far) at once an entire dissolution of the bands of government."[32]

In short, tempered in its presentation by his conservatism and moderation, Blackstone's teaching on revolution is in principle indistinguishable from Locke's. He presents as much of Locke's teaching as he
dares, even on occasions where he might have avoided speaking of it altogether, and rather than squarely confront it, prefers to soft-pedal
(without ever genuinely contradicting) its more upsetting aspects.
Take, for example, this plea for moderation in studying the Glorious
Revolution, delivered with a glance toward the far more frightening
memory of the civil war of the 1640s:

> But care must be taken not to carry this enquiry farther than
> merely for instruction or amusement. The idea, that the con-
> sciences of posterity were concerned in the rectitude of their ances-

tors' decisions, gave birth to those dangerous political heresies, which so long distracted the state, but at length are all happily extinguished. I therefore rather chuse to consider this great political measure, upon the solid footing of authority, than to reason in it's [*sic*] favour from it's justice, moderation, and expedience: because that might imply a right of dissenting or revolting from it, in case we should think it unjust, oppressive, or inexpedient. Whereas, our ancestors having most indisputably a competent jurisdiction to decide this great and important question, and having in fact decided it, it is now become our duty at this distance of time to acquiesce in their determination; being born under that establishment which was built upon this foundation, and obliged by every tie, religious as well as civil, to maintain it.[33]

This is a valiant but not quite successful attempt to lead the reader to derive a prescriptive duty merely from an existing state of affairs, since it rests on the expedient of averting one's eyes from the fact that that state of affairs is the result of a legitimate revolutionary act. What was done once may need doing again, as even Blackstone's contemporary Edmund Burke could not quite deny.[34] But both Blackstone and Burke are concerned with downplaying the whole business of revolutionary action, as too great an attention to it may lead some men to advocate it for what the Declaration of Independence called "light and transient causes."

Despite his strictures on Parliament's absolute power, therefore, Blackstone's endorsement of the right of revolution indicates his belief in limited government and in consent as its foundation. It might be possible to believe in both these things without legitimizing revolution, but both are absolutely necessitated by any doctrine that holds revolution legitimate. Revolution is the withdrawal of consent, and that which was never given cannot be withdrawn. For Blackstone as well as Locke, the threat of revolution is the limit par excellence on those who govern.

The theme of consent permeates Blackstone's account of the English polity. It is directly involved, of course, in the constitution of the Commons[35] and indirectly in that of Parliament as a whole.[36] It even forms the basis of the king's title,[37] notwithstanding that the dynasty has sometimes been changed by force.[38] Prerogative itself is traced to a contract—apparently distinct from the primary social contract, though Blackstone calls it "original"—"between the prince and the subject."[39] That this contract takes a back seat to the primary one is indicated when Blackstone concedes that all the king's powers are subject to the control of the whole legislative power of which he forms a part.[40] Even the regal inheritance has been made conditional by law.[41]

Most striking of all, the common law itself is held to be founded on consent. To the questions, How are its maxims known? and How is their validity determined? Blackstone answers, "by the judges in the several courts of justice."[42] But quite another question is, from what source do the maxims of the common law derive their authority? They rest "entirely upon general reception and usage," i.e., the ancient and continuous consent of the people.[43] As the common law evolves in the hands of the judges, they must be guided by certain principles, such as that customs "must be *reasonable.*"[44] But the proof that the common law rests on tacit consent and not on some inherent judicial authority is that express consent (i.e., a statute) always takes precedence when in conflict with the common law.[45] In Blackstone's account of legislative power, this priority of statute over common law holds even when an unreasonable statute supplants a reasonable maxim of great antiquity in the common law.[46]

But has the reader not been told that the law of nature is found out by reason, that it forms the standard by which positive law is to be measured, and that judges are to be guided above all by reason? If so, then why should the judges not be considered as having a natural-law jurisdiction to correct, revise, or invalidate acts of Parliament in the name of reason? Like Hobbes's judges, Blackstone's are expected to interpret rationally in the interstices of the written law. But as in Locke, so in Blackstone: "The original power of judicature, by the fundamental principles of society, is lodged in the society at large."[47] From this it follows, that, since society lodges (quasi-)sovereignty, or the supreme ordinary power subject only to its own, in the legislature, adjudication is placed at a still further remove, subordinate to the legislative authority. Indeed, in England, the judicial power originated twice removed from the sovereign legislative as an arm of the executive.[48]

It is no depreciation of the contribution of Blackstone's judges, whether in the common law or by statutory construction, to say that the principal contributor to English liberty in the *Commentaries* is the mixed-regime character of the sovereign legislature—and coming in a close second is the separation of powers. Virtually all the most dearly bought freedoms of the English are embodied in statutes.[49] The ultimate security is the regime's foundation on consent, backed up by the threat of revolution.

The condemnation of natural-law jurisprudence implicit in Locke is explicit in Blackstone. For judges to attempt to control parliament, even when it "positively enact[s] a thing to be done which is unreasonable," would be "to set the judicial power above the legislature, which is subversive of all government."[50] We have already seen enough of his endorsement of Locke's teaching on usurpation to say that for Blackstone as well such judicial activism is corrosive of the social contract itself, for judges who engage in such a practice "make Laws without Authority, which the People are not therefore bound to obey,"[51] and come perilously close to necessitating the reversion of sovereign authority into the hands of the people at large.

Blackstone does come closer to constitutionalism than his predecessors did, for his detailed consideration of the rules of legal reasoning and statutory construction was to prove indispensable to the exercise of judicial review under a written constitution.[52] And his emphasis, much greater than that of Hobbes or Locke, on the constraints of law on the actions of those who most immediately govern the lives of private individuals (namely, executive and judicial magistrates) lights the way more brightly toward the sovereignty of laws—and hence of reason itself. But ultimately, for him too, the responsibility for the justice and rationality of the positive law is located in the sovereignty of men—immediately in the sovereignty of the ordinary legislators, finally in the sovereignty of the collected individuals who made that power what it is. Judges loom larger in the *Commentaries,* but their role remains ancillary, subordinate, even tertiary as a security for citizens' lives and liberties.

CHAPTER ELEVEN

Conclusion: Living Constitutionally

Whatever the misunderstandings in his quarrel with William Blackstone, James Wilson did put his finger on the great point of pride that Americans might celebrate as progress over the liberalism of Oxford's Vinerian Professor of Law: "The formation and establishment of constitutions are an immense *practical* improvement, introduced by the Americans into the science of government and jurisprudence."[1] But what changes theoretically about the principles discussed in the three preceding chapters? Everything—and nothing.

Theoretically, a written constitution clarifies the popular sovereignty that stands somewhat murkily behind Blackstone's "omnipotent" Parliament, Locke's "supream Legislative," and even (to a certain extent) Hobbes's absolute sovereign. The Constitution of the United States even emerges from the quasi-revolutionary act of supplanting the failed Articles of Confederation. As such, it is an exercise of sovereign legislative authority, delegating only so much power to the ordinary legislative, executive, and judicial magistracies as "We the People" choose to give. Such a commitment to writing of delegations and limits is no small addition to the social contract theory that the framers inherited. Yet on a theoretical plane it only formalizes and institutionalizes the social control of government that was informally present, but no less present in principle, in Locke and Blackstone.

Readers familiar with the titanic series of debates between Abraham Lincoln and Stephen A. Douglas in the 1858 Illinois campaign for the U.S. Senate may pause to wonder at my use of the phrase "popular sovereignty," which had been Douglas's favored expression for his policy of leaving the fate of slavery in the territories to the decision of local democratic majorities (though Lincoln's "second Freeport question" gave him no end of trouble in maintaining even that morally empty policy with any consistency).[2] But as Lincoln made plain more than once, Douglas's "popular sovereignty" was a misnomer: the genuine article "took tangible form in the noble words" of the Declaration of Independence, when a self-governing people chose to test majority rule against a set of self-evident truths that at once legitimized and set the limits of such rule.[3] Although Lincoln is remembered for emphasizing the just limits on popular sovereignty, it should not be forgotten that he just as consistently dedicated himself to the proposition that over the people of the United States there is no higher human power—certainly there is (in James Madison's words) no "will in the community independent of the majority."[4]

As James Wilson indicated, the signal advantages of written constitutions are practical ones. The people attain greater certainty regarding the powers of government and thus advance, perhaps immeasurably, toward a more reliably limited government. Institutional arrangements are rendered more permanent and sure: citizens know (and give it little further thought) how their public officials are chosen, who may be chosen and when,[5] what broad purposes they are responsible for carrying out, and what procedures may appropriately be used for effecting those purposes—none of which is nearly so permanent and sure wherever the supreme and ordinary legislative authorities are not practically as well as theoretically distinguished.

But perhaps the single greatest advantage of a constitution, as both charter of government and educational device (for citizens and public servants alike) is that, if well designed and amendable, it imparts a durability that makes the threat of social revolution recede well into the background. Jefferson to the contrary, a little revolution now and then is not a good thing; far better to have a frame of government strong enough to come through even the "house divided" of the Civil War fundamentally preserved and needing only amendment. And as that war proved, for one of the two parties of combatants at least, the Constitution had acquired, as intended, "that veneration which time bestows on everything."[6] Not only can such a constitution withstand the tests of time and crisis through its own intrinsic hold on the public mind, it can, as Madison hoped when proposing amendments in 1789, "by establish[ing] the public opinion in [its] favor" become "one mean to controul the majority from those acts to which they might be otherwise inclined."[7]

But surely, it will be said, there is a judicial role in that preservation.

That is true, but like many true things is taken by its proponents to such an extent as to swallow up other truths. The argument might run as follows: insofar as the Constitution creates a judiciary arguably co-equal with the other national branches, rather than distinctly subordinate to the legislative, it may be said that the framers rejected the teaching on the judicial function of those thinkers considered in Part Three. The Constitution, after all, seeks to "establish Justice" and "secure the Blessings of Liberty," in accordance with the "Laws of Nature and of Nature's God" of which the Declaration speaks, and establishes branches of government "so far connected and blended as to give to each a constitutional control over the others."[8] Taking these thoughts together, for instance, Sylvia Snowiss has recently suggested that an earlier notion should be recaptured of judicial review as "a substitute for revolution,"[9] defending "fundamental law" through "restraints on sovereign power."[10]

This, however, is to commit two serious errors. The first is to don blinkers and suppose judicial review to be equivalent to constitutionalism as such. *Constitutions* are a substitute for revolution, or more accurately, an expedient for forestalling them as long as humanly possible; judicial review, as I have argued repeatedly throughout this study, is not even the most important practical contributor to the preservation of constitutions.

The second error, into which Snowiss falls by confusing sovereignty with the ordinary legislative power, is to suppose that sovereign power is subject to the restraints of any "fundamental law" to be enforced from outside itself. The sovereign people are *morally* obliged to constitute government in accordance with the laws of nature; whether they do this job well or badly, they cannot be *practically* obliged by any subordinate power they have created to live any other way than by the contract they have settled among themselves. Richard Stevens has written that, through a written constitution, it "is as though that great, limitless power of the people, the Supreme Power, or the Legislative Power in the most comprehensive sense, shackled itself in its most sober moments so that when it should become drunk with passion it would be unable to execute the injustice wrought by passion."[11] This is the "reflection and choice" of which Hamilton speaks in *Federalist* No. 1.[12] But, adding to what Stevens has said, according to the politico-legal theory essentially attached to the Constitution, no one can be supposed to be more sober than the people were at the time they made their sober choice.

Our earliest jurists recognized this unlimited character of the power of a sovereign people. The frequency of approving citations of Blackstone, with suitable adaptation to the context of constitutionalism, is testimony to this. In Chapter 6, I have described how John Marshall adopted, as his standard of judicially cognizable law, Blackstone's definition of positive law.[13] More pointedly still, William Paterson, endorsing Blackstone's statement that "absolute despotic power . . . must in all governments reside somewhere," brought this principle firmly within the context of written constitutions, calling them "the work or will of the people themselves, in their original, sovereign and unlimited capacity."[14] Even that avowed adversary of Blackstone, James Wilson, echoed him (wittingly or not) when he said that from the people's "authority the constitution originates: for their safety and felicity it is established: in their hands it is as clay in the hands of the potter: they have the right to mould, to preserve, to improve, to refine, and to finish it as they please."[15]

Any advocate of a judicial authority to command what the Constitution does not command and to prohibit what the Constitution does not prohibit runs into insuperable difficulties. First, as Leslie Friedman Goldstein has pointed out with admirable simplicity, Articles III and VI speak of a judicial power and a supremacy principle explicitly linked to "this Constitution" and to nothing else.[16] Second, as Robert L. Clinton has painstakingly established, and as I too have argued in Chapter 4, judicial review does not even legitimately extend to violations under every part of the written Constitution.[17] How, if not even the whole of the Constitution is amenable to judicial enforcement, are we then to suppose a power that enforces what is "beyond the Constitution"?

Even if overcoming these hurdles were possible, a further obstacle awaits, that of finding the interpretive aids that can reliably lead to decision. Hadley Arkes's "appeal to reason" is far too facile, for as Locke said, the ignorance and interest of men (including judges) make the law of nature far more difficult to apply in "particular cases" than "an *establish'd,* settled, known [positive] *Law.*"[18] Appealing to the authority of the Declaration of Independence is an attractive prospect for some. But Madison, writing to Jefferson in 1825 on the subject of appropriate readings for the law school at the University of Virginia and recommending that "the true doctrines of liberty, as exemplified in our Political System, should be inculcated on those who are to sustain and may administer it," admitted that:

It is, at the same time, not easy to find standard books that will be both guides & guards for the purpose. Sidney & Locke are admirably calculated to impress on young minds the right of Nations to establish their own Governments, and to inspire a love of free ones; but afford no aid in guarding our Republican Charters against constructive violations. The Declaration of Independence, tho' rich in fundamental principles, and saying every thing that could be said in the same number of words, falls nearly under a like observation.[19]

Even Lincoln, while castigating Chief Justice Taney's *Dred Scott* opinion for doing "obvious violence to the plain unmistakable language of the Declaration," said that on "the merits of the decision . . . I could no more improve on McLean and Curtis, than [Stephen Douglas] could on Taney."[20] Neither McLean nor Curtis had relied in any way on the Declaration in his dissenting opinion.[21]

The Declaration itself, in keeping with the thesis of the last three chapters, locates the enforcement of the "Laws of Nature and of Nature's God" in one place only: the sovereign people. It is they who give their consent to the formation of government, delegating to it only "just powers" that it may secure the unalienable rights derived from human equality. They might consent to a government of greater power than it is wise to give, or they might witness a constructive expansion of their government of limited powers into one capable of a despotism they never intended. But the teaching of constitutionalism that emerges from the Declaration considers the people to be the sovereign lawgivers, and whatever the limits they may have omitted to place on political power through "some solemn and authoritative act,"[22] those cannot be imposed by judges, in whom citizens confide only one part of the trust to preserve the popularly created fundamental positive law. So long as the political process is still viable, democratic elections may provide the solution. Failing that, the Constitution contemplates one remedy for such a dilemma, in the amending process, although this too relies greatly on the integrity of elections. The Declaration contemplates the only other remedy: revolution, or the withdrawal of consent whenever a "long train of abuses and usurpations" shows the government to be destructive of the purposes of the social contract.

Snowiss has correctly noted that the "notion of a social contract [is] unintelligible outside the natural law tradition."[23] It is also quite consistently the case that the notion of a natural-law jurisdiction for judges is unintelligible *within* the social contract tradition. For the framers as for their philosophic teachers, the sovereignty of law depends radically on the sovereignty of men. The consistent avoidance of natural-law jurisprudence beyond the bounds of the written Constitution by our earliest jurists, documented in Chapter 6, stemmed precisely from a recognition of how the law of nature could be said to govern the universe of constitutional law: in establishing the solid ground for government by consent, the modern doctrine of natural law itself forbids judicial recourse to the laws of nature, in constitutional cases, where the positive law of the Constitution is silent.

Americans were fortunate to be blessed in the earliest generations of the republic with jurists who recognized a sovereign will when they saw one and recognized what that will had delegated them to do: not "adjust . . . clashing interests" with a view to the "public good"[24] nor "intermeddle with the prerogatives" of the other branches of government, but to maintain their courts' integrity as arenas for "decid[ing] on the rights of individuals."[25] (And by now it should be plain that what those rights *are*, in the large sense, is not for judges to decide.)

Beyond this formal responsibility under the Constitution, there is only one additional duty that the justices should perform. As I contended in Part I, they should undertake the informal rhetorical function of cementing the people's attachment to constitutional self-government. This, as I have argued, is properly a rhetoric neither deliberative nor forensic, but epideictic. It has the aim of keeping alive and vibrant the people's appetite for and ethic of genuine republican liberty. Joseph Story understood how much this appetite and this ethic are the true preservative forces of the Constitution:

> The structure has been erected by architects of consummate skill and fidelity; its foundations are solid; its compartments are beautiful, as well as useful; its arrangements are full of wisdom and order; and its defences are impregnable from without. It has been reared for immortality, if the work of man may justly aspire to such a title. It may, nevertheless, perish in an hour by the folly, or corruption, or negligence of its only keepers, THE PEOPLE. Republics are created by the virtue, public spirit, and intelligence of the citizens. They fall, when the wise are banished from the public councils, because they dare to be honest, and the profligate are rewarded, because they flatter the people, in order to betray them.[26]

In 1793, as one of our first justices of the Supreme Court, James Wilson had occasion to display the epideictic rhetoric appropriate to jurists in a republic:

To the constitution of the United States the term *sovereign* is to-tally unknown. There is but one place where it could have been used with propriety. But even in that place, it could not, perhaps, have comported with the delicacy of those who ordained and established that constitution. They might have announced themselves *sovereign* people of the United States: but serenely conscious of the past, they avoided the ostentatious declaration.[27]

The generation alive today, sadly, is not so conscious of the past as that which ordained and established the Constitution. When it comes to that document, we are foxes knowing many small things, and not at all hedgehogs who know the one big thing. We live with a judiciary so profligate that it hardly bothers any longer to flatter us as it betrays us. As part of the project of recapturing a proper sense of our own past, we, with our judiciary full of would-be "statesmen" claiming the final say over the meaning of the fundamental law, and regularly importing into that law such famous nonsense as rights "implicit in the concept of ordered liberty,"[28] may have to risk the indelicacy of ostentatiously declaring our sovereignty over our judicial servants. We may thank the structures of republican government for giving us a variety of opportunities to do so.

CHAPTER ONE. INTRODUCTION

1. I take the phrase from Walter Berns, *Taking the Constitution Seriously* (New York: Simon and Schuster, 1987).

2. Alexander M. Bickel, *The Least Dangerous Branch: The Supreme Court at the Bar of Politics,* 2d ed. (New Haven, Conn.: Yale University Press, 1986), 16.

3. Leslie Friedman Goldstein, *In Defense of the Text: Democracy and Constitutional Theory* (Savage, Md.: Rowman & Littlefield, 1991).

4. The phrase is from Hadley Arkes, *Beyond the Constitution* (Princeton, N.J.: Princeton University Press, 1990).

5. See Robert Lowry Clinton, *Marbury v. Madison and Judicial Review* (Lawrence: University Press of Kansas, 1989), 11–15.

6. Senate Committee on the Judiciary, *Nomination of Robert H. Bork To Be Associate Justice of the Supreme Court of the United States,* 100th Cong., 1st sess., 1987 (Washington, D.C.: Government Printing Office, 1989), 713–14.

7. 1 Cranch 137 (1803).

8. Senate Committee on the Judiciary, *Nomination of David H. Souter To Be Associate Justice of the Supreme Court of the United States,* 101st Cong., 2d sess., 1990 (Washington, D.C.: Government Printing Office, 1991), 329. Earlier, Judge Souter had deftly avoided the import of a question from Senator Charles Grassley (R-Iowa), who echoed Abraham Lincoln's concern that Court rulings make policy that is "irrevocably fixed" and thus prevent the people from being "their own rulers" (ibid., 141).

9. Senate Committee on the Judiciary, *Nomination of Judge Clarence Thomas To Be Associate Justice of the Supreme Court of the United States,* 102d Cong., 1st sess., 1991 (Washington, D.C.: Government Printing Office, 1993), pt. 1, 496.

10. Quoted by Senator Specter in Senate Committee on the Judiciary, *Nomination of Anthony M. Kennedy To Be Associate Justice of the Supreme Court of the United States,* 100th Cong., 1st sess., 1987 (Washington, D.C.: Government Printing Office, 1989), 221.

11. Quoted by Senator Specter in ibid., 222.

12. Ibid.

13. 376 U.S. 254 (1964).

14. Senate Committee, *Nomination of Anthony M. Kennedy*, 223–24.

15. Alexander Hamilton, James Madison, and John Jay, *The Federalist Papers*, ed. Clinton Rossiter (New York: Mentor, 1961), no. 51, 322.

16. Senate Committee, *Nomination of David H. Souter*, 142; emphasis added.

17. Ibid., 240.

18. 347 U.S. 483 (1954).

19. Senate Committee, *Nomination of David H. Souter*, 241.

20. Ibid., 240–41.

21. 410 U.S. 113 (1973).

22. The speech, given at New York University School of Law, is excerpted in "The Case Against the Case: Ruth Bader Ginsburg's Concerns About the Abortion Ruling," *Washington Post*, 20 June 1993, C3.

23. Quoted in Joan Biskupic, "Looking at Human Problems, with Judicial Restraint," *Washington Post*, 20 July 1993, A1, A6; emphasis in original.

24. Joan Biskupic, "Ginsburg Endorses Right to Choose Abortion, ERA," *Washington Post*, 22 July 1993, A1, A10.

25. 369 U.S. 186 (1962).

26. Joan Biskupic, "Ginsburg Hearings Elicit Sketchy View," *Washington Post*, 26 July 1993, A6.

27. Senate Committee, *Nomination of Robert H. Bork*, 97.

28. 381 U.S. 479 (1965).

29. 316 U.S. 535 (1942).

30. Compare Tribe's prepared testimony in Senate Committee, *Nomination of Robert H. Bork*, 1276–83, with the committee report, ibid., 6199–6205.

31. Ibid., 6199.

32. 6 Cranch 87 (1810).

33. 9 Cranch 43 (1815).

34. Joseph R. Biden, Jr., "Law and Natural Law: Questions for Judge Thomas," *Washington Post*, 8 September 1991, C1, C4.

35. See another attempt by Senator Biden to shore up such a distinction in response to an op-ed piece of my own; both articles appear as, "Is There a Hidden 'Litmus Test' for Nominees?," *Wilmington* (Del.) *Sunday News Journal*, 6 December 1992, F7, F10.

36. Senate Committee, *Nomination of Judge Clarence Thomas*, pt. 1, 2.

37. The reference is to *Lochner* v. *New York*, 198 U.S. 45 (1905), holding invalid a New York statute limiting the hours of work for bakers.

38. Senate Committee, *Nomination of Judge Clarence Thomas*, pt. 1, 2–3.

39. Ibid., 3.

40. 388 U.S. 1 (1967), holding invalid a Virginia antimiscegenation statute.

41. 262 U.S. 390 (1923), holding invalid a Nebraska statute prohibiting the teaching of modern foreign languages to children below the ninth grade.

42. 268 U.S. 510 (1925), holding invalid an Oregon statute effectively closing all private schools in the state, and requiring the attendance of virtually all children in public schools.

43. Senate Committee, *Nomination of Judge Clarence Thomas*, pt. 1, 4.

44. See Laurence H. Tribe, " 'Natural Law' and the Nominee," *New York Times*, 15 July 1991, A15.

45. 16 Wallace 130 (1873). Professor Tribe also cited *Bowers* v. *Hardwick,* 478 U.S. 186 (1986), in " 'Natural Law' and the Nominee."

46. Tribe, " 'Natural Law' and the Nominee."

47. Senate Committee, *Nomination of Judge Clarence Thomas,* pt. 1, 2.

48. Both Biden and Tribe also ascribed to the Court in *Bradwell* a dictum from Justice Bradley's concurring opinion—which will seem very sexist to many people today—about what nature intends as women's social functions.

49. Tribe, " 'Natural Law' and the Nominee."

50. I do not say that the charge of legal positivism has been proven against Judge Bork; yet ironically, in an otherwise fine article, he unjustly repeated the charge of "natural-law judging" against Justice Thomas. See Bork, "Natural Law and the Constitution," *First Things* 15 (March 1992): 16.

51. The entire speech appears in Senate Committee, *Nomination of Judge Clarence Thomas,* pt. 1, 150–67. Excerpts compiled by Senator Biden's staff of this and other Thomas speeches appear in ibid., 117–26. Colloquies about the Macedo remark appear in ibid., 111–16, 426–28.

52. Ibid., 166. The first two sentences here, along with the preceding one on Macedo, are included in the Biden staff compilation, ibid., 124–25—interestingly, under the following compiler's heading: "These quotes suggest Thomas will not support radical change in the Court's treatment of economic rights."

53. See, e.g., ibid., 189, 241–42, 270–71, 275–77.

PART ONE. POLITICAL PRUDENCE VS. JURIS PRUDENCE

1. See *U.S.* v. *Butler,* 297 U.S. 1 (1936), at 62, for a conspicuous and much-criticized example.

2. Morton J. Frisch and Richard G. Stevens, "Introduction," in Frisch and Stevens, eds., *American Political Thought: The Philosophic Dimension of American Statesmanship,* 2d ed. (Itasca, Ill.: F. E. Peacock, 1983), 6.

3. Ibid., 7.

4. Ibid.

5. Aristotle, *The Nicomachean Ethics,* trans. H. Rackham (Cambridge, Mass.: Harvard University Press/Loeb Classical Library, 1926, 1934), bk. 6, 1140b, p. 337; hereafter cited as *Ethics,* followed by book and Bekker pagination. I have corrected the translation in places.

6. Ibid., 1141a.

7. Ibid., 1141b.

8. Alexander Hamilton, James Madison, and John Jay, *The Federalist Papers,* ed. Clinton Rossiter (New York: Mentor, 1961), no. 78, 465.

9. See Gary L. McDowell, *Equity and the Constitution* (Chicago: University of Chicago Press, 1982).

10. See Donald L. Horowitz, *The Courts and Social Policy* (Washington, D.C.: Brookings Institution, 1977); Nathan Glazer, "Towards an Imperial Judiciary?" *The Public Interest* 41 (Fall 1975): 104–23.

11. See *Missouri* v. *Jenkins,* 495 U.S. 33 (1990).

12. *Ethics,* bk. 6, 1141b.

13. See ibid., 1141b–1143a.

14. Ibid., 1143a.

15. Ibid., 1143b.

16. My thanks to Professor Christopher Wolfe for suggesting this distinction.

17. Aristotle, *The "Art" of Rhetoric*, trans. J. H. Freese (Cambridge, Mass.: Harvard University Press/Loeb Classical Library, 1926), bk. 1, 1355b, p. 15; hereafter cited as *Rhetoric*, followed by book and Bekker pagination.

18. Ibid., 1357a.

19. Ibid., 1358a–b. See Larry Arnhart, *Aristotle on Political Reasoning: A Commentary on the "Rhetoric"* (DeKalb: Northern Illinois University Press, 1981), 48–50.

20. Arnhart, *Aristotle on Political Reasoning*, 58.

21. This is qualified by the need for equity's occasional correction of the written law (*Rhetoric*, bk. 1, 1374a–b; Arnhart, *Aristotle on Political Reasoning*, 106–7).

22. See Kathleen Hall Jamieson and Karlyn Kohrs Campbell, "Rhetorical Hybrids: Fusions of Generic Elements," *Quarterly Journal of Speech* 68 (1982): 146–57.

23. *Rhetoric*, bk. 1, 1359b, 1360b, 1362a.

24. Aristotle, *The Politics*, trans. Carnes Lord (Chicago: University of Chicago Press, 1984), bk. 3, 1286a–1287b, pp. 111–15.

25. Walter Berns, "Judicial Rhetoric," in Glen Thurow and Jeffrey D. Wallin, eds., *Rhetoric and American Statesmanship* (Durham, N.C.: Carolina Academic Press, 1984), 49.

CHAPTER TWO. STATESMANSHIP AND THE JUDICIARY

1. Alexis de Tocqueville, *Democracy in America*, ed. J. P. Mayer (Garden City, N.Y.: Doubleday Anchor, 1969), 150–51.

2. 492 U.S. 490 (1989).

3. *Marbury* v. *Madison*, 1 Cranch 137 (1803), at 177.

4. Diane Sawyer, anchoring ABC's "World News Tonight," 29 June 1989, referring to *Stanford* v. *Kentucky*, 492 U.S. 361 (1989).

5. *Planned Parenthood of Southeastern Pennsylvania* v. *Casey*, 112 S.Ct. 2791 (1992), Scalia, J., concurring in the judgment in part and dissenting in part, at 2884–85.

6. Ibid., at 2882.

7. Michael J. Perry, *The Constitution, the Courts, and Human Rights* (New Haven, Conn.: Yale University Press, 1982), 101.

8. Owen M. Fiss, "Two Models of Adjudication," in Robert A. Goldwin and William A. Schambra, eds., *How Does the Constitution Secure Rights?* (Washington, D.C.: American Enterprise Institute, 1985), 44.

9. Leonard W. Levy, *Original Intent and the Framers' Constitution* (New York: Macmillan, 1988), 396. See Lino A. Graglia's review of this book in *The Public Interest* 97 (Fall 1989): 97–105.

10. John Agresto, *The Supreme Court and Constitutional Democracy* (Ithaca, N.Y.: Cornell University Press, 1984), 143. At first glance, Agresto's view may seem quite similar to the one expressed by Walter Berns, quoted in Part I at note 25. But a closer look indicates that Agresto goes much further in his expectations for the Court.

11. Gary J. Jacobsohn, *Pragmatism, Statesmanship, and the Supreme Court*

(Ithaca, N.Y.: Cornell University Press, 1977). I think this thoughtful effort ultimately founders, not least in its concluding chapter, which upholds as a model of statesmanship Chief Justice Charles Evans Hughes's opinion for the Court in *Home Building and Loan Association* v. *Blaisdell,* 290 U.S. 398 (1934)—perhaps the most egregious disregard of the Constitution's plain meaning in the twentieth century.

12. Harry M. Clor, "Judicial Statesmanship and Constitutional Interpretation," *South Texas Law Journal* 26 (1985): 397–433. Like Jacobsohn, Clor's case is weakest in his choice of unfortunate examples of judicial "statesmanship": *Fletcher* v. *Peck,* 6 Cranch 187 (1810) (cf. the different treatment of this in Chapter 6); *Palko* v. *Connecticut,* 302 U.S. 319 (1937); *U.S.* v. *Reynolds,* 98 U.S. 145 (1879); *Pierce* v. *Society of Sisters,* 268 U.S. 510 (1925); *Shelley* v. *Kraemer,* 334 U.S. 1 (1948); and *Miller* v. *California,* 413 U.S. 15 (1973). In my view, only *Fletcher* and *Reynolds* were based on sound constitutional principles, though *Palko* was correct in its result. See also the reply to Clor by Lino A. Graglia, "Judicial Review on the Basis of 'Regime Principles': A Prescription for Government by Judges," *South Texas Law Journal* 26 (1985): 435–52.

13. Harry V. Jaffa, "What Were the 'Original Intentions' of the Framers of the Constitution of the United States?" *University of Puget Sound Law Review* 10 (1987): 351–448, reprinted in Jaffa, *Original Intent and the Framers of the Constitution: A Disputed Question* (Washington, D.C.: Regnery Gateway, 1994). See also Jaffa, letter to editor, *Commentary* (October 1987): 4; "Judge Bork's Mistake," *National Review,* 4 March 1988, 38; "A Right to Privacy?" *National Review,* 24 March 1989, 51; and letter to editor, *National Review,* 19 May 1989, 4.

14. There are others. See Paul Eidelberg, *The Philosophy of the American Constitution* (New York: Free Press, 1968; reprint, Lanham, Md.: University Press of America, 1986), 244–46; Robert Kenneth Faulkner, *The Jurisprudence of John Marshall* (Princeton, N.J.: Princeton University Press, 1968), vii, xv, 233, 237; John Hart Ely, *Democracy and Distrust: A Theory of Judicial Review* (Cambridge, Mass.: Harvard University Press, 1980), chaps. 4–6; Eugene Hickok, "On Federalism," *Benchmark* 3 (1987): 238.

15. Justice Antonin Scalia, in his concurring opinion in *Webster* v. *Reproductive Health Services,* appears at least to be moving in the right direction: "The outcome of today's case will doubtless be heralded as a triumph of judicial statesmanship. It is not that, unless it is statesmanlike to prolong this court's self-awarded sovereignty over a field where it has little proper business, since the answers to most of the cruel questions posed are political, not juridical—a sovereignty which therefore quite properly, but to the great damage of the court, makes it the object of the sort of organized pressure that political institutions in a democracy ought to receive" (492 U.S. 490 [1989], Scalia, J., concurring in part and concurring in the judgment, at 532). The justice recognizes the crucial difference between the political and the juridical without quite seeing the incongruity of judicial statesmanship—or rather, without quite seeing that it invariably results in the kind of "self-awarded sovereignty" that he condemns here. His opinion in *Casey,* quoted in the text at note 5, comes nearer to the mark.

16. Tocqueville, *Democracy in America,* 270.

17. Marvin Zetterbaum has noticed this; see his "Alexis de Tocqueville," in

Leo Strauss and Joseph Cropsey, eds., *History of Political Philosophy,* 3d ed., (Chicago: University of Chicago Press, 1987), 774.

18. A modern-day Tocqueville might not reach the same conclusions about the relation between the legal class and democratic majorities. Benjamin R. Twiss suggested over fifty years ago that this relationship went awry roughly contemporaneously with the creation of elite professional bar societies, including the American Bar Association, in the 1870s. See Twiss, *Lawyers and the Constitution* (Princeton, N.J.: Princeton University Press, 1942).

19. Tocqueville, *Democracy in America,* 269.

20. Ibid.

21. Ibid.

22. Ibid., 270.

23. Ibid., 150–51.

24. Ibid., 150.

25. Clor, "Judicial Statesmanship," 399–400.

26. Tocqueville, *Democracy in America,* 150.

27. Clor, "Judicial Statesmanship," 400.

28. Joseph Story, *Commentaries on the Constitution of the United States,* 1st ed. abridged (Boston: Hilliard, Gray, 1833; reprint, Durham, N.C.: Carolina Academic Press, 1987), sec. 908 (sec. 1736 in unabridged 1st ed.). The words quoted originally appear in Story's opinion for the Court in *Martin* v. *Hunter's Lessee,* 1 Wheaton 304 (1816), at 346–47; Story uses them in the *Commentaries* without quotation or attribution. This passage does not appear in the second edition (2 vols., Boston: Little, Brown, 1851), apparently omitted only for the sake of lengthier quotations from the *Federalist* and from Supreme Court rulings on the jurisdictional issues discussed at this point.

29. Story, *Commentaries,* 1st or 2d ed., sec. 424. See the similar depreciation by Hamilton of men's motives in supporting or opposing the Constitution, in Alexander Hamilton, James Madison, and John Jay, *The Federalist Papers,* ed. Clinton Rossiter (New York: Mentor, 1961), no. 1, 34–36. Hereafter cited as *Federalist.*

30. Story, *Commentaries,* 1st or 2d ed., sec. 426.

31. Lincoln's reply to Douglas, Ottawa debate, 21 August 1858, in Roy P. Basler, ed., *The Collected Works of Abraham Lincoln,* 9 vols., (New Brunswick, N.J.: Rutgers University Press, 1953), 3:27. It is noteworthy that Lincoln made this remark in the midst of an extended criticism of the Supreme Court's most notorious attempt to play the "statesman," *Dred Scott* v. *Sandford,* 19 Howard 393 (1857).

32. *Cohens* v. *Virginia,* 6 Wheaton 264, at 418 (1821).

33. "Statesman": *Federalist* 58:360; "statesmen": ibid. 10:80, 12:91, 36:219, and 70:424. See Thomas Engeman, Edward Erler, and Thomas Hofeller, *The Federalist Concordance* (Chicago: University of Chicago Press, 1988), 520.

34. *Federalist* 58:360.

35. *Federalist* 10:80.

36. Ibid., 77. See Martin Diamond, *The Founding of the Democratic Republic* (Itasca, Ill.: F. E. Peacock, 1981), 70–78; Marc F. Plattner, "American Democracy and the Acquisitive Spirit," in Robert A. Goldwin and William A. Schambra, eds., *How Capitalistic Is the Constitution?* (Washington, D.C.: American Enterprise Institute, 1982), 1–21; and Paul Peterson, "The Rhetorical Design and

Theoretical Teaching of *Federalist* No. 10," *Political Science Reviewer* 17 (1987): 193–218.

37. *Federalist* 10:83.

38. Excluding present members, justices of the Supreme Court historically have averaged roughly sixteen years of service. See Henry J. Abraham, *Justices and Presidents,* 2d ed. (New York: Oxford University Press, 1985), Appendix D, 386–91.

39. *Federalist* 70:423.

40. *Federalist* 71:432.

41. Ibid., 432–33.

42. Ibid., 434.

43. See Hamilton's warning in *Federalist* 72 (435–40) that an executive not indefinitely reeligible would, among other things, be dangerously prone to pandering to the people. The Twenty-second Amendment may be teaching us this lesson anew.

44. *Federalist* 62:380.

45. Ibid., 379.

46. *Federalist* 63:385.

47. Ibid., 384.

48. *Federalist* 51:324.

49. David F. Epstein, *The Political Theory of the Federalist* (Chicago: University of Chicago Press, 1984), 186. I shall argue a "somewhat apart from politics" thesis that provides greater distance than Epstein's argument. On the unusual publication history of the judiciary essays, see also James R. Stoner, Jr., *Common Law and Liberal Theory: Coke, Hobbes, and the Origins of American Constitutionalism* (Lawrence: University Press of Kansas, 1992), 197. I am indebted to Professor Stoner for pointing to the passage quoted from Epstein.

50. *Federalist* 78:471.

51. A recent variation on the usual interpretation of no. 78 is Robert A. Burt, *The Constitution in Conflict* (Cambridge, Mass.: Harvard University Press, Belknap Press, 1992). Burt drives a contrived wedge between Hamilton and Madison by overinflating the former's argument for judicial review into one for judicial supremacy and by missing the latter's consistent commitment to a limited version of judicial review; see pp. 52–66. See my review of his book in *Review of Politics* 56 (1994): 398–402. There is a brief treatment of Madison in Chapter 4, which may be compared to what is said of Hamilton here.

52. *Federalist* 78:466; emphasis added.

53. Fuller discussions of this issue appear in Chapters 4 and 5.

54. *Federalist* 78:470.

55. Ibid., 469.

56. Ibid., 470–71.

57. Ibid., 465.

58. Ibid.

59. Ibid., 466. Two who have are Christopher Wolfe, *The Rise of Modern Judicial Review: From Constitutional Interpretation to Judge-made Law* (New York: Basic Books, 1986), 75, and Robert Lowry Clinton, *Marbury v. Madison and Judicial Review* (Lawrence: University Press of Kansas, 1989), 70–71.

60. *Federalist* 78:465–66; emphasis added.

61. Ibid., 470–71; emphasis added.

62. See the similar usage of the word "rights" to denote not individual liberties but the rightful powers of a political office, in Madison's *Federalist* 51: "The interests of the man must be connected with the constitutional rights of the place" (322). It was common at the time of the founding to use "right" and "power" interchangeably in a way that can confound the modern reader; see also Thomas Hobbes, *Leviathan,* ed. Michael Oakeshott (New York: Collier, 1962), 134 ("From this institution of a commonwealth are derived all the *rights*" of a sovereign; emphasis in original); and John Locke, *Two Treatises of Government,* ed. Peter Laslett (New York: Mentor, 1965), bk. 2, sec. 3 ("*Political Power* then I take to be *a Right* of making Laws"; emphasis in original).

63. See Benjamin F. Wright, *The Growth of American Constitutional Law* (New York: Holt, Rinehart, and Winston, 1942; reprint, Chicago: University of Chicago Press, Phoenix Books, 1967), 24–25; and Robert G. McCloskey, *The American Supreme Court* (Chicago: University of Chicago Press, 1960), 9.

64. Clor, "Judicial Statesmanship," 399.

65. *Federalist* 78:470.

66. Stoner, *Common Law and Liberal Theory,* 204.

67. Epstein, *Political Theory,* 189. See also the casual and implausible description of this passage as expressing a Hamiltonian endorsement of extraconstitutional invalidation by courts of legislation advantaging certain interest groups or classes, in Howard Gillman, *The Constitution Besieged: The Rise and Demise of Lochner Era Police Powers Jurisprudence* (Durham, N.C.: Duke University Press, 1993), 32.

68. Apparently only Gary L. McDowell has noticed this aspect of *Federalist* 78 and connected it to the explicit discussion of equity in nos. 80 and 83. See McDowell, *Equity and the Constitution: The Supreme Court, Equitable Relief, and Public Policy* (Chicago: University of Chicago Press, 1982), 40–42.

69. Ibid., 42; emphasis added.

70. *Federalist* 80:480.

71. *Federalist* 78:470.

72. See Ann Stuart Diamond, "The Anti-Federalist 'Brutus,' " *Political Science Reviewer* 6 (1976): 269. See also Ralph A. Rossum, "The Courts and the Judicial Power," in Leonard W. Levy and Dennis J. Mahoney, eds., *The Framing and Ratification of the Constitution* (New York: Macmillan, 1987), 234; and Stoner, *Common Law and Liberal Theory,* 208.

73. Ann Stuart Diamond points out that "what Hamilton is really doing is trying to put the cat back *into* the bag; he is trying to make the best of Brutus' charges and turn the flank of a very dangerous argument" ("The Anti-Federalist 'Brutus,' " 277; emphasis in original). Ralph Rossum, arguing that no. 78 "fail[s] to provide much support for the inference that the Framers intended judicial review," contends (following Leonard Levy) that Hamilton's response to Brutus was merely tactical and points out that Hamilton never mentions judicial review in *Federalist* 33, on the limits of implied powers, or in *Federalist* 84, on enforcement of a bill of rights ("The Courts and the Judicial Power," 234–35). But if Hamilton was essentially in agreement with Madison that judicial review was limited to cases of "a judiciary nature" (Madison, quoted by Rossum, 236)—a subject discussed in Chapters 4 and 5—these omissions should not be surprising. And if Hamilton the clever tactician did not himself believe in judicial review as an inference from the Constitution, his easiest and most effective reply to Brutus would simply be to deny its existence.

74. *Federalist* 78:468–69.

75. See Brutus's essays nos. 11 through 15, in Herbert J. Storing, ed., *The Complete Anti-Federalist*, 7 vols. (Chicago: University of Chicago Press, 1981), 2:417–42.

76. *Federalist* 81:482; emphasis in original.

77. Brutus no. 11, in Storing, ed., *Complete Anti-Federalist*, 2:419. See the discussion of Hamilton's limited view of the equity power, text at notes 65–71.

78. *Federalist* 78:466; 81:482; emphasis added. See also Wolfe, *Rise of Modern Judicial Review*, 77.

79. *Federalist* 81:484–85.

80. Ibid., 485.

81. *Federalist* 78:471, 468–69, 465; 81:485.

82. Brutus no. 15, in Storing, ed., *Complete Anti-Federalist*, 2:440; emphasis in original.

83. Jesse H. Choper, *Judicial Review and the National Political Process* (Chicago: University of Chicago Press, 1980), 50.

84. Agresto, *Supreme Court and Constitutional Democracy*, 120.

85. Ibid.

86. See George Anastaplo, *The Constitution of 1787* (Baltimore: Johns Hopkins University Press, 1989), 33: "No other branch or officer of government can counteract what Congress does here, no matter how mistaken or wrong-headed Congress may be." But for an argument that the words "high Crimes and Misdemeanors" are limiting, see Raoul Berger, *Impeachment: The Constitutional Problems* (Cambridge, Mass.: Harvard University Press, 1973), esp. chap. 2, 53–102.

87. McCloskey, *American Supreme Court*, 47.

88. William H. Rehnquist, *Grand Inquests: The Historic Impeachments of Justice Samuel Chase and President Andrew Johnson* (New York: William Morrow, 1992), 134.

89. See Richard E. Ellis, *The Jeffersonian Crisis: Courts and Politics in the Young Republic* (New York: Oxford University Press, 1971), chaps. 5–7, 69–107. See also Berger, *Impeachment,* who argues that "his factional acquittal was a miscarriage of justice" (224).

90. Henry Adams, *History of the United States of America During the Administrations of Thomas Jefferson* (New York: Library of America, 1986), 465–66. Of the eight articles of impeachment prosecuted against Chase by the House of Representatives, only three (Articles III, IV, and VIII) commanded majority votes for a conviction in the Senate, though none drew the constitutionally required two-thirds vote for conviction. Questions of the factual truth of any of the charges to one side, these three articles no less than the other five (and in some respects more than those others) contained allegations of politically motivated improprieties that were difficult if not impossible to tie to the particulars of existing criminal law or even to the prevailing procedural expectations of judges in courts of law. See Samuel H. Smith and Thomas Lloyd, *Trial of Samuel Chase, an Associate Justice of the Supreme Court of the United States, Impeached by the House of Representatives for High Crimes and Misdemeanors, Before the Senate of the United States,* 2 vols. (Washington, D.C.: 1805; reprinted, New York: Da Capo Press, 1970), 2:485–92. The highest vote (nine-

teen of thirty-four senators voting to convict) came on the most politically charged of the allegations: Article VIII, which accused Chase of an "inflammatory political harangue" in charging a Maryland grand jury (ibid., 491). See also Eleanore Bushnell, *Crimes, Follies, and Misfortunes: The Federal Impeachment Trials* (Urbana: University of Illinois Press, 1992), chap. 4, 57–88. It bears noting that, insofar as Chase's impeachment came about as a result of his deeds and words while presiding over trials and grand jury proceedings on circuit, the debates during and outcome of his trial can shed very little light on the proper boundaries of the congressional impeachment power when applied to Justices of the Supreme Court sitting in their appellate capacity.

91. The possibility of abuse of the impeachment power where judges were concerned worried John Marshall, who wrote to Samuel Chase just before the latter's trial: "The present doctrine seems to be that a Judge giving a legal opinion contrary to the legislature is liable to impeachment. . . . I think the modern [i.e., recent] doctrine of impeachment shoud [sic] yield to an appellate jurisdiction in the legislature. A reversal of those legal opinions deemd [sic] unsound by the legislature woud [sic] certainly better comport with the mildness of our character than a removal of the Judge who has renderd [sic] them unknowing of his fault" (Marshall to Chase, January 23, 1805, in Herbert A. Johnson et al., eds., *The Papers of John Marshall*, 7 vols. to date [Chapel Hill: University of North Carolina Press, 1974–], 6:347).

Leonard Levy regards the letter as a "desperate plan for congressional review of the Court" to override judicial review (Levy, *Original Intent,* 84), but that both exaggerates and misses the point. First, Marshall's letter was a private one of sympathy for Chase, not a "plan" of some kind that Marshall ever considered making public. Second, the "legal opinions" that landed Chase in trouble with the Republicans were not given in the course of exercising judicial review, but in the course of instructing juries on circuit. Third, in this private letter Marshall may be engaging in a bit of bitter humor at the turn of events leading to Chase's trial. That is, one may take his reference to the "modern doctrine of impeachment" as a grimly mocking one, ridiculing the notion that Congress should take its impeachment power so far as to punish Chase for what he regarded as, at worst, a sort of intemperance from the bench. Nevertheless, the reference to an "appellate jurisdiction in the legislature" may be a sign of Marshall's acceptance of the coordinate power of Congress to interpret the Constitution with an authority, under many circumstances, equal to the judges'. Finally, it is plausible that Marshall subscribed to the view of impeachment offered by Hamilton in *Federalist* 81, since here he condemns that expedient only when it is used against a judge "unknowing of his fault," a description he apparently thought fit Chase.

92. Story, *Commentaries,* 2d ed., sec. 1635 (1st ed., sec. 1629).

93. In considering what are impeachable offenses, Story elsewhere rejects the notion of finding them only in criminal statutes but also recoils from absolute congressional discretion, preferring a middle ground that recurs to "parliamentary practice, and the common law" as "the only safe guide" (*Commentaries,* 2d ed., sec. 797; 1st ed., sec. 795). Since he also clearly regards impeachment as a "political" act (2d ed., sec. 786; 1st ed., sec. 784), there seems to be wide latitude for Congress to consider judicial invasions of its own authority as within the purview of impeachment.

94. *Federalist* 81:482; emphasis in original; 78:466, 469.

95. *Federalist* 81:483.

96. Clor, "Judicial Statesmanship," 407.
97. Perry, *The Constitution, the Courts, and Human Rights*, 101.

CHAPTER THREE. JOHN MARSHALL ON STATESMANSHIP

1. Felix Frankfurter, "John Marshall and the Judicial Function," in Frankfurter, *Of Law and Men: Papers and Addresses of Felix Frankfurter,* ed. Philip Elman (New York: Harcourt, Brace & World, 1956; reprint, Hamden, Conn.: Archon Books, 1965), 4.
2. Leonard W. Levy, *Original Intent and the Framers' Constitution* (New York: Macmillan, 1988), 44. See also Levy, "Marshall Court," in Leonard W. Levy, Kenneth L. Karst, and Dennis J. Mahoney, eds., *Encyclopedia of the American Constitution,* 4 vols. (New York: Macmillan, 1986), 3:1211–18.
3. Levy, *Original Intent,* chaps. 4, 7, 13.
4. Ibid., 88, 122.
5. Alexander Hamilton, James Madison, and John Jay, *The Federalist Papers,* ed. Clinton Rossiter (New York: Mentor, 1961), no. 1:33; hereafter cited as *Federalist.*.
6. See, e.g., Sanford Levinson, "Can One Account for Tastes in Constitutional Interpretation?" and Gary J. Jacobsohn, "Rules Are Not Enough: An Argument for Principled Unpredictability," in Sarah Baumgartner Thurow, ed., *Constitutionalism in Perspective* (Lanham, Md.: University Press of America, 1988); and Sotirios A. Barber, *On What the Constitution Means* (Baltimore: Johns Hopkins University Press, 1984), 154–59.
7. Robert H. Bork, *The Tempting of America: The Political Seduction of the Law* (New York: Free Press, 1989), 21. See my review in *Interpretation: A Journal of Political Philosophy* 19 (1991): 78–84.
8. Bork, *Tempting of America,* 21.
9. See, e.g., David P. Currie, *The Constitution in the Supreme Court: The First Hundred Years, 1789–1888* (Chicago: University of Chicago Press, 1985), 196–99.
10. Bork, *Tempting of America,* 28.
11. Edward S. Corwin, *John Marshall and the Constitution* (New Haven, Conn.: Yale University Press, 1919), 67, 124.
12. James Bradley Thayer, *John Marshall* (Boston: Houghton Mifflin, 1901), 57.
13. Albert J. Beveridge, *The Life of John Marshall,* 4 vols. (Boston: Houghton Mifflin, 1919), 3:132, 142.
14. Frankfurter, "John Marshall and the Judicial Function," 6; compare Beveridge, *Life of Marshall,* 1:v.
15. Frankfurter, "John Marshall and the Judicial Function," 5; compare Thayer, *John Marshall,* 63, and also Thayer, "The Origin and Scope of the American Doctrine of Constitutional Law," *Harvard Law Review* 7 (October 1893): 130ff.
16. Frankfurter, "John Marshall and the Judicial Function," 8; compare Corwin, *Marshall and the Constitution,* 124.
17. All the authors quoted in this paragraph published their views of Marshall in the twentieth century. Yet an earlier author, almost hagiographical in his treatment and writing approvingly of Marshall's jurisprudence for the most part, gives an assessment with which Thayer, Beveridge, Corwin, and Frank-

furter would probably agree: Allan B. Magruder, *John Marshall* (Boston: Houghton Mifflin, 1885, 1899).

18. Robert Kenneth Faulkner, *The Jurisprudence of John Marshall* (Princeton, N.J.: Princeton University Press, 1968), xvi.

19. Ibid., xii, xix.

20. Morton J. Frisch, "John Marshall's Philosophy of Constitutional Republicanism," *Review of Politics* 20 (1958): 34–45.

21. See ibid., pt. 2, 38–40.

22. This chapter and the two that follow are considerably indebted to three scholars who have influenced my reading of Marshall's judicial opinions: Wallace Mendelson, "Was Chief Justice Marshall an Activist?" in Mendelson, *Supreme Court Statecraft* (Ames: Iowa State University Press, 1985), 84–103; Christopher Wolfe, *The Rise of Modern Judicial Review: From Constitutional Interpretation to Judge-made Law* (New York: Basic Books, 1986) (see also Wolfe's "John Marshall and Constitutional Law," *Polity* 25 [1982]: 5–25, and "How to Read and Interpret the Constitution," in Thurow, ed., *Constitutionalism in Perspective*, 3–22); and Robert Lowry Clinton, *Marbury v. Madison and Judicial Review* (Lawrence: University Press of Kansas, 1989). None of these gentlemen, of course, is responsible in any way for the opinions I express here.

23. *Federalist* 10:80.

24. Ibid., 78.

25. *Federalist* 78:471.

26. At this point some readers will point to *Brown* v. *Board of Education,* 347 U.S. 483 (1954) as showing the Court at its finest, awakening the nation to the evils of segregation and inspiring action to combat racism. Whatever the constitutional merits of *Brown,* even if such an aberrant event were taken to be the hook on which a whole theory of judicial power is hung, such a view distorts history. Although the emerging activism of the modern civil rights movement, and the pressure for national legislation, have some links to the "new law" proclaimed in *Brown,* it remains true, as Wallace Mendelson has written, that "the real victories are won in legislatures and at the polls." Mendelson also notes that notable "southern desegregation did not come until Congress enacted the Civil Rights Act of 1964, along with the Voting Rights Act and the Elementary and Secondary Education Act of 1965. Revolutionary changes followed" (*Supreme Court Statecraft,* 156–57). See also Gerald N. Rosenberg, *The Hollow Hope: Can Courts Bring About Social Change?* (Chicago: University of Chicago Press, 1991), chap. 2, 42–71.

27. See generally Beveridge, *Life of Marshall,* 3:chap. 5 passim. See also Marcus Cunliffe's introduction to the only currently available reprint of Marshall's work, published as John Marshall, *George Washington,* 5 vols. (New York: Chelsea House, 1983), which is the 2d ed. of 1832, without the colonial history; hereafter cited as Marshall, *Life of Washington.* For a jaundiced view of Marshall's skills and integrity as a historian, see William A. Foran, "John Marshall as a Historian," *American Historical Review* 43 (1937): 51.

28. Jefferson to William Johnson, March 4, 1823, quoted in Beveridge, *Life of Marshall,* 3:267.

29. Quoted in Magruder, *John Marshall,* 233–34.

30. Ibid., 236.

31. Beveridge, *Life of Marshall,* 3:223.

32. Cunliffe, "Introduction," in Marshall, *Life of Washington,* vol. 1, eleventh and twelfth pages (the pages of this introduction are not numbered).

33. Robert K. Faulkner, "John Marshall," in Morton J. Frisch and Richard G. Stevens, eds., *American Political Thought: The Philosophic Dimension of American Statesmanship,* 2d ed. (Itasca, Ill.: F. E. Peacock, 1983), 106.

34. See, e.g., Samuel Cooper Thatcher in the *Monthly Anthology and Boston Review,* 1808, quoted in Beveridge, *Life of Marshall,* 3:269–70.

35. Marshall, *Life of Washington,* 1:165–66.

36. Ibid., 3:32.

37. Ibid., 121.

38. Ibid., 119–20n.

39. Ibid., 4:110.

40. Ibid., 149.

41. 9 Wheaton 1 (1824).

42. 6 Wheaton 264 (1821).

43. Marshall, *Life of Washington,* 4:147–63.

44. Ibid., 5:25. On the origins of the parties generally, see ibid., 4:247–48; 5:22–35.

45. *United States* v. *Maurice,* 2 Marshall's C.C. 96 (C.C.D.Va. 1823), reprinted in Philip B. Kurland and Ralph Lerner, eds., *The Founders' Constitution,* 5 vols. (Chicago: University of Chicago Press, 1987), 4:113.

46. Marshall, *Life of Washington,* 5:137–38.

47. Ibid., 138.

48. Ibid., 139.

49. Ibid., 152, 191. See Alexis de Tocqueville's use of Marshall to make much the same argument, in *Democracy in America,* ed. J. P. Mayer (Garden City, N.Y.: Doubleday Anchor, 1969), 229–30.

50. Marshall, *Life of Washington,* 5:166.

51. Ibid., 166–67.

52. First inaugural address, in Thomas Jefferson, *Writings,* ed. Merrill Peterson (New York: Library of America, 1984), 492–93.

53. *Federalist* 63:384.

54. Marshall, *Life of Washington,* 5:86.

55. Ibid., 283–84.

56. Ibid., 176–77.

57. Ibid., 106–7. For more on the positions of Jefferson and Hamilton while serving together, see ibid., 26–29.

58. Ibid., 4:195–97, 200–201.

59. 2 Dallas 409 (1792).

60. 3 Dallas 171 (1796).

61. 3 Dallas 199 (1796).

62. 2 Dallas 419 (1793).

63. Marshall, *Life of Washington,* 4:189–91.

64. Ibid., 192–95.

65. Ibid., 240–43; 5:n. 5.

66. Ibid., 5:10–11.

67. Ibid., 56–61.

68. Ibid., 201–7.

69. Arthur Conan Doyle, "The Adventure of Silver Blaze," in Doyle, *The Illustrated Sherlock Holmes* (New York: Crown, 1984), 172.

70. Marshall, *Life of Washington,* 4:191.

71. Ibid., 5:10. Washington vetoed the bill.

72. *Marbury* v. *Madison,* 1 Cranch 137 (1803).

CHAPTER FOUR. THE BREADTH OF NATIONAL JUDICIAL POWER
IN THE MARSHALL ERA

1. G. Edward White, *The Marshall Court and Cultural Change, 1815–1835,* abridged ed. (New York: Oxford University Press, 1991), 427. See also an earlier statement by the same author: "Marshall declared the independence of judges in *Marbury* v. *Madison,* making the appellate judiciary the final interpreter of the supreme law of the land" (*The American Judicial Tradition* [New York: Oxford University Press, 1976], 9).

2. *Marbury* v. *Madison,* 1 Cranch 137 (1803). For just a small sample of the prevailing view on *Marbury* and its significance, see Albert J. Beveridge, *The Life of John Marshall,* 4 vols. (Boston: Houghton Mifflin, 1919), 3:101–56; Leonard W. Levy, *Original Intent and the Framers' Constitution* (New York: Macmillan, 1988), 75–88; Robert G. McCloskey, *The American Supreme Court* (Chicago: University of Chicago Press, 1960), 26–53; Benjamin Fletcher Wright, Jr., *The Growth of American Constitutional Law* (New York: Holt, Rinehart and Winston, 1942; reprint, Chicago: University of Chicago Press, Phoenix Books, 1967), 33–54; Archibald Cox, *The Role of the Supreme Court in American Government* (New York: Oxford University Press, 1976), 9–16; Cox, *The Court and the Constitution* (Boston: Houghton Mifflin, 1987), 44–71; Alexander M. Bickel, *The Least Dangerous Branch: The Supreme Court at the Bar of Politics,* 2d ed. (New Haven, Conn.: Yale University Press, 1986), 1–33; Alpheus Thomas Mason, *The Supreme Court: Palladium of Freedom* (Ann Arbor: University of Michigan Press, 1962), 83; William W. Van Alstyne, "A Critical Guide to *Marbury* v. *Madison,*" *Duke Law Journal* (1969): 1; Susan Low Bloch and Maeva Marcus, "John Marshall's Selective Use of History in *Marbury* v. *Madison,*" *Wisconsin Law Review* (1986): 301. See also, at random, virtually any textbook on American government or casebook on constitutional law. The locus classicus of the *Marbury*-as-Federalist-politics thesis is Martin Van Buren, *Inquiry into the Origin and Course of Political Parties in the United States* (New York: Hurd and Houghton, 1867; reprint, New York: Augustus M. Kelley, 1967), 280–310.

3. See, e.g., John Agresto, *The Supreme Court and Constitutional Democracy* (Ithaca, N.Y.: Cornell University Press, 1984); Robert K. Faulkner, "John Marshall," in Morton J. Frisch and Richard G. Stevens, eds., *American Political Thought: The Philosophic Dimension of American Statesmanship,* 2d ed. (Itasca, Ill.: F. E. Peacock, 1983); and Gary J. Jacobsohn, *The Supreme Court and the Decline of Constitutional Aspiration* (Totowa, N.J.: Rowman and Littlefield, 1986). For a judicial "finalist" who eschews judicial statesmanship as well as activism, see Raoul Berger, *Congress v. the Supreme Court* (Cambridge, Mass.: Harvard University Press, 1969).

4. Robert Lowry Clinton, *Marbury v. Madison and Judicial Review* (Lawrence: University Press of Kansas, 1989). See also the excellent treatments by Wallace Mendelson, "Was Chief Justice Marshall an Activist?" in Mendelson, *Supreme Court Statecraft* (Ames: Iowa State University Press, 1985); Christopher Wolfe, *The Rise of Modern Judicial Review: From Constitutional Interpretation to Judge-made Law* (New York: Basic Books, 1986), 74–89; and P. Allan Dionisopoulos and Paul Peterson, "Rediscovering the American Origins of Judicial Review," *John Marshall Law Review* 18 (Fall 1984): 49. The most extensive critique of Clinton's analysis of *Marbury* is Dean Alfange, Jr., "Marbury v. Madison and Original Understandings of Judicial Review: In Defense of

Traditional Wisdom," *Supreme Court Review* (1993): 329–446 (pp. 332–35, and 385–413 are devoted expressly to Clinton), which unfortunately fails to come to grips with the full range of Clinton's argument and evidence.

5. 12 Serg. & Rawle 330 (Pa. 1825). The alleged incompatibility was first asserted in 1893 by James Bradley Thayer, "The Origin and Scope of the American Doctrine of Constitutional Law," *Harvard Law Review* 7 (1893): 49–132.

6. In the order given in this paragraph, the myths are refuted in Clinton, *Marbury and Judicial Review,* as follows: (1) chaps. 2 and 3, 31–55; (2) chap. 4, 56–77; (3) through (6) chap. 5, 81–101; (7) chap. 8, 128–38; (8) chap. 1, 4–30, and chap. 5, 81–101. For more on Clinton's book, see my review in *Review of Politics* 52 (1990): 485–87.

7. Clinton, *Marbury and Judicial Review,* 19–20, quoting William Blackstone, *Commentaries on the Laws of England* (Oxford: Clarendon Press, 1765–1769; facsimile reprint, Chicago: University of Chicago Press, 1979), 1:91. Blackstone himself cites as authority for this rule the famous decision of Sir Edward Coke in *Dr. Bonham's Case,* 8 Coke's Reports 107a (1610), at 118. For an excellent discussion of Coke and *Bonham's Case,* see James R. Stoner, Jr., *Common Law and Liberal Theory: Coke, Hobbes, and the Origins of American Consitutionalism* (Lawrence: University Press of Kansas, 1992), 48–68.

8. Clinton, *Marbury and Judicial Review,* 18, quoting Max Farrand, ed., *The Records of the Federal Convention of 1787,* rev. ed., 4 vols. (New Haven, Conn.: Yale University Press, 1937), 2:430. See also Clinton, *Marbury and Judicial Review,* 56–77. Cf. Robert A. Burt, *The Constitution in Conflict* (Cambridge, Mass.: Harvard University Press, Belknap Press, 1992), 57.

9. Clinton, *Marbury and Judicial Review,* 20, 24–30.

10. 1 Cranch 137, at 176–80. See Clinton, *Marbury and Judicial Review,* 16–18.

11. See the literature summarized, and the position taken, by Susan R. Burgess, *Contest for Constitutional Authority: The Abortion and War Powers Debates* (Lawrence: University Press of Kansas, 1992). For a critique of coordinate review, see Wolfe, *Rise of Modern Judicial Review,* 94–101; for a reply to Wolfe, see Clinton, *Marbury and Judicial Review,* 230–33.

12. See McLaughlin's view quoted and critiqued in Edward S. Corwin, *"Marbury* v. *Madison* and the Doctrine of Judicial Review," *Michigan Law Review* 12 (1914): 538–72, reprinted in Richard Loss, ed., *Corwin on the Constitution,* 3 vols. (Ithaca, N.Y.: Cornell University Press, 1987), 2:91, 99–103.

13. See William Winslow Crosskey and (in vol. 3) William Jeffrey, Jr., *Politics and the Constitution in the History of the United States,* 3 vols. (Chicago: University of Chicago Press, 1953–1980), 2: 938–1046. The quotation is from p. 1035. On this same page, however, Crosskey, while remarking that *Marbury* was "on its actual facts" a case within this "tripartite" theory, claims: "But the Supreme Court did not so treat the Marbury case; the right of reviewing the constitutionality of all acts of Congress was claimed generally; and there can be no reasonable doubt the Court intended so to claim it."

14. Ralph Rossum, "The Courts and the Judicial Power," in Leonard W. Levy and Dennis J. Mahoney, eds., *The Framing and Ratification of the Constitution* (New York: Macmillan, 1987), 236.

15. R. Kent Newmyer, "Marshall, John," in Kermit L. Hall, ed., *The Oxford Companion to the Supreme Court of the United States* (New York: Oxford University Press, 1992), 524. Cf. Burt, *Constitution in Conflict,* 119–20.

16. Corwin, "*Marbury* v. *Madison* and the Doctrine of Judicial Review," in Loss, ed., *Corwin on the Constitution,* 2:99.

17. 1 Stat. 20, 73–93. See Clinton, *Marbury and Judicial Review,* 63–66. For a denial that Articles III and VI call forth by their own terms an appellate power in the Supreme Court over state tribunals in cases involving questions of national power or the application of the federal Constitution to state acts, a claim that section 25 of the Judiciary Act was unwarranted and part of an underhanded Hamiltonian agenda of centralization, and a baffling attempt to tie all this to *Marbury,* see Van Buren, *Origin and Course,* 294–302.

18. 19 Howard 393 (1857). See Roy P. Basler, ed., *The Collected Works of Abraham Lincoln,* 9 vols. (New Brunswick, N.J.: Rutgers University Press, 1953), 2:387–88, 398–410, 494–96, 516–18; 3:89, 232–33, 255, 277–79, 316–17, 421, 435, 450–51, 460, 543–46; 4:268. See Clinton, *Marbury and Judicial Review,* 113–15. *Dred Scott,* of course, was the second invalidation of an act of Congress by the Court. In various passages cited above, Lincoln makes it plain that he did not merely think the decision wrong and in need of reversal; he thought the issue of the Missouri Compromise was none of the Court's business, and deserving of being ignored by the other branches as a "political rule." Whether he had in mind anything like a "cases of a judiciary nature" principle cannot be determined. On the debate and passage of the act of 1862, prohibiting slavery in the territories in the face of *Dred Scott,* see Henry Wilson, *History of the Antislavery Measures of the Thirty-seventh and Thirty-eighth United States Congresses, 1861–64* (Boston: Walker, Wise, 1864), 92–109.

19. Clinton himself does not provide a detailed breakdown of the Constitution along the lines that follow, though he does give examples of particular provisions. One should proceed here with some caution. Although it is fair to say, as Clinton does, that judicial review is "a special case of statutory construction" (see text at note 9 above), statutory construction is itself but an occasional recourse of common law courts in the decision of particular legal disputes. Hence, while it is true that statutes control common law precedent, and the Constitution controls statute law, the effort of the judge in any particular case is to do justice by the parties according to *the* law, meaning whatever manner of law appropriately applies. This understanding of the essence of the judicial function encourages a sober resistance to any temptation toward facile compartmentalization of the Constitution's provisions with respect to "final" and "non-final" judicial decision-making. I am indebted to Professor James R. Stoner, Jr., for his urging of such sobriety in these matters. For a sensitive account of the common law elements in American constitutionalism, see his *Common Law and Liberal Theory,* esp. 5–9, 205–11, 216–25 (although it may become clear to readers of Part Three how much I disagree with Stoner's argument that "in the founding of American law and the establishment of the Constitution as law, it is more accurate to say that liberal insights are assimilated into a common law context than to argue the reverse" [ibid., 178], unless we are prepared to say that that which is assimilated comes to dominate and dictate the shape of that into which it is assimilated).

20. Clinton, *Marbury and Judicial Review,* 29.

21. *Marbury,* at 176; emphasis added.

22. Ibid., at 177.

23. Mason, *Supreme Court: Palladium of Freedom,* 94.

24. *Marbury,* at 178.

25. Ibid., at 179. Robert A. Burt, like most who read *Marbury,* sees only

three examples here, omitting the first for reasons explored in the text (*The Constitution in Conflict*, 119). Robert Clinton has combined the second and third into one example but thus includes, in his list of three, all four of the examples I have identified (*Marbury and Judicial Review*, 135).

26. *Marbury*, at 178.

27. Ibid., at 178.

28. For an example of judicial refusal to give effect to such an act, see *United States* v. *Klein*, 13 Wallace 128 (1872).

29. *Marbury*, at 179.

30. Ibid., at 170. See Clinton, *Marbury and Judicial Review*, 90, 99.

31. *Marbury*, at 179.

32. Ibid., at 174–75.

33. 2 Dallas 297 (1793). Charles Lee cited this case erroneously, attempting to make another point while arguing *Marbury*, at 148. See Clinton, *Marbury and Judicial Review*, 84–85.

34. 6 Wheaton 264 (1821), at 399–402. See Clinton, *Marbury and Judicial Review*, 96–97.

35. *Cohens*, at 404–5.

36. *Marbury*, at 170.

37. Ibid., at 179. Clinton raises the possibility that such a case might come to the Court from the state courts, under section 25 of the Judiciary Act of 1789, with the result that the Court could affirm a state judgment against the tax. But he finds no final authority present in such an instance. Clinton, *Marbury and Judicial Review*, 136.

38. As an aside, it should be noted that Congress would probably not call it an export tax—more likely something such as an exporter's license fee, charged on a sliding scale according to a previous year's shipments. What then for the Court? Is this a "tax or duty" within the prohibition? Opinions will differ, and Congress's will prevail over the Court's if it is determined.

39. 5 Cranch 115 (1809), at 136.

40. Ibid., at 139–40.

41. 5 Cranch 303 (1809). See David P. Currie's discussion of this case, in *The Constitution in the Supreme Court: The First Hundred Years, 1789–1888* (Chicago: University of Chicago Press, 1985), 89.

42. 5 Cranch 344 (1809).

43. 5 Peters 1 (1831).

44. 3 Cranch 159 (1805).

45. 6 Cranch 307 (1810).

46. See discussion of these cases in Gary L. McDowell, *Curbing the Courts: The Constitution and the Limits of Judicial Power* (Baton Rouge: Louisiana State University Press, 1988), 124. See also the citation of *Durousseau* in *ex parte McCardle*, 7 Wallace 506 (1869), at 513.

47. 3 Wheaton 336 (1818).

48. 5 Cranch 61, at 86, 91. See Currie, *Constitution in the Supreme Court*, 85–89. The first point here was obviated by the act incorporating the Second Bank; see *Osborn* v. *Bank of the United States*, 9 Wheaton 738 (1824).

49. 5 Cranch 61, at 83. See also *Cohens* v. *Virginia*, 6 Wheaton 264 (1821), at 404.

50. Clinton, *Marbury and Judicial Review*, 20.

51. For an excellent treatment of those canons of interpretation, applying equally to statutory and constitutional construction, see Wolfe, *Rise of Modern*

Judicial Review, 18–19; and Wolfe, "How to Read and Interpret the Constitution," in Sarah Baumgartner Thurow, ed., *Constitutionalism in Perspective,* (Lanham, Md.: University Press of America, 1988), 4–14.

52. 2 Cranch 445 (1804). See Currie, *Constitution in the Supreme Court,* 82–84.

53. 6 Cranch 332 (1810).

54. 1 Peters 511 (1828).

55. See the reliance on *Canter* by Justices McLean and Curtis, dissenting in *Dred Scott,* 19 Howard 393, at 540–41, 613, and Curtis's citation of *Sere* in ibid., at 613.

56. 10 Wheaton 152 (1825).

57. See also Clinton, *Marbury and Judicial Review,* 116–27, for a comprehensive review of all the Supreme Court opinions through 1983 in which *Marbury* was cited as precedent.

58. 6 Wheaton 264 (1821).

59. Beveridge, *Life of Marshall,* 4:342–70.

60. Currie, *Constitution in the Supreme Court,* 102.

61. Beveridge remarks: "In *Cohens* v. *Virginia,* John Marshall stamped upon the brow of Localism the brand of illegality. If this is not the true interpretation of his opinion in that case, all of the exalted language he used is mere verbiage" (*Life of Marshall,* 4:353).

62. 6 Wheaton 264, at 383.

63. Ibid., at 415.

64. Ibid., at 384, 388, 391; emphasis added.

65. See Clinton, *Marbury and Judicial Review,* 25–26. See also Wallace Mendelson, "Jefferson on Judicial Review: Consistency Through Change," in Mendelson, *Supreme Court Statecraft,* 215–25. For a recent account of Jefferson's evolving thought on judicial power, see David N. Mayer, *The Constitutional Thought of Thomas Jefferson* (Charlottesville: University Press of Virginia, 1994), 257–94. Mayer argues that the "tripartite doctrine was fully developed in Jefferson's mind by the time of his presidency," that the *Marbury* case was decided on a "really quite narrow principle" that made no claim "that the Court's judgment was superior to that of other branches," and that the *Marbury* result thus "accorded logically with [Jefferson's] own constitutional theory" (ibid., 268, 273).

66. Farrand, ed., *Records of the Federal Convention,* 2:430. See generally Clinton, *Marbury and Judicial Review,* 56–66.

67. Clinton, *Marbury and Judicial Review,* 26–28. See also Madison's "Helvidius" no. 1, 24 August 1793, in William T. Hutchinson et al., eds., *The Papers of James Madison,* 22 vols. to date (Chicago: University of Chicago Press [vols. 1–10], 1962–1977; Charlottesville: University Press of Virginia [vols. 11–22], 1977–), 15:73; hereafter cited as *Papers of Madison.*

68. Alexander Hamilton, James Madison, and John Jay, *The Federalist Papers,* ed. Clinton Rossiter (New York: Mentor, 1961), no. 44:286; emphasis added; hereafter cited as *Federalist.*

69. Madison, "Helvidius" no. 2, *Papers of Madison,* 15:83; emphasis in original.

70. Ibid., 84.

71. Ibid., 17:311.

72. Ibid.

73. Ibid.; emphasis in original.

74. Madison to Roane, 2 September 1819, in Marvin Meyers, ed., *The Mind of the Founder: Sources in the Political Thought of James Madison* (Indianapolis: Bobbs-Merrill, 1973), 458.

75. Ibid., 459–60.

76. Letter to *North American Review,* 28 August 1830, in ibid., 538.

77. "Notes on Nullification," in ibid., 568.

78. "Observations on a Draught of a Constitution for Virginia," in *Papers of Madison,* 11:293.

79. Madison to Jefferson, 24 October/1 November 1787, in James Morton Smith, ed., *The Republic of Letters: The Correspondence between Thomas Jefferson and James Madison, 1776–1826,* 3 vols. (New York: W. W. Norton, 1995), 1:503. Also see *Federalist* 84:510–20.

80. Jefferson to Madison, 6 February 1788, in Smith, ed., *Republic of Letters,* 1:530.

81. Madison to Jefferson, 17 October 1788, in ibid., 565.

82. Ibid., 566; emphasis in original.

83. Jefferson to Madison, 15 March 1789, in ibid., 587.

84. Speech of 8 June 1789, in *Papers of Madison,* 12:206–7.

85. Ibid., 206.

86. Ibid., 201–2.

87. Ibid., 203.

88. Ibid., 200.

89. Ibid., 206.

90. Ibid., 201–2.

91. Ibid., 206–7.

92. Ibid., 206; emphasis added.

93. Ibid., 207; emphasis added.

94. Ibid., 205.

95. Ibid., 204–5.

96. *Federalist* 78:466.

97. Rossum, "The Courts and the Judicial Power," 234–35.

98. Hamilton, "Opinion on the Constitutionality of an Act to Establish a Bank," in Harold C. Syrett et al., eds., *The Papers of Alexander Hamilton,* 26 vols. (New York: Columbia University Press, 1961–1979), 8:97–134.

99. Joseph Story, *Commentaries on the Constitution of the United States,* 2d ed., 2 vols. (Boston: Little, Brown, 1851), 1: secs. 373–96.

100. This narrowing was accomplished chiefly by an insistence on a "textually demonstrable constitutional commitment" of an issue to some branch other than the judiciary, in *Baker* v. *Carr,* 369 U.S. 186 (1962), at 217.

101. Story, *Commentaries,* 1:sec. 374; emphasis added.

102. *Gibbons* v. *Ogden,* 9 Wheaton 1 (1824), at 197.

103. Story, *Commentaries,* 1:sec. 375.

104. Burt, *Constitution in Conflict,* 148.

105. Note here that near the end of the work, in discussing the supremacy clause, Story says of federal laws invading the reserved powers of the states that "they will be merely acts of usurpation, and will deserve to be treated as such"—but by whom he does not say (*Commentaries,* 2:sec. 1837).

106. Ibid., 1:sec. 376.

107. Ibid., sec. 383.

108. Ibid., 2:sec. 1865, quoting James Kent, *Commentaries on American*

Law, 1st ed., 2 vols. (New York: O. Halsted, 1826; reprint, New York: Da Capo Press, 1971), 2:6.

109. When discussing the Sedition Act of 1798 in his treatment of freedom of the press, Story refers to the act as having been "deliberately affirmed by the courts of law, and in a report made by a committee of congress," a characterization that certainly gives no priority to the judgment of the former over that of the latter. Story, *Commentaries,* 2:sec. 1892.

110. Ibid., secs. 1768–72.

111. Ibid., secs. 1782–94.

112. Ibid., sec. 1646; emphasis in original.

113. Ibid.

114. Ibid., sec. 1647.

115. Ibid., 1:sec. 374.

116. Franck, review of *Marbury v. Madison and Judicial Review,* by Robert Lowry Clinton, *Review of Politics* 52 (1990): 487.

117. *Cooper* v. *Aaron,* 358 U.S. 1 (1958), at 18.

CHAPTER FIVE. THE "NATIONALISM" OF *MCCULLOCH V. MARYLAND*

1. John Taylor, *Construction Construed and Constitutions Vindicated* (Richmond, Va.: Shepherd and Pollard, 1820; reprint, New York: Da Capo Press, 1970), 84, 103.

2. 9 Wheaton 1 (1824).

3. 12 Wheaton 419 (1827). Note that in this case Marshall, supposing a hypothetical federal license tax on exporters (contrary to Art. I, sec. 9), asks how Congress could "shield itself" from "just censure" for such a law; he does not ask how it could shield itself from a judicial invalidation of the law (ibid., at 445). See Chapter 4, text accompanying notes 30–37.

4. 4 Peters 410 (1830).

5. 4 Wheaton 316 (1819).

6. Albert J. Beveridge, *The Life of John Marshall,* 4 vols. (Boston: Houghton Mifflin, 1919), 4:282.

7. Edward S. Corwin, *John Marshall and the Constitution* (New Haven, Conn.: Yale University Press, 1919), 128.

8. Robert Kenneth Faulkner, *The Jurisprudence of John Marshall* (Princeton, N.J.: Princeton University Press, 1968), 102.

9. For rare contrary views see Christopher Wolfe, *The Rise of Modern Judicial Review: From Constitutional Interpretation to Judge-made Law* (New York: Basic Books, 1986), 41; Wallace Mendelson, *Supreme Court Statecraft* (Ames: Iowa State University Press, 1985), 92–93; and Robert Lowry Clinton, *Marbury v. Madison and Judicial Review* (Lawrence: University Press of Kansas, 1989), 194–96.

10. Richard E. Ellis, "*McCulloch* v. *Maryland,*" in Kermit L. Hall, ed., *The Oxford Companion to the Supreme Court of the United States* (New York: Oxford University Press, 1992), 537. See also, for a less moderate—and thus more typical—view, Leonard W. Levy, "*McCulloch* v. *Maryland,*" in Leonard W. Levy, Kenneth L. Karst, and Dennis J. Mahoney, eds., *Encyclopedia of the American Constitution,* 4 vols. (New York: Macmillan, 1986), 3:1234–37.

11. John Marshall, "A Friend of the Constitution," no. 4, 3 July 1819, in

Gerald Gunther, ed., *John Marshall's Defense of McCulloch v. Maryland* (Stanford, Calif.: Stanford University Press, 1969), 182.

12. Following some introductory remarks, the first question is treated on pp. 401–25 of 4 Wheaton, the second question on pp. 425–37.

13. See Clinton, *Marbury and Judicial Review,* 194–96.

14. David P. Currie, *The Constitution in the Supreme Court: The First Hundred Years, 1789–1888* (Chicago: University of Chicago Press, 1985), 160.

15. 1 Stat. 20, at 73–93; reprinted in Henry Steele Commager, ed., *Documents of American History,* 5th ed. (New York: Appleton-Century-Crofts, 1949), 153–55.

16. 4 Wheaton 316, at 402, 404, 408, 409, 410, 412, 413, 417, 418–19, 419 (twice).

17. Ibid., at 402.

18. Ibid., at 404.

19. Ibid., at 408–9.

20. Ibid., at 409.

21. Ibid., at 412.

22. Ibid., at 413.

23. Ibid., at 419.

24. Corwin, *Marshall and the Constitution,* 130. Cf. Leonard W. Levy, "Marshall Court," in Levy, Karst, and Mahoney, eds., *Encyclopedia of the American Constitution,* 3:1214.

25. These essays by "Amphictyon" (probably William Brockenbrough) and "Hampden" (definitely Spencer Roane), along with Marshall's pseudonymous articles in reply, are reprinted in Gunther, ed., *Marshall's Defense.* For the charge of "travelling out of the case," see "Amphictyon," no. 1, 30 March 1819, 55; "Hampden," no. 1, 11 June 1819, 110–11.

26. Marshall, "A Friend of the Constitution," no. 1, 30 June 1819, in ibid., 158. See also his "A Friend to the Union," nos. 1 and 2, 24 and 28 April 1819, in ibid., 82–84, 104–5.

27. "Hampden," no. 1, 11 June 1819, in ibid., 110.

28. *McCulloch* v. *Maryland,* 4 Wheaton 316, at 402.

29. Ibid., at 401.

30. Ibid., at 402.

31. Ibid., at 401.

32. 5 Cranch 61 (1809).

33. 4 Wheaton 316, at 401.

34. Marshall, "A Friend to the Union," no. 2, 28 April 1819, in Gunther, ed., *Marshall's Defense,* 104.

35. *United States* v. *Fisher,* 2 Cranch 358 (1805).

36. John Marshall, *The Life of George Washington,* 2d ed. (1832); reprinted as *George Washington,* 5 vols. (New York: Chelsea House, 1983), 4:240–43; hereafter cited as Marshall, *Life of Washington.*

37. Ibid., 5:note 5, pp. 4–8 of notes. This was note 3 in the first edition of 1807 and was reproduced unchanged in the second edition of 1832. Compare it with the opinions in Thomas Jefferson, *Writings,* ed. Merrill Peterson (New York: Library of America, 1984), 416–21; and Harold C. Syrett et al., eds., *The Papers of Alexander Hamilton,* 26 vols. (New York: Columbia University Press, 1961–1979), 8:97–134. Comparison of the note with Marshall's *McCulloch* opinion is also fruitful.

38. Currie, *Constitution in the Supreme Court,* 165.

39. 4 Wheaton 316, at 423; emphasis added. See also ibid., at 419.

40. Marshall, *Life of Washington,* 5:note 5, p. 8 of notes.

41. 4 Wheaton 316, at 420. See also Marshall, "A Friend to the Union," no. 2, 28 April 1819, and "A Friend of the Constitution," no. 3, 2 July 1819, in Gunther, ed., *Marshall's Defense,* 96–97, 176.

42. See "A Friend of the Constitution," nos. 1, 4, and 5, 30 June and 3 and 5 July 1819, in ibid., 156–57, 182–84, 186–87, 190.

43. 2 Cranch 358 (1805), at 396.

44. Ibid.

45. Alexander Hamilton, James Madison, and John Jay, *The Federalist Papers,* ed. Clinton Rossiter (New York: Mentor, 1961), no. 23:153; emphasis in original. Hereafter cited as *Federalist.*

46. Ibid., 156.

47. Ibid.

48. Currie, *Constitution in the Supreme Court,* 165.

49. Ibid., 325 n. 284.

50. 4 Wheaton 316, at 400–401.

51. Ibid., at 400.

52. 6 Wheaton 264 (1821), at 424–25.

53. 4 Wheaton 316 (1819), at 401.

54. Max Farrand, ed., *The Records of the Federal Convention of 1787,* rev. ed., 4 vols. (New Haven, Conn.: Yale University Press, 1937), 1:164–68.

55. 4 Wheaton 316, at 423; emphasis added.

56. 6 Wheaton 264 (1821), at 404–5.

57. 4 Wheaton 316, at 423.

58. Ibid., at 421.

59. Ellis, *"McCulloch* v. *Maryland,"* in Hall, *Oxford Companion to the Supreme Court,* 538.

60. Marshall, "A Friend to the Union," no. 2, 28 April 1819, in Gunther, ed., *Marshall's Defense,* 103.

61. Andrew Jackson, veto message, 10 July 1832, in James D. Richardson, ed., *A Compilation of the Messages and Papers of the Presidents,* 20 vols. (New York: Bureau of National Literature, 1897), 3:1146.

62. Webster's remarks in the Senate are excerpted in Louis Fisher, *American Constitutional Law* (New York: McGraw-Hill, 1990), 81.

63. Beveridge, *Life of Marshall,* 4:533.

64. Marshall, "A Friend to the Union," no. 2, 28 April 1819, in Gunther, ed., *Marshall's Defense,* 104–5.

PART TWO. NATURAL LAW IN THE SUPREME COURT

1. Alexander Hamilton, James Madison, and John Jay, *The Federalist Papers,* ed. Clinton Rossiter (New York: Mentor, 1961), no. 51:324.

2. Richard G. Stevens, "Liberal Democracy and Justice in the Constitution of Walter Berns," *Political Science Reviewer* 22 (1993): 85; emphasis in original.

3. Thomas C. Grey, "Do We Have an Unwritten Constitution?" *Stanford Law Review* 27 (1975): 703, and "Origins of the Unwritten Constitution: Fundamental Law in American Revolutionary Thought," ibid. 30 (1978): 843; Harry V. Jaffa, "What Were the 'Original Intentions' of the Framers of the Constitution of the United States?" *University of Puget Sound Law Review* 10

(1987): 351, and "The Closing of the Conservative Mind," *National Review,* 9 July 1990, 40. See also the contributions by Hadley Arkes, Russell Hittinger, and William Bentley Ball to "Natural Law and the Law: An Exchange," *First Things* 17 (May 1992): 45–54.

4. Gary L. McDowell, *Curbing the Courts: The Constitution and the Limits of Judicial Power* (Baton Rouge: Louisiana State University Press, 1988), 49; emphasis in original. This remark appears in one of the most cogent reviews available of recent constitutional theorizing, criticizing most sharply the work of R. Dworkin, J. H. Ely, J. Choper, L. Lusky, L. Tribe, M. Perry, P. Bobbitt, and A. S. Miller. See McDowell's chap. 1 passim.

5. Roscoe Pound, "Liberty of Contract," *Yale Law Journal* 18 (1909): 454.

6. Benjamin Fletcher Wright, Jr., *American Interpretations of Natural Law: A Study in the History of Political Thought* (Cambridge, Mass.: Harvard University Press, 1931; reprint, New York: Russell and Russell, 1962), 280–306.

7. Edward S. Corwin, *The Twilight of the Supreme Court* (New Haven, Conn.: Yale University Press, 1934; reprint, Hamden, Conn.: Archon Books, 1970), 52–101.

8. Walter Berns, "Judicial Review and the Rights and Laws of Nature," *Supreme Court Review* (1982): 49–83; reprinted in Berns, *In Defense of Liberal Democracy* (Chicago: Regnery Gateway, 1984), 29–62.

9. Gary J. Jacobsohn, "E.T.: The Extra-Textual in Constitutional Interpretation," *Constitutional Commentary* 1 (1984): 21–42.

10. Leonard W. Levy, *Original Intent and the Framers' Constitution* (New York: Macmillan, 1988), 124–36.

11. Robert H. Bork, *The Tempting of America: The Political Seduction of the Law* (New York: Free Press, 1989), 19–49.

12. Levy, *Original Intent,* 130.

13. Ibid., 397.

14. Bork, *Tempting of America,* 20.

15. 2 Dallas 304 (1795).

16. 3 Dallas 386 (1798).

17. 6 Cranch 87 (1810).

18. 9 Cranch 43 (1815).

19. 6 Fed. Cas. no. 3230 (C.C.E.D.Pa. 1823).

20. 12 Wheaton 213 (1827).

21. 2 Peters 627 (1829).

22. See Pound, "Liberty of Contract," 464–66; Wright, *American Interpretations,* 305–6; and Corwin, *Twilight of the Supreme Court,* 55–62. For recent interpreters who follow this pattern, see James W. Ely, Jr., *The Guardian of Every Other Right: A Constitutional History of Property Rights* (New York: Oxford University Press, 1992), 81, and Howard Gillman, *The Constitution Besieged: The Rise and Demise of Lochner Era Police Powers Jurisprudence* (Durham, N.C.: Duke University Press, 1993), 45–60.

23. Leonard W. Levy, Kenneth L. Karst, and Dennis J. Mahoney, eds., *Encyclopedia of the American Constitution,* 4 vols. (New York: Macmillan, 1986).

24. Frank R. Strong, "Fundamental Law and the Supreme Court," in ibid., 2:827–28.

25. Thomas C. Grey, "Higher Law," in ibid., 2:914–17.

26. Laurence H. Tribe, "Substantive Due Process of Law," in ibid., 4:1796–1803.

27. 8 Wallace 603 (1870).

28. 20 Wallace 655 (1874).

29. 165 U.S. 578 (1897).

30. 198 U.S. 45 (1905).

31. Thomas G. Walker, "Fundamental Rights," in Kermit L. Hall, ed., *The Oxford Companion to the Supreme Court of the United States* (New York: Oxford University Press, 1992), 323. See also, in the same volume, historical linkages of varying subtlety traced by Stephen B. Presser, "Chase, Samuel" (137); H. Jefferson Powell, "Higher Law" (370); and Christopher Wolfe, "Natural Law" (581).

32. See, generally, Chapter 7, but for a sample, *Calder* is cited in the *Legal Tender Cases,* 12 Wallace 457 (1871), at 670 (Field, J., dissenting); and in *Juilliard* v. *Greenman,* 110 U.S. 421 (1884), at 469–70 (Field, J., dissenting). *Fletcher* is cited in *Legal Tender Cases,* 12 Wallace at 581 (Chase, C. J., dissenting); and in *Chicago, Burlington and Quincy Railroad Co.* v. *Chicago,* 166 U.S. 226 (1897), at 237 (Harlan, J., for the Court). *Corfield* is cited in the *Slaughter-House Cases,* 16 Wallace 36 (1873), at 97 (Field, J., dissenting); ibid., at 116–18 (Bradley, J., dissenting); ibid., at 127 (Swayne, J., dissenting); and in *Butchers' Union Slaughter-House and Live-Stock Landing Co.* v. *Crescent City Live-Stock Landing and Slaughter-House Co.,* 111 U.S. 746 (1884), at 764–65 (Bradley, J., concurring). *Wilkinson* is cited in *Legal Tender Cases,* 12 Wallace at 671 (Field, J., dissenting); and in *Missouri Pacific Railway Co.* v. *Nebraska,* 164 U.S. 403 (1896), at 417 (Gray, J., for the Court).

33. For a classic example of such abuse in a related area, whether deliberately or ignorantly done, see Chief Justice Waite's distortion of Marshall's *Dartmouth College* opinion in his opinion for the unanimous Court in *Stone* v. *Mississippi,* 101 U.S. 814 (1880), at 819–20.

34. See, e.g., Wright, *American Interpretations,* 298–306; Corwin, *Twilight of the Supreme Court,* 90–94; Benjamin R. Twiss, *Lawyers and the Constitution* (Princeton, N.J.: Princeton University Press, 1942); Christopher Wolfe, *The Rise of Modern Judicial Review: From Constitutional Interpretation to Judgemade Law* (New York: Basic Books, 1986), 144–50; Paul Kens, *Judicial Power and Reform Poliitcs: The Anatomy of Lochner v. New York* (Lawrence: University Press of Kansas, 1990), 60–114; Ely, *Guardian of Every Other Right,* 59–100; and Gillman, *Constitution Besieged,* 19–99.

35. Some recent authors have reviewed these cases more sympathetically than is conventional. See David P. Currie, *The Constitution in the Supreme Court: The First Hundred Years, 1789–1888* (Chicago: University of Chicago Press, 1985), 41–49, 127–59; and Jacobsohn, "E.T.," 33–41. The most moderate of these commentators has remarked of the "temptation of 'natural justice' review" that "such a form of judicial review was very rare," that it was often contained in mere dicta and that it was "outside the mainstream of early U.S. constitutional history" (Wolfe, *Rise of Modern Judicial Review,* 108).

CHAPTER SIX. THE EARLY CASES ON "NATURAL LAW"

1. *Sturges* v. *Crowninshield,* 4 Wheaton 122 (1819), at 202.

2. Robert Lowry Clinton, *Marbury v. Madison and Judicial Review* (Lawrence: University Press of Kansas, 1989), 15–18, and chap. 5 passim.

3. 2 Dallas 304 (1795), at 320.

4. Leonard W. Levy, *Original Intent and the Framers' Constitution* (New York: Macmillan, 1988), 130–32. A similarly mistaken characterization is given by Clinton, *Marbury and Judicial Review,* 146–47, and by James W. Ely, Jr., *The Guardian of Every Other Right: A Constitutional History of Property Rights* (New York: Oxford University Press, 1992), 63.

5. 2 Dallas 304, at 319–20. Here Paterson also considered, and dismissed as groundless, a claim that the repeal was ex post facto within the meaning of Art. I, sec. 10.

6. Ibid., at 307–16.

7. Levy, *Original Intent,* 131. See also Christopher Wolfe, *The Rise of Modern Judicial Review: From Constitutional Interpretation to Judge-made Law* (New York: Basic Books), 109; and Ely, *Guardian of Every Other Right,* 63.

8. Levy, *Original Intent,* 131, quoting 2 Dallas 304, at 311.

9. 2 Dallas 304, at 311.

10. See Raoul Berger, " 'Law of the Land' Reconsidered," in Berger, *Selected Writings on the Constitution* (Cumberland, Va.: James River Press, 1987), 139.

11. Dallas reports (2 Dallas 304, at 310) that the "judge then read the 1st, 8th, and 11th articles of the declaration of rights; and the 9th and 46th sections of the constitution of Pennsylvania." The relevant portions read as follows: "I. That all men are born equally free and independent, and have certain natural, inherent and inalienable rights, amongst which are, the enjoying and defending life and liberty, acquiring, possessing and protecting property, and pursuing and obtaining happiness and safety. . . . VIII. That every member of society hath a right to be protected in the enjoyment of life, liberty and property, and therefore is bound to contribute his proportion towards the expence of that protection, and yield his personal service when necessary, or an equivalent thereto: But no part of a man's property can be justly taken from him, or applied to public uses, without his own consent, or that of his legal representatives. . . . XI. That in controversies respecting property, and in suits between man and man, the parties have a right to trial by jury, which ought to be held sacred. . . . Sect. 9. . . . The general assembly . . . shall have power to . . . prepare bills and enact them into laws; . . . and shall have all other powers necessary for the legislature of a free state or commonwealth: But they shall have no power to add to, alter, abolish, or infringe any part of this constitution. . . . Sect. 46. The declaration of rights is hereby declared to be a part of the constitution of this commonwealth, and ought never to be violated on any pretence whatever"(Francis N. Thorpe, ed., *The Federal and State Constitutions, Colonial Charters, and Other Organic Laws of the States, Territories, and Colonies Now or Heretofore Forming the United States of America,* 7 vols. [Washington, D.C.: Government Printing Office, 1909], 5:3082, 3083, 3084–85, 3091). When he finished reading the above, Paterson resumed: "From these passages, it is evident" (2 Dallas 304, at 310)—and thus began his discussion of natural rights and limited government.

12. 2 Dallas 304, at 310, 312.

13. Ibid., at 311.

14. Ibid., at 312–15.

15. Ibid., at 315.

16. Levy, *Original Intent,* 130, 132.

17. 2 Dallas 304, at 307, quoting William Blackstone, *Commentaries on the*

Laws of England, 4 vols. (Oxford: Clarendon Press, 1765–1769; facsimile reprint, University of Chicago Press, 1979), 1:156.

18. 2 Dallas 304, at 308.

19. Ibid.

20. See Levy, *Original Intent,* 64–74. But see Clinton, *Marbury and Judicial Review,* 144, for a single paragraph that disposes of Levy's ten pages of confusion.

21. Recently this conventional wisdom has cropped up again in Kermit L. Hall, ed., *The Oxford Companion to the Supreme Court of the United States* (New York: Oxford University Press, 1992). See H. Jefferson Powell, "Higher Law," ibid., 370; William M. Wiecek, "History of the Court: Establishment of the Union," ibid., 374; Christopher Wolfe, "Natural Law," ibid., 581. More careful in comparing Chase and Iredell is Powell, *"Calder v. Bull,"* ibid., 114–15.

22. Wolfe, "Natural Law," in ibid., 581. See also Wolfe, *Rise of Modern Judicial Review,* 108–9.

23. Robert H. Bork, *The Tempting of America: The Political Seduction of the Law* (New York: Free Press, 1989), 19, 20.

24. Leonard W. Levy, *"Calder v. Bull,"* in Leonard W. Levy, Kenneth L. Karst, and Dennis J. Mahoney, eds., *Encyclopedia of the American Constitution,* 4 vols. (New York: Macmillan, 1986), 1: 194–95. It should be noted that Chase's was only the first and not the "main" opinion, the justices, as was customary then, writing seriatim from most junior to most senior member. See also Stephen B. Presser, "Chase, Samuel," in Hall, ed., *Oxford Companion,* 137.

25. See note 20; also see Justice Johnson, concurring in *Satterlee v. Matthewson,* 2 Peters 380 (1829), at 414–16, 681–87.

26. See Robert L. Clinton, "The Obligation Clause of the United States Constitution: Public and/or Private Contracts," *University of Arkansas at Little Rock Law Journal* 11 (1988–1989): 43. See also Wallace Mendelson, "B. F. Wright on the Contract Clause: A Progressive Misreading of the Marshall-Taney Era," *Western Political Quarterly* 38 (1985): 262–75; Albert P. Melone, "Mendelson v. Wright: Understanding the Contract Clause," ibid. 41 (1988): 791–99; and Mendelson, "Bootstraps v. Evidence: a Response to Professor Melone," ibid.: 801–5.

27. The relevant portions provide: "That all, and every the Subjects of Us, Our Heirs, or Successors, which shall go to inhabit within the said Colony, and every of their Children, which shall happen to be born there, or on the Seas in going hither, or returning from thence, shall have and enjoy all Liberties and Immunities of free and natural Subjects within any the Dominions of Us, Our Heirs or Successors, to all Intents, Constructions and Purposes whatsoever as if they and every of them were born within the realm of *England"*; emphasis in original; and: "That it shall and may be lawful to and for the Governor, or Deputy-Governor, and such of the Assistants of the said Company for the Time being as shall be assembled in any of the General Courts aforesaid . . . to erect and make such Judicatories, for the hearing, and determining of all Actions, Causes, Matters and Things . . . which shall be in Dispute, and Depending there, as they shall think Fit, and Convenient, and also from Time to Time to Make, Ordain, and Establish all manner of wholesome and reasonable Laws, Statutes, Ordinances, Directions, and Instructions, not Contrary to the Laws of this Realm of *England"*; emphasis in original (Thorpe, ed. *Federal and State Constitutions,* 1:533).

28. 3 Dallas 386, at 387 (Chase, J.).

29. Ibid., at 395–96 (Paterson, J.), 398 (Iredell, J.).

30. Ibid., at 387 (Chase, J.).

31. Ibid., at 387–88.

32. Ibid., at 388.

33. Ibid., at 387; emphasis added.

34. Ibid., at 388.

35. Harry V. Jaffa, "The Closing of the Conservative Mind," *National Review,* 9 July 1990, 41.

36. 3 Dallas 386, at 388 (Chase, J.).

37. Ibid.

38. *Hurtado* v. *California,* 110 U.S. 516 (1884), at 536.

39. See note 27.

40. 3 Dallas 386, at 388 (Chase, J.).

41. Ibid., at 388–89.

42. Ibid., at 389.

43. Ibid., at 394.

44. Ibid.

45. *Barron* v. *Baltimore,* 7 Peters 243 (1833).

46. 3 Dallas 386, at 392–93 (Chase, J.).

47. Ibid., at 395.

48. Compare *Stone* v. *Mississippi,* 101 U.S. 814 (1880) (police powers override the contract clause), and *Covington and Lexington Turnpike Road Co.* v. *Sandford,* 164 U.S. 578 (1896) (substantive due process held to be a firmer ground than contract clause for limiting police power).

49. See Blackstone, *Commentaries,* 1:46, 91, 134–35.

50. See note 27.

51. Blackstone, *Commentaries,* 1:91.

52. John Hart Ely, *Democracy and Distrust: A Theory of Judicial Review* (Cambridge, Mass.: Harvard University Press, 1980), 210.

53. 3 Dallas 386, at 392 (Chase, J.).

54. *Ware* v. *Hylton,* 3 Dallas 199 (1796), at 223.

55. 3 Dallas 386, at 398 (Iredell, J.).

56. Ibid.

57. Ibid., at 399.

58. Ibid.

59. *Fletcher* v. *Peck,* 6 Cranch 87 (1810), at 137 (Marshall, C. J., for the Court). See also note 26.

60. For recent treatments, see Levy, *Original Intent,* 132–33; Bork, *Tempting of America,* 25–26; Wolfe, *Rise of Modern Judicial Review,* 109–10; Gary J. Jacobsohn, "E.T.: The Extra-Textual in Constitutional Interpretation," *Constitutional Commentary* 1 (1984): 38–39; and David P. Currie, *The Constitution in the Supreme Court: The First Hundred Years, 1789–1888* (Chicago: University of Chicago Press, 1985), 128–36.

61. 6 Cranch 87, at 133. See Albert J. Beveridge, *The Life of John Marshall,* 4 vols. (Boston: Houghton Mifflin, 1919), 3:588.

62. 6 Cranch 87, at 132 (Marshall, C. J., for the Court).

63. Ibid., at 133–34. This lengthy discourse on the equity problem in fraud cases was probably prompted by the similar arguments by Joseph Story, counsel for Peck in this case.

64. Ibid., at 133.

65. Ibid., at 133–34.

66. Ibid., at 134.

67. Ibid., at 135.

68. Ibid.; emphasis added.

69. Ibid., at 135–36.

70. See, e.g., Bork, *Tempting of America,* 25; Currie, *Constitution in the Supreme Court,* 130–31; and Beveridge, *Life of Marshall,* 3:590.

71. Alexander Hamilton, James Madison, and John Jay, *The Federalist Papers,* ed. Clinton Rossiter (New York: Mentor, 1961), no. 37:228; hereafter cited as *Federalist.*

72. 6 Cranch 87, at 136 (Marshall, C. J., for the Court).

73. "But it is not on slight implication and vague conjecture that the legislature is to be pronounced to have transcended its powers, and its acts to be considered as void. The opposition between the constitution and the law should be such that the judge feels a clear and strong conviction of their incompatibility with each other" (ibid., at 128).

74. Wolfe, *Rise of Modern Judicial Review,* 109.

75. 6 Cranch 87, at 139 (Marshall, C. J., for the Court).

76. Currie, *Constitution in the Supreme Court,* 132.

77. 6 Cranch 87, at 143 (Johnson, J., dissenting).

78. Ibid., at 142 (Marshall, C. J., for the Court).

79. Ibid., at 139.

80. Ibid., at 133.

81. Ibid., at 139.

82. See ibid., at 144 (Johnson, J., dissenting).

83. Ibid., at 143.

84. Blackstone, *Commentaries,* 1:40. See also Montesquieu, *The Spirit of the Laws,* ed. Anne Cohler, Basia Miller, and Harold Stone (New York: Cambridge University Press, 1989), 3.

85. 6 Cranch 87, at 143.

86. Ibid., at 143, 145.

87. Given Johnson's doubts in *Fletcher* as to the contract clause's extension to public grants, his very unfocused opinion here may also indicate an already developing doubt that the ex post facto clause applied only to the criminal law. See his concurrence in *Satterlee* v. *Matthewson,* 2 Peters 380 (1829), at 414–16, 681–87.

88. 6 Cranch 87, at 144.

89. Ibid.

90. Ibid.

91. *Federalist* 49:313, 315.

92. Sandra F. VanBurkleo, "Johnson, William," in Hall, ed., *Oxford Companion,* 450.

93. 12 Wheaton 213, at 332 (Marshall, C. J., dissenting).

94. 4 Wheaton 122 (1819).

95. See, e.g., James Bradley Thayer, *John Marshall* (Boston: Houghton Mifflin, 1901), 94; Edward S. Corwin, *John Marshall and the Constitution* (New Haven, Conn.: Yale University Press, 1919), 190; and Currie, *Constitution in the Supreme Court,* 150–56.

96. Wolfe, *Rise of Modern Judicial Review,* 55–57; and Mendelson, "B. F. Wright on the Contract Clause," 346–48.

97. Jaffa, "Closing of the Conservative Mind," 41. Currie even suggests a

slight hint of the later doctrine of "freedom of contract," in *Constitution in the Supreme Court,* 153. Somewhat ambiguous on this point is Robert Kenneth Faulkner, *The Jurisprudence of John Marshall* (Princeton, N.J.: Princeton University Press, 1968), 26–30.

98. 12 Wheaton 213, at 344, 345, 347, 353–54 (Marshall, C. J., dissenting).

99. See Washington's opinion, ibid., at 257–59.

100. Ibid., at 339–40 (Marshall, C. J., dissenting).

101. Ibid., at 344.

102. Ibid., at 347.

103. Ibid., at 353–54.

104. Ibid., at 347, 350, 354.

105. Oliver Wendell Holmes, Jr., "Natural Law," in Max Lerner, ed., *The Mind and Faith of Justice Holmes,* 2d ed. (New York: Modern Library, 1943), 396.

106. 12 Wheaton 213, at 347 (Marshall, C. J. dissenting).

107. Blackstone, *Commentaries,* 1:44. Consider the similarity to Hobbes's definition of civil law, in Thomas Hobbes, *Leviathan,* ed. Michael Oakeshott (New York: Collier, 1962), 198.

108. Blackstone, *Commentaries,* 1:41–42.

109. Ibid., 91.

110. 4 Wheaton 518 (1819), at 666. Unlike Livingston, Johnson did not join in the opinions of Washington and Story as well.

111. 12 Wheaton 213, at 290 (Johnson, J.). See also 282, 287, 291.

112. Ibid., at 282.

113. Ibid., at 290.

114. Ibid., at 292.

115. Ibid., at 303–4 (Thompson, J.).

116. Ibid., at 304; see also 312.

117. Ibid., at 298.

118. 9 Cranch 43 (1815), at 44–45.

119. Ibid., at 54. In his final paragraph, Story summarized his holding as the opinion only of "the majority of the court," but no justice went on the record as dissenting from any part of his opinion (ibid., at 55).

120. Ibid., at 47.

121. Ibid., at 48.

122. Ibid., at 49.

123. Ibid., at 50.

124. Ibid., at 52.

125. Levy, *Original Intent,* 135–36; Currie, *Constitution in the Supreme Court,* 138–41; and Jacobsohn, "E.T.," 39–40.

126. 9 Cranch 43, at 45.

127. Gary L. McDowell, *Equity and the Constitution: The Supreme Court, Equitable Relief, and Public Policy* (Chicago: University of Chicago Press, 1982), 77. See chap. 4 passim for Story's views on equity jurisprudence.

128. Ibid., 75.

129. Ibid., 76, quoting Joseph Story, *Commentaries on Equity Jurisprudence,* 3d ed., 2 vols. (Boston: Little, Brown, 1842), 1:19.

130. Thorpe, ed., *Federal and State Constitutions,* 7:3813–14. Note also that the Fifth Amendment requires due process for the deprivation of property and compensation when taken for public use; but neither provision was then held to

apply to state governments (nor should the latter be so held now, "incorporation" doctrine to the contrary notwithstanding).

131. See Washington's concurring opinion in *Trustees of Dartmouth College v. Woodward,* 4 Wheaton 518 (1819), at 663–65; Story's concurring opinion in ibid., at 695; and Story, *Commentaries on the Constitution of the United States,* abridged 1st ed. (Boston: Hilliard, Gray, 1833; reprint, Durham N.C.: Carolina Academic Press, 1987), sec. 706.

132. *Federalist* 78:470.

133. Ibid.

134. 9 Cranch 43, at 52.

135. See McDowell, *Equity and the Constitution,* chap. 5 passim.

136. 9 Cranch 43, at 52.

137. Ibid.

138. Currie, *Constitution in the Supreme Court,* 139. A similar error is made by R. Kent Newmyer, "Story, Joseph," in Hall, ed., *Oxford Companion,* 843: In "*Terrett* v. *Taylor* (1815) and *Town of Pawlet* v. *Clark* (1815), [Story] fused natural-law principles with the Contracts Clause to void state acts confiscating land." Enough has been said of *Terrett* in the text to set the record straight on that case. But Newmyer's error regarding *Town of Pawlet* (9 Cranch 292) is fourfold: 1. Story does not refer to any "natural-law principles" in this case; 2. *Town of Pawlet* is not a case involving the contract clause, or any other provision of the federal Constitution except that which gives jurisdiction to the federal courts in controversies "between Citizens of the same State claiming Land under Grants of different States" (Art. III, sec. 2); 3. no act of any state is held void by the Court; and 4. no act at issue in this case was an attempt to confiscate land.

139. That the equity power is exercised distinctly from the power of constitutional review is indicated by Hamilton in *Federalist* 78:470 (and see Chapter 2 at notes 65–71). Hamilton also intimated this distinction in *Federalist* 80: 479–80. There, replying to the fears raised by the Anti-Federalist "Brutus" that cases in equity "arising under this Constitution" would free judges to interpret by the "reasoning spirit" of the text as opposed to its letter, Hamilton stresses the tradition of equity courts "reliev[ing] against what are called hard bargains." More important, by all the examples he gives, Hamilton seems to foresee that the cases in equity that will "aris[e] under this Constitution" will typically be keyed to the various modes of diversity jurisdiction, where the nature of the parties and not the federal nature of the issues will bring the case into the federal courts. Cf. Brutus, essay 11, in Herbert J. Storing, ed., *The Complete Anti-Federalist,* 7 vols. (Chicago: University of Chicago Press, 1981), 2:417–22.

140. See Wolfe, *Rise of Modern Judicial Review,* 362 n.50, and Jacobsohn, "E.T.," 36–38.

141. 2 Peters 627, at 657. The succeeding sentence cites *Terrett.*

142. Ibid. See Thorpe, ed., *Federal and State Constitutions,* 6:3215. See also Justice Johnson's association of *Calder* and *Wilkinson,* concurring in *Satterlee v. Matthewson,* 2 Peters 380 (1829), at 681.

143. 2 Peters 627, at 657.

144. Ibid., at 658.

145. Ibid.

146. Ibid.; emphasis added.

147. Ibid., at 660.

148. Ibid., at 660–63.

149. Jacobsohn writes that *Wilkinson* had "to be decided on the basis of an interpretation of the Federal Constitution" ("E.T.," 37). In fact, no federal issue entered into Story's holding, although he came briefly within hailing distance of the ex post facto clause (2 Peters 627, at 661).

150. Thorpe, ed., *Federal and State Constitutions*, 6:3215.

151. Indeed, Story ruled for a unanimous Court in *Watson* v. *Mercer*, 8 Peters 88 (1834) (following Washington's lead in *Satterlee* v. *Matthewson*, 2 Peters 380 [1829]) that retrospective civil laws are constitutional, even if adversely affecting private rights, if no obligation of contract is impaired. The nearest Story came to natural law on any other occasion was in *Prigg* v. *Pennsylvania* (1842), when he wrote that by "the general law of nations," slavery has no obligatory extraterritorial status but is supported by "mere municipal regulation"—for this he had ample precedents at common law (16 Peters 539, at 611–12). This point was made also by Justice McLean, dissenting in *Dred Scott* v. *Sandford*, 19 Howard 393 (1857), at 534–36, 547–49. Justice Curtis, also dissenting in *Dred Scott*, at 624, declared this principle to be "inferable from the Constitution." All three justices rested this inference on the language of the fugitive slave clause.

152. Thomas M. Cooley, *A Treatise on the Constitutional Limitations Which Rest upon the Legislative Power of the States of the American Union* (Boston: Little, Brown, 1868; reprint, New York: Da Capo, 1972), 164. Cooley rejected natural-law review on one page and embraced substantive due process on another without any apparent sense of irony.

153. Ibid., 166.

154. See discussion of this case in Chapter 7.

155. *Butchers' Union Co.* v. *Crescent City Co.*, 111 U.S. 746 (1884), at 762–65 (Bradley, J., concurring).

156. 6 Fed. Cas. no. 3230 (C.C.E.D.Pa. 1823), reprinted in Philip B. Kurland and Ralph Lerner, eds., *The Founders' Constitution*, 5 vols. (Chicago: University of Chicago Press, 1987), 4:501. The quotation is on p. 503; emphasis added.

157. Bradley's paraphrase of *Corfield* in his *Butchers' Union* opinion dropped this from view altogether. Field's dissent in *Slaughter-House* quotes the passage in full, then rushes ahead, oblivious to Washington's crucial qualification (16 Wallace 36 [1873], at 97).

CHAPTER SEVEN. THE METAMORPHOSIS OF THE EARLY
PRECEDENTS

1. Dissenting in *Loan Association* v. *Topeka*, 20 Wallace 655 (1875), at 669. Erwin C. Surrency, writing the entry on Clifford in Kermit L. Hall, ed., *The Oxford Companion to the Supreme Court of the United States* (New York: Oxford University Press, 1992), reports that Clifford's "greatest constitutional decision was in *Loan Association* v. *Topeka* (1874) [*sic*], where he wrote the majority opinion holding that the Court could declare unconstitutional any statute of Congress on grounds other than a stated constitutional provision" (161). Yet not only did *Topeka* involve no act of Congress, but Clifford *in dissent* also repudiated, as the quotation in the text shows, exactly the view Surrency attributes to him, a view that can be attributed to the man who actually wrote the majority opinion, Justice Samuel F. Miller. Howard Gillman errs as well in mis-

taking the date of this case and characterizes it as a unanimous decision (*The Constitution Besieged: The Rise and Demise of Lochner Era Police Powers Jurisprudence* [Durham, N.C.: Duke University Press, 1993], 68).

2. Christopher Wolfe argues that a "first victory"—albeit "a rather ambiguous one"—for substantive due process as a truly ascendant doctrine arrived in *Chicago, Milwaukee and St. Paul Railroad* v. *Minnesota*, 134 U.S. 418 (1890); see Wolfe, *The Rise of Modern Judicial Review: From Constitutional Interpretation to Judge-made Law* (New York: Basic Books, 1986), 149. The doctrine came into its own less ambiguously in *Allgeyer* v. *Louisiana*, 165 U.S. 578 (1897).

3. Thomas M. Cooley, *A Treatise on the Constitutional Limitations Which Rest upon the Legislative Power of the States of the American Union* (Boston: Little, Brown, 1868; reprint, New York: Da Capo Press, 1972), 397, 16. Only one of these, *Conner* v. *Elliott* (18 Howard 591 [1856]), was a Supreme Court case, and it did not cite *Corfield*.

4. Raoul Berger, *Government by Judiciary: The Transformation of the Fourteenth Amendment* (Cambridge, Mass.: Harvard University Press, 1977), chaps. 2 and 3 passim.

5. *Corfield* still plays a small role in debates over the congressional intent regarding the relation between the Fourteenth Amendment and the Bill of Rights. See Michael Kent Curtis, *No State Shall Abridge: The Fourteenth Amendment and the Bill of Rights* (Durham, N.C.: Duke University Press, 1986), 66–67, 114–15; Raoul Berger, *The Fourteenth Amendment and the Bill of Rights* (Norman: University of Oklahoma Press, 1989), 34–36, 105; and Earl M. Maltz, *Civil Rights, the Constitution, and Congress, 1863–1869* (Lawrence: University Press of Kansas, 1990), 109, 118–19.

6. 16 Wallace 36 (1873).

7. Ibid., at 76 (Miller, J., for the Court). Miller also on this page cites *Ward* v. *Maryland*, 12 Wallace 418 (1872), which in turn did not cite *Corfield* but did cite the page of Cooley's *Treatise* where *Corfield* was cited. *Ward*, at 430.

8. *Slaughter-House Cases*, 16 Wallace 36 (1873), at 96–98 (Field, J., dissenting).

9. Ibid., at 118 (Bradley, J., dissenting).

10. See, e.g., *Edwards* v. *California*, 314 U.S. 160 (1941), at 180 (Douglas, J., concurring). *Corfield* did crop up twice in Justice Hugo Black's lengthy appendix to his dissent in *Adamson* v. *California*, 332 U.S. 46 (1947), at 105–6, 115, as he reproduced congressional statements supporting his position on total incorporation of the Bill of Rights by section 1 of the Fourteenth Amendment. However—no surprise from Justice Black—no hint of any "natural-law" reading of *Corfield* surfaced there or in his dissent proper, where the case is not cited at all.

11. See *Poe* v. *Ullman*, 367 U.S. 497 (1961), at 541 (Harlan, J., dissenting).

12. 2 Peters 380, at 414.

13. 6 Howard 507, at 539.

14. 7 Howard 1, at 66.

15. 244 U.S. 205, at 227.

16. 11 Wallace 259, at 267.

17. 12 Wallace 457.

18. See text at notes 31–61.

19. 13 Wallace 654, at 662.

20. *Taylor* v. *Porter*, 4 Hill 140 (N.Y. 1843); *Wynehamer* v. *People*, 13 Kernan 378 (N.Y. 1856).

21. 15 Wallace 610, at 623.

22. *Sinking Fund Cases,* 99 U.S. 700 (1878), at 765; *Juilliard* v. *Greenman,* 110 U.S. 421 (1884), at 469.

23. 20 Wallace 655, at 668–69.

24. 6 Cranch 87 (1810), at 135–36 (Marshall, C. J., for the Court).

25. 2 Peters 380, at 413 (Washington, J., for the Court).

26. 8 Peters 88, at 110 (Story, J., for the Court).

27. 1 Black 358, at 365–66. Counsel also trotted out a number of English and state cases, including *Dr. Bonham's Case,* 8 Co. Rep. 107 (1610); *Bowman* v. *Middleton,* 1 Bay 252 (S.C. 1792); *Gardner* v. *Newburgh,* 2 Johns. Ch. 162 (N.Y. 1816); and *Taylor* v. *Porter,* 4 Hill 140 (N.Y. 1843).

28. 1 Black 358, at 373–74.

29. *United States* v. *Arredondo,* 6 Peters 691 (1832), at 714–15.

30. *Drehman* v. *Stifle,* 8 Wallace 595 (1870), at 603 (Swayne, J., for the Court). Swayne mistakenly referred here to *"Williamson* v. *Leland,"* but his citation was correct.

31. 8 Wallace 603 (1870).

32. David Currie finds at least an implication that Chase condemned the act's prospective application in *Hepburn* and notes that Chase made this explicit in dissent a year later (*The Constitution in the Supreme Court: The First Hundred Years, 1789–1888* [Chicago: University of Chicago Press, 1985], 321 n. 255).

33. In an article published shortly after the *Hepburn* decision, Henry Adams reviewed the original passage of the 1862 legal tender statute. In his account, Chase as treasury secretary had initially opposed legal tender but yielded to the idea only when (in Chase's view) satisfactory arrangements for bank credit could not be worked out. Chase "had been drawn into it against his most deeply rooted convictions and his better judgment; but no sooner was the decision made, than he threw his whole weight in favor of the bill" ("The Legal-Tender Act," *North American Review,* April 1870; reprinted in Adams, *The Great Secession Winter of 1860–61 and Other Essays,* ed. George E. Hochfield [New York: A. S. Barnes, 1963], 146).

34. *Hepburn* v. *Griswold,* 8 Wallace 603, at 625 (Chase, C. J., for the Court).

35. Ibid., at 610–22.

36. Ibid., at 622–23. See Miller's reply in dissent, at 637.

37. Ibid., at 624; emphasis added.

38. Currie, *Constitution in the Supreme Court,* 327.

39. 8 Wallace 603, at 637 (Miller, J., dissenting).

40. Curiously, Potter does not appear at all in Benjamin R. Twiss's excellent account, *Lawyers and the Constitution* (Princeton, N.J.: Princeton University Press, 1942), of the ABA's origins and its role in encouraging conservative judicial activism.

41. *Legal Tender Cases,* 12 Wallace 457, at 488–91 (argument of counsel Potter). See Justice Strong for the Court, at 539, where he states that "we are not judges of the appropriateness" of acts of Congress. See ibid., at 542.

42. Ibid., at 501–7 (argument of counsel Potter).

43. Ibid., at 502. But see the contrary view held by all the Justices, majority and minority, in *Rice* v. *Railroad Co.,* 1 Black 358 (1862), and the *Sinking Fund Cases,* 99 U.S. 700 (1878).

44. *Legal Tender Cases,* 12 Wallace 457, at 502 (argument of counsel Potter).

45. Ibid., at 503–4.

46. *Ogden* v. *Saunders,* 12 Wheaton 213 (1827), at 303–4, 312. See Chapter 6 at note 115.

47. *Legal Tender Cases,* 12 Wallace 457, at 581 (Chase, C. J., dissenting).

48. Ibid., at 506 (argument of counsel Potter).

49. Ibid., at 580 (Chase, C. J., dissenting).

50. Ibid., at 551 (Strong, J., for the Court).

51. Ibid., at 580 (Chase, C. J., dissenting).

52. See text at notes 24 and 25 and Chapter 6 at notes 69–71.

53. *Legal Tender Cases,* 12 Wallace 457, at 581.

54. Ibid., at 582.

55. *Calder* v. *Bull,* 3 Dallas 386 (1798), at 388 (Chase, J.).

56. *Legal Tender Cases,* 12 Wallace 457, at 618 (Clifford, J., dissenting). Clifford also cited Marshall's opinion in *Sturges* v. *Crowninshield* (4 Wheaton 122 [1819]) in much the same carefree manner (ibid., at 619–20). On *Sturges,* see also ibid., at 667 (Field, J., dissenting).

57. Ibid., at 640–43, 647–48 (Field, J. dissenting). Field's eagerness to enlist Marshall even led him to attribute to Marshall, not Story, the Court's opinion in *Martin* v. *Hunter's Lessee* (1 Wheaton 304 [1816]; ibid., at 664).

58. Ibid., at 670.

59. Ibid., at 671.

60. Ibid., at 672.

61. Ibid., at 671, quoting "*Wilkeson* [sic] v. *Leland,*" 2 Peters 627 (1829), at 657.

62. Loren P. Beth, "Field, Stephen Johnson," in Hall, ed., *Oxford Companion,* 290.

63. See, e.g., Sumner's essay "Democracy and Plutocracy," in Robert C. Bannister, ed., *On Liberty, Society, and Politics: The Essential Essays of William Graham Sumner* (Indianapolis: Liberty Fund, 1992), chap. 13 passim. For differing views on the fairness and accuracy of the term "Social Darwinism" to describe the conservatism of the late nineteenth century, see Richard Hofstadter, *Social Darwinism in American Thought,* rev. ed. (Boston: Beacon Press, 1955), and Bannister, *Social Darwinism: Science and Myth in Anglo-American Social Thought* (Philadelphia: Temple University Press, 1979). Each has a chapter devoted to Sumner: Hofstadter, 51–66; Bannister, 91–113.

64. For representative samples, see the *Slaughter-House Cases,* at 83–111 (Field, J., dissenting); *Munn* v. *Illinois,* 94 U.S. 113 (1877), at 136–54 (Field, J., dissenting); *Sinking Fund Cases,* 99 U.S. 700 (1878), at 750–69 (Field, J., dissenting); *Juilliard* v. *Greenman,* 110 U.S. 421 (1884), at 451–70 (Field, J., dissenting); and *Butchers' Union Co.* v. *Crescent City Co.,* 111 U.S. 746 (1884), at 754–60 (Field, J., concurring).

65. *Pollock* v. *Farmers' Loan and Trust Co.,* 158 U.S. 601 (1895).

66. 94 U.S. 113 (1877), at 142 (due process clause protects the pursuit of happiness), 148 (quoting *Wilkinson*) (Field, J., dissenting).

67. *Allgeyer* v. *Louisiana,* 165 U.S. 578 (1897), at 589–90 (Peckham, J., for the Court), quoting *Butchers' Union Slaughter-House Co.* v. *Crescent City Live-Stock Landing Co.,* 111 U.S. 746 (1884), at 764 (Bradley, J., concurring), which in turn quoted Justice Washington's circuit ruling in *Corfield.*

68. Wolfe, *Rise of Modern Judicial Review,* 144.

69. Ibid.

70. 3 Dallas 171 (1796).

71. 9 Wheaton 1 (1824).

72. *United States* v. *E. C. Knight Co.*, 156 U.S. 1 (1895); *Pollock* v. *Farmers' Loan and Trust Co.*, 158 U.S. 601 (1895).

73. *Slaughter-House,* at 78.

74. Robert Lowry Clinton, *Marbury v. Madison and Judicial Review* (Lawrence: University Press of Kansas, 1989), 166.

75. Ibid., 161–91.

76. 198 U.S. 45 (1905).

77. Paul Kens, *Judicial Power and Reform Politics: The Anatomy of Lochner v. New York* (Lawrence: University Press of Kansas, 1990).

78. Gillman, *Constitution Besieged.*

79. Kens, *Judicial Power and Reform Politics,* 64.

80. Ibid., 66.

81. Ibid., 75.

82. Ibid., 87.

83. Ibid., 88.

84. Ibid., 93, discussing *Bartmeyer* v. *Iowa,* 18 Wallace 129 (1873), at 137ff. (Field, J., concurring).

85. Ibid., 105, discussing the *Slaughter-House Cases,* at 83 ff. (Field, J., dissenting).

86. Ibid., 117.

87. Ibid., 105.

88. Gillman, *Constitution Besieged,* 5, 10.

89. Ibid., 50–60, 86–92.

90. Ibid., 64–75, 104–31.

91. Ibid., 38, 44.

92. Ibid., 21.

93. Ibid., 54.

94. 300 U.S. 379 (1937).

95. Gillman, *Constitution Besieged,* 193.

96. Ibid., 32, quoting Garry Wills, *Explaining America: The Federalist* (New York: Doubleday, 1981), 205. Wills's thesis on this page, that the purpose of a multiplicity of factions is "to *block them all*" (emphasis in original) and thus produce a "self-defeating squabble" above which "virtuous men" govern, cannot account for the following remarks of Publius: "The regulation of these various and interfering interests forms the principal task of modern legislation and involves the spirit of party and faction in the necessary and ordinary operations of government"; and "It is in vain to say that enlightened statesmen will be able to adjust these clashing interests and render them all subservient to the public good. Enlightened statesmen will not always be at the helm" (Alexander Hamilton, James Madison, and John Jay, *The Federalist Papers,* ed. Clinton Rossiter [New York: Mentor, 1961], no. 10:79, 80). For better interpretations of the framers' views of factions, and especially of *Federalist* 10, see Martin Diamond, "Democracy and *The Federalist:* A Reconsideration of the Framers' Intent," *American Political Science Review* 53 (1959): 52–68, reprinted with other fine essays on the *Federalist* and related subjects in William A. Schambra, ed., *As Far as Republican Principles Will Admit: Essays by Martin Diamond* (Washington, D.C.: AEI Press, 1992), 17–36; David F. Epstein, *The Political Theory of the Federalist* (Chicago: University of Chicago Press, 1984), 59–110; Paul Peterson, "The Rhetorical Design and Theoretical Teaching of *Federalist* No. 10," *Political Science Reviewer* 17 (1987): 193–218; and Paul A. Rahe,

Republics Ancient and Modern: Classical Republicanism and the American Revolution (Chapel Hill: University of North Carolina Press, 1992), 589–90, 596–97, 614–15.

97. Gillman, *Constitution Besieged*, 32.

98. Ibid., 33.

99. See Kens, *Judicial Power and Reform Politics*, 93–97. In this connection it should be noted that Gillman's account of *Holden* v. *Hardy*, 169 U.S. 366 (1898), a ruling upholding an eight-hour workday for miners, and of that case's doctrinal connection to *Lochner* is less persuasive than that of Kens. Cf. Gillman, *Constitution Besieged*, 120–31, esp. 123, with Kens, *Judicial Power and Reform Politics*, 108–27.

100. See, e.g., Gillman, *Constitution Besieged*, 72–73.

101. See Marvin Meyers, *The Jacksonian Persuasion: Politics and Belief* (Stanford, Calif.: Stanford University Press, 1957; reprinted with new preface, New York: Vintage, 1960), 101–41, 163–205; Eric Foner, *Free Soil, Free Labor, Free Men: The Ideology of the Republican Party Before the Civil War* (New York: Oxford University Press, 1970), 11–39; J. David Greenstone, *The Lincoln Persuasion: Remaking American Liberalism* (Princeton, N.J.: Princeton University Press, 1993), 230–40, 249–51, 277, 284; and Harry V. Jaffa, *Crisis of the House Divided: An Interpretation of the Issues in the Lincoln-Douglas Debates* (Garden City, N.Y.: Doubleday, 1959; reprint, Chicago: University of Chicago Press, Phoenix Books, 1982), 318–21.

102. William Graham Sumner, "Socialism," in Bannister, ed., *On Liberty, Society, and Politics*, 172.

103. Sumner, "Republican Government" (1877), in ibid., 90–91.

104. Sumner, "Socialism," in ibid., 170.

105. Ibid., 177.

106. Abraham Lincoln, speech at Springfield, Illinois, 26 June 1857, in Roy P. Basler, ed., *The Collected Works of Abraham Lincoln*, 9 vols., (New Brunswick, N.J.: Rutgers University Press, 1953), 2:401.

107. Ibid. 4:268. See Rahe, *Republics Ancient and Modern*, 780–82.

108. 198 U.S. 45 (1905), citing *Allgeyer* at 53 (Peckham, J., for the Court).

109. 262 U.S. 390 (1923), citing, inter alia, *Slaughter-House, Butchers' Union, Allgeyer,* and *Lochner* at 399 (McReynolds, J., for the Court).

110. 268 U.S. 510 (1925), citing *Meyer* at 534 (McReynolds, J., for the Court).

111. 367 U.S. 497 (1961), citing *Meyer* at 517 (Douglas, J., dissenting); and citing *Allgeyer, Meyer,* and *Pierce* at 543 (Harlan, J., dissenting).

112. 381 U.S. 479 (1965), citing *Meyer* and *Pierce* at 481 (Douglas, J., for the Court), at 488, 495 (Goldberg, J., concurring), and at 502, 503n. (White, J., concurring).

113. 410 U.S. 113 (1973).

114. *Poe* v. *Ullman*, 367 U.S. 497 (1961), citing *Corfield* and *Calder* at 541 (Harlan, J., dissenting); *Griswold* v. *Connecticut*, 381 U.S. 479 (1965), citing *Calder* at 490n. (Goldberg, J., concurring).

PART THREE. AMERICA'S PHILOSOPHIC TEACHERS AND THE JUDICIAL FUNCTION

1. See, e.g., Walter F. Murphy, "The Art of Constitutional Interpretation: A Preliminary Showing," in M. Judd Harmon, ed., *Essays on the Constitution of*

the *United States* (Port Washington, N.Y.: Kennikat Press, 1978), 130–59, and Paul G. Kauper, "The Higher Law and the Rights of Man in a Revolutionary Society," in *America's Continuing Revolution* (Garden City, N.Y.: Doubleday Anchor, 1976), 41–67.

2. See Christopher Wolfe, *The Rise of Modern Judicial Review: From Constitutional Interpretation to Judge-made Law* (New York: Basic Books, 1986), 108–13.

3. See Leslie Friedman Goldstein, "Judicial Review and Democratic Theory: Guardian Democracy vs. Representative Democracy," *Western Political Quarterly* 40 (1987): 391–412; reprinted in Goldstein, *In Defense of the Text: Democracy and Constitutional Theory* (Savage, Md.: Rowman and Littlefield, 1991), 125–51.

4. Walter Berns, "Judicial Review and the Rights and Laws of Nature," *Supreme Court Review* (1982): 49–83; reprinted in Berns, *In Defense of Liberal Democracy* (Chicago: Regnery Gateway, 1984), 29–62.

5. Goldstein, "Judicial Review and Democratic Theory."

6. Wolfe, *Rise of Modern Judicial Review.*

7. Hadley Arkes, *Beyond the Constitution* (Princeton, N.J.: Princeton University Press, 1990).

8. Ibid., 17.

9. Ibid.; emphasis in original.

10. Ibid., 38; emphasis in original.

11. Cf. ibid., 213–18, 245–46, with the careful reasoning on enumerated and implied powers by Hamilton, "Opinion on the Constitutionality of an Act to Establish a National Bank," in Harold C. Syrett et al., eds., *The Papers of Alexander Hamilton,* 26 vols. (New York: Columbia University Press, 1961–1979), 8:97–134. For a fully Hamiltonian reminder of the principle at stake, see Martin Diamond, "The Forgotten Idea of Enumerated Powers," in William A. Schambra, ed. *As Far as Republican Principles Will Admit: Essays by Martin Diamond* (Washington, D.C.: AEI Press, 1992), 179–85. See also *McCulloch* v. *Maryland,* 4 Wheaton 316 (1819) (and the discussion in Chapter 5), and *Gibbons* v. *Ogden,* 9 Wheaton 1 (1824). Controversies over the reach of congressional power continue on the Court: see, e.g., *National League of Cities* v. *Usery,* 426 U.S. 833 (1976); *Garcia* v. *San Antonio Metropolitan Transit Authority,* 469 U.S. 528 (1985); and *United States* v. *Lopez,* _____ U.S. _____ (1995).

12. Arkes, *Beyond the Constitution,* 66; emphasis in original. When I had an opportunity to ask Professor Arkes in a public forum (at the Heritage Foundation, Washington, D.C., in June 1993) whether Abraham Lincoln, consistent with Arkes's principles, should have applauded a hypothetical "*Dred Scott* in reverse"—i.e., a ruling by the Court that slavery was everywhere unconstitutional as contrary to natural right—his answer was "no," insofar as the Constitution in 1857 left states the power to legislate the institution. This was a perfectly reasonable reply. I suggested then and suggest now that no reader of Professor Arkes's book could expect an answer other than "yes" to this question.

13. On the basis of a conventional reading of several of the cases discussed in Chapter 6, Arkes praises Samuel Chase's opinion in *Calder* v. *Bull* (3 Dallas 386 [1798]) (ibid., 10), and Johnson's dissent in *Fletcher* v. *Peck* (6 Cranch 187 [1810], at 271) (ibid., 20, 28). On the basis of a few dicta, he molds Marshall's *Fletcher* opinion into a shape the chief justice would not recognize (ibid., 24–28). And though he will not defend it unequivocally as leading to the correct

result, he has much praise for Salmon Chase's opinion for the Court in *Hepburn* v. *Griswold* (8 Wallace 603 [1870]) (ibid., 33–35).

14. Ibid., 78.

15. Ibid., 70; emphasis in original.

16. Ibid., 71.

17. In this vein, Arkes blithely supports the overthrow of *Barron* v. *Baltimore* and the judicial enforcement of the Bill of Rights against the states, by virtue of nothing more solid than "the *implications that* [are] *simply necessary to the rendering of justice*" (ibid., 162; emphasis in original). Later he dismisses the debate over "incorporation" as "a problem without substance" (ibid., 167).

18. Ibid., 18.

19. Ibid., 247.

20. See ibid., 106–7.

21. *Calder* v. *Bull,* 3 Dallas 386 (1798), at 399.

22. Arkes, *Beyond the Constitution,* 163.

23. Alexander Hamilton, James Madison, and John Jay, *The Federalist Papers,* ed. Clinton Rossiter (New York: Mentor, 1961), no. 9:72.

24. See Leslie Friedman Goldstein's criticism of what she takes to be Walter Berns's working assumption (in "Judicial Review and the Rights and Laws of Nature") that we can understand the founders by understanding Locke, Hobbes, Vattel, and Pufendorf, in "Popular Sovereignty, the Origins of Judicial Review, and the Revival of Unwritten Law," *Journal of Politics* 48 (1986): 51 n. 1. Also on this question of influence, see Thomas L. Pangle, *The Spirit of Modern Republicanism: The Moral Vision of the American Founders and the Philosophy of Locke* (Chicago: University of Chicago Press, 1988), esp. 124–27, 276–79; and Paul A. Rahe, *Republics Ancient and Modern: Classical Republicanism and the American Revolution* (Chapel Hill: University of North Carolina Press, 1992), esp. 545–72.

25. See Richard G. Stevens, "The Constitutional Completion of the Liberal Philosophy of Hobbes and Locke," *Political Science Reviewer* 17 (1987): 267–84; Patrick Coby, "The Law of Nature in Locke's *Second Treatise:* Is Locke a Hobbesian?" *Review of Politics* 49 (1987): 3–28; and Rahe, *Republics Ancient and Modern,* esp. 364–98.

CHAPTER EIGHT. SOVEREIGNTY AND JUDGING IN HOBBES'S *LEVIATHAN*

1. Thomas Hobbes, *A Dialogue Between a Philosopher and a Student of the Common Laws of England,* in William Molesworth, ed., *The English Works of Thomas Hobbes,* 11 vols. (London: John Bohn, 1839–1845; reprint, Darmstadt, Germany: Scientia Verlag Aalen, 1966), 6:5.

2. Walter Berns, "Judicial Review and the Rights and Laws of Nature," *Supreme Court Review* (1982): 61.

3. Richard G. Stevens, "The Constitutional Completion of the Liberal Philosophy of Hobbes and Locke," *Political Science Reviewer* 17 (1987): 273. See also Leo Strauss, *Natural Right and History* (Chicago: University of Chicago Press, 1953), 165–251; and Paul A. Rahe, *Republics Ancient and Modern: Classical Republicanism and the American Revolution* (Chapel Hill: University of North Carolina Press, 1992), 362–63, 462, 493, 499.

4. In an essay first published in 1954, Norberto Bobbio wrote that "one of

the fundamental problems which allow us to touch the most sensitive points of Hobbes's clever and systematic mechanism is the problem of *the relationship between natural law and civil law.* . . . [W]e may consider it as one of the most vexed questions in all of Hobbes's juridical and political work" ("Natural Law and Civil Law in the Political Philosophy of Hobbes," in Bobbio, *Thomas Hobbes and the Natural Law Tradition* [Chicago: University of Chicago Press, 1993], 115; emphasis in original).

5. Ibid., 117–18. My answer to this question will differ somewhat from Bobbio's.

6. Laurence Berns, "Thomas Hobbes," in Leo Strauss and Joseph Cropsey, eds., *History of Political Philosophy,* 3d ed. (Chicago: University of Chicago Press, 1987), 408. See also Leo Strauss, "On the Basis of Hobbes's Political Philosophy," in Strauss, *What Is Political Philosophy?* (New York: Free Press, 1959; reprint, Westport, Conn.: Greenwood Press, 1973), 194.

7. Thomas Hobbes, *Leviathan,* ed. Michael Oakeshott (New York: Collier, 1962), 101.

8. Ibid., 39, 48.

9. Thomas Hobbes, *De Cive or the Citizen,* ed. Sterling P. Lamprecht (New York: Appleton-Century-Crofts, 1949; reprint, Westport, Conn.: Greenwood Press, 1982), 57–58. Thus even though Hobbes explicitly denies that there is a "summum bonum" (*Leviathan,* 80), there does appear to be what may be called a universal "minimum bonum," making possible all the other freely sought goods of "commodious living" (ibid., 102) or the "contentments of life" (ibid., 247).

10. Hobbes, *Leviathan,* 113, 108, 113.

11. Ibid., 132; emphasis in original. I will refer throughout, unless otherwise indicated, to Hobbes's sovereign as a single individual, as he consistently does, although he admits that sovereignty may be lodged in the few or the many as well as the one.

12. Hobbes, *Leviathan,* 132.

13. Ibid., 135.

14. Ibid., 229.

15. Ibid., 135.

16. Ibid., 136.

17. Ibid., 138.

18. Ibid., 199.

19. Ibid., 132.

20. Ibid., 157.

21. Ibid., 136.

22. Ibid., 123.

23. Ibid., 187.

24. Ibid., 120; emphasis in original.

25. Ibid., 247; emphasis added.

26. Ibid., 253–54.

27. Ibid., 118, 121, 122, 192, 214, 234, 253–54; Hobbes, *De Cive,* 148, 153, 165; and Hobbes, *The Elements of Law, Natural and Politic,* ed. Ferdinand Tönnies, 2d ed. (London: Frank Cass, 1969), 88, 93. More than once Hobbes objects to calling this proportional equality by the name distributive justice, apparently because of his narrow definition of the noun in that phrase. See *Leviathan,* 118; and *Elements of Law,* 88.

28. Hobbes, *Dialogue,* in Molesworth, ed., *English Works,* 6:25–26.

29. Hobbes, *Leviathan*, 214, but cf. ibid., 199.

30. Ibid., 218–19.

31. Ibid., 230.

32. Ibid., 233.

33. Ibid., 234.

34. Ibid., 161; see also 247.

35. Ibid., 247; emphasis in original.

36. See Strauss, *Natural Right and History*, 170, 198–99.

37. Hobbes, *Leviathan*, 51.

38. Ibid., 104; emphasis in original.

39. Ibid.; emphasis in original.

40. Ibid., 124.

41. Bobbio, *Hobbes and the Natural Law Tradition*, 166–67.

42. Strauss, *Natural Right and History*, 181. Paul Rahe, while referring to Hobbes's rejection of a summum bonum, and ably accounting for his depreciation of logos (*Republics Ancient and Modern*, 372–75), refers to Hobbes's "partially concealed teleology" (ibid., 397)—but this is a decidedly strange use of that noun.

43. Leo Strauss, "On Natural Law," in Strauss, *Studies in Platonic Political Philosophy* (Chicago: University of Chicago Press, 1983), 144.

44. Hobbes, *Leviathan*, 102.

45. Ibid., 124.

46. Strauss, *Natural Right and History*, 166.

47. Ibid., 198–99 n. 43.

48. Hobbes, *Leviathan*, 490–91. My thanks to Professor Thomas K. Lindsay for alerting me to this passage. Whether Hobbes fairly characterizes Aristotle need not concern us here.

49. See ibid., chap. 25, on the difference between counsel and command.

50. Ibid., 198.

51. Ibid., 482.

52. Ibid., 62. For the basis of this belief, see ibid., 98.

53. Ibid., 234.

54. Ibid., 135; emphasis added.

55. Ibid., 167.

56. As Paul Rahe writes, "It was not difficult to transform Hobbes's teaching into a doctrine of anticipation, resistance, and rebellion" (*Republics Ancient and Modern*, 480).

57. Hobbes, *Leviathan*, 231.

58. Ibid., 257.

59. Ibid., 201.

60. Ibid., 199. For an astute discussion of this problematic sentence, see Bobbio, *Hobbes and the Natural Law Tradition*, 129–30.

61. One could say that criticizing Coke is the theme of Hobbes's *Dialogue*. See James R. Stoner, Jr., *Common Law and Liberal Theory: Coke, Hobbes, and the Origins of American Constitutionalism* (Lawrence: University Press of Kansas, 1992), chap. 7 passim. I am indebted to Professor Stoner for enriching my understanding of the issues between Coke and Hobbes.

62. Hobbes, *Leviathan*, 201–2; emphasis in original. Interestingly, Hobbes cites Coke's *Institutes* here, not his famous remark in *Bonham's Case* that the the common law may "sometimes adjudge" an act of Parliament to be "against common right and reason" and therefore "utterly void" (8 Coke's Reports 107,

118 [1610]). In the famous "writs of assistance" case of 1761, James Otis had taken *Bonham's Case* as asserting an independent judicial power to conform the positive law to the natural. But Otis was plainly mistaken in that reading, as what Coke had meant was that judges must give statutes an interpretation that presumes the reasonableness of the legislator and resolves any internal contradictions. See Bernard Bailyn, *The Ideological Origins of the American Revolution* (Cambridge, Mass.: Harvard University Press, 1967), 176–77; Robert Lowry Clinton, *Marbury v. Madison and Judicial Review* (Lawrence: University Press of Kansas, 1989), 37–40. See also Stoner, *Common Law and Liberal Theory*, chap. 3 passim, for the most thorough discussion of *Bonham's Case*. William Blackstone considered *Bonham's Case* within the rule of his doctrine of parliamentary supremacy; see his *Commentaries on the Laws of England,* 4 vols. (Oxford: Clarendon Press, 1765–1769; facsimile reprint, Chicago: University of Chicago Press, 1979), 1:91. Hobbes's silence on the case indicates that at least he was not the originator of Otis's mistake.

63. Hobbes, *Leviathan,* 205.
64. Ibid.
65. Ibid., 209. See Blackstone, *Commentaries,* 1:91, and note 62, above.
66. Hobbes, *Leviathan,* 207.
67. Ibid., 160–61.
68. Ibid., 172.
69. Ibid., 169.
70. Ibid., 126.
71. Ibid., 132.
72. Ibid., 130.
73. Ibid., 132.
74. See ibid., 246.
75. See Bobbio, *Hobbes and the Natural Law Tradition,* 171.

CHAPTER NINE. THE MOVEMENT TOWARD
CONSTITUTIONALISM IN LOCKE'S *SECOND TREATISE*

1. John Locke, *Two Treatises of Government,* ed. Peter Laslett (New York: Mentor, 1965), bk. 1, section 106.
2. Ibid., bk. 2, secs. 123, 124; emphasis in original.
3. See Richard G. Stevens, "The Constitutional Completion of the Liberal Philosophy of Hobbes and Locke," *Political Science Reviewer* 17 (1987): 273.
4. Locke, *Two Treatises,* bk. 2, sec. 90; see also secs. 13, 93. Cf. Thomas Hobbes, *Leviathan,* ed. Michael Oakeshott (New York: Collier, 1962), 157, on the stark alternative between absolutism and the anarchy of war.
5. Locke, *Two Treatises,* bk. 2, sec. 180.
6. Hobbes, *Leviathan,* 151.
7. However, it has been cogently argued that the true ground of both limited government and the right of revolution is in Locke's absolute prohibition of suicide (Gary D. Glenn, "Inalienable Rights and Locke's Argument for Limited Government: Political Implications of a Right to Suicide," *Journal of Politics* 46 [1984]: 80–105).
8. Hobbes, *Leviathan,* 134; emphasis in original.
9. Locke, *Two Treatises,* bk. 2, sec. 3.
10. Ibid., sec. 131; emphasis in original.

11. Ibid., sec. 225.

12. See ibid., secs. 212–20.

13. 1 Cranch 137 (1803), at 176.

14. Locke, *Two Treatises*, bk. 2, sec. 138.

15. Ibid., sec. 94.

16. See Stevens, "Constitutional Completion," 274–79.

17. Locke, *Two Treatises*, bk. 2, secs. 4, 6, 61 (twice), 69, 83, 108, 115. The second of these passages refers to the sovereignty of God. In all the other passages, Locke uses the term in a context in which he rejects or disparages traditional claims of sovereignty.

18. See ibid., secs. 87, 88, 89, 127, 131, 132, 134, 135, 136, 141, 149, 150, 157, 168, 212. Not all of these passages use identical language, but each speaks to the issue of the location of supreme power.

19. Ibid., sec. 97; emphasis in original.

20. Ibid., sec 127; emphasis in original. See also ibid., secs. 88, 212, and especially 89, where each man "authorizes the Society, or which is all one, the Legislative thereof to make Laws for him."

21. Ibid., sec. 157; see also secs. 131, 168.

22. Ibid., sec 134; emphasis in original.

23. Ibid.; emphasis in original.

24. Ibid., sec. 96; emphasis in original.

25. Ibid., sec. 149; emphasis in original.

26. Ibid., sec. 150; emphasis in original. See also ibid., secs. 168, 243.

27. Ibid., sec. 135; emphasis in original.

28. Stevens, "Constitutional Completion," 281.

29. Locke, *Two Treatises*, bk. 2, secs. 143, 144.

30. Alexander Hamilton, James Madison, and John Jay, *The Federalist Papers*, ed. Clinton Rossiter (New York: Mentor, 1961), no. 47:301.

31. Locke, *Two Treatises*, bk. 2, sec. 149; and see chap. 14, "Of Prerogative," especially secs. 162, 163.

32. Ibid., sec. 12; emphasis in original.

33. Ibid., sec. 124; emphasis in original.

34. Ibid., sec. 136; emphasis in original.

35. See, e.g., ibid., secs. 19, 20, 89, 125, 131, 136.

36. Ibid., sec. 96.

37. See ibid., secs. 38, 45, 50, 138.

38. Stevens, in "Constitutional Completion," 280, writes that "one sees in Locke's *Letter on Toleration* that what can be tolerated is, after all, only what is tolerable."

39. Locke, *Two Treatises*, bk. 2, sec. 220.

40. Whether Hobbes seriously contends for any such thing as natural justice, his counsel to prudent sovereigns speaks in that language.

41. Leo Strauss, "Plato," in Leo Strauss and Joseph Cropsey, eds., *History of Political Philosophy*, 3d ed. (Chicago: University of Chicago Press, 1987), 37.

42. Hadley Arkes, *Beyond the Constitution* (Princeton, N.J.: Princeton University Press, 1990), 163.

43. As late as 1896, this was recognized as central to constitutional government by Justice John Marshall Harlan I, dissenting in *Plessy* v. *Ferguson*, 163 U.S. 537 (1896), at 558–59.

44. Locke, *Two Treatises*, bk. 2, secs. 221, 242; emphasis in original.

45. Ibid., sec. 214; emphasis in original.

46. Ibid., sec. 212; emphasis in original.

47. Ibid., sec. 197; emphasis in original.

48. Ibid., sec. 199; emphasis in original.

49. Ibid., sec. 227; emphasis in original.

50. Ibid.; emphasis in original.

51. See William Blackstone's very Lockean account of that event, in his *Commentaries on the Laws of England*, 4 vols. (Oxford: Clarendon Press, 1765–1769; facsimile reprint, Chicago: University of Chicago Press, 1979), 1:204–6, 238.

52. The other two were Francis Bacon and Isaac Newton. See Jefferson to John Trumbull, 15 February 1789, in Thomas Jefferson, *Writings,* ed. Merrill Peterson (New York: Library of America, 1984), 939–40.

CHAPTER TEN. THE POLITICAL SCIENCE OF BLACKSTONE'S *COMMENTARIES*

1. William Blackstone, *Commentaries on the Laws of England*, 4 vols. (Oxford: Clarendon Press, 1765–1769; facsimile reprint, Chicago: University of Chicago Press, 1979), 1:121.

2. See Dennis Nolan, "Sir William Blackstone and the New Republic," *Political Science Reviewer* 6 (1976): 283–324.

3. Robert G. McCloskey, ed., *The Works of James Wilson*, 2 vols. (Cambridge, Mass.: Harvard University Press, 1967), 1:77–80, 103–13, 168–85.

4. On Blackstone's Lockeanism, see Herbert J. Storing, "William Blackstone," in Leo Strauss and Joseph Cropsey, eds., *History of Political Philosophy*, 3d ed. (Chicago: University of Chicago Press, 1987), 622–34. Storing does not mention Wilson's critique, but placing Storing's Blackstone side by side with Wilson's will bear out the suggestion offered here.

5. Blackstone, *Commentaries*, 1:123.

6. Ibid. Readers of *Leviathan* can hardly come away thinking this is Hobbes's last word on the subject, but his explicit teaching is that "tyranny" is only monarchy "misliked"—a name given by those "that are discontented under monarchy" (Thomas Hobbes, *Leviathan,* ed. Michael Oakeshott [New York: Collier, 1962], 142).

7. John Locke, *Two Treatises of Government*, ed. Peter Laslett (New York: Mentor, 1965), bk. 2, sec. 127.

8. Blackstone, *Commentaries*, 1:122, citing Locke, *Two Treatises*, bk. 2, sec. 57.

9. Blackstone, *Commentaries*, 1:38.

10. See note 3.

11. Blackstone, *Commentaries*, 1:39–40.

12. Ibid., 41.

13. Ibid., 40–41. Blackstone quickly adds that "holy scriptures" comprise a "revealed or divine law" of equal or higher obligation, though not found out by reason (ibid., 42). See Paul A. Rahe, *Republics Ancient and Modern: Classical Republicanism and the American Revolution* (Chapel Hill: University of North Carolina Press, 1992), 530.

14. Blackstone, *Commentaries*, 1:43.

15. Samuel Pufendorf, *On the Duty of Man and Citizen According to Natural Law,* ed. James Tully (New York: Cambridge University Press, 1991), xxi, 117–

18. Compare Pufendorf's bk. 2, chaps. 1 (quoted here) and 5 with Hobbes, *Leviathan,* chaps. 13 and 17, and Locke, *Two Treatises,* bk. 2, chaps. 2, 3, and 7.

16. Blackstone, *Commentaries,* 1:44.

17. Ibid., 202–3.

18. Ibid., 47.

19. See Pufendorf, *On the Duty of Man and Citizen,* 116–17.

20. Blackstone, *Commentaries,* 1:47.

21. Compare ibid., 48, 52, 172, 178, 192–93, 204–6, 230, 243–44.

22. Ibid., 46.

23. See above, Chapter 9, text at notes 19–26.

24. Blackstone, *Commentaries,* 1:156.

25. Ibid., 157.

26. Cf. McCloskey, ed., *Works of Wilson,* 1:77–79, with Storing, "William Blackstone," 626–27.

27. Locke, *Two Treatises,* bk. 2, sec. 150; emphasis in original.

28. On the Constitution's contemplation of its own perpetuity, in an opinion that recognizes both the theoretical legitimacy and the extralegality of revolution, see *Texas* v. *White,* 7 Wallace 700 (1869), at 724–26.

29. Blackstone, *Commentaries,* 1:204.

30. Ibid., 205.

31. Ibid., 206.

32. Ibid., 51–52, citing Locke, *Two Treatises,* bk. 2, sec. 212.

33. Blackstone, *Commentaries,* 1:205.

34. See Burke draw much the same distinction as does Blackstone in the passage quoted in the text: "No government could stand a moment, if it could be blown down with any thing so loose and indefinite as an opinion of '*misconduct.*' They who led at the Revolution, grounded the virtual abdication of King James upon no such light and uncertain principle. They charged him with nothing less than a design, confirmed by a multitude of illegal overt acts, to *subvert the Protestant church and state,* and their *fundamental,* unquestionable laws and liberties: they charged him with having broken the *original contract* between king and people. This was more than *misconduct.* A grave and overruling necessity obliged them to take the step they took, and took with infinite reluctance, as under that most rigorous of all laws. Their trust for the future preservation of the constitution was not in future revolutions. The grand policy of all their regulations was to render it almost impracticable for any future sovereign to compel the states of the kingdom to have again recourse to those violent remedies" (Edmund Burke and Thomas Paine, *Reflections on the Revolution in France* and *The Rights of Man* [Garden City, N.Y.: Doubleday Anchor, 1973], 39); emphasis in original.

35. Blackstone, *Commentaries,* 1:164.

36. Ibid., 178.

37. Ibid., 183.

38. Ibid., 192–93.

39. Ibid., 230. Writing that Blackstone "recoiled from the consequences" of Locke's theory, Paul Rahe remarks that he "preferred to speak of there being a contract between the ruler and the ruled and not to describe government as a trust temporarily conferred." But Rahe appears to recognize Blackstone's cautious deeper teaching, fundamentally consistent with Locke's (*Republics Ancient and Modern,* 531).

40. Blackstone, *Commentaries,* 1:243.

41. Ibid., 210–11.

42. Ibid., 69.

43. Ibid., 68; see also 78.

44. Ibid., 77; emphasis in original.

45. Ibid., 89.

46. Ibid., 91.

47. Ibid., 257.

48. Ibid.

49. See ibid., 129–35.

50. Ibid., 91. See James Madison's similar remark in 1788, quoted above in Chapter 4, text at note 78.

51. Locke, *Two Treatises,* bk. 2, sec. 212.

52. See Robert Lowry Clinton, *Marbury v. Madison and Judicial Review* (Lawrence: University Press of Kansas, 1989), chaps. 2 and 3; and Christopher Wolfe, *The Rise of Modern Judicial Review: From Constitutional Interpretation to Judge-made Law* (New York: Basic Books, 1986), chap. 1. For an account of Blackstone that differs somewhat from my own, but with which I agree that "Blackstone is able to succeed where Hobbes failed in taming common lawyers," see James R. Stoner, Jr., *Common Law and Liberal Theory: Coke, Hobbes, and the Origins of American Constitutionalism* (Lawrence: University Press of Kansas, 1992), chap. 10; the quotation is from p. 175.

CHAPTER ELEVEN. CONCLUSION

1. Robert G. McCloskey, ed., *The Works of James Wilson,* 2 vols. (Cambridge, Mass.: Harvard University Press, 1967), 1:303; emphasis added.

2. Harold Holzer, ed., *The Lincoln-Douglas Debates: The First Complete, Unexpurgated Text* (New York: HarperCollins, 1993), 96.

3. Abraham Lincoln, speech at Paris, Illinois, 7 September 1858, in Roy P. Basler, ed., *The Collected Works of Abraham Lincoln,* 9 vols. (New Brunswick, N.J.: Rutgers University Press, 1953), 3:90.

4. Alexander Hamilton, James Madison, and John Jay, *The Federalist Papers,* ed. Clinton Rossiter (New York: Mentor, 1961), no. 51:323; hereafter cited as *Federalist.*

5. Occasional controversy does erupt even over a point this basic and embroils the Supreme Court in matters that it would be better to leave alone; see *U.S. Term Limits, Inc. v. Thornton,* _____ U.S. _____ (1995).

6. *Federalist* 49:314. See Lincoln's early effort in this regard (address before the Young Men's Lyceum of Springfield, Illinois, 27 January 1838, in Basler, ed., *Works of Lincoln,* 1:108–15).

7. See Chapter 4 text at note 95.

8. *Federalist* 48:308.

9. Sylvia Snowiss, *Judicial Review and the Law of the Constitution* (New Haven, Conn.: Yale University Press, 1990), 2, 6, 78, 113. For a fuller account, see my review of Snowiss's book in *Review of Politics* 54 (1992): 471–74.

10. Snowiss, *Judicial Review and the Law of the Constitution,* 197.

11. Richard G. Stevens, "The Constitutional Completion of the Liberal Philosophy of Hobbes and Locke," *Political Science Reviewer* 17 (1987): 282.

12. *Federalist* 1:33.

13. See Chapter 6 text at notes 106, 107.

14. See Chapter 6 text at notes 17–19.

15. McCloskey, ed., *Works of Wilson*, 1:304.

16. Leslie Friedman Goldstein, "Judicial Review and Democratic Theory: Guardian Democracy vs. Representative Democracy," *Western Political Quarterly* 40 (1987): 403–4. Reprinted in Goldstein, *In Defense of the Text: Democracy and Constitutional Theory* (Savage, Md.: Rowman and Littlefield, 1991). Goldstein also points in this article to the significant rejection of a Council of Revision in which judges would serve.

17. Robert Lowry Clinton, *Marbury v. Madison and Judicial Review* (Lawrence: University Press of Kansas, 1989).

18. John Locke, *Two Treatises of Government*, ed. Peter Laslett (New York: Mentor, 1965), bk. 2, sec. 124. See also *Calder* v. *Bull*, 3 Dallas 386 (1798), at 399 (Iredell, J.).

19. Madison to Jefferson, 8 February 1825, in James Morton Smith, ed., *The Republic of Letters: The Correspondence Between Thomas Jefferson and James Madison, 1776–1826*, 3 vols. (New York: W. W. Norton, 1995), 3:1924.

20. Speech at Springfield, 26 June 1857, in Basler, ed., *Collected Works of Lincoln*, 2: 405, 400. Harry Jaffa has suggested that the only adequate grounds for refuting Taney's *Dred Scott* opinion are in the Declaration, and that Lincoln himself would have welcomed a judicial determination that the Constitution *required* Congress to keep slavery out of the territories ("The Closing of the Conservative Mind," *National Review*, 9 July 1990, 43; "What Were the 'Original Intentions' of the Framers of the Constitution of the United States?" *University of Puget Sound Law Review* 10 [1987]: 444). The first contention is preposterous; the second is mythical and would subject Lincoln to his own criticism of Stephen Douglas: that he was "for Supreme Court decisions when he like[d] and against them when he [did] not like them" (Lincoln, speech at Springfield, 17 July 1858, in Basler, ed., *Collected Works of Lincoln*, 2:517–18).

21. 19 Howard 393 (1857), at 529–64 (McLean, J. dissenting), and 564–633 (Curtis, J. dissenting).

22. *Federalist* 78:470.

23. Snowiss, *Judicial Review and the Law of the Constitution*, 66.

24. *Federalist* 10:80.

25. *Marbury* v. *Madison*, 1 Cranch 137 (1803), at 170.

26. Joseph Story, *Commentaries on the Constitution of the United States*, abridged 1st ed. (Boston: Hilliard, Gray, 1833; reprint, Durham, N.C.: Carolina Academic Press, 1987), sec. 1016.

27. *Chisholm* v. *Georgia*, 2 Dallas 419 (1793), at 454; emphasis in original.

28. *Palko* v. *Connecticut*, 302 U.S. 319 (1937), at 325.

BIBLIOGRAPHY

BOOKS

Abraham, Henry J. *Justices and Presidents*. 2d ed. New York: Oxford University Press, 1985.

Adams, Henry. *The Great Secession Winter of 1860–61 and Other Essays*. Edited by George E. Hochfield. New York: A.S. Barnes, 1963.

_____. *History of the United States of America During the Administrations of Thomas Jefferson*. New York: Library of America, 1986.

Agresto, John. *The Supreme Court and Constitutional Democracy*. Ithaca, N.Y.: Cornell University Press, 1984.

America's Continuing Revolution. Garden City, N.Y.: Doubleday Anchor, 1976.

Anastaplo, George. *The Constitution of 1787*. Baltimore: Johns Hopkins University Press, 1989.

Aristotle. *The "Art" of Rhetoric*. Translated by J. H. Freese. Cambridge, Mass.: Harvard University Press/Loeb Classical Library, 1926.

_____. *The Nicomachean Ethics*. Translated by H. Rackham. Cambridge, Mass.: Harvard University Press/Loeb Classical Library, 1926.

_____. *The Politics*. Translated by Carnes Lord. Chicago: University of Chicago Press, 1984.

Arkes, Hadley. *Beyond the Constitution*. Princeton, N.J.: Princeton University Press, 1990.

Arnhart, Larry. *Aristotle on Political Reasoning: A Commentary on the "Rhetoric."* DeKalb: Northern Illinois University Press, 1981.

Bailyn, Bernard. *The Ideological Origins of the American Revolution*. Cambridge, Mass.: Harvard University Press, 1967.

Bannister, Robert C. *Social Darwinism: Science and Myth in Anglo-American Social Thought*. Philadelphia: Temple University Press, 1979.

Bannister, Robert C., ed. *On Liberty, Society, and Politics: The Essential Essays of William Graham Sumner*. Indianapolis: Liberty Fund, 1992.

Barber, Sotirios A. *On What the Constitution Means*. Baltimore: Johns Hopkins University Press, 1984.

Basler, Roy P., ed. *The Collected Works of Abraham Lincoln.* 9 vols. New Brunswick, N.J.: Rutgers University Press, 1953.

Berger, Raoul. *Congress v. the Supreme Court.* Cambridge, Mass.: Harvard University Press, 1969.

———. *The Fourteenth Amendment and the Bill of Rights.* Norman: University of Oklahoma Press, 1989.

———. *Government by Judiciary: The Transformation of the Fourteenth Amendment.* Cambridge, Mass.: Harvard University Press, 1977.

———. *Impeachment: The Constitutional Problems.* Cambridge, Mass.: Harvard University Press, 1973.

———. *Selected Writings on the Constitution.* Cumberland, Va.: James River Press, 1987.

Berns, Walter. *In Defense of Liberal Democracy.* Chicago: Regnery Gateway, 1984.

———. *Taking the Constitution Seriously.* New York: Simon and Schuster, 1987.

Beveridge, Albert J. *The Life of John Marshall.* 4 vols. Boston: Houghton Mifflin, 1919.

Bickel, Alexander. *The Least Dangerous Branch: The Supreme Court at the Bar of Politics.* 2d ed. New Haven, Conn.: Yale University Press, 1986.

Blackstone, William. *Commentaries on the Laws of England.* 4 vols. Oxford: Clarendon Press, 1765–1769. Facsimile reprint, Chicago: University of Chicago Press, 1979.

Bobbio, Norberto. *Thomas Hobbes and the Natural Law Tradition.* Chicago: University of Chicago Press, 1993.

Bork, Robert H. *The Tempting of America: The Political Seduction of the Law.* New York: Free Press, 1989.

Burgess, Susan R. *Contest for Constitutional Authority: The Abortion and War Powers Debates.* Lawrence: University Press of Kansas, 1992.

Burke, Edmund, and Thomas Paine. *Reflections on the Revolution in France and The Rights of Man.* Garden City, N.Y.: Doubleday Anchor, 1973.

Burt, Robert A. *The Constitution in Conflict.* Cambridge, Mass.: Harvard University Press, Belknap Press, 1992.

Bushnell, Eleanore. *Crimes, Follies, and Misfortunes: The Federal Impeachment Trials.* Urbana: University of Illinois Press, 1992.

Cahn, Edmond, ed. *Supreme Court and Supreme Law.* Bloomington: Indiana University Press, 1954. Reprint, New York: Clarion/Simon and Schuster, 1971.

Choper, Jesse H. *Judicial Review and the National Political Process.* Chicago: University of Chicago Press, 1980.

Clinton, Robert Lowry. *Marbury v. Madison and Judicial Review.* Lawrence: University Press of Kansas, 1989.

Commager, Henry Steele, ed. *Documents of American History.* 5th ed. New York: Appleton-Century-Crofts, 1949.

Cooley, Thomas M. *A Treatise on the Constitutional Limitations Which Rest upon the Legislative Power of the States of the American Union.* Boston: Little, Brown, 1868. Reprint, New York: Da Capo Press, 1972.

Corwin, Edward S. *John Marshall and the Constitution.* New Haven, Conn.: Yale University Press, 1919.

———. *The Twilight of the Supreme Court.* New Haven, Conn.: Yale University Press, 1934. Reprint, Hamden, Conn.: Archon Books, 1970.

Cox, Archibald. *The Court and the Constitution.* Boston: Houghton Mifflin, 1987.

_____. *The Role of the Supreme Court in American Government.* New York: Oxford University Press, 1976.

Crosskey, William Winslow, and (in vol. 3) William Jeffrey, Jr. *Politics and the Constitution in the History of the United States.* 3 vols. Chicago: University of Chicago Press, 1953–1980.

Currie, David P. *The Constitution in the Supreme Court: The First Hundred Years, 1789–1888.* Chicago: University of Chicago Press, 1985.

Curtis, Michael Kent. *No State Shall Abridge: the Fourteenth Amendment and the Bill of Rights.* Durham, N.C.: Duke University Press, 1986.

Diamond, Martin. *The Founding of the Democratic Republic.* Itasca, Ill.: F. E. Peacock, 1981.

Doyle, Arthur Conan. *The Illustrated Sherlock Holmes.* New York: Crown, 1984.

Eidelberg, Paul. *The Philosophy of the American Constitution.* New York: Free Press, 1968. Reprint, Lanham, Md.: University Press of America, 1986.

Ellis, Richard E. *The Jeffersonian Crisis: Courts and Politics in the Young Republic.* New York: Oxford University Press, 1971. Reprint, New York: W. W. Norton, 1974.

Ely, James W., Jr. *The Guardian of Every Other Right: A Constitutional History of Property Rights.* New York: Oxford University Press, 1992.

Ely, John Hart. *Democracy and Distrust: A Theory of Judicial Review.* Cambridge, Mass.: Harvard University Press, 1980.

Engeman, Thomas, Edward Erler, and Thomas Hofeller. *The Federalist Concordance.* Chicago: University of Chicago Press, 1988.

Epstein, David F. *The Political Theory of the Federalist.* Chicago: University of Chicago Press, 1984.

Farrand, Max. *The Records of the Federal Convention of 1787.* Rev. ed. 4 vols. New Haven, Conn.: Yale University Press, 1937.

Faulkner, Robert Kenneth. *The Jurisprudence of John Marshall.* Princeton, N.J.: Princeton University Press, 1968.

Fisher, Louis. *American Constitutional Law.* New York: McGraw-Hill, 1990.

Foner, Eric. *Free Soil, Free Labor, Free Men: The Ideology of the Republican Party Before the Civil War.* New York: Oxford University Press, 1970.

Frankfurter, Felix. *Of Law and Men: Papers and Addresses of Felix Frankfurter.* Edited by Philip Elman. New York: Harcourt, Brace, and World, 1956. Reprint, Hamden, Conn.: Archon Books, 1965.

Frisch, Morton J., and Richard G. Stevens, eds. *American Political Thought: The Philosophic Dimension of American Statesmanship.* 2d ed. Itasca, Ill.: F. E. Peacock, 1983.

Gillman, Howard. *The Constitution Besieged: The Rise and Demise of Lochner Era Police Powers Jurisprudence.* Durham, N.C.: Duke University Press, 1993.

Goldstein, Leslie Friedman. *In Defense of the Text: Democracy and Constitutional Theory.* Savage, Md.: Rowman and Littlefield, 1991.

Goldwin, Robert A., and William A. Schambra, eds. *How Capitalistic Is the Constitution?* Washington, D.C.: American Enterprise Institute, 1982.

_____. *How Does the Constitution Secure Rights?* Washington, D.C.: American Enterprise Institute, 1985.

Greenstone, J. David. *The Lincoln Persuasion: Remaking American Liberalism.* Princeton, N.J.: Princeton University Press, 1993.

Gunther, Gerald, ed. *John Marshall's Defense of McCulloch v. Maryland.* Stanford, Calif.: Stanford University Press, 1969.

Hall, Kermit L., ed. *The Oxford Companion to the Supreme Court of the United States.* New York: Oxford University Press, 1992.

Hamilton, Alexander, James Madison, and John Jay. *The Federalist Papers.* Edited by Clinton Rossiter. New York: Mentor, 1961.

Harmon, M. Judd, ed. *Essays on the Constitution of the United States.* Port Washington, N.Y.: Kennikat Press, 1978.

Hobbes, Thomas. *De Cive or the Citizen.* Edited by Sterling P. Lamprecht. New York: Appleton-Century-Crofts, 1949. Reprint, Westport, Conn.: Greenwood Press, 1982.

_____. *The Elements of Law, Natural and Politic.* Edited by Ferdinand Tönnies. 2d ed. London: Frank Cass, 1969.

_____. *Leviathan.* Edited by Michael Oakeshott. New York: Collier, 1962.

Hofstadter, Richard. *Social Darwinism in American Thought.* Rev. ed. Boston: Beacon Press, 1955.

Holzer, Harold, ed. *The Lincoln-Douglas Debates: The First Complete, Unexpurgated Text.* New York: HarperCollins, 1993.

Horowitz, Donald L. *The Courts and Social Policy.* Washington, D.C.: Brookings Institution, 1977.

Hutchinson, William T., et al., eds. *The Papers of James Madison.* 22 vols. to date. Chicago: University of Chicago Press (vols. 1–10), 1962–1977; Charlottesville: University Press of Virginia (vols. 11–22), 1977–.

Jacobsohn, Gary J. *Pragmatism, Statesmanship, and the Supreme Court.* Ithaca, N.Y.: Cornell University Press, 1977.

_____. *The Supreme Court and the Decline of Constitutional Aspiration.* Totowa, N.J.: Rowman and Littlefield, 1986.

Jaffa, Harry V. *Crisis of the House Divided: An Interpretation of the Issues in the Lincoln-Douglas Debates.* Garden City, N.Y.: Doubleday, 1959. Reprint, Chicago: University of Chicago Press, Phoenix Books, 1982.

_____. *Original Intent and the Framers of the Constitution: A Disputed Question.* Washington, D.C.: Regnery Gateway, 1994.

Jefferson, Thomas. *Writings.* Edited by Merrill Peterson. New York: Library of America, 1984.

Johnson, Herbert A., et al., eds. *The Papers of John Marshall.* 7 vols. to date. Chapel Hill: University of North Carolina Press, 1974–.

Kens, Paul. *Judicial Power and Reform Politics: The Anatomy of Lochner v. New York.* Lawrence: University Press of Kansas, 1990.

Kent, James. *Commentaries on American Law.* 1st ed. 2 vols. New York: O. Halsted, 1826. Reprint, New York: Da Capo Press, 1971.

Kurland, Philip B., and Ralph Lerner, eds. *The Founders' Constitution.* 5 vols. Chicago: University of Chicago Press, 1987.

Lerner, Max, ed. *The Mind and Faith of Justice Holmes.* 2d ed. New York: Modern Library, 1943.

Levy, Leonard W. *Original Intent and the Framers' Constitution.* New York: Macmillan, 1988.

Levy, Leonard W., Kenneth L. Karst, and Dennis J. Mahoney, eds. *Encyclopedia of the American Constitution.* 4 vols. New York: Macmillan, 1986.

Levy, Leonard W., and Dennis J. Mahoney, eds. *The Framing and Ratification of the Constitution.* New York: Macmillan, 1987.

Locke, John. *Two Treatises of Government.* Edited by Peter Laslett. New York: Mentor, 1965.

Loss, Richard, ed. *Corwin on the Constitution.* 3 vols. Ithaca, N.Y.: Cornell University Press, 1981–1988.

McCloskey, Robert G. *The American Supreme Court.* Chicago: University of Chicago Press, 1960.

McCloskey, Robert G., ed. *The Works of James Wilson.* 2 vols. Cambridge, Mass.: Harvard University Press, 1967.

McDowell, Gary L. *Curbing the Courts: The Constitution and the Limits of Judicial Power.* Baton Rouge: Louisiana State University Press, 1988.

_____. *Equity and the Constitution: The Supreme Court, Equitable Relief, and Public Policy.* Chicago: University of Chicago Press, 1982.

Magruder, Allan B. *John Marshall.* Boston: Houghton Mifflin, 1885, 1899.

Maltz, Earl M. *Civil Rights, the Constitution, and Congress, 1863–1869.* Lawrence: University Press of Kansas, 1990.

Marshall, John. *The Life of George Washington.* 2d ed., 1832. 2 vols. Reprinted as *George Washington.* with introduction by Marcus Cunliffe. 5 vols. New York: Chelsea House, 1983.

Mason, Alpheus Thomas. *The Supreme Court: Palladium of Freedom.* Ann Arbor: University of Michigan Press, 1962.

Mayer, David N. *The Constitutional Thought of Thomas Jefferson.* Charlottesville: University Press of Virginia, 1994.

Mendelson, Wallace. *Supreme Court Statecraft.* Ames: Iowa State University Press, 1985.

Meyers, Marvin. *The Jacksonian Persuasion: Politics and Belief.* Stanford, Calif.: Stanford University Press, 1957. Reprinted with new preface, New York: Vintage, 1960.

Meyers, Marvin, ed. *The Mind of the Founder: Sources in the Political Thought of James Madison.* Indianapolis: Bobbs-Merrill, 1973.

Molesworth, William, ed. *The English Works of Thomas Hobbes.* 11 vols. London: John Bohn, 1839–1845. Reprint, Darmstadt, Germany: Scientia Verlag Aalen, 1966.

Montesquieu [Charles de Secondat, Baron de]. *The Spirit of the Laws.* Edited by Anne Cohler, Basia C. Miller, and Harold S. Stone. New York: Cambridge University Press, 1989.

Pangle, Thomas L. *The Spirit of Modern Republicanism: The Moral Vision of the American Founders and the Philosophy of Locke.* Chicago: University of Chicago Press, 1988.

Perry, Michael J. *The Constitution, the Courts, and Human Rights.* New Haven, Conn.: Yale University Press, 1982.

Pufendorf, Samuel. *On the Duty of Man and Citizen According to Natural Law.* Edited by James Tully. New York: Cambridge University Press, 1991.

Rahe, Paul A. *Republics Ancient and Modern: Classical Republicanism and the American Revolution.* Chapel Hill: University of North Carolina Press, 1992.

Rehnquist, William H. *Grand Inquests: The Historic Impeachments of Justice Samuel Chase and President Andrew Johnson.* New York: William Morrow, 1992.

Richardson, James D., ed. *A Compilation of the Messages and Papers of the Presidents.* 20 vols. New York: Bureau of National Literature, 1897–1917.

Rosenberg, Gerald N. *The Hollow Hope: Can Courts Bring About Social Change?* Chicago: University of Chicago Press, 1991.

Schambra, William A., ed. *As Far as Republican Principles Will Admit: Essays by Martin Diamond.* Washington, D.C.: AEI Press, 1992.

Smith, James Morton, ed. *The Republic of Letters: The Correspondence Between Thomas Jefferson and James Madison, 1776–1826.* 3 vols. New York: W. W. Norton, 1995.

Smith, Samuel H., and Thomas Lloyd. *Trial of Samuel Chase, an Associate Justice of the Supreme Court of the United States, Impeached by the House of Representatives for High Crimes and Misdemeanors, Before the Senate of the United States.* 2 vols. Washington, D.C., 1805. Reprint, New York: Da Capo Press, 1970.

Snowiss, Sylvia. *Judicial Review and the Law of the Constitution.* New Haven, Conn.: Yale University Press, 1990.

Stoner, James R., Jr. *Common Law and Liberal Theory: Coke, Hobbes, and the Origins of American Constitutionalism.* Lawrence: University Press of Kansas, 1992.

Storing, Herbert J., ed. *The Complete Anti-Federalist.* 7 vols. Chicago: University of Chicago Press, 1981.

Story, Joseph. *Commentaries on Equity Jurisprudence.* 3d ed. 2 vols. Boston: Little, Brown, 1842.

———. *Commentaries on the Constitution of the United States.* Abridged 1st ed. Boston: Hilliard, Gray, 1833. Reprint with introduction by Ronald D. Rotunda and John E. Nowak, Durham, N.C.: Carolina Academic Press, 1987.

———. *Commentaries on the Constitution of the United States.* 2d ed. 2 vols. Boston: Little, Brown, 1851.

Strauss, Leo. *Natural Right and History.* Chicago: University of Chicago Press, 1953.

———. *Studies in Platonic Political Philosophy.* Chicago: University of Chicago Press, 1983.

———. *What Is Political Philosophy?* New York: Free Press, 1959. Reprint, Westport, Conn.: Greenwood Press, 1973.

Strauss, Leo, and Joseph Cropsey, eds. *History of Political Philosophy.* 3d ed. Chicago: University of Chicago Press, 1987.

Syrett, Harold C., et al., eds. *The Papers of Alexander Hamilton.* 26 vols. New York: Columbia University Press, 1961–1979.

Taylor, John. *Construction Construed and Constitutions Vindicated.* Richmond, Va.: Shepherd and Pollard, 1820. Reprint, New York: Da Capo Press, 1970.

Thayer, James Bradley. *John Marshall.* Boston: Houghton Mifflin, 1901.

Thorpe, Francis N., ed. *The Federal and State Constitutions, Colonial Charters, and Other Organic Laws of the States, Territories, and Colonies Now or Heretofore Forming the United States of America.* 7 vols. Washington, D.C.: Government Printing Office, 1909.

Thurow, Glen, and Jeffrey D. Wallin, eds. *Rhetoric and American Statesmanship.* Durham, N.C.: Carolina Academic Press, 1984.

Thurow, Sarah Baumgartner, ed. *Constitutionalism in Perspective.* Lanham, Md.: University Press of America, 1988.

de Tocqueville, Alexis. *Democracy in America.* Edited by J. P. Mayer. Garden City, N.Y.: Doubleday Anchor, 1969.

Twiss, Benjamin R. *Lawyers and the Constitution*. Princeton, N.J.: Princeton University Press, 1942.

U.S. Congress. Senate. Committee on the Judiciary. *Nomination of Anthony M. Kennedy To Be Associate Justice of the Supreme Court of the United States.* 100th Cong., 1st sess., 1987. Washington, D.C.: Government Printing Office, 1989.

_____. *Nomination of David H. Souter To Be Associate Justice of the Supreme Court of the United States.* 101st Cong., 2nd sess., 1990. Washington, D.C.: Government Printing Office, 1991.

_____. *Nomination of Judge Clarence Thomas to Be Associate Justice of the Supreme Court of the United States.* 102nd Cong., 1st sess., 1991. Washington, D.C.: Government Printing Office, 1993.

_____. *Nomination of Robert H. Bork to Be Associate Justice of the Supreme Court of the United States.* 100th Cong., 1st sess., 1987. Washington, D.C.: Government Printing Office, 1989.

Van Buren, Martin. *Inquiry into the Origin and Course of Political Parties in the United States.* New York: Hurd and Houghton, 1867. Reprint, New York: Augustus M. Kelley, 1967.

White, G. Edward. *The American Judicial Tradition.* New York: Oxford University Press, 1976.

_____. *The Marshall Court and Cultural Change, 1815–1835.* Abridged ed. New York: Oxford University Press, 1991.

Wills, Garry. *Explaining America: The Federalist.* New York: Doubleday, 1981.

Wilson, Henry. *History of the Antislavery Measures of the Thirty-seventh and Thirty-eighth United States Congresses, 1861–64.* Boston: Walker, Wise, 1864.

Wolfe, Christopher. *The Rise of Modern Judicial Review: From Constitutional Interpretation to Judge-made Law.* New York: Basic Books, 1986.

Wright, Benjamin Fletcher, Jr. *American Interpretations of Natural Law: A Study in the History of Political Thought.* Cambridge, Mass.: Harvard University Press, 1931. Reprint, New York: Russell and Russell, 1962.

_____. *The Growth of American Constitutional Law.* New York: Holt, Rinehart, and Winston, 1942. Reprint, Chicago: University of Chicago Press, Phoenix Books, 1967.

ARTICLES

Alfange, Dean, Jr. "Marbury v. Madison and Original Understandings of Judicial Review: In Defense of Traditional Wisdom." *Supreme Court Review* (1993): 329–446.

Arkes, Hadley, Robert H. Bork, Russell Hittinger, and William Bentley Ball. "Natural Law and the Law: An Exchange." *First Things* 17 (May 1992), 45–54.

Berns, Walter. "Judicial Review and the Rights and Laws of Nature." *Supreme Court Review* (1982): 49–83.

Bloch, Susan Low, and Maeva Marcus. "John Marshall's Selective Use of History in *Marbury v. Madison.*" *Wisconsin Law Review* (1986): 301–37.

Bork, Robert H. "Natural Law and the Constitution." *First Things* 15 (March 1992): 16–20.

Clinton, Robert L. "The Obligation Clause of the United States Constitution:

Public and/or Private Contracts." *University of Arkansas at Little Rock Law Journal* 11 (1988–1989): 343–67.

Clor, Harry M. "Judicial Statesmanship and Constitutional Interpretation." *South Texas Law Journal* 26 (1985): 397–433.

Coby, Patrick. "The Law of Nature in Locke's *Second Treatise:* Is Locke a Hobbesian?" *Review of Politics* 49 (1987): 3–28.

Diamond, Ann Stuart. "The Anti-Federalist 'Brutus.' " *Political Science Reviewer* 6 (1976): 249–81.

Dionisopoulos, P. Allan, and Paul Peterson. "Rediscovering the American Origins of Judicial Review." *John Marshall Law Review* 18 (1984): 49–76.

Foran, William A. "John Marshall as a Historian." *American Historical Review* 43 (1937): 51–64.

Franck, Matthew J. Review of *Judicial Review and the Law of the Constitution,* by Sylvia Snowiss. *Review of Politics* 54 (1992): 471–74.

――――. Review of *Marbury v. Madison and Judicial Review,* by Robert Lowry Clinton. *Review of Politics* 52 (1990): 485–87.

――――. Review of *The Constitution in Conflict,* by Robert A. Burt. *Review of Politics* 56 (1994): 398–402.

――――. Review of *The Tempting of America: The Political Seduction of the Law,* by Robert H. Bork. *Interpretation: A Journal of Political Philosophy* 19 (1991): 78–84.

Frisch, Morton J. "John Marshall's Philosophy of Constitutional Republicanism." *Review of Politics* 20 (1958): 34–45.

Glazer, Nathan. "Towards an Imperial Judiciary?" *The Public Interest* 41 (Fall 1975): 104–23.

Glenn, Gary D. "Inalienable Rights and Locke's Argument for Limited Government: Political Implications of a Right to Suicide." *Journal of Politics* 46 (1984): 80–105.

Goldstein, Leslie Friedman. "Judicial Review and Democratic Theory: Guardian Democracy vs. Representative Democracy." *Western Political Quarterly* 40 (1987): 391–412.

――――. "Popular Sovereignty, the Origins of Judicial Review, and the Revival of Unwritten Law." *Journal of Politics* 48 (1986): 51–71.

Graglia, Lino A. "Judicial Review on the Basis of 'Regime Principles': A Prescription for Government by Judges." *South Texas Law Journal* 26 (1985): 435–52.

――――. Review of *Original Intent and the Framers' Constitution,* by Leonard W. Levy. *The Public Interest* 97 (Fall 1989): 97–105.

Grey, Thomas C. "Do We Have an Unwritten Constitution?" *Stanford Law Review* 27 (1975): 703–18.

――――. "Origins of the Unwritten Constitution: Fundamental Law in American Revolutionary Thought." *Stanford Law Review* 30 (1978): 843–93.

Hickok, Eugene. "On Federalism." *Benchmark* 3 (1987): 229–38.

Jacobsohn, Gary J. "E.T.: The Extra-Textual in Constitutional Interpretation." *Constitutional Commentary* 1 (1984): 21–42.

Jaffa, Harry V. "The Closing of the Conservative Mind." *National Review,* 9 July 1990, 40.

――――. "Judge Bork's Mistake." *National Review,* 4 March 1988, 38.

――――. "A Right to Privacy?" *National Review,* 24 March 1989, 51.

――――. "What Were the 'Original Intentions' of the Framers of the Constitution of the United States?" *University of Puget Sound Law Review* 10 (1987): 351–448.

Jamieson, Kathleen Hall, and Karlyn Kohrs Campbell. "Rhetorical Hybrids: Fusions of Generic Elements." *Quarterly Journal of Speech* 68 (1982): 146–57.

Melone, Albert P. "Mendelson v. Wright: Understanding the Contract Clause." *Western Political Quarterly* 41 (1988): 791–99.

Mendelson, Wallace. "B. F. Wright on the Contract Clause: A Progressive Misreading of the Marshall-Taney Era." *Western Political Quarterly* 38 (1985): 262–75.

———. "Bootstraps v. Evidence: A Response to Professor Melone." *Western Political Quarterly* 41 (1988): 801–5.

Nolan, Dennis. "Sir William Blackstone and the New Republic." *Political Science Reviewer* 6 (1976): 283–324.

Peterson, Paul. "The Rhetorical Design and Theoretical Teaching of *Federalist* No. 10." *Political Science Reviewer* 17 (1987): 193–218.

Pound, Roscoe. "Liberty of Contract." *Yale Law Journal* 18 (1909): 454–87.

Stevens, Richard G. "The Constitutional Completion of the Liberal Philosophy of Hobbes and Locke." *Political Science Reviewer* 17 (1987): 267–84.

———. "Liberal Democracy and Justice in the Constitution of Walter Berns." *Political Science Reviewer* 22 (1993): 74–123.

Thayer, James Bradley. "The Origin and Scope of the American Doctrine of Constitutional Law." *Harvard Law Review* 7 (1893): 49–132.

Van Alstyne, William W. "A Critical Guide to *Marbury* v. *Madison.*" *Duke Law Journal* (1969): 1–47.

Wolfe, Christopher. "John Marshall and Constitutional Law." *Polity* 25 (1982): 5–25.

CASES

Adamson v. *California,* 332 U.S. 46 (1947).

Allgeyer v. *Louisiana,* 165 U.S. 578 (1897).

American Insurance Co. v. *Canter,* 1 Peters 511 (1828).

Baker v. *Carr,* 369 U.S. 186 (1962).

Bank of the United States v. *Deveaux,* 5 Cranch 61 (1809).

Barron v. *Baltimore,* 7 Peters 243 (1833).

Bartmeyer v. *Iowa,* 18 Wallace 129 (1873).

Bowers v. *Hardwick,* 478 U.S. 186 (1986).

Bowman v. *Middleton,* 1 Bay 252 (S.C. 1792).

Bradwell v. *Illinois,* 16 Wallace 130 (1873).

Brown v. *Board of Education,* 347 U.S. 483 (1954).

Brown v. *Maryland,* 12 Wheaton 419 (1827).

Butchers' Union Slaughter-House and Live-Stock Landing Co. v. *Crescent City Live-Stock Landing and Slaughter-House Co.,* 111 U.S. 746 (1884).

Calder v. *Bull,* 3 Dallas 386 (1798).

Cherokee Nation v. *Georgia,* 5 Peters 1 (1831).

Chicago, Burlington and Quincy Railroad Co. v. *Chicago,* 166 U.S. 226 (1897).

Chicago, Milwaukee and St. Paul Railroad v. *Minnesota,* 134 U.S. 418 (1890).
Chisholm v. *Georgia,* 2 Dallas 419 (1793).
Cohens v. *Virginia,* 6 Wheaton 264 (1821).
Conner v. *Elliott,* 18 Howard 591 (1856).
Corfield v. *Coryell,* 6 Fed. Cas. no. 3230 (C.C.E.D.Pa. 1823).
Covington and Lexington Turnpike Road Co. v. *Sandford,* 164 U.S. 578 (1896).
Craig v. *Missouri,* 4 Peters 410 (1830).
Dr. Bonham's Case, 8 Co. Rep. 107 (1610).
Dred Scott v. *Sandford,* 19 Howard 393 (1857).
Drehman v. *Stifle,* 8 Wallace 595 (1870).
Durousseau v. *United States,* 6 Cranch 307 (1810).
Eakin v. *Raub,* 12 Serg. and Rawle 330 (Pa. 1825).
Edwards v. *California,* 314 U.S. 160 (1941).
Elmendorf v. *Taylor,* 10 Wheaton 152 (1825).
Ex parte McCardle, 7 Wallace 506 (1869).
Fletcher v. *Peck,* 6 Cranch 187 (1810).
Garcia v. *San Antonio Metropolitan Transit Authority,* 469 U.S. 528 (1986).
Gardner v. *Newburgh,* 2 Johns. Ch. 162 (N.Y. 1816).
Gibbons v. *Ogden,* 9 Wheaton 1 (1824).
Griswold v. *Connecticut,* 381 U.S. 479 (1965).
Gunn v. *Barry,* 15 Wallace 610 (1873).
Hayburn's Case, 2 Dallas 409 (1792).
Hepburn v. *Ellzey,* 2 Cranch 445 (1804).
Hepburn v. *Griswold,* 8 Wallace 603 (1870).
Hodgson and Thompson v. *Bowerbank,* 5 Cranch 303 (1809).
Holden v. *Hardy,* 169 U.S. 366 (1898).
Home Building and Loan Association v. *Blaisdell,* 290 U.S. 398 (1934).
Hurtado v. *California,* 110 U.S. 516 (1884).
Hylton v. *United States,* 3 Dallas 171 (1796).
Juilliard v. *Greenman,* 110 U.S. 421 (1884).
Legal Tender Cases, 12 Wallace 457 (1871).
Loan Association v. *Topeka,* 20 Wallace 655 (1875).
Lochner v. *New York,* 198 U.S. 45 (1905).
Loving v. *Virginia,* 388 U.S. 1 (1967).
Luther v. *Borden,* 7 Howard 1 (1849).
McCulloch v. *Maryland,* 4 Wheaton 316 (1819).
McVeigh v. *United States,* 11 Wallace 259 (1871).
Marbury v. *Madison,* 1 Cranch 137 (1803).
Martin v. *Hunter's Lessee,* 1 Wheaton 304 (1816).
Meyer v. *Nebraska,* 262 U.S. 390 (1923).
Miller v. *California,* 413 U.S. 15 (1973).
Missouri v. *Jenkins,* 495 U.S. 33 (1990).
Missouri Pacific Railway Co. v. *Nebraska,* 164 U.S. 403 (1896).
Munn v. *Illinois,* 94 U.S. 113 (1877).
National League of Cities v. *Usery,* 426 U.S. 833 (1976).
Ogden v. *Saunders,* 12 Wheaton 213 (1827).
Osborn v. *Bank of the United States,* 9 Wheaton 738 (1824).
Osborn v. *Nicholson,* 13 Wallace 654 (1872).
Owings v. *Norwood's Lessee,* 5 Cranch 344 (1809).
Palko v. *Connecticut,* 302 U.S. 319 (1937).
Pierce v. *Society of Sisters,* 268 U.S. 510 (1925).

Planned Parenthood of Southeastern Pennsylvania v. *Casey,* 112 S.Ct. 2791 (1992).
Plessy v. *Ferguson,* 163 U.S. 537 (1896).
Poe v. *Ullman,* 367 U.S. 497 (1961).
Prigg v. *Pennsylvania,* 16 Peters 539 (1842).
Rice v. *Railroad Co.,* 1 Black 358 (1863).
Roe v. *Wade,* 410 U.S. 113 (1973).
Satterlee v. *Matthewson,* 2 Peters 380 (1829).
Sere v. *Pitot,* 6 Cranch 332 (1810).
Shelley v. *Kraemer,* 334 U.S. 1 (1948).
Sinking Fund Cases, 99 U.S. 700 (1878).
Skinner v. *Oklahoma,* 316 U.S. 535 (1942).
Slaughter-House Cases, 16 Wallace 36 (1873).
Southern Pacific Co. v. *Jensen,* 244 U.S. 205 (1916).
Stanford v. *Kentucky,* 492 U.S. 361 (1989).
Stone v. *Mississippi,* 101 U.S. 814 (1880).
Sturges v. *Crowninshield,* 4 Wheaton 122 (1819).
Taylor v. *Porter,* 4 Hill 140 (N.Y. 1843).
Terrett v. *Taylor,* 9 Cranch 43 (1815).
Texas v. *White,* 7 Wallace 700 (1869).
Town of Pawlet v. *Clark,* 9 Cranch 292 (1815).
Trustees of Dartmouth College v. *Woodward,* 4 Wheaton 518 (1819).
United States v. *Arredondo,* 6 Peters 691 (1832).
United States v. *Bevans,* 3 Wheaton 336 (1818).
United States v. *Butler,* 297 U.S. 1 (1936).
United States v. *Fisher,* 2 Cranch 358 (1805).
United States v. *Klein,* 13 Wallace 128 (1872).
United States v. *Lopez,* _____ U.S. _____ (1995).
United States v. *Maurice,* 2 Marshall's C.C. 96 (C.C.D.Va. 1823).
United States v. *More,* 3 Cranch 159 (1805).
United States v. *Peters,* 5 Cranch 115 (1809).
United States v. *Reynolds,* 98 U.S. 145 (1879).
U.S. Term Limits, Inc. v. *Thornton,* _____ U.S. _____ (1995).
Van Horne's Lessee v. *Dorrance,* 2 Dallas 304 (1795).
Ward v. *Maryland,* 12 Wallace 418 (1871).
Ware v. *Hylton,* 3 Dallas 199 (1796).
Watson v. *Mercer,* 8 Peters 88 (1834).
Webster v. *Reproductive Health Services,* 492 U.S. 490 (1989).
West River Bridge Co. v. *Dix,* 6 Howard 507 (1848).
Wilkinson v. *Leland,* 2 Peters 627 (1829).
Wynehamer v. *People,* 13 Kernan 378 (N.Y. 1856).